COMING TO CLASS

Also in the CrossCurrents Series

COMING TO CLASS

Pedagogy and the Social Class of Teachers

EDITED BY

Alan Shepard,
John McMillan, and
Gary Tate

New Perspectives in Rhetoric and Composition
CHARLES I. SCHUSTER, SERIES EDITOR

Boynton/Cook Publishers
HEINEMANN
Portsmouth, NH

Boynton/Cook Publishers, Inc.
A subsidiary of Reed Elsevier Inc.
361 Hanover Street
Portsmouth, NH 03801-3912
http://www.heinemann.com

The authors and publisher wish to thank those who granted permission to reprint borrowed material:

"Digging Deep" by Louise DeSalvo. Copyright © by Louise DeSalvo. Reprinted by permission of the author.

"The Job, the Job: The Risks of Work and the Uses of Texts" by Janet Zandy. Copyright © by Janet Zandy. Reprinted by permission of the author.

Library of Congress Cataloging-in-Publication Data
CIP is on file with the Library of Congress.
ISBN 0-86709-451-6

Consulting Editor: Charles Schuster
Production: Melissa L. Inglis
Cover design: Barbara Werden
Manufacturing: Courtney Ordway

Printed in the United States of America on acid-free paper
02 01 00 99 98 DA 1 2 3 4 5

Contents

Preface

This is not the first book about academics and social class. In the past few years, several others have been published. Any list of notable contributions to this vital topic would include *This Fine Place So Far From Home*, a collection edited by C. L. Barney Dews and Carolyn Leste Law; Victor Villanueva's *Bootstraps*; and *Liberating Memory*, edited by Janet Zandy. These three volumes, along with others, have helped to recover the voices of academics from the working class, many of whom have spent their careers trying to conform to the elitist assumptions about class that pervade the academy, and some of whom are actively engaged in changing the climate of higher education. That climate has been in flux for several decades now. In the second half of this century a number of demographic changes, furthered by the G. I. bill, federal student loans, affirmative action programs, the enormous growth of community colleges, and open admissions, have fundamentally altered the landscape of U.S. colleges and universities. In some important ways, these changes were carefully observed in the 1960s and 1970s. Sociologists of education in this nation and abroad paid close attention, for example, to the effects of students' social class origins on academic performance. Curiously, their *teachers'* own class origins were largely taken to be irrelevant to what was taught to students, and how.

Coming to Class: Pedagogy and the Social Class of Teachers complements this work, in the sense that it aims to uncover what are often unspoken class suppositions and strictures in American higher education and record the effects of some of those fundamental demographic changes. Yet *Coming to Class* also takes the discussion of the role of class in higher education in new directions. We have asked the contributors, who come from a wide range of backgrounds, to trace the effects of their own class histories on their teaching. We believe this to be the first book to focus on how social class shapes the ways a teacher works in the classroom or in a particular course.

While all of the contributors are involved with the teaching of "English" in one way or another, representing the several subfields that constitute the discipline today, they are writing from a number of points of view. Along one axis we have a range of social class origins. Along another axis we have writers who are at various points along the academic chain of being, or who possess varying amounts of the profession's symbolic capital, from a graduate student (who is also a coeditor of this volume) to tenured full professors who hold chairs, from a community college professor to those who teach in private institutions that cater to children of the upper middle class, from those working toward tenure to those who are retired, from those teaching basic writing to those teaching the most ethereal literature.

Amidst these variations in class origins or present status or subject position, and with two or three notable exceptions, the majority of our contributors are coming to the topic of pedagogy as a function of social class for the first time: hence our title, *Coming to Class*. We consider this to be a strength of the collection, in part because that is where most people who teach in American colleges and universities are presently at—just coming to recognize the role of social class in their own pedagogical practices. Several contributors stated that this was one of the most difficult writing assignments they had ever accepted—difficult because class is still so invisible in higher education. As teachers, we hope that this collection will further the several conversations about social class that are vigorously under way in this country.

1

Class and Classroom
Going to Work

Jim Daniels

This essay will be informal and personal—that is my teaching style. But it will also be blunt and straightforward, for that is also my teaching style. I bring a hard-nosed approach to teaching poetry that makes my courses more difficult than what students often expect, yet I am arguably one of the most available and approachable teachers on campus. While I am no longer a member of the working class, my paradoxical teaching style reflects my background as a working-class kid. When I received a National Endowment for the Arts Creative Writing Fellowship in 1985, I got a card from my oldest brother, Mike, a truckdriver, that said, "Not bad for a poor white boy from Detroit." I've spent a long time convincing my family what hard work it is to be a poet; in the classroom, I spend a lot of time convincing my students of the same thing.

I have been teaching creative writing at Carnegie Mellon University (CMU), an expensive private school in Pittsburgh, since 1981, and I am now a full professor. It's a university named after two of the most famous local robber barons, Andrew Carnegie and Andrew Mellon. Andrew Carnegie founded it in 1900 as Carnegie Tech, a school for the children of steelworkers. Legend has it that the building in which I teach, Baker Hall, with its long, sloped hallway, was designed so that if the school didn't work out, it could be turned into a mill.

I was born in Detroit, where the names were different (Ford, Fisher, etc.), but the industrial history is similar, and I was raised in a neighborhood full of autoworkers and the children of autoworkers. My grandfather worked for Packard Motor Company until it went bankrupt, and my father worked for Ford until he retired. Or Ford's,

1

as we called it, referring to old Henry's place. I worked all through high school as a stockboy at a party store to save money for college, and then I too worked at Henry's place, in the axle plant my father worked at, during summers of my college years.

Much of my own poetry has dealt with this background. In fact, I published an entire book of poems, *Punching Out*, that is set in a factory. Because of my reputation for writing about factory work and the working class, I have often been asked about the irony of my teaching at a major research university named for Carnegie and Mellon where the students often come from privileged backgrounds so different from my own. I had not been around many wealthy people before coming to CMU, and I was forced to get over some blanket resentment of wealth and privilege in order to become an effective classroom teacher for my students.

I took great pride, as many of my generation did, in paying my own way, and when it comes to teaching, I have always expected my students to *pay their own way*. I don't mean pay in the sense of "I had to walk ten miles to school every day in bare feet so you should too." The "paying his/her own way" student is becoming increasingly rare at this and many other private universities. I mean "pay" in the sense of simple personal responsibility in the classroom. In my teaching, I have tried not to let this nostalgia for hard work and earning influence my reactions to students who come to college without having had this experience. But because Carnegie Mellon's tuition is now over $20,000 a year, it does enroll many students from more privileged backgrounds, and in fact aggressively recruits students who can pay that tuition, seeking out international students and targeting affluent areas of the nation. That privilege sometimes breeds a kind of arrogance that raises the working-class hairs on the back of my neck.

When I first started at CMU, I was both scared out of my mind and defensive. I felt like I had scammed everybody to get the job and that at some point the "class police" would show up, inspect my credentials, and give me the boot. Other working-class folks in academia have told me of similar fears. I sometimes would interpret an innocent question as a challenge. I was on a one-year instructor contract, so at the time, my position *was* pretty shaky. It was a rocky start, and my students' evaluations reflected that, though during the second semester I began to settle in a bit, and did well enough to have my contract renewed.

At the end of that first year, I asked Ronald, one of my seniors, what he was going to do after graduation. He said, "I'm going to hang around New York and live off my trust fund for a while." Trust fund? I had never known anyone who had a trust fund. I laughed, surprised. He was a good student—perceptive, funny, quirky. He wasn't afraid to take risks in his writing or his artwork. I thought for a moment and put myself in his place. What if I had a trust fund? I probably would have thought going to New York and hanging out for a while was a pretty damn good idea. Delay my entrance into the working world? As Curly of the Three Stooges would say, "Soitainly." "Have a good time," I told Ronald. That exchange opened my eyes to where many of my students were coming from, and to the different choices open to them that were not available to me.

Taking my cue from Ronald, after my first year of teaching, I went on a two-month bicycle trip through Europe. Yes, it was Europe, but I had to do it the hard way—pedaling a bike—to *earn* the trip and alleviate the strange class guilt I felt. It was the first time in my life I could afford such a trip, the first summer since I was thirteen years old in which I had not worked. I was reaping one of the spoils of academic life, the privilege of time, and was doing something my friends back home would probably never be able to do. When I returned, I suddenly had more in common with my students, many of whom typically either spend a summer in Europe during their college years or study abroad for a semester. The fine lines between classes I had always so firmly drawn were already beginning to fade.

Poetry has a history of being associated with the leisure class, those who had the time and the education to write, so in a way I already had experience crossing over through the simple act of writing poetry. It is only in the second half of this century that much poetry has come from the working class. Part of my job as a teacher is to show students that poetry both *is* work and can *do* work. It is work in that it requires a great deal of effort, not simply "inspiration." It can do work in that it can help provide insight into the human condition for both writer and reader.

One of the issues that always comes up in my classes is accessibility. Some people feel that in order to be good, poetry has to be hard to understand—that poetry is too sophisticated for the masses, etc. I've always associated this attitude with class bias. Primo Levi (1989) wrote, ". . . talking to one's fellow man in a language that he cannot understand . . . is . . . an ancient repressive artifice, known to all churches, the typical vice of our political class, the foundation of all colonial empires. It is a subtle way of imposing one's rank" (174). I tell my students that if I have a bias as a poet, it is a bias toward clarity. It's *not* okay if no one understands it. We cannot dismiss readers so cavalierly. The easiest poem to write is one that no one will understand, and if no one understands it, what value does it have? What work does it do?

Once during a class discussion, when the class couldn't figure out one student's poem, the student replied, "Oh, it must be a cultural thing." My reply was that *all writers* have an obligation to reach out to their readers, and especially to bridge cultural divides. At the beginning of each semester, I read my own poetry to my classes to let them know a little more about me as a writer and as a person. They seem to respond better to poems they can immediately relate to—poems about high school, teenage relationships, drinking, getting in trouble, and so on—rather than poems about working on an assembly line. Most of them have never known any factory workers. The experience is so far removed from their own that I use that fact as a lesson, discussing the challenge all writers face of making their life and experience more familiar to readers. I talk about how the challenge for me was to bring the reader into the factory to see and experience that world through my poems.

I also use my poems as examples of how you can write poems about *anything*—of how poetry can be about our daily struggles, and doesn't have to be about lofty subjects in arcane language. As James Wright (1983) said, "Anything can be the location of a poem as long as the poet is willing to approach that location with the appropriate reverence. Even very ugly places" (195). The poet Jonathan Holden (1983) has written, "The emotional urgency which energizes a poem of any value cannot be faked" (168). I want my students to have an emotional stake in what they're writing about, which often means getting closer to their daily lives, not farther away. Because of the misconception that poetry is an idle pursuit removed from our daily lives, and because of my own background, which disdained any "idle pursuit," I am exceedingly intolerant of a poem that the poet doesn't seem personally invested in. Writing poetry is not just playing around with words; it is using language to convey meaning and emotion.

The poet Richard Hugo (1979) once wrote, "A creative writing class is one of the last places in the world where your life still matters" (65). I use that quote as an epigraph for my classes. The first poetry assignment I give asks students to write a "questionnaire" or "resume" poem in which they introduce themselves, and from there we begin the work of making meaning of their lives. I often learn a great deal about their histories from this assignment. Generally, many beginning poets write autobiographical poems, so I quickly learn about my students' backgrounds. As a result, we are all more conscious of social class than we might be in, for example, a math class. This is particularly true in workshop classes; the main texts are student poems, and we spend a great deal of class time reading about each other's lives.

Creative writing is a subject that some academics have always viewed with suspicion. Perhaps they believe the courses are easy, are too touchy-feely, and, as a result, are "impossible to grade." Even at

CMU, where we offer one of the country's few undergraduate creative writing degrees, these false assumptions persist—even among students. I am quick to set them straight.

My syllabi are very detailed, particularly when it comes to evaluation and grading. I insist that all work be turned in on time. No waiting for the Muse to show up—she has to work nine to five, just like everybody else. Well, maybe she works the afternoon shift, or midnights. She can be temperamental, certainly, but when the alarm clock goes off, the Muse gets up, grumbling, and heads to the shower.

Still, some students don't believe I am serious until they get their grades. Perhaps they have never been in a situation where doing something late or not doing it at all can have serious repercussions—like getting them fired. Just recently, I have had to fail a student for not turning in a final portfolio on time (it was two weeks late, and the student had not even requested an extension). If students have more than two unexcused absences, their grade drops one level. If more than four occur, I ask the student to drop the course. Arriving late more than three times also drops the grade. I try to teach personal responsibility through my example as both a writer and a teacher. I always return assignments promptly, within a week of the due date.

An early mistake I made as a teacher was to try to be friends with my students. I wanted to side with them against authority—the bosses I had resented so much for taking my father away from me on nights and weekends while he was at work, and the ones I had worked for myself in mind-numbing work settings. The problem, of course, is that if students saw me as their friend, they tried to take advantage of me and asked for unnecessary extensions, better grades, and so on. In order to be a good teacher, I had to become more attuned to my job, which is to make them better writers. Being pals with them did not help in that process, so over the years I have strived for a balance.

I begin each class by reading a poem—one chosen by me or by a student. If anyone shows up late, he or she disrupts that poem. That first poem is the factory whistle for my classes: Listen up. We're getting started. This is why we're here.

Once we're started, I work hard to get everyone talking, for my classes are really discussions. I rarely lecture, and then only in the introductory courses. My goal is to create a community of writers. Growing up where I did I could have used more support and encouragement for my ambitions, and more of a sense that I was not alone in my desire to be a poet. Today I try to break down barriers—class, race, sex—because they often create distrust and confrontational discussions or, worse, silence. The one thing that does unite everyone is an interest in poetry, so I try to stay focused on that. Being aware of the class tensions between my background and my position in the university allows me, I think, an advantage in seeing slights or distortions that some might miss, comments that reveal a subtle bias.

When we discuss student work, it is always with an eye toward revision, which is consistent with my emphasis on poetry as work. I require revision in all of my classes, of course, but I think I put extra emphasis on it because of my background. Certainly, some poems are gifts. Occasionally, we do find money on the ground. Most often, we go to work. We earn the poems through trial and error, through working and reworking an idea, an image, a feeling.

Before I take this "production" comparison too far—I was just about to suggest that as a professor I serve as a quality-control inspector—I must point out that one of the big differences between writing poems and making axle parts is the issue of personal stake in the material. I don't want my students to turn out identical poems in an assembly-line fashion, but I do want them to sit down and *attempt* to write poetry on a regular basis, and I want them to write out of an honest examination of their lives. I require students to keep notebooks, as both records of their attempts at writing and as a resource for ideas for future poems. For example, when I make an assignment to write a sonnet, I don't want students thinking only of producing a product—"fourteen lines, iambic pentameter, rhymed"—but I want them thinking of subject matter, thinking of what ideas from their notebooks might work in this form.

One of the things I hated about factory work was the anonymity of it all, and I try to avoid that production-line mentality in my classes. In the factory, if I was doing a good job, I was functioning like a machine. The only time the bosses paid any attention to me was when I screwed up. I want to know my students, and I want to reward them for doing good work. Every professor will tell you this, but at a university that rewards (in terms of raises and promotions) research over classroom effectiveness, it's often not the case.

I require students to see me in my office at least twice a semester, and I always have my workshop students over to my house for dinner so that they can see me more as an individual instead of as The Professor. I had problems with authority growing up at least in part because I associated authority with class oppression and lack of fairness. While I am not afraid to use my authority in the classroom to shape the discussion, correct errors, and so forth, I do want students to be aware of the human being behind that authority—one who cooks, changes diapers, listens to music, etc.

I don't want to be seen as someone who keeps people in their places as a way of maintaining my place. My first book of poems is called *Places/Everyone*—I have always been concerned with how society tries to keep us in our "places" and makes it very difficult to move up from one "place" to another. I want my students instead to see me as someone who knows more about poetry than they do, has more experience reading and writing it, and wants to use that knowledge and experience to help them improve their own reading and writing.

When I meet with students individually, I have them bring in their poems, and we discuss them in more detail than is allowed for during class time. These appointments allow me to get to know my students better, which in turn allows me to respond more effectively to their writing. I get a better idea of their emotional makeup, and that sometimes helps me get a sense for what tone to take when providing critiques of their poems.

Nothing makes me angrier than when a student misses a scheduled appointment. I sit stewing in my office, wasting a half hour waiting for the student to show. The next day in class, I sometimes hear comments like, "Oh, sorry, can we reschedule?" Sometimes there's not even an apology. Such students treat me as a servant, which, in a way, I am. But I am also their boss, in that I evaluate their performance. It is this strange negotiation between being in charge and providing a service that has been most difficult for me to adapt to, given my background. While I don't mind being accountable for how I teach my classes, how I evaluate my students, I do resent being second-guessed by students clearly more interested in getting a high grade than in learning the subject matter. Some students seem to think that paying the high tuition should buy them good grades. In the factory, the roles were much clearer.

Evaluation—grading—*is* an issue in a creative writing class. I have a pretty good idea, after teaching poetry for fifteen years, of who's putting in the effort and improving, and that is what I grade on—my perception of a student's writing, along with his or her performance in classroom discussions. I have much more confidence in my grading than I did when I first started, and that allows me to be tougher. In an environment where the "gentleman's *C*" has been replaced by the "gentleman's *B*," I have been very conscientious about maintaining high standards for my students, and I have a reputation as a tough grader. I hope *tough* means *fair*, for I want all my grades to count, to have meaning. I want students to have a sense of accomplishment when they leave my class with a good grade. It is not something that has been given to them, but something they earned.

While I don't grade individual poems, students clearly know how well they've done through my written comments, all of which are geared toward revision. I cover the poems with comments ranging from suggestions on line breaks to suggestions for rethinking the entire poem. I often ask, "Where is the *poem* in this poem? Where is its emotional core? What is motivating you to write this?" Some students are discouraged by the amount of feedback they get from me. I try to mitigate that somewhat in conferences—to put my comments into perspective and offer as much encouragement as I can. I tell students frequently that it would be much less *work* for me to write "great" or "good work" or *B* on their poems than to write the detailed critiques they get. Those critiques are a concrete sign that I am doing my job.

Because I am teaching poetry, and not applied electronics, I tell my students to be as idealistic as they can for as long as they can. "Don't sell yourself short if you really want to be a writer," I tell them. "If you fail, you can try something else. But are you going to be happy if you don't try?" While many of them can afford to hold onto their idealism longer than I could because of the financial support of their families, what I have found is that students coming from wealthy backgrounds as often as not are pressured to be successful right away, with "success" rather narrowly defined.

One student of mine—his name was Arthur Tillbury III but he went by the name "Tripp"—applied to both law school and graduate programs in creative writing. His father was a lawyer. You can guess where he ended up, and unhappily so, based on the e-mail I've gotten from him. He wants to start a literary magazine for lawyers, and maybe things will work out for him as he emerges from his father's influence, but I felt defeated for him.

Like Tripp, I also had to deal with parental pressure. For me, it was pressure to use my education to better myself, to lift myself up in class and stature. My parents did not, at first, see writing poetry as a way to achieve that. For many of my students, it's pressure not to fall, or lower one's standard of living. We are allies against that kind of pressure.

It's easy to remember my working-class students. They are rare, and becoming more so, and their writing, even their speech, often reveals their class. Many Pittsburghers speak in a clearly identifiable dialect, which include saying "yinz" for "you all," and dropping the infinitive—"the car needs washed." It is both a sign of region *and* of class. CMU students sometimes derogatorily refer to someone who speaks like this as a "yinzer." Karen, a working-class student from Pittsburgh, told me how she tried consciously to lose the dialect to fit in at CMU.

Minority students often seem to gravitate toward minority faculty (particularly at CMU, which has a very small number of minority faculty). I have found that something similar often happens with students from working-class backgrounds, though it may take them a little longer to find me because I am not so easily identifiable. Maybe they'll attend one of my poetry readings, or read a poem of mine somewhere, or hear about me from another student. One thing about class is that you can erase your background if you choose, become someone new, shed class like an old greasy jacket. While I don't wear it everywhere like I used to, I haven't shed that jacket entirely and never will.

I try not to treat my working-class students any differently. In terms of grading, I know I don't. In fact, working-class students tend to get lower grades partly because of the carryover from bad public schools. The best poets coming into my courses are often the ones from the more privileged backgrounds. They usually have gone to private schools where they have had more exposure to poetry, and they have also gotten more attention and encouragement to write their own poems. It's often the working-class, public school kids who have to come the farthest, who in the introductory courses have to play catch-up with everyone else.

One of my first working-class students was Gladys, and from her I learned how poetry can help break down barriers in the classroom. I also began to learn how to negotiate the territory between my own background and that of my students. Gladys worked as a secretary at CMU, and because of her tuition benefit, she was able to take classes for free. She had raised her family, and they were grown and out of the house when she returned to school. She took a couple of my poetry classes and eventually received a degree in creative writing, though it took her many, many years. I confess, I made a special effort to see that she did graduate and waived some meaningless requirements that didn't seem to apply to her. Her husband was a steelworker, and though she had a working-class background, she did not see it as possible subject matter for her poetry.

Gladys's early poems were sappy rhymers. Greeting card verse. She was much older than the other students, and some of them openly patronized her. They had little patience for her corny pieties. I kept telling her to write about her life. It was hard to find Gladys in those poems, or even behind her poems.

Finally, late one semester, Gladys turned in a poem about a group of secretaries who walked together at lunch time. There was spirit, a glimmer of life to it. When we discussed the poem in class, one wild punk rocker looked her in the eye and said, "Gladys, this is good. You're writing about something real here." The moment transformed the class. A warmth spread over the room as Gladys beamed and nodded. Everyone was quick to praise her, recognizing the breakthrough. It was a moment so memorable that fourteen years later when a student from that class who is now teaching at another university introduced me at a poetry reading at his school, he told that story in his introduction.

As a teacher, I also found myself being put off by Gladys's bad rhyming verse, but I didn't want to dismiss her with what I saw as snobbery, class-based scorn. She could have been my mother. My mother, who had taken a writing class at the local community college after all her children had left home. My mother, who had proudly, nervously, shown me a poem she'd written for that course. I wanted to side with Gladys because of our shared backgrounds, but as a teacher, I had to side with the students who recognized her writing as inferior. Later in the semester, when a group of students was driving to my house for the class dinner, Gladys asked them if they should stop and get some Creamsicles for dessert. They stopped, and Gladys went into the store. We had Creamsicles together.

In that situation, poetry was a link, finally, between classes, as well as between my own roles and identities. It provided a natural opportunity to bridge gaps. As I was to find with another working-class student, however, poetry does not always provide *enough* of a link to bridge the gaps. Darlene was a welfare mother who'd had various problems over the years with drugs, the law, etc. She had a big tattoo on one arm, and a big scar on the other where she'd had another tattoo removed. One day, she showed up at my office with some of her writing and told me she was applying to CMU. Somewhere along the line she'd heard me read and decided to study with me. Perhaps she saw me writing about things that she could relate to. Darlene is the kind of person who, once she wants something, will find a way to have it, whether it's drugs or poetry. She'd done very well at the community college, and her poems were full of passion and life, so I wrote a letter to the admissions office requesting they admit her. To their credit, they put together a financial aid package to allow her to enroll.

It angered and amazed her that so many of the students didn't have a clue as to what it was like "out there." She took three busses to get to campus each day and was very restricted by her son's schedule, so every minute was precious to her. She cried when her family somehow finagled to get her a computer so that she wouldn't have to make that long trip to campus to use the computer clusters. Darlene really wanted to come to CMU, but I don't think she had thought much about the other students. Once she enrolled, she realized how much she stood out from the others, and she resented it. She was older, a mother, and poor. She felt the other students were looking down their noses at her.

"They're not all so bad," I kept telling her. "Give them a chance, and they'll give you a chance." She was covering all the students with the blanket of privilege so that she couldn't really *see* any of them. She reminded me of myself when I first came to CMU, though she clearly had more spunk than I ever did. She was always vocal in class, but easily frustrated and easily hurt. She wore her emotions on her sleeve in a way that seemed totally opposite to just about everyone else. While the characteristic attitude of the students then seemed to be what I called "prematurely cynical," Darlene, who had every reason to be cynical, was instead fighting, fighting for hope. I often met with her after class to try to calm her down and put things in perspective for her. The artifice, the pretentiousness of some of the students was certainly there, but I knew from my own experience that the stereotypes did not hold up. Actually, some students were fascinated by Darlene's background and were intimidated by *her*.

While defending the other students, and the institution as a whole, I also found myself wondering, had I mellowed? Had I been co-opted? Had I now become part of this institution of privilege? I had certainly come to appreciate the advantages for me as both a teacher and a writer to be at an expensive research university. My teaching load is two courses per semester, which allows me plenty of time to teach and write with all of my concentration. Would I give up this job to teach more classes, larger classes, with more Darlenes? No. Time to write is something I consider precious, sacred. But these advantages make me even more aware of my special obligation to students like Darlene, someone trying to do what I did.

I directed Darlene's honors thesis, a collection of her poems, so we met every week through her senior year. She had an intense rivalry with another senior, and it seemed to be based in part on class differences. The other student was from England, and Darlene thought she was a snob—maybe it was the British accent. At the end of the year, the dean's office had scheduled Darlene and the other student to present their theses at the same time in different rooms. I attended Darlene's, along with just one other student, another woman from a working-class background who had become good friends with Darlene. I think they both had been drinking beforehand. Darlene had brought the wrong version of her manuscript and couldn't find the second page of one of her poems. She stopped halfway through it and looked for the other page for a good five minutes. In the middle of that, the associate dean came in and sat down. Darlene became embarrassed and fumbled even more, nearly stopping her presentation altogether. At the end, I was furious. She had let *us* down by being unprofessional, by confirming a class stereotype and looking like she wasn't up to the challenge when we both knew she was.

My ears burned as I walked past her out of that room. I couldn't talk to her. I realized later that she knew all along that no one was going to show up, that all the writing students would go hear "one of their own." I couldn't stay mad at her. Particularly when I saw her at graduation, with her son, a hyperactive kid with lots of troubles. At the reception for students and their parents, Darlene did stick out as much as she claimed she did, off to the side, self-consciously eating hors d'oeuvres with her son. I remember her in my office saying, "But Jim Daniels, you more than anyone should understand."

I do. I understand. Without care, a university can be as numbing and impersonal as an auto plant. I try to be open to all my students in a way my father was never open to me—because of work, long hours, frustration, anger. I have modeled myself after the teachers who gave extra attention to both my writing and my life to help me realize my dream of being a poet instead of a factory worker. But with Darlene, I realized that poetry is no savior, that I'm no savior. I think I let *her* down, too.

If social class is like a tattoo, then I think there's a middle ground between showing it off and removing it entirely. In my classes, I search for that elusive middle ground. As Darlene knows now, you can't remove a tattoo without some scarring, and scars are as permanent as tattoos. They both fade some, but never go away.

When I leave the house in the morning, I tell my wife and kids "I'm going to school," not "I'm going to work." I try to never lose sight of how fortunate I am to be able to say that. Yes, it is a job, it is *work*, but it is a place where learning occurs every day in every class, and I am a part of that learning, a part of shaping young lives, shaping them to be open to the world as the best poets are, not to be closed off by prejudice and resentment that eats away at one's soul. I work at a place where I can use a word like *soul* without embarrassment. And yes, it's a privilege—I am privileged now—I have made my own trust fund, and I'm not going to give it back.

Works Cited

Holden, J. 1983. *Chowder Review* (Summer): 18/19, 168.

Hugo, R. 1979. *The Triggering Town: Lectures and Essays on Poetry and Writing*. New York: W.W. Norton.

Levi, P. 1989. "On Obscure Writing." *Other People's Trades,* trans. R. Rosenthal. New York: Summit.

Wright, J. 1983. *Collected Prose,* ed. A. Wright. Ann Arbor: University of Michigan Press.

2

Digging Deep

Louise DeSalvo

It is 1983. I am on a very small airplane, flying from Boston to Maine, to give a series of talks at Colby College about my work on Virginia Woolf. I am teaching at Hunter College (where students, like me, are often the first members of their family to attend college) and have published two books—a study of how Woolf composed her first novel, *The Voyage Out*; and an edition of a more political, radical, earlier draft of that novel. I have the seed of an idea for yet another— a book about Woolf's childhood focusing on the damaging effects of neglectful, abusive child-rearing practices in England's middle and upper classes. Unlike many of my colleagues (whom I refer to, derisively, as "Anglomaniacs"), I find little to admire in what I know about the practices of Woolf's class, though I respect her scathing critique of privilege in works like *Three Guineas*.

This flight to Maine, so far, has been thrilling. The pilot has hugged the magnificent coast. We are flying so low we can see the waves pounding on the rocks, the salt spray pluming in the air.

Soon, the plane banks, heads inland, descends. "Below," the pilot announces, "are the tracks of the Maine Central Railroad." And I burst into tears. For my maternal grandfather, Salvatore Calabrese, worked on these tracks at the beginning of the century.

I am interested in issues of class in my teaching and in my writing because of my working-class origins, and I discuss them whenever I can. In a recent course on Woolf, for example, students in my class have decided to focus on the poorer characters—Charles Tansley, Mrs. Bast, and Mrs. McNab in *To the Lighthouse*, for example— rather than on the middle-class Ramsays. [In time, one student, Kathleen Dobie, publishes "This is the House That Class Built," the first major treatment of class in Woolf's *Jacob's Room*.] We have

13

thought, too, about how poorly Woolf treated her servants—the evidence is in her diaries—and about whether Woolf's attitude to the workers she was creating in the novel shifted and became more sympathetic because when she was writing *Lighthouse* there was a major general strike in England.

But I believe, too, that demythologizing the artistic process is important, both for my students and me, and this is why I have worked on earlier drafts of Woolf's published novels. For without any models in my family for how intellectual work gets done, I have looked to writers like Woolf to learn how. In my composition classes, I have shown beginning writers the earlier drafts of Woolf's published work. My students are always thrilled to see them—to examine the false starts Woolf made, the sharpening of phrases, the eradication of entire trite and overwritten paragraphs, the deepening of meaning through imagery and metaphor. They have learned that, even for writers from privileged classes, getting the meaning you want down on paper is a long, painstaking process. But perhaps most important, they have learned, too, that their first drafts sound no worse (and occasionally sound better) than hers.

As I was growing up in the Italian working-class section of Hoboken, New Jersey, we rarely discussed issues of class, exploitation, or my parents' thwarted desires and their hopes that I would lead a different life. Nonetheless, I learned about the kind of worker I would one day want to be by watching the members of my family bend over their suppers when they came home, exhausted from work, too tired to speak; by seeing their eyes cloud when they spoke of what they had dreamed for themselves when they were young; and by listening to them tell me that what had been impossible for them—doing freely chosen work that satisfied their desires—might one day be possible for me if I worked hard, studied hard, and continued my education as they couldn't.

I work with students, with books, with words because I believe that education can make one's life qualitatively better. My grandfather worked with steel, with pickax and shovel, because he was illiterate, because he had no other way to earn his living. I work, standing in front of a (somewhat comfortable) classroom, talking, or sitting at a desk writing, or reclining on a sofa reading or thinking. My grandfather worked, hunched over, always in pain, always uncomfortable, scraping his way through and across the land, his labor exploited, fixing a railroad line he would never travel upon for pleasure, for he had not the time nor the money. He left his home for months, and, because he couldn't read, couldn't write, there was no word from him until he returned, looking years older, saying little, for there was little to say, looking down, down, down.

In a 1916 essay called "The 'Wop' in the Track Gang," Dominic T. Ciolli reports that railroad men like my grandfather slept in their filthy work clothes—there was no place to wash—on vermin-infested bags of straw, covering themselves with discarded horse blankets, eight men to a roach-infested, windowless boxcar; they awakened at three in the morning, and worked from five until twelve "without rest," had a bread and water lunch, and worked again until four. Once, when a gang of laborers complained that they had no fresh water, Ciolli heard the padrone remark, "These dagoes are never satisfied. . . . They should be starved to death. . . . They don't belong here."

I know that my grandfather's long, hard days of working on the railroad, sometimes repairing the line, sometimes as a cook for the crew, in the heat of the sun, or in the pouring rain, or sleet and snow, living in the conditions Ciolli has described, is why his heart failed him, and why he died so young, leaving my mother and me so hopelessly bereft. I work under far different conditions. I leave home in the late morning, and return in the evening, tired, but exhilarated from a day's work with students, proud of what I've accomplished, eager to return to my reading, my writing, and to dig in, to pick away at the next chunk of meaning. My father, too, was a laborer, though a skilled one—he was a machinist. Though he worked hard, unlike my grandfather he did not work under brutal conditions, and, though he always complained about his bosses, he never complained about his work. He felt privileged by comparison; he had "good benefits": health and life insurance, a retirement plan. To me, his work life was one of dignity, hard work (he retired at eighty). His life, though, was one of thwarted desire (though he still possesses a capacity to find joy in whatever comes his way, to engage with life, and to be voraciously curious about how things work—on a recent trip to Versailles, he used his meager French, learned during World War II, to ask a gardener how the fountains worked).

Thwarted desire. I believe that a life of thwarted desire is a cruel fact of working-class life. For example, as a young man my father had a spectacular untrained tenor voice and wanted to become an opera singer—he had the raw talent and the temperament to become a star. But money was scarce, and he couldn't afford lessons, and besides, he didn't have sufficient schooling; as the only son in a large family, he stopped school in the seventh or eighth grade. He had started working when he was seven years old, helping his mother with the piecework she did at home. So, instead of singing himself, he went to the Metropolitan Opera whenever he could afford it. (At the Met, no one, including me, liked to sit near him because he couldn't control himself from singing along, and loudly, with the arias he had started to memorize when he was just a boy.)

And my mother, too, never realized her desires. She worked as a
"salesgirl" selling shoes and couldn't use the scholarship she was
awarded to go to college. It was the thirties; her family was in desperate financial shape, and she needed to start work immediately after
high school. Throughout my youth, my mother let me examine the
medal, engraved with her name, that she had been awarded for her
writing in high school. She wore it proudly on the lapel of her Sunday
suit throughout her life. And though she was the best writer in her
class and hoped to someday become a writer, in adulthood the only
writings she ever managed were her exquisitely phrased, weekly letters to my children when they were in college.

How has my family background, my class origin, affected my pedagogy when I teach literature and writing?

I have chosen to teach students who, like myself, are the first in
their families to attend college. Often, they are self-supporting, working full-time while attending college, sometimes raising children.
Hunter is racially and ethnically diverse. Many students are poor;
many come from the latest wave of New York City immigrants. Some
are activists (or were in their country of origin). Though some of my
colleagues lambast the City University's open admissions policy and
developmental courses, I applaud them. In my experience, students
work hard to become literate; many achieve, in college, a prose
fluency that I had not yet attained in graduate school. When they are
in major courses in literature, my students often write publishable
papers. So I believe the City University system works, and I believe
that attempts to erode it are racist and classist attacks on the only
education available to the poor in New York City.

I believe that my students deserve the finest teachers, and I try to
be the finest teacher I can be for them. This means that I take every
opportunity I can to learn about them as individuals (without violating
their privacy), to support their efforts, to show that I value and respect
their work. Though I require them to set high standards for themselves, I show them how to be successful in my classroom. The
antithesis of the teacher I want to be is teacher as overseer (like the
padrone who oversaw my grandfather's work)—one who holds students in contempt, who stifles and suppresses them, who tells them
what to do but not how to do it, and who usually tells them that what
they have done hasn't been done well enough.

More important, though, my working-class origin shows in the
way I teach—in how I organize a classroom. Underlying everything I
do is a belief that it is my responsibility to provide an opportunity for
my students to allow themselves to recognize their desires as human
beings, and that I work with them as a partner in enabling them to

learn ways in which their life's work and their desires can become congruent. I want to work in a way that will enable them to follow their desires rather than to frustrate them, to act as agents of their desire rather than of someone else's. I believe that this is fundamentally what a radical educator does.

I am passionate about this because, like the working-class writer D. H. Lawrence, I believe that the most pernicious aspect of a hierarchical class system is not only that the privileged exploit the labor of workers, but also that in a hierarchical class system, the working class is prevented from ever having what they want (chosen, valued work, perhaps; or work done in safe and aesthetically pleasing surroundings; free time; safe streets and beautiful homes and neighborhoods).

This means that in every class I teach (literature or writing), I begin by asking my students to think and talk and write about what *they* desire—in their lives, in their careers, and in this class. (There is substantial evidence that doing this regularly means the difference between achieving one's desires and not.) I want them to learn what is important to them, rather than force them to learn what is important to me. I ask them to imagine what they want to have accomplished twenty years from now; I ask them what they could do during our semester's work together to help them realize this dream. We freewrite about this in class or at home in diaries or the journals I suggest they keep for class. By way of example, so they can understand their preoccupations by contrasting them with mine, I read what I have written in my journal about what is occupying me right now, and how it differs from what I focused upon in the past. Now, for example, because I am in my mid-fifties, and because I want to continue to lead a vital life as I age, I am focusing upon the elder characters in Woolf's novels—Mrs. Dalloway, for example—ones I'd previously largely ignored when, as a parent of young children, I focused upon Woolf's descriptions of children and childhood when reading.

In a Virginia Woolf (or any literature) class, having each student recognize what she or he wants sets the focus for that student's work for the semester. Clare, for example, who wants to become an architect, focuses on the description of interior and public spaces; Josh, who plans to be a horticulturist, on Woolf's descriptions of flowers; Ned, who is studying to be a social worker, on class differences; Tom, unwillingly separated from his children, on father/child relationships; Eliza, already in the fashion industry, on Woolf's description of clothing.

In my writing classes, I invite my students to imagine the careers they would like for themselves. I share my past and current dreams (and challenges and frustrations, too), and those of other writers. I read to them from my journals and those of writers and artists such as

Virginia Woolf, May Sarton, and Anne Truitt—and I tell, specifically, how I work toward my goals, also suggesting concrete ways in which they might work toward theirs. I do this because I believe it is important to show students how successful writers work so that they might organize a life for themselves with these models in mind. I suggest that they keep a journal—most published writers do. That they find or make a network of writers—Howard Gardner's *Creating Minds* (1993) indicates that peer groups of writers help one another become successful in ways in which writers who are isolated can't. That they set a schedule—Virginia Woolf wrote from ten to one in the mornings, and in the afternoons, she typed her work and read; Anne Morrow Lindbergh, too, reserved her mornings for her writing; the novelist, essayist, and poet Jay Parini makes sure he works daily, in the mornings, switching from one project to another; in her diaries May Sarton often complained that her voluminous correspondence took too much time away from her creative work, yet she felt obligated to answer all her mail before beginning her own work—a mistake, I think.

Always, though, these are suggestions. I believe that student writers must find ways of working that are congenial to themselves, not merely imitative of the ways other writers work. I invite students to become self-reflective—to experiment with a way of working or with a schedule or with setting a series of self-determined goals (to work on dialogue or to work with sense data in memoir, for example), and then to reflect on whether that way of working makes sense for them. In this way, student writers and critics learn a sense of *control* over the way they work that contributes to their sense of autonomy and authority.

I work in this way because I believe that my primary purpose as a working-class intellectual is to share with my students what I know about the process of how one does this kind of work, and to show them where to find this kind of information for themselves. Keeping the process hidden, I believe, disables working-class students. For without the kinds of connections that come with privilege, my students need to learn an arsenal of strategies to enable them to fulfill their desires, for opportunities will not come to them as easily as they might come to more privileged writers. So, I show my student writers how I work, how other writers work, by looking at letters, diaries, notebooks, early drafts. I teach my student writers how work gets published, and I show them how to get theirs published. This is important, for many don't know how the publishing industry works, and how long it takes, for example, to get a work published. I tell them, for example, that, before acceptance, my first novel was rejected twenty-five times. And I teach them to take themselves and their work seriously, and that their work matters. (One student, John

Champagne, published a novel he'd written with me, *The Blue Lady's Hands*, before he graduated.)

The aim of this pedagogy for student majors in English is three-fold: first, to demystify what a working writer's life, what a critic's work life is like; second, to teach by providing an example against which students can formulate their own ways of working; third (and crucial), to show the steps by which one goes about enacting one's desire.

Always, I insist that they take their work, and the work of their peers, seriously, and that they respect one another's work. In my judgment, the pedagogy in many creative writing classroom permits vicious assaults of student writers in the guise of group critiquing. This has never made much sense to me, for I believe it undermines the self-confidence and self-determination that beginning working-class writers require to continue their work. Can you imagine, I ask my students, such a class with William Faulkner and Ernest Hemingway? Faulkner would tell Hemingway to write longer sentences; Hemingway would tell Faulkner to shorten his. Critiquing, I believe, is often nothing more than a report of personal preference. Worse, it teaches students to look to others for suggestions about what needs doing or confirmation of the worth of their work, rather than to develop the skills necessary to determine this on their own. I believe the most innovative, most radical, most important work is written by writers who eschew outside criticism, at least until a draft of the work is finished.

When we do read our work to one another in writing classes, or in literature classes (and I write with students), I insist that we point to facets of the work that succeed, not critique aspects of the work that fail. I loathe the word *fail*. For, truly, where there is risk, there can be no such thing as failure; it is often in writing something that doesn't quite work that we are moving toward something that does. I encourage students, though, to tell their peers when something is unclear or when they'd like to hear more about a subject, for I believe that working-class students are often reluctant to say all that they might about a given subject, having internalized the view that what they say isn't valuable and therefore must be said quickly and succinctly. I've discovered, over the years, that providing active support for what is beginning to work or what works, and encouraging students to amplify what they've already written, enable them to set the highest standards for themselves.

In my classes, we sit in a circle, so that we can see one another and interact with one another, and so that everyone will take equal responsibility for participation. I encourage my students to actively listen to one another. My ideal aim is to have each student speak dur-

ing each class. I do this because I believe that there is nothing sweet-
er than the sound of student voices in synergistic communion with
each other. I do this because I learn more about each book I teach, and
about the act of writing, by listening to my students than by telling
them what I know. Of course, I learn, too, about them. I want to provide my students with a model of teacher, not as an authority—though
I am authoritative—but as a lifelong learner. My favorite times are
when students are meeting in small groups, reading their work to each
other or discussing a passage in a literary work. As I circle the room
to ask how they're doing, I take great pride and pleasure in their interactions, and, when I see them smiling with the joy they're taking in
each other's insights, when I watch them lean into the circle in intellectual and emotional communion, I know I've created the classroom
atmosphere I value.

Focusing on helping students value and understand the *process* of
work in a creative writing classroom, rather than focusing on the *product* of work is a direct outgrowth of my class background. Focusing on
process, I believe, allows egalitarian interactions in a way that focusing
on product does not. Focusing on process invites a moment-by-
moment appreciation of how work happens; it teaches that we can
control the way we work—that we can make our work time productive
and perhaps even pleasurable. Inviting students to think about the ways
in which their process of writing, of reading, can be managed to yield
maximum pleasure and personal benefit turns the tables on the
definition of work that most (that I) have internalized—of work as
something someone else tells you to do for someone else's benefit,
work that is unpleasant, rather than rewarding and pleasurable.

And so we go around the room and I ask, say, "How is your work
going right now?" or "What is your greatest challenge right now?" or
"What worked last week?" As each student answers, we listen, offer
corresponding or differing experiences and suggestions and support.
Each semester, I ask my students many questions about their work.
What is the most significant challenge in your work right now? What
are you enjoying in your work right now? What have you learned
about your best times to work? What do you need to do before working? Where do you work best? What have you accomplished? What
do you still want to do? What changes do you want to make? How do
you imagine the shape of your finished piece?

Often, my class and I talk about workspaces. I ask them where
they work, where they like to work, what their ideal writing place
would be. I ask this question each semester because I know my students often live in cramped and noisy quarters, and I want to share
what I know about writers who began their careers with similar (supposed) impediments, for, I think, one way of silencing people is to

have them think they need ideal conditions to do their work. I talk about William Faulkner, for example, who wrote one of his novels with the noise of a boiler accompanying him, for he worked while on the job; about Toni Morrison, who continued a line of poetry after her son vomited on her paper by writing right around it; about Henry Miller, who lived on the streets, using his manuscripts as a pillow, who without a centime to his name, sat, writing, on the terrace of the Dome in Paris, waiting for someone to come by to pay his bill; how D. H. Lawrence, during a period of illness and extreme poverty, sat, his back to a granite boulder, overlooking the sea, penning a draft of *Women in Love*; how I have found a quiet, rarely used wood-paneled reading room in a nearby library, yet how I wrote, too, with my babies splashing in a wading pool on a summer day. And my students share free or cheap writing spaces they know of that are beautiful and quiet: Central Park, during warm weather; a coffee shop in Greenwich Village where they don't chase you away; or the patio on the seventh floor of Hunter College. I believe that writing in public spaces automatically makes you think of yourself as a writer, and that if I can get my students to write in public, it gets them to take themselves seriously as writers; it enables them to place themselves in the tradition of writers such as Beauvoir and Sartre, who did it too.

All those years ago, the moment when I realized I was flying over the rails of the Maine Central Railroad that my grandfather had worked on during the beginning of the century as I was on my way to deliver my lecture about my work on Virginia Woolf has stood, for me, as an emblem of the tremendous, almost unspeakable irony of my life. Everything I have done as a teacher, as a writer—who I teach, and why, and what, and how—I now read against the context of my grandfather's work, and against that of my working-class mother and my father.

And when, in one of my literature classes, one of my writing classes, I hear myself ask a student, "Can you dig deeper into the meaning of this passage?" or "Can you dig deeper into what you felt then, into what you focused on as it was happening?" or "Can you dig more deeply into why you responded to that character in that way?" I understand that this is how I have always described my work, as if I am using pickax and shovel, like my grandfather, as if digging into meaning is something like digging into hard earth, which it is and which it isn't. And it isn't until I write this essay that I understand that, in the language I use as I go about my intellectual work—in consistently asking my students and myself to dig deep—that I am trying to retain my connection with my grandfather, and with his hard, manual labor.

Note

On May 26, 1998, The Board of Trustees of The City University of New York approved a proposal barring students who have not yet passed proficiency exams, effectively ending its "Open Admissions" policy instituted in the 1970s.

Works Cited

Ciolli, D. T. 1916. "The 'Wop' in the Track Gang." *The Immigrants in America Review.* (July).

Gardner, H. 1993. *Creating Minds.* New York: HarperCollins.

3

One Hundred Friends and Other Class Issues
Teaching Both In and Out of the Game

John Ernest

Trippers and askers surround me,
People I meet. . . . the effect upon me of my early life. . . . of
the ward and city I live in. . . . of the nation,
The latest news. . . . discoveries, inventions, societies. . . .
authors old and new,
My dinner, dress, associates, looks, business, compliments,
dues,
The real or fancied indifference of some man or woman I
love,
The sickness of one of my folks—or of myself. . . . or ill-
doing. . . . or loss or lack of money. . . . or depressions or
exaltations,
They come to me days and nights and go from me again,
But they are not the Me myself.
                            —Walt Whitman, *Leaves of Grass*

My favorite line (among many favorites) from the poem eventually
entitled "Song of Myself" follows shortly after the lines I have used in
the epigraph. Whitman continues directly with the assertion, "Apart
from the pulling and hauling stands what I am." He then characterizes

I would like to thank Rebecca Mays Ernest and Avy Trager for their help with this essay, with
special thanks to Rebecca for the term *pericultural*. I am grateful also to Alan Howard for conversations years ago that eventually led me to this essay.

"what I am": the way that it "Stands amused, complacent, compas-
sionating, idle, unitary"—the way, in my favorite line, "what I am" is
"Both in and out of the game and watching and wondering at it"
([1855] 1996, 30). If I had been asked many years ago, when I first
started thinking about this poem, to identify the presence of class in
the above lines, I would have focused on the lines beginning with
"People I meet," including upbringing, geographical location, and
various cultural badges and rituals of identity: "dinner, dress, associates, looks, business, compliments, dues." And it would have been
easy, as indeed it was, to find myself in the line about being both in
and out of the game. I was a white middle-class male from the out-
skirts of Toledo, Ohio, who believed that the suburbs were liminal
enough to allow for some flexibility in one's cultural script. People
like me, with a fondness for literature, indulge in Kerouac dreams
when we're young; when we get older, we're likely to become academics raging against, say, the tyranny of narrative, or maybe finding
ways to think of academics as an oppressed class. Our own narratives, if generally predictable, are relatively unobstructed; self-creation and revision seem endlessly possible.

This relative freedom of movement, geographical and social, has
long been an influential presence in the white middle class—rendering the social terms of identity at once more fluid and less secure.
Examining what many take to be the centerpiece of American national mythology, the belief that "class background is not fate" (Lindberg
1982, 5), Gary Lindberg considers the effects generally of migrations
and cultural adaptations from other countries, and the effects
specifically of ongoing internal migrations and adaptations in the
United States. "This repeated movement," Lindberg argues,

> has had some obvious consequences. It has made many Americans
> restless, unstable, thirsty for novelty. It has loosened family and
> community bonds and has encouraged people to dwell imaginative-
> ly in the future. Institutions that depend on stable residence, like
> primogeniture and apprenticeship, have lost their power, and per-
> sonal facility has been given a correspondingly wider field. In social
> relations this ceaseless movement has weakened the familiar pat-
> terns of identification. Instead of relying on family background, class
> habits, inherited manners, many Americans have had to confront
> each other as mere claimants, who can at best try to persuade each
> other who they in fact are. (5)

Of course, Lindberg's list of "familiar patterns of identification" is
decidedly limited; some of the familiar patterns—one thinks especially of race and gender—are alive and well, though selectively
assigned, and carrying the weight of social identification for us all.
And class is rendered all the more slippery, its dynamics relocated to

the ideological fields of race, gender, sexual orientation, or just to the hazy realm of *difference*. Class background may not be fate, but there are still established scripts, roles to play or resist, narratives to read or misread. The belief that one can be both in and out of the game is itself part of the game. In this way, people like me are part of a proud tradition in a nation in which, as Lindberg has so importantly argued, "the confidence man is a representative American, perhaps even our covert hero" (3).

But while I recognize that the social field is more complex than Lindberg here suggests, I am still drawn to his analysis as it relates to the issue of class as a dynamic in the classroom, for in a nation of confidence men, confidence is hard to come by—and confidence, trust, is essential to education. We come to a classroom as "mere claimants" involved in a kind of performance, hoping others will accept our assumed credentials (as students, as teachers), trying to get something from one another (from good grades to a reason to believe in great ideals) on the basis of a created confidence. These days, in other words, I find my definition of class not just in the middle lines of this essay's epigraph, not just in the badges and rituals of identity, but in the whole set, beginning with "Trippers and askers surround me" and ending with the assertion, "But they are not the Me myself." I take the game to be the complex social play scripted from familiar cultural signifiers: race, class, and gender (the three most familiar categories), national and regional affiliations, occupational ties, freedom of movement, age, height, intelligence—the list goes on, many items open to a range of interpretations (intelligence, for example). Each individual is identified by more than one of these categories, these narrative threads, and the importance of each category is influenced by its association with the others. Hair color, for example, is an identifying characteristic that is treated differently when considered with another characteristic, gender—the process by which complex individuals are rendered *blonds*, *brunettes*, or *redheads*, each a label that comes with a cultural script of identity. All of these narrative threads enter the classroom and become part of that complex group performance that, when it works, is the drama of education.

But I'm getting ahead of Myself. My understanding of class, and the role it plays in the classroom, extends from my own narrative, the story that I've alternately discovered and constructed about myself.

One Hundred Friends, Two Worlds, and the Calibration of Identity

The story could begin at various points. Here, I'll begin it with my marriage at the age of eighteen, allowing the decision to marry to remain, as it truly is, inexplicable. A marriage required income; accordingly, I dropped out of college after two years (I had started at sixteen, so this was viewed by my parents as a significant shift in my developing life story) and took a job in a film-processing plant. I left that for what seemed a more attractive possibility of selling pianos and organs. I was laid off, and I applied for a position with an insurance agency (a friend had connected me to the opportunity), where after a salaried training period of some six months I would sell insurance on commission. To get this position, I had to first take an aptitude test. The appropriate answers to the various questions were, I thought, fairly clear (it was multiple choice), so I answered in such a way as to present myself—social, outgoing, and so on—as a good bet for an insurance salesman. I was given the position, and I was given my first assignment: Put together a list of one hundred friends to whom I could sell insurance.

I should have saved the list: One hundred friends are hard to come by, and I'm sure I've lost contact with almost everyone on that list, though not, I'm happy to report, because I tried to sell them insurance. I quit after calling the second person on the list, my favorite professor, who seemed surprised to hear from me in that capacity. His surprise pushed me out of the insurance business. It was not the first time that my idealization of education had served me well—this time, inspiring shame for following through on a shameless listing of names—and it wasn't the last, either. But the list would be, at least, a curiosity to me now. Until they were transformed by their inclusion on the list, the one hundred people whose names I used were not exactly *friends*. I hardly knew many of them. They were names of just about anybody I could think of: some friends, friends of friends, friends of my parents, people I had encountered along the way. What brought them together on the list was that they were all theoretically approachable for one reason or another; and most of the reasons had to do with the context in which I had met the one hundred people— that is, class. The listing of one hundred friends, each of whom has his or her own implicit listing of another one hundred, with the hundreds of friends serving as both entrance to and foundation for a career— this seems to me a significant manifestation of what class is and how it operates. Class is, most fundamentally, a cultural grouping that serves as both entrance to and foundation for one's public life.

To speak of the life scripts made possible and shaped by one's class, though, is not to speak of narrative coherence or ideological unity. Certainly, this was clear to me in the years after my short and disastrous stay with the insurance company (you don't want to know about my first and only attempt to make a sale). Eventually—I'll spare you the slide show of the journey—I found myself working the evening shift at a machine shop in Owego, New York, and spending many of my days haunting the campus (not as a student) of Cornell University in Ithaca, something under an hour's drive away. In other words, I found myself inhabiting two strikingly different worlds. My background provided me access to both worlds but prepared me for neither. One could find friends who had left the suburbs for something like a working-class life; and one could certainly think of many who had moved on to Cornell or other prestigious institutions. But I had come from a mechanically challenged family; to the others at the shop, I was something of a curiosity, the college boy, someone to test verbally and, at times, physically. On the other hand, "college," for my family, was an important but generic concept; going to Cornell—or living a life that might prepare one, socially, intellectually, to go to Cornell—simply wouldn't occur to anyone. Any college would do. I was conscious of the split represented by the two worlds; in fact, I'm pretty sure I dramatized it for myself and others. And I was conscious, also, that living in and with that split was probably more true to my nature than inhabiting either world would be. I did not feel that I belonged in either world, though I was drawn to both.

No doubt, I did dramatize the romantic tragedy of my time in the two worlds, and I continue to do so—for, in fact, I credit my self-consciousness about that split with my success in finding my way to my present life. The terms of identity are both positive and negative; we define ourselves both according to who we are and according to who we are not, often going to some trouble to identify outsiders to establish ourselves as insiders. Accordingly, if one wants to avoid becoming an unselfconscious creation of one's class, it can be of some value to discover oneself living both in and out of the game, and to develop a way of understanding what to make of this. As it sometimes does, experience provided the guiding analogy: the machine shop I worked at did precision machining—and there I learned that precision is a matter of careful (and sometimes creative) imprecision. We would drill holes within .001 inch of where they should be; we would control the roughness of surfaces that needed to be perfectly smooth; we would make sure that all the various aspects of a complex design, imprecise individually, would still be sufficiently precise in relation to one another. Similarly, I learned, from my experience in the two worlds, to look for myself less by trying to be precisely "the Me myself" than by trying to find a life that was less imprecisely fitted to me. The difference was that I had no blueprint for "the Me myself"; I could discover the contours of this self only by noting when and in what ways I did or did not "fit" in my environment. Not having a sense of self to move toward, it helped to have a few possible selves to move away from; and to be in but not of two worlds so attractive, so familiar and foreign at the same time, helped me to calibrate my backward journey, to achieve an increasingly precise imprecision of self-performance.

My experiences have emphasized to me what should have been obvious from the start—that class is both defined and experienced relationally. I think, then, in terms of what I call *multiply contingent identity*, by which I mean that the social role of each member of the community is contingent upon the culturally coordinated roles of a number of others. Each act, word, and gesture is, in this scheme of identity, a kind of performance (sometimes habitual, sometimes self-conscious); and the realization or fulfillment of identity is always delayed and in danger of being undermined as our performance awaits verifying responses, reciprocal performances, in the field of social relations. If relational identity is revealed in the persona we assume with our friends or parents, or in the ways in which we are transformed by a new environment (professional or social), then multiply contingent identity would be the performance of selfhood that we face when we are with friends and parents at the same time, or when we encounter professional colleagues in an unexpected context. We are suddenly forced to determine the relations among the various roles we play in various situations. Often, we discover that the drama of selfhood has a problem with coherence and unity. Class, the social and perspectival field that offers a kind of unity to our various performances, is then a mode of interpretation and of motivated misinterpretation (if only in the form of assumptions about the singular integrity of the cultural script we should follow). Class teaches us how to see, which of course means that it teaches us at times also how not to see other possibilities, other ways of viewing and understanding the demands and possibilities of life. Confronted by selves that seem to challenge the terms of selfhood, we misread the performances of others (taking what they see as principled, for example, and viewing it as repressed, or reading someone who *seems* defensive as someone who *is* offensive) to preserve the integrity of our own (so that we do not have to encounter our own relaxation of principle, perhaps, or ask why someone should feel defensive around us).

Imperfect Liberty: The Culture of the Academy

As a teacher of literature, I recognize that the multiply contingent interpretations of social identity are at the heart of my pedagogical responsibilities; and as a teacher of African American literature at a predominantly white institution, I cannot separate issues of class from the issues usually placed under the vexed heading of *diversity*. As I see it, my role is to introduce students to a specific field of literature, draw them into the demands and pleasures of the field, help them develop and refine their analytical skills, and reach the point where together we can appreciate once again the extent to which literature is both a manifestation of and entrance into worlds of understanding. My goal each semester is to orchestrate and sustain a communal engagement in a series of literary texts. I try to teach my students to be responsive to the demands of individual literary texts even as we work to construct an understanding of a broader literary period, and much of the work we do over the course of the semester is a matter of identifying and responding to such demands.

Many of my students know very little or nothing about African American history and literature, and many have no *conscious* experience thinking or talking about race, though their initial responses to the material reveal much about the power of cultural scripts of identity, particularly in terms of the discourse of race. In his study of the cultural dynamics of racism, David Theo Goldberg (1993) argues that the "discourse underlying racism" converges with "related discourses" and is "interiorized by the individual," defining "not only subjectivity but otherness also." One's understanding of such basic concepts as individual identity and value is fundamentally influenced, Goldberg explains, by the discourses that provide the grounds for moral action: "Subjects' actions are rendered meaningful to themselves and others in light of the values that this discourse, among others, makes available or articulates to the parties involved. In this way, racialized discourse—reproduced, redefined perhaps, and acted upon—reconstitutes the relations of power that produced them" (57). In short, "To succeed so long in effecting the materiality of differential exclusions," Goldberg argues, "racialized discourse has to be grounded in the relations of social subjects to each other and in ways of seeing, of relating to, (other) subjects" (53). And these ways of seeing, of course, enter the classroom, culturally prepared to respond to, forestall, or deny the validity of encounters with history or literature designed to challenge the terms of the racist culture. Such encounters are complicated still further by the fact that American higher education itself is deeply implicated in ideologies of race, gender, and class. Many in the academy have responded to this history by developing approaches to teaching designed to recognize the authority of the various cultures represented by our students, and thereby to facilitate a sort of cultural multilingualism as we teach them academic modes of research, interpretation, and writing. Too often, though, teachers conceptualize, essentialize, and thereby appropriate the cultural backgrounds of their students while sustaining, however unintentionally, the mystical authority of academic modes of understanding—as if the academy were capable of encompassing all cultures, and of being encompassed by none.

Issues of the relation between the cultural background of the student and the culture of the academy become especially evident, and are especially contested, in the field of academic reading and writing. I'll offer one quirky example of the cultural background of academic standards: In a reading comprehension test used not long ago at the learning center of a major university, students encountered a passage from *The Conquest of Mexico*, a history written by William H. Prescott and published in 1843. This is, of course, a rather extreme manifestation of ways in which academic standards of literate achievement are grounded in nineteenth-century ideological discourses. Many, if not most, academics today, of whatever background, would not look to Prescott for a model of reading, writing, or historical analysis. But the example is useful all the same, for in "Chateaubriand's English Literature," one of his many reflections on composition, Prescott wrote,

> Every man, at least every man with a spark of originality in his composition, has his own peculiar way of thinking, and, to give it effect, it must find its way out in its own peculiar language. Indeed, it is impossible to separate language from thought in that delicate blending of both which is called style; at least, it is impossible to produce the same effect with the original by any copy, however literal. We may imitate the structure of a sentence, but the ideas which give it its peculiar propriety we cannot imitate. (1875, 251)

These and similar reflections eventually led Prescott to a style for which he was justly praised in his own time and often since then (as his presence in the reading comprehension test suggests). However, for those currently teaching college-level composition (in advanced literature classes or first-year courses) to students not uniformly or even predominantly white, male, aristocratic, or otherwise culturally empowered, the institutionalization of Prescott's style underscores the problems posed by Prescott's reflections on the relations among style, thought, and identity. For many students and teachers alike, the models and standards of university-level writing are the academy's most direct act of cultural imperialism. However much teachers might value individual manifestations of Prescott's ideal union of "peculiar way[s] of thinking" and peculiar ways of writing, they are faced with the task of teaching students to, in effect, "imitate the structure of a sentence" (and, beyond that, of a paragraph, and of an entire essay)— and thereby to imitate the structure of an identity that fits snugly into what is for many students a threatening culture.

Of course, education, however one approaches it, requires students to negotiate a delicate balance between individual development and socialization; the process of establishing, refining, and maintaining that balance is itself the process of education. But experience suggests that many students feel that the scales have been fixed, and that both the means and the ends of nominal "individual development" have been predetermined by the institution and embedded in the syllabus, the textbook, and even the teacher's pedagogical assumptions and methods. Students have spent a lifetime in the educational system, and many understand things about it that some faculty members either never have learned or have forgotten. Like Arlo Guthrie at the recruiting station, students have been selected, inspected, affected, and often rejected. Some have learned to play the game successfully; some have decided that the game requires sacrifices—of time, of pride, of identity—that they are not willing to make. Moreover, students recognize what many administrative speakers try both to encourage and to contain—that classroom education and dorm-room study are only a part of their college experience. They accordingly look for ways to reap the greatest dividends (the grades on which their future career options will depend, and that both the academy and their families use to gauge their progress) from the least possible effort (so that they will have time to pursue the interests that seem more directly related to their personal development and satisfaction).

In the classroom, students' perceptions of the nature of academic life and culture can lead them to follow the rules without attending to the meaning of the game. The instructor who concentrates on helping students develop their individual voices—to confront without risk of academic failure the challenge of language and identity—faces the risk of sending the students on to impending doom in other, more conventional classes. An oasis offers relief from the desert, but it doesn't offer a safe exit to a more congenial environment. Instructors who attempt to lead their students from individual expression to the academic voice, from the narrative to the formal essay, run the risk of discrediting those cultural voices that do not fit neatly into academic structures. Instructors who try to help their students negotiate a balance of their individual voice and the academic mode run the risk of seeming condescending, insincere, manipulative, or worse. In Herman Melville's *Typee* ([1846] 1968), the narrator, Tommoo, is pressured by the Typees to have his face tattooed. Recognizing that the tattoo is a mark of socialization, indicating social status and even religious allegiance, and unwilling to break irrevocably from his own culture, Tommoo naturally resists. Perceiving his resistance, the islanders assure Tommoo that he is "at perfect liberty" to choose the style of the tattoo, including that reserved for the highest ranks of Typee society (220). Many of those students whom we group under the heading of cultural diversity have, I believe, a similar view of the liberty available to them in the academy.

I cannot talk about class and pedagogy, in other words, without considering the class system of the academy itself, a system that defines insiders and outsiders, and even degrees of citizenship, in various ways (institutional affiliation, publishing history, teaching load, etc.). And this is a powerful culture, particularly in its occasional tendency to view itself as a place where class can be transcended, where one can escape one's implication in a racist culture, or where one can otherwise write oneself out of or above one's historical, national, regional, and cultural setting. Too often, in this world, our expressed concern for cultural diversity translates into the integration of cultural concerns within the unifying framework of academic modes of thought. That is, we present—implicitly, perhaps inadvertently, but powerfully—the culture of the academy as an effectively transcultural authority, a perspective capable of accounting for (and thereby subordinating) the perspectives available to less encompassing cultures. This is not appreciation but appropriation, for the culture of academic writing—including certain methods of analysis, clear modes of comparison, concrete argumentative "points," and conventional structures and strategies for organizing and presenting "one's views"— imposes its authority on (in effect, *authorizes*) the cultural subjects it studies. Beyond academic writing, the culture of the academy in various ways imposes its authority—and, in effect, authorizes—the subjects (students) whose task, according to a fiction of pedagogy, is to study and to begin to take power over academic modes of thought.

In other words, the dominant cultural difference we face in the classroom is that between the academy itself and those who are contained by it, between relative insiders and outsiders. This dominant difference creates a wall between the instructor and each student—a wall that is often noticed but seldom confronted formally. Too often, instructors say of their most needful students that they simply don't know how to think; students, in their dorms and in teaching evaluation forms, often return the compliment, accusing their teachers of being either confusing or boring. Instructors, of course, take this condemnation as a validation of their own view, arguing that students find the class boring *because* they are lazy or ineffective thinkers. Since every teacher is blessed each semester with a few or more students who find the course genuinely interesting, he or she is all too likely to allow the disenfranchised students to suffer the consequences of their "poor attitudes."

This dominant cultural difference we face in our classrooms— between the institution and its subjects—includes differences of educational perspectives, differences that often constitute the central dynamic of the classroom process and of teacher-student relationships. Our educational system has both an official and an underground identity. The official identity is publicized by administrators, catalogues, and brochures, and is represented by, for example, the university's faculty and its library. According to the official academy, education is a high ideal, a shining city on the intellectual and social hill, a lifetime pursuit, both the means and an end in itself. The underground identity is publicized by student grapevines, and is represented most prominently by the "study aids" section of any popular bookstore. Many, if not most, of our best and brightest students are graduates of both systems. Whether or not we believe in the value of, say, *The Princeton Review—Cracking the System,* a guide to the SAT, it is prudent to note that many students either do believe in its value or at least feel that there is a "system" capable of being "cracked." They are, in short, both in and out of the game.

And that's a good place to be. We may know that education is all-encompassing and all-inclusive, a mysterious journey that has no end, but many students perceive it to be a peculiar nut to crack, and look for their educational ideals outside the classroom. Perhaps, though, the two views are not as different as they seem; perhaps students learn as much about our world and about themselves by taking short-cuts as they would by walking down a broader, longer path. It is difficult to convince students that education is a journey that each individual must discover and explore in his or her own way when students have a long background of experience with standardized tests. In any event, we are more likely to draw students into an expansive, challenging, and rewarding view of education by accommodating their perspective than by simply resisting or ignoring it. For beyond this dominant cultural difference is an important conceptual difference, and those of us who inescapably represent the institution of education have much to learn from the conceptual strategies students have spent a lifetime formulating. There are lessons to be learned from those who live in the vast and various underground— and you needn't go looking; they'll come to you.

A Pericultural Model and a Class Act

I confess that I take seriously the conventional academic essay with a clear thesis, focused topic sentences, a careful interpretive method, and informed textual and contextual evidence. Indeed, my syllabus for every class includes an increasingly detailed "Guide for Papers" (now up to fifteen pages and counting!), in which I explain and provide models for writing this kind of paper. It is not that I believe that the academic essay is particularly graceful; nor do I believe that the protocols of close reading or theoretically informed analysis are the only or even the best reading game in town. But I do believe that the

conventional academic essay and formal approaches to detailed interpretation are valuable pedagogical tools, often forcing students (and I
remain a student in this and other regards) to confront the limitations
and the possibilities of their understanding at any given moment—
drawing them to recognize that they do not know how to get from one
insight to another in their explanation, that there seems to be a reveal-
ingly hazy realm in their response to a text, and that literary understanding requires self-awareness, intellectual discipline, and more
than a dash of humility.

We have much to teach each other, and we can't afford to let the
overruling class system of academic culture stand in the way. Each
semester, then, I continue to work my way toward what might be
called a pericultural model of teaching. A pericultural model of teaching envelops the academy by identifying it as a particular cultural
community, one among many others, with fundamental structures of
thought and standards of validity, and thereby enables students to
understand the nature and terms of voluntary citizenship—temporary,
permanent, or provisional—within that community. Each semester,
each course offers a new community, with multiple performances of
selfhood, and multiple perspectives not only on the material we are
studying but on the process of the study itself. And these multiple performances are multiply contingent, as we respond to one another,
challenge one another, and modify the terms of reciprocal identity.
Incomplete in vision and understanding individually, we can learn to
see together by conflict, negotiation, and mutual revision. My job is to
encourage my students to say, with Whitman, "I resist anything better
than my own diversity" (43); my job is to be both in and out of the
game, to play with authority as slyly as does Whitman when he
writes, "You shall not look through my eyes either, nor take things
from me, / You shall listen to all sides and filter them from yourself," or when he advises, "All I mark as my own you shall offset it
with your own, / Else it were time lost listening to me" (28, 45).

In other words, I try to demystify the culture of the academy, not
by trying to pretend that it doesn't exist, but by frankly acknowledging the nature and terms—and the limitations—of the *class* that I
most directly represent, and by building into my approach to teaching
my own ongoing conflicts with, constructions of, and occasional
alienation from that representative identity. We cannot escape the
labyrinth of cultural diversity and social practice to reach the common
ground of clarity and understanding, nor should we want to try. We
can only acknowledge that it *is* a labyrinth, that inevitably we all
stand at different points within the labyrinth, and that the academy has
developed a way of giving its section of the labyrinth the appearance
of independence and order. Much as I might like to, I cannot build a

bridge that will take me where my students live; I cannot understand them simply by learning more about their backgrounds. But I can take what I learn to understand more fully where I live, and the terms of my life there. The best way to build bridges between cultures, it seems to me, is not to start from the other shore, but to explore the geography and shifting sands of the shore upon which one stands—to examine and reveal the assumptions, beliefs, and limitations of the culture one knows best. The acknowledgement of distance, joined with a desire to reach across that distance, is usually a more effective and respectful approach to human understanding than is the pretention of closeness and empathy. Gerald Graff (1989), discussing the place of critical theory in literature classes, notes that "people need a sense of what an institution as a corporate body stands for in order to be able to enter—or want to enter—into its issues, methods, and modes of talking and thinking. . . . The legibility of the texts we teach depends on the legibility of the institutions in which we teach them" (256). Basically, Graff argues that we need to take the students behind the academic scenes, to reveal to them the assumptions and conflicts that underlie our professed certainty (or at least assurance) in the classroom. Such examinations enable us to reveal ourselves, and the system we represent, to the students, to make ourselves vulnerable before them, and thus to reveal to them the infrastructure of the culturally limited but institutionally inescapable authority of the academic mode of thinking and writing.

Not "apart from" but *within* "the pulling and hauling stands what I am . . . Both in and out of the game and watching and wondering at it." My backward journey continues, in other words, as my one hundred friends and I enter a larger and more diverse society involved in the mutually dependent calibrations of community. And this is a community that, at its best, finds strength in the imprecisions of selfhood. It seems like a good place to live.

Works Cited

Goldberg, D. T. 1993. *Racist Culture: Philosophy and the Politics of Meaning*. Cambridge, MA: Blackwell.

Graff, G. 1989. "The Future of Theory in the Teaching of Literature." In *The Future of Literary Theory*, ed. Ralph Cohen, 250–267. New York: Routledge, Chapman and Hall.

Lindberg, G. 1982. *The Confidence Man in American Literature*. New York: Oxford University Press.

Melville, H. [1846] 1968. *Typee: A Peep at Polynesian Life*. Chicago: Northwestern-Newberry.

Prescott, W. H. 1875. "Chateaubriand's English Literature." In *Biographical and Critical Miscellanies*, 227–271. Philadelphia: Lippincott.

Robinson, A., and J. Katzman. 1989. *The Princeton Review—Cracking the System: The SAT and PSAT*. New York: Villard.

Whitman, W. [1855] 1996. *Poetry and Prose*, ed. Justin Kaplan. Library of America College Edition. New York: Literary Classics of the United States.

4

Truth and the Working Class in the Working Classroom

Carol Faulkner

When I first began teaching composition, I didn't really imagine how my teaching could or would grow out of who I am, out of the paint-blistered house I grew up in, the factories my parents worked in, the hard-working, rough-edged lives of the people I cared about, out of the stories my family did and did not tell. In fact, early in my teaching career, I saw my class background in the same way I saw other factors such as my youth and inexperience—as weaknesses, drawbacks, things to be overcome. It's taken me a long time to understand and accept how profoundly class has influenced my pedagogy, how inseparable it is from the way I teach. My class identification has influenced everything from my attitude toward authority to the way I privilege meaning over form. My most fundamental attitudes toward language spring from my past.

In my house, we didn't grow up believing in Santa Claus. That would have been a lie. Language carried a moral responsibility. Words were about saying what you really thought. They were about speaking the truth. This attitude toward language was not just an idiosyncrasy of my family, but something that we shared with others of the same social class.

In her 1983 study, *Ways with Words*, Shirley Brice Heath compared how two working-class communities in the Piedmont region, one black and one white, used language differently. On the one hand, in the African American community, "good story-tellers . . . may base their stories on an actual event, but they creatively fictionalize the details surrounding the real event, and the outcome of the story may not even resemble what indeed happened" (166). Exaggeration, imagination, and embellishment are not only tolerated, they are admired. On the other hand, as Heath writes:

Children [of white working-class families] are not allowed to tell
stories, unless an adult announces that something which happened to
a child makes a good story and invites a retelling. When children are
asked to retell such events, they are expected to tell non-fictive stories which "stick to the truth." Adults listen carefully and correct
children if their facts are not as the adult remembers them. In contrast, fictive stories which are exaggerations of real-life events, modeled on plots or characters children meet in storybooks, are not
accepted as stories, but as "lies," without "a piece of truth." (158)

Heath's account of the way the white working-class community
approaches storytelling is an accurate description of the way my
family approached it. Such an introduction to words has left me with
a particular perception of truth, a rather literal one that doesn't stop
with stories but is pretty fundamental to the way I look at language in
general.

This emphasis on truth is central to my pedagogy. It means that I
don't see speech in any form as just an exercise. It explains why I
could never give assignments in which students are asked to argue the
opposite of what they believe. That would be a violation of the ethics
of language for me. It also makes a lot of sense that I never could
relate to teaching the modes. It always seemed to me essentially
pointless to ask students to detail how to bake a cake or classify the
three types of instructors. For me, such assignments shift attention
from what writing is really about. They give the impression that
words are just things to be manipulated (and manipulation is a very
bad word where I come from) rather than tools that enable a person to
express some deeply held belief. By separating form from content,
such assignments eliminate from the classroom the things that really
count—the ideas that motivate students. They break the link between
writing and why writing matters.

By contrast, I operate on the assumption that writing improves
when people strive to say something that matters to them. I think it's
wrong to ask students to compartmentalize their values, and that is
precisely what we suggest they do when we "grade for grammar" or
give assignments that imply that form and content are distinct from
each other, that the classroom is somehow separate from their lives,
that the things they write about have nothing to do with the things
they believe. Outside of a grade, I can't see any reason for students to
want to put any effort into writing a paper that asks them to practice a
form. For the vast majority of students that's not enough reason to
take writing seriously; besides, I don't want to encourage students to
write only for a grade or to live only for a paycheck or to otherwise
separate meaning from action. For meaning and action to be integrated, students must feel that the whole writing process counts, that they
cannot write well without saying something worthwhile, that what

they do for the class is somehow part of their life. This is an issue Paulo Freire writes about in "The 'Banking' Concept of Education," an essay I often teach in my writing classes and one that encompasses many of my concerns as a teacher. Like Freire, I believe that the ways one teaches send subtle messages to the students about how the world operates. If we teach via authoritarian methods in classrooms that separate the subject matter from students' life experiences, we teach not how to alter students' circumstances but how to adapt to existing ones (211). Students learn to replace what is important to them with what is important to the teacher. This is exactly antithetical to what I believe are the goals of true education: to understand one's own and one's community's circumstances and to develop the skills to change them for the better. The more one's circumstances need to be changed, the more crucial it is that the methods of education show the integral nature of life, and become part of the mechanism for change.

Of course, I can't just assume that students will share with me this same sense of earnestness about the value of words. Even if they do, they may not connect that value with an English class. I have to find ways to set up my classes so that students feel that there is something at stake beyond a grade. I often begin writing courses with a discussion of literacy and what it means in the world beyond the classroom. It is my hope to connect reading and writing with political participation and power, not in any theoretical way, but in the most basic sense of becoming part of an informed and critical citizenry, which is so necessary to the democratic process. This discussion easily segues into the focus of my teaching, which is critical thinking. I ask students to examine the assumptions of the arguments they read and make and to try to extend that examination to the institutions that surround and shape all of us. I stress how important it is to be able to recognize whose interests are being served by the way that an argument or an institution or a belief system is constructed, to question what is left out and why, to pursue areas of inquiry suggested in Bartholomae and Petrosky's *Ways of Reading* (1996, 12–13). This emphasis has obvious roots in my own concerns with class structure and gender issues, but beyond that it reaches back toward the value of words and gives all students, whatever their career or academic goals, an equal stake in the class if they want to have it.

For the most part, I see my stress on the integrity of language as a positive component of my pedagogy. At the same time, I know I need to recognize and compensate for the weaknesses inherent in viewing language the way I was taught to view it. Especially in students who share my class background, I've noticed there's a sense that tailoring one's approach to one's audience is dishonest or manipulative, somehow not being straight. Some students almost make a virtue of offending their audience. Many are reluctant to practice different rhetorical strategies and so limit the effective delivery of their ideas. They have to be reminded how often all of us choose our words carefully when speaking with friends, coworkers, family.

More important, though, truth and meaning are more complicated than believing or not believing in Santa Claus. I think there's a tendency amongst my social class to view truth reductively, as if we could just say it if we were only honest or courageous enough. Many of us are not inclined to recognize the difficulty of finding it buried under or inside cultural and personal narratives, squirreled away with our fears and inherited assumptions. I think of my father sitting in that little circle of lamplight reading the newspaper or watching Huntley and Brinkley, but never venturing into a novel, not seeing the value in reading about something that didn't actually happen, not seeing that truth is more than sticking to the facts or that facts themselves can be untrue. I used to think of literature as art for the poor because, unlike ballet or music or painting, it is truly open to everyone who can read, but I have come to understand that it's not open to everyone in exactly the same way. Students who come from backgrounds such as mine have to learn to go beyond a simplistic understanding of truth and reality if they are to develop an appreciation for various types of literature. I try to encourage this in my freshman composition classes by choosing a text that contains many essays that may reach provisional conclusions via circuitous routes, but never profess to find them easily or to settle on one too firmly. They are essays that defy either/or constructions of truth, that require very close reading, and that, by their very form, insist on the complexity of reality.

Taken to its extreme, the working-class attitude toward language can be restrictive and anti-imaginative. In my own writing this is not so much a problem when I'm working on an essay such as this one, but as a fiction writer, I still feel those constraints practically every time I write a story. For me, it's not a simple struggle to free imaginative depictions from their real-life antecedents or from the limits of time or space or perspective. It's more that words themselves feel like borrowed tools to be used ever so carefully so as to be returned to their rightful owners undamaged. It's as if my words are all subjected to some referential ruler of truth that makes me feel inhibited—fearful of experimenting with them, and of highlighting the playful qualities of language, the delight in sound, incongruity, rhythm. I love the sort of tumbling, seemingly carefree profusion of writers like Virginia Woolf, for instance, but that quality is rare in my own writing. It's not until I've gained a sense of ownership over words (something I must do over and over and over again) that I feel my writing take off.

It's this sense of ownership that I believe is missing in so many of my working-class students. In Heath's book, she reports the comments teachers made about their white working-class pupils who weren't doing well: "little ability to interpret or go beyond minimal requirements . . . little imagination or extension of ideas," "rarely asks questions in class, but is always the first to volunteer answers for review questions" (269). Indeed, I can see myself in these descriptions. In many ways I guess I teach to my earlier self, organize my class around the things that would have made me a better teacher and writer from the beginning. The assignments I give ask students to apply the theories we read about to their own lives, to ask how those theories matter and how valid they are, measured against their own experience. What I'm looking for in their essays is that they have found the ideas we've read and discussed useful in some way to them. I'm not looking for a complete understanding so much as I'm looking for evidence that they find the reading and writing we do to be connected and applicable to themselves. I have gotten the most remarkable papers from my students: a paper on the ritual of fishing and an analysis of its cultural significance inspired by an anthropological study we read; an examination of abusive relationships using Paulo Freire's "banking concept of education"; a discussion from a millworker about his need for a literal and figurative room of his own. I have learned so much from my students that I never could have learned had I tried to direct them more closely. Many times students have told me that they will never forget the essays that we've read. The ideas we've discussed have entered their consciousnesses, have become tools for them to analyze the world in a more complex way.

Such complexity of thought requires a broadened sense of truth that is hindered by a cramped imagination. Unfortunately, there's almost a fear of imagination in the way I learned to think about language. I think my parents saw believing in Santa Claus and other fairy tales as bad because it led to double the grief; it added disillusionment to the already difficult act of facing harsh reality. I watched my parents come home from factories every day, and I saw the ways that their lives were constrained by class: physically, economically, and psychologically. As a working-class woman, I could never see myself as an independent agent operating free from social factors. I grew up with such a heavy sense of being determined by the hardships awaiting me—in many ways *too* heavy a sense. While I don't want to transfer that weight to my students' shoulders, neither do I want simply to reinforce the cultural narrative of individualism, the notion that we each rise and fall completely independently of the people and institutions that surround us. I think this is very easily and subtly done when students are not asked to respond to each other. For me, that's what the classroom community is about. It's about creating an atmosphere in which we all, students and teachers alike, recognize the impact we have on each other, recognize that none of us can be or even should be completely independent of others. I try to de-emphasize competition between students while emphasizing cooperation. I have them constructively criticize each other's papers, and I structure the discussion in a way that encourages them to see themselves as part of a collective search for meaning. For instance, I ask questions such as, "What does it mean to be fully human and what things inside or outside of us prevent us from achieving our full humanity?" This is a question that asks students not to judge and refute each other's answers as right or wrong, but to think about how those ideas contribute to and broaden their own understanding. I avoid pro-con debates because I don't think they invite listening so much as they encourage people to think of communication in terms of winning and losing. I want my classroom to be a place where there is a genuine search for truth and a struggle to express it, not a place where shouting at each other passes for dialogue. That's a model we see all the time in the public and political domain, and one that education ought to correct rather than mimic.

Classroom discussion functions as a reminder of our interconnectedness. That's why I think it's vital to hold students responsible for listening and responding to their classmates. Not asking students to consider and respond to others—for instance, allowing them to write about anything they want within a given format or mode of development—suggests a very individualistic model, which paradoxically devalues the individual. It implies that ideas are conceived by the individual, that they owe nothing to an intellectual community. But at the same time, the individual's ideas are undermined because they have no impact on the community. I see those kinds of "open" assignments as the embodiment of false choices for students, offering the illusion of freedom without any of the substance, sort of like asking students to choose the color of crayons they'll use while making sure they stay in the lines. Such assignments don't ask them to examine the ways they are learning nor to relate the material in a substantial way to their lives. Without such corresponding responsibilities, there are no real freedoms. I once had a student tell me about a class he had failed. The teacher let him write about anything he wanted. "That showed he didn't care what I thought," he said. If a student doesn't have to grapple with other people's ideas, surely the message is that no one has to grapple with his. Such isolated shouting into the wilderness may fit neatly into a system in which everyone is graded individually, but it hasn't much application beyond the classroom. Where in this world do people really succeed or fail completely on their own?

Still, real classroom dialogue is not easy because genuinely listening to what others have to say suggests that one may actually change one's mind. I know that for me changing an opinion is more than just a process of sorting through the best evidence, and I know this is true for many of my students too. One of the qualities most valued in the culture I come from is loyalty, and that applies not only to people, but also to ideas and ways. There's a sense of loss of identity that comes with changing one's mind. I still feel it in my resistance to becoming an "academic," the fear that I'm being disloyal, that I'm leaving behind the people I love, that I will wake up and not recognize myself. I know that if I feel my sense of identity threatened, I loyally retreat to the point of view I grew up with. My flexibility of mind, my sense of imaginative freedom, the possibility of intellectual movement disappear. For that reason, I don't want to corner my students. I don't want to cause them to fall back into a narrowed perspective. We all have our points of view born of our pasts. There's nothing wrong with that. What is wrong is not being flexible enough to move in and out of them, to recognize that ours is only one perspective among many. It's that flexibility that is threatened when people are confronted harshly. So far as many working-class students go, this only serves to separate them further from educational opportunities that I want them to have. To deal with this, the best I can do is create a nonthreatening classroom atmosphere where confrontation is a gentle process, and where I am generously listening to students, genuinely trying to understand what they mean—and thus risking change myself. Students have changed me, and I'm conscientious about letting them know when they have. That's a vital part of my teaching. It's also risky both to me and to my students, but if I won't risk it, I can't expect them to. I just can't set myself apart from my students the way I once imagined teachers were supposed to.

My emphasis on discussion and classroom community suggests that the writing process will be much messier than thinking up a thesis and then supporting it. Since my early thesis statement workshops I've asked myself, What does it mean to know what you have to say before you even start to say it? There's an assumption of authority over one's words and ideas, a posture that seems especially difficult for groups of students who feel disenfranchised by their minority, gender, or class status, not to mention just their subservient position as student to begin with. For me, the solution is not to teach them how to posture with confidence. That would imply that the fault is just with them, that all they need to do is step over to the other side where right-thinking people express their opinions with deserved confidence. While I want my students to develop a strong sense of personal authority, a belief in the validity of their own points of view, I see a certain amount of tentativeness as a very healthy sign of open-mindedness. I encourage students to see their conclusions as provisional, to keep their minds open to the possibilities of new information, to temper their opinions with a bit of self-doubt. Within moderation, I want students to use phrases such as "I think" because these phrases diminish the godlike qualities of the disembodied writer. I think the world would be a better place if more people did so.

Establishing this balance between a sense of personal authority and a healthy self-doubt is complicated by a too-deferential attitude toward authority, which is implicit in how white working-class children learn to tell stories. One waits until asked, doesn't venture out on one's own to interpret. In many ways, that's the kind of student I learned to be. It made me a successful student and it provided an entry into the world of academia, but it also made me too accepting of traditional approaches that had grown out of other lives than mine. I was too eager to be welcomed on the inside to be critical of the system I was entering. As a teacher, I adopted the forms that I imagined the teaching of writing to entail even though I didn't like many of those techniques. I'm sure my early students learned something and some even became better writers. But I think what they learned most was what I had unconsciously absorbed: a passive attitude toward authority and a self-deprecating attitude toward my own sense of reality. In those first few years of teaching, I felt constantly inadequate and stressed because while I was trying to tell them to write in their own voice, I was teaching in someone else's.

I could not come to such realizations just by reading about voice, which I certainly read a lot about. I came to it experientially, which is, I believe, a hallmark of the way my class acquires and values knowledge. Just as we value a literal quality of truth, we place value on concrete knowledge. We trust less in the abstractions of classroom theory and more in the apprenticeship of experience. As I become more myself as a teacher, I find more ways to allow my own experience to shape the way I respond to students and to validate my place in the college classroom. In spite of its drawbacks, I feel fortunate that I grew up with a strong working-class identity. It gave me enough of a sense of what matters to me or enough discomfort with what doesn't that I had to find my own way, true to myself, true to my class.

Works Cited

Bartholomae, D., and A. Petrosky. 1996. *Ways of Reading: An Anthology for Writers*. New York: St. Martin's Press.

Freire, P. 1993. "The 'Banking' Concept of Education." In *Ways of Reading*, ed. David Bartholomae et al., 207–219. New York: St. Martin's Press.

Heath, S. B. 1983. *Ways with Words*. New York: Cambridge University Press.

5

Production Values and Composition Instruction
Keeping the Hearth, Keeping the Faith

Karen Fitts and Alan W. France

The lower middle class, deified generically by conservatives as "small business," is often characterized by a range of qualities peculiarly American: from self-reliance to militant individualism, from cautious frugality to hard-bitten calculation, from provinciality to prejudice, and from commonsensical ingenuity to downright anti-intellectualism. It is from this social location and with these cultural affiliations that we each have entered the academic world. In this essay, we explore the consequences of being "in between," of belonging neither to the working class nor to an affluent, postindustrial elite. This social experience has significantly shaped our views of the world, including our commitments to teaching.

The discipline of reading and writing our ideologies, which we so often ask our students to do, has been quite instructive to us. In the course of this essay, we will be relying on a Marxist-feminist interpretation of social experiences, thus foregrounding our class and gender relations to accumulated capital. Our aim, therefore, is to historicize both ourselves and our approaches to pedagogy. But first we begin, as we encourage our students to do, with personal narratives.

Narratives We Were Taught

Karen

In my Southern, rural background, it was owning land that set my family apart from those who worked for wages, and lack of capital that marked us as different from more comfortable, genteel landed families. My brother and I loved the stories we were told of our parents: a young couple laboring, following the grain and fruit harvests through the West, saving their money to buy Grandfather Fitts's 160-acre homestead in west central Louisiana. Their few photographs of this period showed a carelessly beautiful couple in the company of others like them, with exotically bulbous vehicles nearby. In one, they stood in a small group near a roadside overlook, the horizon dropping away behind them. My dad's arm was draped over my mom's shoulder; her hands were folded in front of her. In another, my dad sat on a motorcycle. Looking back, I think that what we loved most about the stories of their early years was the idea of our parents roaming the countryside, money in a bank somewhere, looking carefree. For even as children, my brother and I knew what was never articulated: The farm might be a priceless resource but it was also a grim taskmaster and—once it became my parents' property—it owned us rather than the other way around.

Being landowners rather than working for someone else for a paycheck conditioned my parents' view of who they and their children were, particularly in relation to others in the close-knit community of Toro. All around were numerous people poorer than we were. But an occasional spread was held by prosperous landowners, with ties to business and government. Our place in the community fell "in between," where we labored to improve the land and to increase its yield. It was a monumental and all-encompassing struggle, according to the family narrative, in which the most effective instrument at hand—the attribute that enabled us to avoid falling into dependence if not poverty—was self-reliant individualism, put to work in a world in which justice could be counted on to follow from diligence and hard work.

However, I have since come to question the twin narratives of individuality and justice, which, when used as standards for judging rural agrarian society (or urban academic culture, for that matter), mask more than they illuminate. In my experience of farm labor, it was conducted under largely separate and unequal conditions, defined for men as the struggle against nature, for women as the enduring service to it. Herein was reproduced the always already undervalued status of the woman farmer or, perhaps more accurately, of the farmer's woman.

For example, in terms of her relation to capital, my hardworking, faithful mother was consigned for many years to proletariat status both outside and inside our middle-class family. I say "for many years" because now, a retired teacher and a widow, she is less subject to patriarchal hierarchy than ever before in her life: Her teacher's pension is as secure as any pension ever is and, since my father's death, she speaks for herself. As a female schoolteacher in 1950s-to-1980s Louisiana, however, the fruits of her labor were consistently minimized, in terms of both salary and upward mobility, because she was inherently ineligible for promotion. Although my mother is respected and loved by generations of Vernon Parish students and school employees, her labor nonetheless was symbolically appropriated for decades by the principal, a position roughly equivalent in rural school systems to that of an entrepreneur. His was a position to which she could not reasonably aspire because it inevitably was held by a male. Whoever he might be personally—wise and reflective or small-minded and petulant—his position authorized him to supervise, grant or withhold rewards, and set limits in a gendered system of work.

At home with my father, she knew other forms of symbolic division and expropriation of labor. Although I have never known two persons more dedicated to the twin ideals of self-reliance and a just society, they faced a remorseless dragon, the profoundly classed and gendered system of familial duty. As Friedrich Engels wrote in *The Origin of the Family, Private Property, and the State* ([1845] 1972), middle-class women experience gender differently from working-class women. Breadwinners among other breadwinners, working-class women retain greater in-home status than their middle-class sisters, a reflection of their more equal wage-earning potential outside the home (79).

At home as at school, division of labor was absolute: My mother's labor produced and nurtured human beings; my father's labor produced crops, fences, and barns. While neither was dispensable, clearly her work signified less. For, as dictated by community, class-based standards, it was his farm production—not her production of human beings—that made us a middle- rather than a working-class family. Also as expected by the community, it was my father who spoke for the farm (and thus the family) on public matters. He was not at all an arrogant man; in fact, this power appeared more foisted upon him than relished. However, his familial designation as husband and father subordinated her considerable talents and powers as wife and mother, my role model for adult life. In her life on the farm, her status as a woman (propertyless) married to a man (propertied) mirrored her position as a teacher working for a principal.

As I have striven to take my place in the world and in my own family, this configuration of the professional and the familial has resurfaced, to my dismay, time after time. Once I taught seventh grade where the principal, a former coach, blasted a referee's whistle whenever he desired that everyone in the hallway stop, get quiet, and turn toward him. He desired this several times each day. For many women I knew, to enter his office alone was to invite arch questions and lewd comments. Several years later, as my first marriage was dissolving and I was facing single motherhood, my employer at the time, whom I had imagined thought me indispensable to his success, earnestly suggested that *he* was to blame for my divorce: He had "given" me such a good job that I no longer seemed to need the security of marriage.

Of course, I couldn't just decide not to work in order to avoid having employers like these. I wanted to work, but also I needed to work. So in the long run, these experiences from the work world thoroughly discredited my childhood lessons of "personal freedom" and "individual self-reliance." According to those lessons, I could have avoided and/or triumphed over these humiliating and painful incidents if I had just tried hard enough. But the principal held the whistle and the superintendent decided who got which jobs. Their actions couldn't just be ignored, and neither was I likely to change their assumptions.

Looking back and sorting through the contradictions—egalitarian ideals on one side, constrained realities on the other—I divide my experience into pregendered and postgendered lives. Before adolescence I absorbed the message that I "could do anything if I worked at it." I could be President, lead the union, be a nurse, a math whiz, a farmer. The revelation that I was bound by indelible markers of class and gender (as my parents had been before me) hit hard. As my body changed during pubescence, it began to attract new attentions; the eyes of acquaintances and strangers traced its lines, exploring and measuring in an offhand way. At the same time, the attentions I was familiar with—my parents, teachers, and friends seeing me as inherently important and intellectually promising—began to evaporate or, even more threatening, to transform radically. This pubescent body I lived in called up in others, and unfortunately in me, peculiar new assumptions about who I was. I seemed headed toward passive death of the intellect and active construction of the sexual. During this time there seemed to be no question but that the body (mine and my female friends') would be on display: the neckline low, hemline high, waist cinched, wrists and throat roped with jewelry. The last two years of high school I lightened my hair to a brazen copper and heavily blackened my eyelids and lashes. But above all I smiled, nodded, listened, and agreed. This strange mixture of the insistently voluptuous with the retiringly chaste is what I remember most clearly about young adulthood. Cherished values seemed merely to veil an ugly underlying doctrine, the real "American way": maximum exploitation of resources, natural and human.

Alan

Although very different on the surface, my classically petite-bourgeois upbringing in the urban Northeast was similar to Karen's in some important ways. My father and grandfather were small-scale entrepreneurs and the family business determined their consciousness of themselves, their values, and their relation to others. My earliest memories were conditioned by narratives belonging to the "gospel of success" genre. According to family lore, Grandfather France built the inventory of his Brooklyn-based rosin-import business by ascetic practices of Franklinesque proportion. As a young man, according to one story, he daily denied himself lunch, ingesting instead the aroma of food emitted from a restaurant's sidewalk grate. He brought into the business his only son, who promptly married the firm's most capable young secretary. Emulating the elder generation, my parents lived arduously and inexpensively, reinvesting profits in the business. Seven decades after its formation, France, Campbell, and Darling, Inc., by now a small chemical manufacturing business, was sold to an international conglomerate, thus concluding the France family's contribution to America's entrepreneurial history. The next chapter, the globalization of capitalism, would go on without them.

Coming of age at this juncture between the nineteenth-century ascetic mode of capital accumulation and the postwar, postindustrial hedonism of consumer capitalism, the regime of flexible accumulation, as it is called, I have spent most of my adult life trying to reconfigure the pieces of a tradition that has landed on the scrap heap of history. This experience of anomie (which I imagine to be fairly common in the American academy) has shaped my intellectual self-consciousness and my vocation as teacher. And like Karen's, my alienation has been deeply inflected by a masculinist division of the world into a dominant public sphere, men's competitive struggle to achieve "success" through work in a secular vocation, and a subordinate domestic sphere occupied by women and children. This late Victorian division of labor was supported by a romantic mythology that, though it accords even less with the material realities of their world, our students still find persuasive.

The basic problem is that the success ethic, in practice, turns out to be inimical to "family values." There is a mythologized "founding father" who succeeds through an act of will. The myth is silent about founding mothers and about any psychic costs of success for all family members. The price is high, though, in my experience. The father's attention to accumulation and his devotion to the values of rational calculation that maximize it starve the family of a male intimacy. For male children of the third generation, the founding-father myth—the story of accumulation itself—often becomes not a "success" story, but a deeply frustrating story about emotional autism and lost opportunities for love.

And yet, in many ways, I share a deep, even visceral, belief in the virtues of my fathers: modesty, frugality, the value of hard work, the stewardship of nature (all of which were frequently violated in practice, of course). My father often contradicted those who made disparaging remarks about garbage men or ditch diggers. He would say, "There's nothing shameful about honest work." He thought display was "vulgar" and idleness a vice. He even said about marriage that a man and a woman should "pull in harness together," although I'm not sure what he meant by it. In any case, these values are either quaint, oppressive, or ridiculous in the context of consumer capitalism. Physical labor is odious to most, a mark not so much of social as of personal inferiority (with a token nod to all the money that plumbers make). And the idea that spending money to acquire commodities is not a primary source of happiness in life—that it may indeed distract from more important things—seems positively medieval. Yet, in the midst of this free-market orgy of consumption, we still hear the old homilies about freedom and equality of opportunity, family values and hard work, abstaining from sex, saying no to drugs, and attending the church of your choice on Sunday. Thus do these values live on in the half-life of late capitalist ideology serving, as platitudes, to obscure the degradation of labor and to ennoble consumption.

How, then, did this class "positionality" work to produce the teacher-scholar-critic whom I've become? Only in retrospect can I recognize the profound resentment of my status, torn as I was between the professional and working classes. In the midst of 1950s suburban abundance, my father's reputation for gravity and frugality was peculiar—or worse. I literally wore this contradiction. As I approached high school, neighborhood boys began, under pressure from family, to appear in brand-name chinos and penny loafers; sweaters multiplied and softened in color and texture; well-made suits, wool overcoats, starched shirts, and wing-tipped shoes distinguished the better sort of boys at church and other social occasions. Other symptoms of social differentiation became apparent as well: the country club, Saturday golf, formal dances, and weekend trips in the fall to rumored places like Cambridge, Massachusetts, and Princeton, New Jersey, for football games and, as I now know, for building intergenerational social networks.

On the other side of town, meanwhile, different changes were taking place. There were black slacks, pointed-toe shoes with steel-cleated heels, long hair, and fistfighting. There were street rods and serious courtships, and maybe most attractive of all, black R & B: Johnny Ace, Ivory Joe Hunter, Shirley and Lee, the Chantels. My heart was on this side of town, although I was totally unfit for labor, force-fed as I had been on the American Dream, the protestant ethic, and the Horatio Alger myth. With my self-importance and soft hands— and no inkling of what to do with tools—I had a great need for the emollients of bourgeois status.

This was clearly a case for higher education, and after high school, I spent sixteen of the next twenty-five years in various universities. But as we well know, English departments are no place to escape class distinctions, which go to the very soul of work and study. English departments are divided, like Berkeley Heights, New Jersey, into the laboring class and the better sort. There is a corridor through the department, to use Jim Berlin's (1996) image, which divides rhetoric from poetic (xiii), and those of us on the rhetoric side (when we haven't been physically banished to the basement or to mobile units) are familiar enough with not-so-benign neglect, condescension, and occasionally, overt contempt.

My first full-time position was an instructorship at a large state university, as part of a composition motor pool serving the literacy needs of underprepared first-year students. After my first year, the department chair moved all the instructors from the offices we shared with professorial faculty to windowless attic cubicles, known collectively as "the garret." Some of my best students were athletes, some white but most black, from the "other side" of towns across the South. Many of them came on scholarship with big hopes and left on crutches. I at least landed on the street with both knees intact.

It was only during my final stint in graduate school that the politics of my personal and professional experiences began to coalesce. Even then, I began my doctoral studies in English hoping to specialize in nineteenth-century British literature. It was only after I stumbled on the family bastard, rhetoric, that I began to understand that composition, the production of texts, belonged to a noble tradition. From Jim Corder and Win Horner, among others, I learned that rhetoric *is* the English department corridor on which all offices open as well as the universal corrosive that might dissolve the hauteur of bourgeois and belletristic privilege.

Teaching in Class/Class in Teaching

What if our parents and our parents' parents had known what we would learn from their stories? We see the ideology we imbibed growing up as describing a society different from the one we inhabit as adults and as teachers. In our fathers' and mothers' version of America, virtue and hard work were rewarded and justice was even-handedly conferred. Embedded in their hopes were myths about patriarchy, told by and about fathers who needed to conquer an adversarial public world (and in one way or another be excused from family life) and mothers who needed to believe that their isolation as lone adults among children was virtuous, or at least workable.

Obviously, we see differently. But the question we must answer here is how did we, nurtured in the bosom of our reasonably sane and loving families, emerge so disaffected? A big part of the answer, of course, belongs to the dynamic of recent history, in particular the Civil Rights Movement, Vietnam, and the women's movement. But many of our contemporaries in the academy have shared these experiences without coming to reject, as we do, the free market and the nuclear family.

A more particular answer to this question, we think, is that our lives are revisions, more than rejections, of family narratives. We have made central to the story parts that to our forebears were implicit or peripheral. These revisions illustrate, mundanely enough, how hegemony builds its own dialectical resistance: The ongoing penetration of capital into every human relation continually produces a class of disaffected bourgeois critics too engaged with the earlier ideological formation ever to accept the new one. In *Bread and Wine* (1937), Antonio Gramsci's comrade in the Italian Communist Party, Ignazio Silone, has Don Paolo explain the process this way:

> if one takes seriously [the principles taught us] and uses them as a standard to test society as it is organized . . . it becomes evident that there is a radical contradiction between the two. Our society in practice ignores these principles altogether. . . . But for us they are a serious and sacred thing . . . the foundation of our inner life. (157–158)

Although those who taught us were courageous and admirably wily, they didn't mean exactly what they said. Or what they said was not intended to produce what we thought and took to heart.

The radical contradiction between articulated ideal and social reality underlies our approach to literary and cultural criticism, rhetoric, and composition pedagogy. In our syllabuses and in our daily interactions with students and their texts, we work to emphasize the dissonance between appearance and reality, between ideals and their material bases, by underscoring in our teaching language's powers of ambiguity and duplicity. Individual experience, we have learned, is inadequate to self-knowledge; without a context within which to view experience, one is unable to address—for purposes either of affirmation or of resistance—power relationships. In our essay "Advocacy and Resistance in the Writing Class" (Fitts and France 1994), we described our pedagogical objectives in the following way:

> to awaken students to the role of culture in giving meaning to—or overlaying with significance—female or male physiology, to use a prominent example. In short, we consider our role to be that of teaching resistance to cultural definitions of biological sex by provoking dissonance between egalitarian expectations, on the one hand, and social and cultural asymmetries of power and perceived worth, on the other. (15)

This objective echoes the classical Western philosophical opposition between appearance and reality formulated by Plato's cave. The metaphors employed here suggest an unveiling of the deceptions of language. We want to "awaken" the (sleeping) student to the "role" of culture (implying a distinction between the fictional and the "real") and to the "dissonance" between surface expectations and underlying realities of power and value. In practice, our pedagogies strive to unveil the radical discrepancy between an ideal—or ideological—world (of family, school, church, and country) and the real world of the commodity, in which all local value is transmuted into exchange value, and of patriarchy, in which all local power is distributed according to sex.

How, then, does this rhetoric of revelation take pedagogical form?

Karen

Unveiling the work of ideology is, of course, a work in progress. On the occasions when teaching well is most difficult, I attribute the trouble to knowing what I know and trying to teach responsibly based on that knowledge: that power, or the lack of power, overdetermines exchanges among people. Occasionally memories arise of that middle school principal, whistle in mouth, eyebrow raised, or the superintendent who dexterously mixed management and marital counseling. In addition, different schools, with their varying missions, student populations, and institutional traditions have interacted in complex ways with my classed and gendered loyalties.

As an adjunct, for example, teaching largely first-generation college students, I saw myself as an advocate of students, articulating the two-way flow of learning and teaching in the classroom, foregrounding their intellectual labor, and minimizing my teacherly authority. In

my best Freirean manner, I emphasized the necessity that learning be
relevant to them and asked them to remember their own experiences
with "banking" and "problem-posing" educational strategies. Deeply
invested in the privileges conferred by the credentials of an education—any old kind of education—the students wrestled confoundedly
with this new understanding of institutional power gone awry and of
foundational inequities. As for me, having struggled with similar
painful issues, I found these years and these students gratifying.

In another setting, where students represented the very elites I
previously had wanted to make more accountable, I had less success.
To speak generally, I perceived the students to be diligent, well-pre-
pared for college work, and polite; I saw them also as maddeningly
compliant and dangerously insulated from societal ills. Defensiveness
on my part (very difficult readings, a stinging grade system) mixed
with condescension (refusal to acknowledge their ability to engage
the work I had set for us to do) miserably undercut my Freirean mission of making learning relevant to those who would learn. Since
those years, I've (re)learned that a teacher's task always remains the
same—to begin with students from where they are—and that the most
effective teaching and learning take place dialectically.

For example, I teach an upper-division seminar entitled "Gendered
Rhetorics" with the goal of providing insight into social stratification,
especially as these inequities are maintained or challenged with language. In this class last year, students and teacher faced a frustrating
knot of emotion and logic in the (still) hotly-debated question of whether
women in the 1990s are expected to serve and to consent. Four male
students grumbled about the question itself, asking "Why do we have to
talk about *this*?" and about the answers they were hearing from some of
their classmates. The four urged us to talk about self-reliance, self-
denial, and the "common sense" that tells us that whoever works hardest
gets the prize of self-direction. Five of the women insisted that the question is worth arguing and writing about. They argued that women, in
fact, can't rely on themselves and that neither, in fact, do men. One the-
orized that, if women are expected to be objects of beauty, one who
isn't "attractive" won't get the job. I valued these disagreements, seeing
in them the dialectics that signify that learning is taking place.

In "Gendered Rhetorics," readings from Freud ([1933] 1994) and
Cixous ([1976] 1994) set the stage for an important series of mas-
culinist-feminist dialectics. Both writers link the male and female psyche to male and female bodies, but each posits wildly variant consequences. Freud claims that "portions of the male sexual apparatus also
appear in women's bodies, though in an atrophied state" (21). His
view is that "with the change to femininity the clitoris should wholly
or in part hand over its sensitivity, and at the same time its impor-

tance, to the vagina" (24). Freud's considerations of the female body lead him to assert that women exhibit weak character, physical vanity, and sexual frigidity. By contrast, Cixous admires female physiology with its potential for multiple orgasms, lactation, intellectual suppleness, and feeling. She celebrates the possibilities inherent in woman: "I am spacious, singing flesh, on which is grafted no one knows which I, more or less human, but alive because of transformation" (89).

Building on the gendered discourses of Freud and Cixous—two thinkers so keenly divided on the purposes and values of the female body—I designed a writing project as follows:

> Look for a "real life" situation, or cultural event, in which a gendered discourse and its consequences to all of us are exposed. For example, women and men entering nontraditional jobs often must confront stereotypical assumptions about what it means to be masculine or feminine in the United States. (I'm thinking of women in the service, as supervisors of men, as telephone line repair personnel; of men as nurses, as elementary school teachers, or as day care personnel.) It matters to all of us because our society will be quite different (in ways that you should elucidate) depending upon whether these nonconventional souls are encouraged or discouraged. Consider your findings in light of the theories we are reading and on which we are relying this semester to gain a better understanding of discourse as gendered. Ideally, this kind of assignment will illustrate the conventions that maintain gendered roles.

Upon thinking over the assignment, a student I will call Janet wrote an examination of pop culture she entitled "Girls Talk." In it, she argued that significant change will occur only when young women begin to feel comfortable using profanity in public places and in mixed (male and female) company. "Obscenity used by women," she asserted, "may help break down the stereotypes that serve to divide [women and men]." She began the essay with this example:

> The opening scene in Quentin Tarantino's film *Pulp Fiction* is, as the rest of the film, startling and funny. A man and woman turn from a couple exchanging sweet nothings in a diner booth to a couple of criminals. The man stands on the booth seat. "Everybody stay cool. This is a robbery!" he announces. Then his lover, a slight blonde with a reedy voice, climbs on top of a counter and shouts "If any one of you motherfuckers moves I'll shoot every last one of ya!" The comedy from this scene comes partly from the woman's use of the f-word—such a big, bad noise coming out of this little woman. Our laughter at the scene betrays what we think about women: it's not their job to talk dirty.

Janet pointed out, though, that contemporary rock musician Liz Phair—in songs such as "Supernova" (where her guy is "a frictional blast") and "Fuck and Run" ("a lament for bad judgment and guys who do what the title says")—is appropriating the (largely) male prerogative of vulgarity.

It's clear to Janet that Phair's obscenity—Janet's mother responds with "no end to lip-pursing"—is not just for shock value. Neither is Phair attempting to be seductive; as Janet pointed out, "her memorable lines really have nothing to do with sex." Instead, Phair's use of the f-word "helps to clear a space to tell women's side of the story," enabling her to challenge "years of sexist rock." Janet concluded:

> Listen up, Phair's music says to men and women. And it's a bullseye shot to every groupie draped over every bass player, every chick used as scenery in a video, every backup singer, every woman trapped in the largely masculine discourse of pop music: this f-word's for you.

Janet's essay illustrates a shrewd understanding of the possibility that language uses us more subtly than we use it. Our words, our tone, our manner announce information about us that we may not have authorized. Janet had argued that, in Phair's case, the user challenges rather than tolerates the gendered assumptions implicit in language.

Alan

As teachers most of us hope we are changing the world, one day and one student at a time, for the better. Teaching is the exercise of authority and as such it must have some social purpose, whether or not the teacher cares to examine it closely. For the Marxist or feminist teacher, the emphasis on change becomes a primary pedagogical objective. As a Marxist rhetorician and writing instructor, I aspire to the status of the Gramscian "organic intellectual," which Eagleton (1991) defines as one who

> is less a contemplative thinker, in the old idealist style of the intelligentsia, than an organizer, constructor, "permanent persuader", who actively participates in social life and helps bring to theoretical articulation those positive political currents already contained within it. . . . The function of the organic intellectual, in other words, is to forge the links between "theory" and "ideology", creating a two-way passage between political analysis and popular experience. (119–120)

What Karen and I have offered to this point seems to me to be a subjective version of how two people came to be "organic intellectuals," how our specific historical experiences led us to reject the dominant ideology of our adult lives. But "reject" implies a conscious decision, a heroic or visionary insight into the way things really are. While I may have consciously adopted my own political and pedagogical commitments, it has been (to echo Marx) not under circumstances I myself have chosen. To recapitulate, Karen and I have described the context of our "progressive pedagogy" as a collision between two fields of social organization; the collision allowed us to escape—or perhaps expelled us from—the gravitational pull of either. To some degree, we all share the experience of simultaneous alienation and liberation, the "freedom" released by the corrosive penetration of capital into ever more intimate social forms and relations. A big part of my job as teacher, as I see it, is to encourage students to be more aware of this "in between" state and to recognize the revolutionary potential that lies within it.

In attempting to teach the process of cultural critique, I am always conscious of the ideological veil that permits students to hold true to propositions they themselves judge irrational. Those, for example, who know that their state's AFDC payments are less than $100 monthly per child will insist that "welfare mothers have children to collect more money." Or those who believe, in the face of staggering empirical—and often personal—evidence to the contrary, that racism is not a significant factor in contemporary American society. For those on the cushy side of structural inequalities, it *is* hard to see the structures, easy to accept the meritocratic ideology of each rising to his or her "God-given" level of competence, each deserving of the rewards tendered by the invisible hand of the "free market." What my assignments try to do is to put this faith to the test, to help students to part the veil, and to place into confrontation the ideal and the material.

To illustrate, let me take that most obvious of mystifications, the supposed absence of social class in this country. While social class is an unquestionable reality, only some of us can see this "Caruso's footprint" (Brantlinger 1990) in the sand of our common culture. My objective is to make it apparent to those who cannot see it—to the end, ultimately, of persuading students to value work and workers more equally. My strategy is to play off what is already known about our social and economic hierarchy against what might be or is to be learned from an alternative theoretical perspective. Here's how I tried to accomplish this in a sophomore writing course ("Writing from Personal Experience") in the spring semester of 1996.

The assignment began with the careful reading of Shana Alexander's (1995) *New Yorker* essay, "Ain't No More Middle Class," which closely examines the travails and rewards of an American working-class family. Alexander's essay presents itself as pure journalism preoccupied with the quotidian details of the Mertens's daily lives, the specifics of their earnings and expenditures.

We learn what Kenny Merten earns as a highway construction laborer, how much he spends on breakfast (Pepsi and doughnuts), what it costs to take his two teenage sons to McDonald's for lunch on Saturday. We learn about Bonnie's routine as an attendant at a nursing home, how much she earns, and what it's spent on. We get a detailed itinerary of the Mertens's daily lives in interaction with kin, friends, and the larger Indianapolis community they belong to. Of course, Alexander chose her subject wisely: The warts-and-all details add up to a deeply human—if slightly condescending—portrait of "the salt of the earth." But the essay supplies the raw materials for another perspective on the American dream, one untinted by the rosy glass of bourgeois ideology.

To draw back the veil so that students may confront their own "persuadedness" (or "interpellation" as Althusser named it) as bourgeois subjects, I borrowed a technique from Peter Caulfield (1995), the "Attitudes and Attributes List." List objects and events, I instructed students, that seem "Familiar"; list the kinds of things your family would say or do, that represent attitudes and values your family holds. Then make a second list, the "Unfamiliar," of things foreign to your own experience, things that seem weird, silly, naive, dumb, or gross. (Peter calls these the "Me" and the "Not Me" lists.) Here, of course, we are looking for attributes that distinguish the working class from the middle class—attributes that can make visible the differences normally imperceptible to many college students.

Lots of things are common to the Mertens and my students. They identify with their cars (Kenny spends a lot on his Chevy Blazer because, as he says, "A man's got his ego"), eat at fast-food restaurants often, commemorate anniversaries with diamond rings, demand Nike Air athletic shoes (like Christopher, the Mertens's twenty-year-old autistic son), go shopping at malls for fun, place a high value on family vacations, and so on.

But lots of things clashed with students' attitudes and experiences. They found it bizarre that Bonnie didn't have a driver's license, that the family never ate salads or green vegetables. They noticed the insistent "bad grammar" (Kenny solemnly says to Bonnie about their marriage, "I don't have no regrets") and the missing signs of literacy: books, papers, a computer. They were uncomfortable with the state of the Mertens's finances: bounced checks, exceeded credit card limits, the imminent threat of bankruptcy. Then there were the Mertens's jobs, each requiring a uniform and paying less than $15,000 a year.

But what they found most troubling (several did not shy away from calling it a moral failure) was the Mertens's *attitude* toward their plight: They did nothing to improve it. Neither tried very hard to get a better job or considered "going back to school" to acquire new skills. Kenny's anguished declaration that forms the story's title, "Ain't No More Middle Class," is uttered from his La-Z-Boy recliner. He's tired from assembling and disassembling highway barricades all day, contemplating bankruptcy, and he's out of hope for a better future. The students say things like "He needs to take control of his life" and "He needs to keep trying to get a better job." I ask why we—me, too!—feel that the simple virtues of hard, useful work and of family solidarity and intimacy aren't enough.

After the class discussion I ask students to write an essay exploring the conflict between family values and the success ethic (the "getting ahead" imperative) in their own lives. The assignment asks

> How did you learn which way "ahead" is? Is it the same way for women as well as men? Remember that nobody thought Bonnie wasn't striving hard enough. Is our middle-class success ethic a recipe for materialism and absent fatherhood? Isn't Ken Merten a better role model for family life than an executive who has devoted his (or her) life to the competitive struggle in the workplace? You might also examine how your attitude toward manual labor (that it's only for a "loser" like Kenny) was formed.

In their essays, of course, most students defended traditional gender-inflected middle-class social ideals. But the assignment did force them to confront the basic class conflict that our bourgeois ideology renders invisible, and it did part, however fleetingly, the veil of appearances. As such, it is an expression of that method of inquiry known as cultural studies, which makes visible the workings of acculturation, a persuasive force and therefore a rhetorical one (see Brummett 1994, 110–154).

We find cultural studies a useful approach to writing pedagogy, because it suggests to students that one's consciousness (including their own) is the outcome of a sociohistorical process. Cultural studies calls upon students not merely to exercise their ideology but to "read" it, making critical thinking an essential element in the processes of writing: invention, discovery, drafting, and revising. Because history is culture over time, practicing cultural studies can more fully integrate the intellectual work of composition—teaching and learning, reading and writing, reflecting and arguing, affirming and resisting— into themes and narratives of history. That has been our experience.

Works Cited

Alexander, S. 1995. "Ain't No More Middle Class." *The New Yorker*, 13 October, 38+.

Berlin, James A. 1996. *Rhetorics, Poetics, and Cultures: Refiguring College English Studies*. Urbana, IL: National Council of Teachers of English.

Brantlinger, P. 1990. *Caruso's Footprints: Cultural Studies in Britain and America*. New York: Routledge.

Brummett, B. 1994. *Rhetoric of Popular Culture*. New York: St. Martin's Press.

Caulfield, P. 1995. "Teaching Rhetoric as a Way of Knowing." In *Left Margins: Cultural Studies and Composition Pedagogy*, ed. K. Fitts and A. France, 157–172. Albany: SUNY Press.

Cixous, H. [1976] 1994. "The Laugh of the Medusa." In Roman, Juhasz, and Miller, 78–93.

Eagleton, T. 1991. *Ideology: An Introduction*. London: Verso.

Engels, F. [1845] 1972. *The Origin of the Family, Private Property and the State*. New York: International Publishers.

Fitts, K., and A. France. 1994. "Advocacy and Resistance in the Writing Class: Working Toward Stasis." In *Pedagogy in the Age of Politics: Writing and Reading (in) the Academy*, ed. P. Sullivan and D. Qualley. Urbana, IL: National Council of Teachers of English.

Freud, S. [1933] 1994. "Femininity." In Roman, Juhasz, and Miller, 20–36.

Ohmann, R. 1987. *Politics of Letters*. Hanover, NH: Wesleyan University Press.

Roman, C., S. Juhasz, and C. Miller, eds. 1994. *The Women and Language Debate: A Sourcebook*. New Brunswick, NJ: Rutgers University Press.

Silone, I. 1937. *Bread and Wine*. Trans. G. David and E. Mosbacher. New York: Harper and Brothers.

6

Stupid Clown of the Spirit's Motive
Class Bias in Literary and Composition Studies[1]

Olivia Frey

It is the business of a university to train the mind to think,
and to impart solid knowledge, not to turn out nimble
penmen who may earn a living as the clerks and salesmen
of literature.

Lane Cooper, "On the Teaching of Written Composition"

"Some of the tenured members of the department are concerned that
your work is not at the Core of Literary Studies." I can hear in his
voice the capital *C*, *L*, and *S*. I am having breakfast in a local cafe
with the chair of the English Department of St. Olaf College. It is
1988. We are discussing my "tenure case." For the most part, things
are going well. There are, however, "concerns" about my areas of
expertise: English education and composition. I have, of course, been
hired to teach these subjects, to supervise student-teachers, and to
coordinate the writing program. The college has been compelled to
offer these programs because they attract and serve students, and yet,
obviously, the English department has never embraced them.

"We think that perhaps you should teach more literature courses,
more level-three courses. Perhaps teach a seminar or two," he continues as he butters his toast. "If you taught more literature, and not just
freshmen, these concerns would be allayed."

I feel betrayed, and confused. I have tried to do everything right, and have spent tremendous amounts of energy and countless hours building the Writing Across the Curriculum program—recruiting reticent teachers from other disciplines, even mathematics and the natural sciences, to include writing in their courses. I have led workshop after workshop in the summers, at the expense of my own writing and research. I have written scores of grants for the writing program, but none for myself.

As I sit there, no longer able to eat, I begin to understand my mother's complaints when she worked as a secretary for the doctor in our small town in south Florida. Marjorie Johnson Cool worked six days a week, from 8:00 in the morning until 6:00 or 7:00 at night, sometimes later when there was a shooting or another kind of emergency. She not only assisted Dr. Crissey when he treated patients, did the lab work, and autoclaved the instruments, but she also scrubbed the floors and washed the toilets. And yet she was rarely accorded respect. The patients saved their wrath for her when they were angry with the doctor. They talked through her, as though she were invisible, when the doctor was around. Dr. Crissey would be condescending, and too often disregarded her opinions. She finally was able to quit when I finished college. You could say that she retired, except that she had no retirement benefits.

It was not much different for my father. Cecil Howard Cool left school in Virginia when he was fourteen, and ran away to New York City. He worked odd jobs. He was a butler for a while. Drove a cab in New York and then in Washington, D.C. He finally started working construction, and helped build the Pentagon. He formed his own small construction company after he married my mother and they moved to South Miami, Florida. But he had to quit the construction business after he twisted his back taking down a ladder one summer before a hurricane hit. He found steady work as a salesman for a small Sears and Roebuck catalogue store. He wore the polyester suit, and accepted the indoor work, though he never wore a real tie, only the clip-on variety. He was a salesman, and was accorded the respect that salesmen are usually accorded—that is, little respect or consideration, particularly when the new dishwasher starts leaking. In Lane Cooper's 1909 MLA address quoted at the beginning of this essay (Cooper [1910] 1995), the analogy he chooses leaves no doubt about his regard for clerks and salesmen like my father.

I had wanted my life to be different. I had wanted to be the doctor, the "boss," and I knew that school would be my ticket out of the working class and into a respected profession. But somewhere I must have taken a wrong turn. I had made it. I was the "doctor." Yet, that morning in the little cafe in Minnesota sitting with my "boss," I felt as though I had just finished scrubbing and polishing the floor, and while I stood naively aside waiting for praise, he not only did not acknowledge me, but he walked across the clean floor in his muddy shoes.

It's an old story, and a familiar one to composition teachers: composition's relegation to "low" status (Miller 1991) and its fight for legitimacy within college and university English departments. The regard (disregard) for composition and composition teachers has interesting parallels with the daily struggles of workers and laborers, and their status within society at large.

Many English teachers are aware of the history of composition's tenuous position within the profession of English and literary studies. Composition teachers are part of the underclass at colleges and universities, though possibly are less marginalized at small liberal arts colleges. The original words of the proponents as well as the detractors of the first composition programs across the country expose the deepest roots of conflicted attitudes toward composition that still exist today—intellectual and class bias. Composition programs were first developed, and maintain precarious positions still, within institutions whose motivating force, in spite of occasional mitigating humanitarian rhetoric, is to maintain priviledge and position for those who enter. I think that those within composition itself have conflicted attitudes, which accounts for energetic defensiveness when the credibility of composition studies as a discipline seems in doubt.[2]

Higher education was never intended to be, and it is not now, egalitarian, in spite of efforts in the early twentieth century with the founding of land grant colleges to make it more accessible, and in spite of the tireless efforts of community colleges and some public universities to make higher education more available and affordable. It is a narrow gate through to the academy, and an even narrower passage to the other side. Pedagogies and knowledge constructions privilege the already privileged, and economic demands tax even the most hard-working and personally resourceful students. In *Generation at the Crossroads: Apathy and Action on the American Campus*, Paul Loeb (1994) provides indisputable evidence that college is more and more difficult for working-class students, and for some, entirely inaccessible. In 1969, 43 percent of all college students worked outside jobs while enrolled in school. By 1979, this figure had increased to 51 percent, and by 1990, it was 63 percent. Economic pressures "have increasingly skewed the composition of the academy along class lines," writes Loeb (44–45).

As if economics didn't make it difficult enough, working-class students face an intellectual culture, including teaching practices, that is unfamiliar and, to some, an impediment to "making it." In C. L. Barney Dews's and Carolyn Leste Law's anthology, *This Fine Place So Far From Home* (1995), a collection of searing essays that dramatize the feelings of alienation even among those who have "made it," Irvin Peckham writes,

It seems to me that although the educational institution claims to be promoting universal literacy and egalitarianism, it has embraced a system that institutionalizes difference, and through difference, failure, with the failed ones coming primarily from the working classes (the ones who have different habits of cognition and language). One could not expect otherwise when it is the dominant classes who construct the norms by which one marks success and failure. We pretend the race is even, but I see it as fixed. (275)

In "Freshman Composition as a Middle Class Enterprise," Lynn Z. Bloom (1996) demonstrates that "middle-class standards may operate for the worse, particularly when middle-class teachers punish lower-class students for not being, well, more middle-class" (655).

The earliest colleges and universities in England, and then in colonial America and the United States, were founded for the purpose of educating the intellectual elite: clergy, lawyers and doctors: "A classical education was the avenue to the old professions and especially the ministry. . . . And the desire of the professional classes to maintain their standing as a class apart was one reason why all regularly educated men insisted upon the pre-eminence of that kind of education" (Good 1962, 64).

Education in the classics predominated through the early 1900s and World War I, when a practical (elitist) motivation evolved into a nationalistic (elitist) one. The classics prevailed for reasons of cultural purity and identity and, I would add, class purity. Sanskrit scholar and first German philologist at Oxford Max Müller (1901) outlined his Aryan hypothesis in his autobiography: "In order to know what we are, we have to learn how we have come to be what we are. Our very languages form an unbroken chain between us and Cicero and Aristotle, and in order to use many of our words intelligently, we must know the soil from which they sprang, and the atmosphere in which they grew and developed" (104).

As the shape and content of higher education has changed over the course of this century—and the shape of literature and composition programs within these institutions—one thing remains constant. The emphasis and content of education has served some national, political, and/or economic agenda, and these agendas have rarely served the lower classes and others on the margins of society. When restructuring has not served some patriotic or nationalistic agenda, it has served to shore up fragmented literature departments, or make the study of literature more systematic in order to attain some credibility with the "hard" sciences. That is, restructuring or curricular revision has always worked to consolidate power.

It is into this context of the preservation of privilege and power that modern composition courses and programs were introduced—I say "modern" to distinguish composition courses from the earlier courses in classical oratory and writing.

The establishment of composition was controversial, therefore, from the beginning. Students had always written, of course, but what was significant about the creation of the first composition courses at Harvard in 1869 was the formalization and intentionality of writing instruction. Before 1869, writing, recitation, and oratory accompanied students' work in Latin and Greek, religious instruction, and study of the classics. But when the president of Harvard, Charles W. Eliot, appointed Adams Sherman Hill the first Boylston Professor of Rhetoric and charged him with creating the first modern composition course, he did so with explicit goals in mind.

President Eliot looked out on America and saw a country that was rapidly progressing technologically and industrially. He believed that the mission of Harvard in particular, and colleges in general, should be to educate the future leaders and professionals of the United States. Education in the classics of Latin and Greek civilization alone would no longer be appropriate, or very useful, for citizens of a democratic society of European origin in North America. In this respect, Eliot echoed a larger movement on the part of universities at the time to train specialists in engineering and manufacturing—in mathematics, chemistry, and physics—to answer the needs of an increasingly industrialized nation.

Implied in Hill's and President Eliot's statements at the time regarding the teaching of composition, as well as the opinions of other professors of literature and rhetoric, was the idea that writing instruction was not simply instruction in a skill. The discipline that writing required, the thought that it entailed, and the elevated content that was its subject would produce better citizens within society, and better *American* citizens. Lane Cooper, professor of English and classics at Cornell from 1902 to 1943, explicitly states this moral principle in a 1914 article in *English Journal*, "The Correction of Papers": "What, then, does 'the correction of papers' actually mean? Briefly, it means the correction, or straightening, or normalizing of one personality by another through the instrumentality of truth expressed in language" (292).[3]

In spite of Eliot's attempts to give it high status by means of a nationalistic and moral imperative, Harvard's composition program was attacked almost immediately. One reason for the attack was that Harvard faculty and faculty at other colleges did not look forward to reading and correcting so many student themes, and were loath to give up teaching literature and doing research. Brereton (1995) and Graff (1987) both tell the story of Harvard Professor Francis James Child, who almost defected to Johns Hopkins in 1876 because there he would not have to read any more student themes. He stayed at

Harvard when he was relieved of theme grading and was able to devote all of his time to literature.

But the early writings against a formal composition program suggest that there was more to the professors' displeasure than worries about the hard, boring work to come of grading themes. Teaching composition and correcting themes was not only a tedious task, but also theatened to demean the elevated profession of reading and studying literature. Influential critics such as Cooper, Thomas Raynesford Lounsbury, instructor in English at Yale's Sheffield Scientific School from 1870 to 1908, and William Lyon Phelps, professor of English at Yale, expressed horror at the prospect of making writing common. They believed that there were those who could write, that is, the greats of literature, and those who could be great, that is, those who had "innate ability" (Lounsbury [1911] 1995, 276). Cooper ([1910] 1995) quotes Lord Morley: "It is not everybody who can command the mighty rhythms of the greatest masters of human speech" (258–259). Cooper himself writes later in the same essay,

> No teaching could be too good for our land of promise, with the civilization here to be developed. This is obvious. When we penetrate deeper, we note, first of all, that not every person has the same right to an education in the vernacular. An idiot, for example, has not the same right as a genius, nor in general have those who are below the average in capacity or attainments the same right as those who are above it. Doubtless everyone in a sense has a claim to instruction in English, but the point is that some have a better claim, or a claim to more of it, than others. Who are these? Clearly, as has been suggested, they who have the greater capacity. It is a law of nature that to those who have shall be given. In our teaching we may well observe the tendencies of nature, following her laws, and aiding her in the accomplishment of her purposes. (296)

Lounsbury ([1911] 1995) practically sneers when he observes that "the great American community clings to the faith that anybody and everybody can be taught to use the language" (280). These men imply an intellectual primogeniture. They reject the "popular clamor," the "popular cackle" (Lounsbury [1911] 1995, 265) for universal composition instruction, and they reject the common practice of composition. These self-appointed "guardians of usage" and "corrector[s] of personalities" were also guarding the gate against the low, the common, the popular—by definition, "of the people at large," the "great unwashed." An anonymous article in *Century Magazine* in 1896 claimed that "The best way, indeed, to become a good writer is to be born of the right sort of parents" (793–794).

The content and tenor of Cooper's, Lounsbury's, and others' attacks on composition are decidedly unegalitarian. While it seems that they speak primarily of intellectual capacity and attainments, the particular emphasis of their rhetoric and the kinds of images that they use to disparage universal composition instruction suggest that "attainments" includes material attainments, that is, social position or class and the attainments of good breeding that, they assume, naturally come with elevated social class. The worthy—those who could benefit by learning at the feet of the great masters of literature, and who needed no "common" instruction in composition, indeed, would be hurt by it—are the upper classes. "To develop [ability in expression] in any marked degree, there needs, to be sure, innate capacity in the individual; but if that exists, the education of events is likely of itself to ripen it to its consumate flower of perfection" (Lounsbury [1911] 1995, 277). And what are these events that educate to such advantage? According to Lounsbury, they are to "have been engaged in the conduct of vast business enterprises" or to "have shouldered the burden of heavy responsibilities" or to "have borne a part in the great history of events" (277).

On the other hand, the images of the working class—undoubtedly the common laborers who made "vast business enterprises" possible, or the foot soldiers who played the most immediate role in "the great history of events"—that the detractors of common composition instruction used were scornful and derogatory. I can assume that these English professors were not careless with their analogies and rhetoric, so that their language was either intentional, or unconsciously reflected class bias held by many. Consider again Cooper's statement about the clerks and salesmen of literature; these are not occupations that he thinks highly of. The *Century* writer speaks of the freshman fashioning sentences and paragraphs as like working the "treadmill," in contrast to the boy who "thinks interesting thoughts" and will consequently "write not only more attractively, but more correctly" (241). In his essay "English Composition," Phelps ([1912] 1995) speaks of teaching composition as "brain-fagging toil," and equates the endeavor with "coal-heaving" (288). (A colleague of mine is famous for his statement that with every student composition he reads, "another brain cell dies.") Lounsbury calls composition instruction "drudgery" (262), "the most distasteful of occupations" (270).

The same bias underpins attitudes toward composition today. Composition teachers and researchers have struggled since the beginning to achieve legitimacy, to be considered rigorous, to build a methodology and theory unique to composition, to be recognized as a distinct discipline—in short, to be "professional," and not "common." Ohmann (1976) writes, "we seek to be professional as a way of escaping the powerlessness of ordinary work and the nastier side of economic life in capitalist society. Professionalism is a claim to human

dignity. Unfortunately, we succeed in the claim at a cost to others—
and also at a cost to our perception of the way in which dignity for all
people lies" (251).

I have always taught composition, though in the beginning of my
career, I did not teach it willingly. Teaching "Freshman Comp" was
what graduate students did in the universities in the seventies, and still
do. After I received my degree and began applying for permanent
teaching positions, I was advised to stress my experience and my
"eagerness" to teach more freshman composition. Literature jobs were
scarce, and as a comp teacher, I would be more marketable. My first
job was at Wilkes College in Wilkes-Barre, Pennsylvania, where
abandoned underground coal mines burn, the legacy of a once-boom-
ing coal industry. Most of the residents of Wilkes-Barre are the children and grandchildren of the coal miners who once had work. The
rich industrialists—those "engaged in the conduct of vast business
enterprises"—had long ago moved on. I was hired in a nontenure-
track position where, Phelps would have said, appropriately enough
for the region, I heaved coal. I taught four sections of what we used to
call freshman composition each year, two of which were "remedial"
courses for "basic" writers.

After teaching for two years, I woke up and discovered one
September morning that I actually loved what I was doing. I started
having ideas about what worked and what didn't. You could say I was
formulating composition theory. I developed "assignment sequences"
before articles on this topic began to appear in *College Composition
and Communication*. I experimented with the best ways to have conferences with my students—how much or how little I should say, the
kinds of questions I should ask to help them "fix" their writing. I
divided my classes into small groups in which students helped each
other with their writing. My ideas developed, not as a result of reading about composition theory, which didn't actually exist yet, but as a
result of reading about whole language learning, work that I did for
the Methods of Teaching Elementary Reading class that I taught.

My ideas also developed out of necessity. Teaching grammar and
rhetorical strategies, and carefully marking themes with red ink—
which we were trained to do in graduate school—did not work at
Wilkes College, which in the late 1970s served primarily first-generation college students from working-class families. Confronted with a
theme full of red ink, the students quickly became discouraged and
confused. For most, the red ink was unmistakable evidence that they
were strangers in a strange land.

Some students painstakingly corrected every error. These students built houses with their families, after all, or worked in the fam-
ily-owned grocery stores. Attention to detail was crucial—a two-by-

four cut too short by even a quarter of an inch would not fit. Nevertheless, the essays that had been carefully corrected were still not "good"—they were shallow or uninteresting, or I could not hear the students' voices.

Again, Peckham (1995) suggests perhaps why my conscientious writing pedagogy had backfired. Basing his explanation on the research of Basil Bernstein (1971), Peckham highlights several areas of pedagogy and curriculum in higher education that fit the experiences and histories of privileged students, but that work seriously against the success of students from working-class families. Peckham argues that students from the working class are "position-oriented." That is, "both at home and at work, working-class individuals have clearly defined roles determined by their positions. Lines of authority are firmly established and are rarely subject to rearrangement by negotiation" (269).

Peckham observes that A students are those who question, who problem solve, who "own" their learning. The working-class students who dutifully wrote down my advice about writing, who memorized grammatical and rhetorical rules, and who corrected each error marked in red, did not own their learning or their writing. Of course, much more may have been influencing their stance toward writing, including their developmental levels as college freshmen. But by being good daughters and sons, and adhering to the values generally prescribed in their homes, they were absent as writers in the college classroom, and their writing suffered. I stopped using the strategies that I had adopted in graduate school, and followed my instincts. I stopped talking so much, and asked questions and listened more.

I don't talk anymore about teaching "composition." I "work with students on their writing." I don't "grade papers"—I have in fact stopped using a conventional grading system altogether. I read students' papers, react to what they have written, and talk with them often about their writing. I never assign a letter grade to individual papers. The final letter grades that I turn in to the registrar, students have decided for themselves after writing a lengthy narrative self-evaluation. To say "I work with students on their writing," rather than to say "I teach composition" is not just linguistic sleight of hand, but a genuine conceptual and pedagogic difference. In the 1970s when composition began to shape itself as a distinct discipline to be reckoned with, I was both excited and disappointed. I was excited because now, finally, someone was taking seriously what I had made my professional life. Nancy Sommers's (1980) article, "Revision Strategies of Student Writers and Experienced Adult Writers," was a breakthrough for the profession as well as for me, because her work helped me to define and shape further my strategies for working with students on writing. Sommers's work also gave my pedagogy a theoretical as well as a practical justification based on research.

But I was also disappointed, because teaching writing had been real and immediate to me. As affirming as theory was, "to theorize" took something away. A theoretical framework would distance the students and their lives from the work, and distance me from my students. Before theory, any judgments that I made or that my students made were in the context of immediate, meaningful reactions and palpable consequences. I was an experienced partner who worked right alongside my students. My responses were not based on elaborate rules formulated decades ago mostly by white men who were long dead—which was what the study of literature had started to become for me in graduate school. (At least in composition studies, white women have formulated theory at least as often as white men.)

Teaching writing became "composition studies," an institution created to make the teaching of writing scientific—replete with research methodology, elaborate theory, and a corpus of scholarship and objective research studies—in order to gain legitimacy within the university and compete favorably with literary criticism and research. And because English literature had a literary tradition and heritage, it seemed that composition specialists looked for one too, as Susan Miller (1991) suggests. It was the yearning for legitimacy that led composition specialists to locate the origins of composition in classical rhetoric. As Miller notes, linking composition to rhetoric "established a legitimate past and identified the new field of composition as a revived child of a father who acknowledges it" (36). Teaching writing must be "professional," carrying with it all that being professional requires, lest it be considered "drudgery," akin to heaving coal.

In "The Rhetorician as an Agent of Social Change," Ellen Cushman (1996) includes photos of the tumbled-down stone stairway called the "Approach." The stairway had once served as an approach to Rensselaer Polytechnic Institute (RPI) from the community of Troy, New York. Its decay illustrates the "deeply rooted sociological distances" between colleges and universities and the "communities in which they're located." She writes, "Every day, we reproduce this distance so long as a select few gain entrance to universities, so long as we differentiate between experts and novices, and so long as we value certain types of knowledge we can capitalize on through specialization" (10–11). Cushman also cites S. Michael Halloran (1993) who sees an "apparent lack of interest" in civic public discourse that would connect us with our communities "among new rhetoricians of late twentieth-century English departments" (2).

As a profession, composition studies has erected an imposing structure of theoretical and methodological apparatus, lest the endeavor be considered "common labor," laborious and common, with practitioners fearing most that it might become common. Labor and the working class can always be topics for analysis, as long as theory and methodology guarantee distance between practitioners and their subjects.

One movement that has caused that apparatus to shudder is the autobiographical critical movement. Autobiographical criticism is criticism and analysis that is rooted in and integrated with personal stories. The genre represents the intersection of the personal with the act of knowing, the act of making knowledge, and the act of doing research. Daphne Patai (1994) has labeled and discounted autobiographical criticism as "nouveau solipsism," while others have dismissed it as "soft" (unscientific) and self-absorbed (not sufficiently objective). Charles Schuster, the general editor of Boynton/Cook's CrossCurrents series, which has published this book, cautioned contributors at the outset that he wanted the book "to be something more than just a series of personal stories" (McMillan et al. 1995).

Composition does not want to fight the battle again. Stephen M. North (1987) quotes from the 1962 NCTE Executive Council report published as *Research in Written Composition:*

> the field as a whole is laced with dreams, prejudices, and makeshift operations. Not enough investigators are really informing themselves about the procedures and results of previous research before embarking on their own. Too few of them conduct pilot experiments and validate their measuring instruments before undertaking an investigation. (Braddock, Lloyd-Jones, and Schoer 1963, 5)

North concludes, "the authority of an emerging Composition will derive from inquiry—'research'—modeled in method and rigor on research in the sciences. . . . Practical knowledge, the stuff of teachers' rooms, how-to articles, textbooks and the like, doesn't count as research" (17). Basing generalizations or ideas on somebody's story (autobiography) sounds (again) too much like the "sloppiness" of early composition studies—practices, practical knowledge, what teachers did on Friday, none of which by itself counts for much in the academic world of research. As radical a note as her article sounds, Cushman (1996) herself doesn't feel free to use the photos of the RPI Approach without justifying it with Bakhtinian semiotic theory. Methinks she doth protest too much. It is theory, she implies, not our own perceptions, that "allows us to critique how even the construction and setting of the Approach can take on significance" (25). Practice must be based on research. Practice and the revelations of our very senses must be based on theory. Research and theory guarantee objectivity, what really rules the knowledge communities of academe.

And, again, it is objectivity that aids in distancing the common folk, including the working class, from the uncommon folk. Talking about points Malea Powell makes in an unpublished essay, Cushman writes that "the theorizing of academics necessitates a distance from the daily living of people outside academe, particularly those we study" and constitutes "intellectual colonization" (11). In the strong reactions to the suggestion that we return personal stories to research, theory, and academic writing, we hear again Lounsbury's horror at the "popular clamor," the "popular gabble," the prospect of making language "common."

Autobiography may indeed be common. All of the writing in *This Fine Place So Far From Home* incorporates autobiography as the writers trace the impact that academe has had on their working-class histories and consciousness. Working out the ideas has necessitated autobiography. Irvin Peckham (1995) and others take it one step further to say that folks in the working class are drawn to autobiography. "Inserting my history into this text may be . . . characteristic of working class rhetoric" (Peckham 1995, 265). We are first and foremost storytellers. We "focus on immediate events and concrete experiences" (273). Laurel Johnson Black (1995) sums it up in "Stupid Rich Bastards": "This is not an essay. This is a story. My life is not an essay. We don't live essays or tell them to each other on the front steps on hot nights with beer or iced coffee or pretzels or pass them on to our children or dream them" (14). Which is not to say that we of the working class cannot write essays, or do research, or generate theory. But theory and research are not where we begin, or end. We are drawn to the immediacy of language and events. The concrete—both the kinds of language we use and the stuff we walk on—is familiar and comfortable territory.

In addition to lowering property values in intellectual territory, autobiography threatens to undo the hierarchy in another way. Autobiographical critical writing—and other "nonscholarly" writing within the academy—challenges dominant language and knowledge conventions. It unmasks—it plays the "trickster," in another more playful, positive sense of "clown"—to reveal that knowledge and the words and methods that we use to talk about knowledge are pluralistic, not monistic. Autobiographical criticism in particular demystifies not only the single act of writing, research, or scholarship; it opens up to scrutiny the entire process of making meaning, from the moment that we first choose what we will spend time thinking about, to those final moments of drawing conclusions and passing judgment. The genre is thus inevitably political: The myths have maintained intellectual hegemony for some, while closing out scores of others.

The parallels between teaching writing and laboring as a member of the working class—and the subsequent marginalization of these activities as well as composition's fast and furious efforts to establish itself as a legitimate member of the family—are explainable to me. What I finally seek to understand is Why? Why the class bias, the bias against labor, in the first place? Or, to put it another way, why do we do everything we can to "make something of ourselves," as though to wield a pickax or spread tar on a roof is *not* making something of ourselves? In spite of Marxist rhetoric, and identification with oppressed groups—not to mention the scholarly mileage we get out of these topics—few of us would change places with Judy or DuWayne, the custodians of the building in which the St. Olaf English department is housed, or change places with the woman who carefully folds the end of the toilet paper rolls into a *V* at our MLA conferences. In Ohmann's (1976) words, why do we have such a narrow perception of the "way in which dignity for all people lies"?

Is it that academics don't like physical work because it is too hard? Is it because academics don't like to be dirty? It can't be these reasons, since academics, like most people, garden, repair their cars and renovate their houses, though an important distinction is that it is not this labor that defines them.

It does have something, however, to do with the physical in physical labor, nervousness about the physical, even an aversion to the physical. We do not exist comfortably in our bodies, a student of mine observed. And more so than most, academics do not live comfortably in their bodies. An academic's body, an intellectual's body, is in the words of Delmore Schwartz's (1959) poem, "the heavy bear . . . clumsy and lumbering," "the hungry beating brutish one," the "stupid clown of the spirit's motive." Our bodies drag us down. Our aches and pains, our fatigue, our illnesses, our fading sight prevent us from achieving all that we are capable of. The yearnings of our bodies distract us from achieving the higher good and right conduct.

The greatest crime is that our bodies, we mistakenly think, are contrary to intellect and spirit. They are not just the site of sin, but the impediment to objectivity (Bordo 1993). Our bodies are what separate us from God and the angels. Our bodies are the stupid clown of the spirit's motive. They are the clueless, dumb, outward costume, the awkward representation of the higher thought and the better self. Bordo writes, "what remains the constant element throughout historical variation is the *construction* of body as something apart from the true self (whether conceived as soul, mind, spirit, will, creativity, freedom . . .) and as undermining the best efforts of that self. That which is not-body is the highest, the best, the noblest, the closest to God; that which is body is the albatross, the heavy drag on self-realization" (5).

Physical labor is generally perceived as eminently bodied work. Disregarded is the amount of thought that physical labor requires.

Academic labor is generally perceived as dis-embodied work, unless
of course you labor in the field of composition, in which case you
labor mightily to theorize and abstract it into a higher station. It is the
professional Great Chain of Being. Intellectual pursuit must reach
past and through the body in order to reach inward to the spirit and
upward to God. Here the moralistic, nationalistic agendas of 19th-
and 20th-century educators converge with the spiritual impulses of
"pure" academic endeavors. The social functions of literary studies,
according to Miller, have a "quasi-religious" character that has fueled
the exhortations of canon and cultural heritage. "Timelessness, perfection, and spirituality, the common topics of religious persuasion
. . . constitute the subtext of the 'great tradition'" (22).

When I left my small town in south Florida, I knew I was bound
for such "greatness"—high aspirations, great books, the great tradition, everything above and beyond that low, small, common place on
the map that I called home. I left behind my working-class parents
and their friends and my friends and all they represented to me. In
part, ironically, it has been the literature of the "great tradition" itself
that I have read and taught over the years that has shown me how
wrong I have been—the noble laborers in Wordsworth's and Robert
Frost's poetry and in the novels of George Eliot, the Michaels and the
Adam Bedes and the Maggies. Nevertheless, it has been alternative
traditions that have influenced me the most. Women's literature, like
Susan Glaspell's ([1916] 1985) play *Trifles,* has revealed how profound and how neglected domestic work is, in our lives and in our
critical assessments. Considered until recently marginal literary genres, diaries, letters and autobiographies, like the writings of Frederick
Douglass and Zora Neale Hurston, have spoken forcefully for the
truth in everyday voices and occupations.

Even more than the literature I have read, it has been students
who have compelled me to come home to my working-class values—
the beauty and necessity of labor, the fulfillment that comes with
working with my hands, utility, practicality, immediacy, resourceful-
ness. Students like Erica, who put in her time in the National Guard
because her family couldn't help her at all to pay for her college education, but whose eloquence and poetry were indistinguishable from
her family's story and her own labor.

I teach in a small liberal arts college where "learning for learning's sake" is repeated like a mantra, in part because if we don't
believe it, the college might not survive. And yet, it is primarily the
upper classes—with a great deal of disposable income to spend on
many useless things—who can also afford learning for its own sake.

On the contrary, learning is valuable when I can do something
with it—when it changes how I act or when it has an impact on the

world. That is, when it has utility and when it is practical. Learning is valuable when it is immediate—direct and near—at least within one season. It must bear a fruit that I and my students can sink our teeth into and satisfy our hunger. Learning has that abstract power of deepening our understanding and opening our eyes, but it must also set our hands and our lives in motion. Frederick Douglass (1988) rejoiced at learning to read, because it explained "dark and mysterious things," but reading's true power lay in the fact that it was his "pathway from slavery to freedom" (58–59), actual physical release from bondage as well as spiritual and mental freedom.

Mary Louise Buley-Meissner (1993) reviews four books on teaching literature and writing that give me hope.[4] Of the paradigm shifts that have taken place over the years in composition studies, perhaps we may be taking a needed shift backwards to those days when our hodgepodge of eclectic practices and the serendipitous events of each day mattered, when the events of each day were the "matter" of teaching writing, when what we did was not always driven by theory, but by students' passionate individuality. The writers that Buley-Meissner refers to all demonstrate that "we discover meaning in the reality of immediacy: the faces before us, the eyes alert with comprehension or shadowed with doubt, the hands reaching toward understanding," and claim that "practice *must* lead theory because only practice is intimately connected with students' individual lives" (211–212).

My own teaching has changed to reflect my reconception of knowledge—where it comes from and what it should do. My students and I rarely sit in rooms at desks reading books. We are always busy. Students either bring their lives into the classroom and make these lives the content of the course, or we leave the classroom and work in the community. Students and I have worked on various projects over the years—collecting and publishing original stories and poetry from clients at a drop-in center for poor and homeless people in Minneapolis, and from residents of a battered women's shelter; planting, growing, harvesting, and delivering food in the summer for shareholders of a local community farm, and reading naturalist writers on the side; attending council meetings and community meetings to advocate a safer highway design through Northfield. The latest project that students and I have worked on is to design and implement a new charter school in Northfield—The Village School—where community-based learning will be at the center of the curriculum.

Our collective dream is to eliminate schools altogether, much as Virginia Woolf (1938) advocates in *Three Guineas*: "Let it blaze! Let it blaze! For we have done with this education" (36). We don't really intend to burn schools down, but we want to return learning to our communities, make our lives and our work the sites for learning, much as it was before schools as institutions separate from families and community life were established.

I am frequently considered a clown at St. Olaf, run away to join the circus. My students and I run away to islands that evidence a first encounter between Ojibway peoples and French fur traders; we spend summers in drop-in centers, and in fields growing vegetables and flowers; we spend winters in City Hall and in library meeting rooms, dreaming of the way a city should really look. We burn down the walls of the university, if not literally, then figuratively. All the while, students write and I write, we read, we talk about each others' writing, often while we cook or gather firewood. Our gatherings are unruly, un-ruled, guided only by the contexts of our lives and work, and by our relationships with each other.

Needless to say, there's a great deal of clowning around.

Notes

1. The title of the article is a line from Delmore Schwartz's poem "The Heavy Bear" (1959). Susan Bordo (1993) begins her book *Unbearable Weight: Feminism, Western Culture, and the Body* with Schwartz's poem. A theme of the poem and the book is the historical notion in Western culture that the body is, literally, "a drag," and that the physical self gets in the way of our "higher selves." The "stupid clown" in my essay represents what is unacademic and unintellectual. The clown, of course, is also the trickster figure. The two figures actually merge at the end of the essay in a critique of objectivity as the dominant knowledge construction in literary and composition studies.

2. Douglas Hesse (1991) and Marguerite H. Helmers (1995) are two of many who have mounted a defense against personal writing in academic journals, which they believe could undermine the discipline of composition. Helmers writes, "The personal . . . is at root an anti-intellectual gesture, unlikely to generate either renewed intellectualism or disciplinary respectability for composition" (148).

3. All selections from the debate surrounding the controversial establishment of the first composition program at Harvard are from John C. Brereton (1995).

4. Pat Belanoff, Peter Elbow, and Sheryl Fontaine (1991); Robert E. Brooke (1991); Elizabeth Chiseri-Strater (1991); and Barry M. Kroll (1992).

Works Cited

Belanoff, P., P. Elbow, and S. Fontaine, eds. 1991. *Nothing Begins with N: New Investigations of Freewriting*. Carbondale: Southern Illinois University Press.

Bernstein, B. 1971. "Class and Pedagogies: Visible and Invisible." In *Class, Codes, and Control*. London: Routledge and Kegan Paul, 116–45.

Black, L. J. 1995. "Stupid Rich Bastards." In Dews and Law, 13–25.

Bloom, L. Z. 1996. "Freshman Composition as a Middle-Class Enterprise." *College English* 58 (6): 654–675.

Bordo, S. 1993. *Unbearable Weight: Feminism, Western Culture, and the Body*. Berkeley: University of California Press.

Braddock, R., R. Lloyd-Jones, and L. Schoer. 1963. *Research in Written Composition*. Champaign, IL: National Council of Teachers of English.

Brereton, J. C. 1995. *The Origins of Composition Studies in the American College, 1875–1925: A Documentary History*. Pittsburgh: University of Pittsburgh Press.

Brooke, R. E. 1991. *Writing and Sense of Self: Identity Negotiations in Writing Workshops*. Urbana, IL: National Council of Teachers of English.

Buley-Meissner, M. L. 1993. "Review of 'Reclaiming Personal Knowledge: Investigations of Identity, Difference, and Community in College Education.'" *College English* 53 (2): 211–221.

Chiseri-Strater, E. 1991. *Academic Literacies: The Public and Private Discourse of University Students*. Portsmouth, NH: Boynton/Cook.

Cooper, L. [1914] 1995. "The Correction of Papers." In Brereton, 291–299.

_____. [1910] 1995. "On the Teaching of Written Composition." In Brereton, 251–261.

Cushman, E. 1996. "The Rhetorician as an Agent of Social Change." *College Composition and Communication* 47 (1): 7–28.

Dews, C. L. B. and C. L. Law. 1995. *This Fine Place So Far from Home: Voices of Academics from the Working Class*. Philadelphia: Temple University Press.

Douglass, F. [1845, 1892] 1988. *Narrative of the Life of Frederick Douglass, an American Slave: Written by Himself*. Edited by Benjamin Quarles. Cambridge, MA: Harvard University Press.

Gilbert, S. M., and S. Gubar, eds. 1985. *The Norton Anthology of Literature by Women: The Tradition in English*. New York: W. W. Norton.

Glaspell, S. [1916] 1985. *Trifles*. Gilbert and Gubar, 1389–1399.

Good, H. G. 1962. *A History of American Education*. New York: Macmillan.

Graff, G. 1987. *Professing Literature: An Institutional History*. Chicago: The University of Chicago Press.

Halloran, S. M. 1993. "Afterthoughts on Rhetoric and Public Discourse." In *Pre/Text: The First Decade*, ed. Victor Vitanza, 52–68. Pittsburgh: University of Pittsburgh Press.

Helmers, M. H. 1995. *Writing Students: Composition Testimonials and Representations of Students*. Albany, NY: SUNY Press.

Hesse, D. 1991. "The Recent Rise of Literary Nonfiction: A Cautionary Assay." In *Composition Theory for the Postmodern Classroom*, ed. G. Olson and S. Dobrin, 132–142. Albany: SUNY Press.

Kroll, B. M. 1992. *Teaching Hearts and Minds: College Students Reflect on the Vietnam War in Literature*. Carbondale: Southern Illinois University Press.

Loeb, P. R. 1994. *Generation at the Crossroads: Apathy and Action on the American Campus*. New Brunswick, NJ: Rutgers University Press.

Lounsbury, T. R. [1911] 1995. "Compulsory Composition in Colleges." In Brereton, 261–286.

McMillan, J., A. Shepard, and G. Tate. 18 September 1995. Letter to the author.

Miller, S. 1991. *Textual Carnivals: The Politics of Composition*. Carbondale: Southern Illinois University Press.

Müller, M. 1901. *My Autobiography: A Fragment*. New York: Charles Scribner's Sons.

North, S. M. 1987. *The Making of Knowledge in Composition*. Portsmouth, NH: Boynton/Cook.

Ohmann, R. 1976. *English in America: A Radical View of the Profession*. New York: Oxford University Press.

Patai, D. 1994. "Point of View: The Nouveau Solipsism." *Chronicle of Higher Education* 15 (25): A58.

Peckham, I. 1995. "Complicity in Class Codes: The Exclusionary Function of Education." In Dews and Law, 263–276.

Phelps, W. L. [1912] 1995. "English Composition." In Brereton, 287–291.

Powell, M. 1995. Custer's Very Last Stand: Rhetoric, the Academy, and the Un-seeing of the American Indian. Unpublished essay.

Schwartz, D. 1959. "The Heavy Bear." In *Summer Knowledge: New and Collected Poems 1938–1958*. New York: Doubleday.

Sommers, N. 1980. "Revision Strategies of Student Writers and Experienced Adult Writers." *College Composition and Communication* 31: 378–388.

"Two Ways of Teaching English." 1896. *Century Magazine* 51: 793–794.

Woolf, V. 1938. *Three Guineas*. New York: Harcourt Brace Jovanovich.

7

Class Conflict in the English Profession

Donald Lazere

In a 1977 *New Yorker* article covering the MLA convention job exchange, Calvin Trillin observed that the English profession's employment practices "could have been designed by the manager of a Southern textile mill" (89). These practices derive largely from the distinctive nature of graduate programs in the humanities, which differ in important ways from, say, medical or legal faculties and other disciplines that do not have undergraduate programs and that prepare their graduates for careers outside the academic world.

In English particularly, one of departments' main reasons for being is to staff the Freshman English writing programs that are required of virtually all undergraduate students; yet in most colleges and universities, especially those weighted toward graduate study, the English professors have little or nothing to do with either teaching writing or preparing grad students to do so. These faculties have an intrinsic conflict of interest in relation to their students. In English particularly, graduate students teach Freshman English and grade exams for undergraduate literature courses, thus supplying cheap labor (at near-minimum wage) for this extensive sector of university expenditure and relieving faculty of much drudgery. Moreover, grad students provide warm FTE bodies for graduate seminars, the main focus of whatever teaching many graduate faculty members do. (This is not to imply that graduate faculties have a cushy job; certainly their work advising students, directing dissertations, doing research, writing, consulting, and so on, is ample; still, their position is privileged in many ways in comparison to that of teachers with heavy undergraduate loads, especially in composition and large, general-education courses.) The topics of such seminars are chosen by the instructor, frequently not with an eye toward what will be of most value to the students in their present or future undergraduate teaching, but as a means of advancing, with a handful of acolytes, whatever specialized research he or she happens to be working on at the moment. This system in practice often serves as a valuable apprenticeship and opportunity for students to work at an advanced level with outstanding scholars, and its potential abuses did not become salient earlier in this century when relatively few doctorates were awarded, nor in the post–World War II academic boom when graduate faculties competed to expand their empires and the plentiful number of new jobs available for Ph.D.s made the exploitation of grad students little more than an initiation ritual. Nor was there widespread public questioning of the value of the exponential growth in the GNP of doctoral dissertations and postdoctoral publications in literary scholarship—a field in which the amount of important new knowledge has long been outstripped by the number of practitioners; only when literary scholarship took a leftist turn in the seventies and eighties did all those arcane titles of books and conference papers become a source of ridicule for journalistic and political critics of academia.

This syndrome in the English profession has been intensified by the drastically widening gap between its upper and lower levels in the last three decades. The bottom first dropped out of the literature job market around 1970. At about the same time, the "literacy crisis" came to public and professional attention, with attendant increases in basic writing and other composition programs. Consequently, many of us receiving our doctorates in literature since then have been obliged to take jobs in undergraduate colleges, teaching composition and introductory literature courses remote from the heights of our graduate seminars and dissertation topics. Meanwhile, most of the prestigious university English faculties have not changed the focus of their graduate courses—beyond an occasional composition theory class—or their own scholarly studies to adjust to the difference in the level of teaching concerns of recent graduates compared to earlier generations slated for jobs in other prestige undergraduate and graduate programs. Quite the contrary: With the triumph of structuralist and poststructuralist theory over the past thirty years, the ante has been constantly upped in the pursuit of the most remote speculations. It is as though the very abstractness of contemporary theory has been nourished by its having become an artificial world for those scholars who either need not (because they are established) or cannot (because there are no jobs for them) connect with the real demands of education and society today.

For a quarter century now, the fate of as many as half the graduates of even the most prestigious doctoral schools in English has been a dispiriting cycle of dead-end, one-year lectureships, revolving-door assistant professorships, part-time or academic staff (i.e., nontenure-track) positions in writing programs segregated from English department faculties, or terminal unemployment necessitating a total career change. Such a severe decline in career prospects would have been regarded as a major crisis for the accrediting institutions of any other profession or occupation—certainly any one requiring an average of ten years of graduate education. Most graduate programs in English and other academic subjects, however, basically went on doing business as usual, because their own faculties were tenured and faced little danger of their own positions being eliminated. (As in every occupation in a capitalist economy, when hard times hit, those at the bottom are the first to be laid off and those at the top the last.) When the job market collapsed, most graduate departments did not cut back the number of their admissions in proportion to the reduced prospects of their graduates or give applicants a realistic assessment of their futures. This is only one of many forms of apparent callousness that make it difficult for graduate faculties to deny that they have cynically disregarded the fate of their students in the interests of maintaining the multiple advantages to themselves of having an undiminished corps of Freshman English teachers, graders, and grad-seminar students.

Faculties have additional conflicts of interest here stemming from the anomaly that higher education is virtually the only profession in which the credentialing institutions form part of the same system that is the primary employer of their graduates. Like management in any other occupation, it is to the obvious advantage of academic departments to have a reserve army of the unemployed from which to hire—but these departments also enjoy the unique privilege of controlling the number of candidates that will be on the labor market and thus have a vested interest as employers in continuing to produce a glut of graduates! The academic profession at large, and in English particularly, should long ago have formulated a binding code of ethics to deal honorably with these dangers, but it never has.

Further conflicts stemming from graduate departments' dual identity as both credentialer and employer include the custom of most graduate departments not to hire graduates of their own program as faculty members. This policy did not appear egregious when beginning jobs were plentiful in other departments of the same quality, but such is no longer the case, and few departments to my knowledge have considered altering this custom as a gesture of responsibility toward worthy graduates who have encountered bad luck in the job market.

A similar conflict results from the custom of most Ivy League and other prestigious departments rarely to grant tenure to assistant professors. Again, in more prosperous times, those thus denied tenure

were pretty certain to be able to find an associate professorship at
another university, of good if not equal ranking. In the economic
squeeze since about 1970, however, departments have been forced to
economize in every possible way, including hiring primarily at the
lowest rank—a policy that has also produced a scandalous increase in
the replacement of tenure-track faculty by part-timers and temporary
full-time lecturers. This exigency has predictably encouraged revolving-door hiring and firing practices, with fewer assistant professors
being promoted to associate professor at nearly all universities, and
with few or no hirings at the associate professor level at most. Thus
new Ph.D.s who are overjoyed at getting an assistant professorship at
one of the prestige universities find themselves six or seven years
later out of a job with no place else to go at midcareer—the very
quality of their previous achievements a disadvantage in making them
overqualified for the available positions. I know people in this situation who have begged departments to hire them as an assistant professor, but one of the profession's numerous taboos is that universities
generally will not hire anyone at a lower rank than they have previously attained.

Most discussion of the collapse in the academic job market has
focused on the dearth of entry-level positions, but the situation is
even worse for those who found an initial position and after serving
out their probationary period with service that would previously have
been quite adequate for tenure at their own school or for being hired
as an associate professor elsewhere find themselves in their late thirties or older forced out of the career to which they have devoted
fifteen years, more or less, of their postcollegiate lives, at an age when
changing careers is far more difficult. Gradually through the eighties,
the bust cycle in the academic job market seemed to run its course,
jobs were opening up again, and educational analysts were predicting
a future shortage of teachers. It was wholly predictable, however, that
virtually all of the new jobs were at the beginning assistant-professor
level, leaving in the lurch the entire lost generation of those who
received their doctorates between about 1970 and 1980. With the
recession of the nineties, however, the market took an even worse
nosedive than the first one, so both old and new Ph.D.s are out of luck
again currently. Moreover, many of those who couldn't get initial
jobs have by now taken up other occupations or have survived as
academic gypsies on itinerant lectureships or in academic staff positions; any chance that they may have to get senior-level jobs now
will be further impeded by the lack of regular evaluation of those not
on tenure-track positions and by their inability in most cases to have
produced under adverse circumstances the amount of scholarship
expected of tenure-track faculty.

Even most of those members of the lost generation in English who have been fortunate enough to get tenure-track positions, and then tenure, teaching undergraduate composition and introductory literature courses, have bought a one-way ticket to the Siberia of the English profession. The stigma attached to taking a job in an undergraduate college or a university of lesser prestige, because that was the only kind available, becomes a self-fulfilling prophecy, because those lucky enough to have gotten tenure at the top universities during the golden postwar days continue obliviously to consider taking a job at any lesser institution a sign of inferior abilities and to rule out anyone in such a position from consideration for hiring at a senior level. This is especially true of composition specialists. As distinguished a teacher, publishing scholar, and public intellectual as Mike Rose labored for years in a nontenure-track, staff appointment in the UCLA writing program; when he finally did recently get a tenured position at UCLA, it was not in English but Education. At one point, Rose was on the brink of receiving a senior position at the University of California, San Diego, but he was vetoed by an administrator who deemed composition an unworthy field for a senior professor at that university.

Moreover, the primary criterion for hiring at the associate- or full-professor level is scholarly research and publications. But most faculty at nonelite colleges have little or no time to do research or writing because of heavier teaching and administrative loads than at research universities (which also provide Ph.D. students as assistants who do most grading) and because of the concentration of composition and large undergraduate basic literature courses, in which grading consumes inordinate time. (The problem is compounded for those faculty hired as directors of writing programs who are untenured—one of the more scandalous practices in the profession—a position of double jeopardy in that the additional time spent on administration typically counts for little or nothing toward tenure.) This means that those who must cope in their teaching with the problems that college study presents to the recent pool of students in nonelite schools are not in a position to read and write research and criticism addressing these problems—while the faculties with the leisure of the theory class at research universities have little motivation to address them. Advanced scholarship in English that addressed key questions of undergraduate education would need to focus on practical aspects of critical thinking, cognitive development, sociolinguistics, orality and literacy, political socialization, gender and racial issues, and the influence of mass media and politics on cognition. (Mina Shaughnessy's [1977] *Errors and Expectations*, for example, should be in the theory section of every Ph.D. exam list.) One beneficial spinoff of the whole overheated PC controversy is that it has at least forced many literary scholars down from the theoretical stratosphere to address pedagogical issues.

Needless to say, teachers in elementary and high schools and community colleges face even more daunting problems in teaching, with even less time to seek theoretical guidance. In *The Irrelevant English Teacher*, J. Mitchell Morse (1972) made the iconoclastic proposal that the most senior professors, with their wealth of experience, should be the ones teaching the most demanding course in the curriculum—Freshman English—while the newest Ph.D.s, with the latest scholarship at their command, should be teaching the graduate seminars. I agree with Morse that our profession's priorities are completely upside down. Perhaps elementary school teachers should be expected to hold a doctorate—say, in developmental psychology or sociolinguistics—and perhaps it is they, rather than the gurus of arcane literary theory, who should get regular sabbaticals, grants, and visiting appointments in research universities and humanities centers.

Most detached outsiders hearing of the woes in the lower ranks of the English profession due to nearly three decades of financial austerity would suppose that the first sector of the profession to be targeted for budget cuts certainly should be new hirings from other research university faculties at the most expensive salary level, that of senior "star" professors. Quite the contrary is the case, however. Senior hirings continued with little abatement throughout the worst years of budget crisis; indeed, since about 1970 many of the most prestigious English departments have gotten caught up in a corporate-raiding craze, outbidding one another—often at salaries well beyond set scales for humanities faculty—for the superstars of critical theory, who (in a grotesque simulacrum of the gypsy scholars at the bottom of the ladder) move to one upwardly mobile university for a few years, only until they get a more glamorous offer from another.

It does not seem to occur to those department heads who garner headlines crowing about their latest six-figure-salary faculty star that an action more consistent with the humane values English studies are supposed to embody would be to use that much money to open assistant professor slots for their own unemployed graduates, associate professorships for worthy junior faculty who at present can't get tenure at their university or elsewhere, or full professorships for some of the lost generation who have labored with distinction for years teaching undergraduate composition and literature, directing composition programs, or producing independent scholarship outside conventional academic hierarchies.

It is unseemly enough when department heads in private universities indulge in metaphors of acquiring all-star lineups or blue-chip senior faculties; it is even more so when those in publicly financed universities do it. Several University of California campuses, for example, have gotten into the sweepstakes game for international superstars such as Jacques Derrida and Fredric Jameson—the same campuses whose regular English faculties include few members primarily concerned with undergraduate education and whose vast composition programs are staffed from the reserve army of underemployed temporaries, part-timers, and nontenure-track academic staff, many of whom received their doctorates from these or comparable departments.

The most ironic touch is that the department heads, senior faculty, and roving superstars who perpetuate this farce include a good number of Marxists and deconstructionists, who in their theoretical musings expose the evils of capitalist class divisions or other social and epistemological hierarchies. Their justification for such behavior seems to be that they are undermining the hierarchies of the capitalist system on the phenomenological front—as they claw their way to the top of their own professional hierarchy. As a Marxist myself, I must testify that many (though not all) Marxist, poststructuralist, feminist, and ethnic-studies academic stars are among the most offensive snobs and social climbers I have ever met, and among the most callous toward the forms of class prejudice in their own profession I have surveyed here.

My proposal that graduate faculties redirect the funds they now use to hire senior faculty stars toward salvaging the wrecked careers of the lost generation of their graduates will be met with objections that this would be a variation on affirmative action, devaluing impartial standards of excellence in achievement in favor of redressing social injustices. This argument merits serious consideration, but it must be weighed against the fact that in this instance the social injustices have been perpetrated by the profession itself. Whether those injustices have been deliberate or not, the objective reality remains that university faculties have had a vested interest in maintaining a full complement of graduate students throughout the worst years of the job crisis, as well as a reserve army of unemployed Ph.D.s. Virtually the only way they could prove their good faith now would be to subordinate their premium on recruiting the most accomplished scholars in favor of demonstrating a sense of responsibility to those former students from whose misfortunes they have benefited. It is not as though they would be pressured into hiring scholars who are less than competent; it stands to reason that the decline in available positions has simply shut out many scholars who previously would have been judged worthy of beginning or advanced positions. Surely giving them the opportunity to redeem the time they have lost would result in much worthy scholarly production from these multitudes of otherwise mute, inglorious Miltonists.

When recounting my own experiences as a victim of the great job drought, I am inclined to lapse into the style of W. C. Fields's mock temperance lecture, "That Fatal Glass of Beer," revising it into "That Fatal Class of Comp." "Yes, my friends, I was a highly respectable literature graduate student, slated for the Ivy League fast track, when one fatal day, in desperate financial straits, I foolishly agreed to accept teaching a class of comp. I have to confess I actually enjoyed it, and without realizing the consequences, I took another, and then another, and another, until before I knew it, I had become an incurable . . . Composition Specialist."

As a consequence of the collapse in the English job market around 1970, I came to understand too late some peculiar totems and taboos of the English profession. You start teaching comp courses as an expedient way of making ends meet as a grad student or during a stretch of unemployment. If you keep teaching them year after year, your salary scale goes up at more or less the same rate as on a tenure track, which is good news in keeping one from starving; the bad news is that composition is not considered a legitimate academic specialization by most prestige universities (which of course staff their writing programs with grad students and temporaries like me), so the comp experience and specialty count for little or nothing in getting a tenure-track job—but at the same time, the salary level one attains teaching comp puts one above the beginning assistant-professor level, and hence unemployable at that level even with another, literary speciality—a neat catch-22.

Actually, that error was preceded by my having in my naiveté broken at least a couple of the profession's other taboos. Rather than going to graduate school directly out of college and staying there straight through to the doctorate at the youngest possible age, I dropped in and out of grad school for some ten years, working in journalism in New York, writing free-lance fiction and criticism, traveling in Europe, getting a degree in literature from the Sorbonne, and drafting a book on Albert Camus that eventually became my doctoral dissertation. Between 1965 and 1970, after completing my M.A. at Columbia and while working on my Camus book free-lance, I picked up enough work teaching Freshman English around the San Francisco Bay area, as a nontenure-track instructor, to make nearly a full-time, permanent living at it—which one could do easily enough in those days when jobs were plentiful and inflation hadn't skyrocketed.

I thought then, and still do, that people who went directly from college to graduate school, stayed there through the doctorate, and went directly back into university teaching have an overly restricted view of the world, and conversely that experience of the outside world should be regarded as an asset for teaching undergraduate students, who are in most cases going into that world, not academia. (One also might think the English profession would find value in experience of the world outside academia that has formed the setting for most literature throughout history—that is, until this postwar period, when creative writers too have sought the haven of the university and lost contact with anything to write about except academia itself.)

I eventually learned, however, that experience either outside academia or in teaching without a doctorate counted for less than nothing in the academic job market. Indeed, advanced experience and age were a handicap, both because of the previously mentioned catch-22 regarding salary scale and because such experience made it less easy (in terms of possible grievance actions as well as their own consciences) for hiring departments to hustle beginning assistant professors in and out of the revolving door without granting tenure.

To make things worse, the bust in the temporary job market around 1970 coincided with a backlash against sixties political activism by younger faculty members, mainly around the Vietnam War but also around causes like feminism, ethnic studies, and faculty unionism. The sudden glut of college teachers facilitated a purge of untenured faculty activists, encouraged behind the scenes nationally by the Nixon administration, then at the peak of its pre-Watergate paranoia, and in California by Governor Ronald Reagan and his advisor on campus unrest, Edwin Meese III, the man who, as deputy district attorney of Alameda County in 1964, had persuaded Governor Edmund Brown to call in the riot squad to bust the Free Speech Movement nonviolent sit-in at Berkeley, and who supervised the Reagan-ordered National Guard occupation of Berkeley during the People's Park conflict in 1969, in which Reagan had stated, "If we're going to have a bloodbath, let's get it over with." The signals coming from Washington and Sacramento emboldened nervous administrators to fire the politically active and other "troublemakers," along with anyone else they wanted to get rid of for personal reasons.

I had been teaching for three years on a full-time lectureship at California State University, Hayward, which had been, prior to its recent incorporation in the CSU system, Alameda County Teachers college. The growth of the college in the sixties had enabled the older faculty there to begin hiring M.A.s and Ph.D.s from the prestige universities. Their eagerness to raise the school's esteem, however, was mixed with insecurities in regard to the more accomplished junior faculty members, and when the purge atmosphere developed, the English senior faculty exploited it to indulge their personal caprices.

The department and university administration, retention and promotion committees, and faculty union were all packed with their allies, enabling them to act with impunity. A tenured professor at Purdue, recently widowed with five children, came to Hayward with a contract for two pro forma probationary years before tenure there, but was arbitrarily terminated after those two years. Likewise for a Berkeley Ph.D. who gave up a junior position at Yale; he has never been able to regain a regular faculty position to the time of this writing. Sandra Gilbert—who had recently received her Ph.D. from Columbia, who had already published far more than any senior faculty member at Hayward, who subsequently was hired in senior positions at Indiana, Princeton, and the University of California, Davis, and was elected president of the Modern Language Association—was dismissed after a pretenure review as not meeting the high scholarly standards of this institution. (The general opinion was that the male senior faculty were simply threatened by uppity women. One senior male, when told that Gilbert's book on D. H. Lawrence had been praised by Harold Bloom, grumbled sarcastically, "Who's Harold Bloom?") Likewise with three others, including myself.

In May 1970, I had already been told that I would be rehired for the next academic year, to teach a course on Camus along with writing classes. I had ruffled some feathers in the English department by signing a petition protesting the arbitrary firings, and after the Kent State shootings that month, I gave a speech against the Vietnam war at a campus rally and pointed out two well-known campus policemen dressed in plainclothes in the crowd, photographing me and other speakers. Afterward I wrote the campus president, Ellis McCune (who several years later became temporary Chancellor of the CSU system), asking what the purpose was of this furtive picture taking of campus community members exercising the right of free speech. I never received an answer, and when I called the president's office, I was informed that no such pictures were taken. Two weeks later I was informed by the English department that I would not be retained after all, because I had not completed my doctorate (which was never a condition of my hiring in the first place). In such circumstances, of course, the rhetorical trick is to invent the crime to fit the punishment. Without a contract or probationary faculty status entitling one to grievance procedures, one is helpless to question such procedures, and the administration is free to say, in effect, "We don't need no stinking reasons."

After that, I figured I would be better off with a doctorate and a shot at tenure-track jobs, so I went back to graduate school at Berkeley. There I proposed my Camus book as a dissertation. The English department was resistant to the unorthodox notion of my having written a scholarly book on my own, as a labor of love, outside routine institutional procedures, and on a French author (though it dealt with the American translations and with Camus in relation to American literature and politics). They finally acceded, however—a decision perhaps influenced by the book's having been accepted for publication by Yale University Press.

So by the time I completed my doctorate in 1974 I was nearly forty, had picked up even more teaching experience, had a book published by a top university press along with many articles—and consequently had become virtually unemployable. A temporary lectureship at San Jose State ran out after two years; before, during, and for a year after that, I—along with all the other Ph.D.s who were unemployed at that point—sent out hundreds of job letters to English and comparative literature departments everywhere in the country. I always got interviews at the annual MLA convention slave market—sixteen one year—with Ivy League and other top universities, so I was the envy of all the other hapless applicants I knew. But the upshot of the interviews was always something to the effect of, "Gee, your publications, teaching record, and recommendations are all so great we just had to interview you. But your qualifications are so superior that we'd feel ashamed offering you an assistant professorship—and of course we couldn't hire anyone as an associate professor who hasn't come up the ladder as assistant professor, and we don't have any money to hire at that level, anyway."

In those days a whole crowd of us—Berkeley assistant professors who hadn't gotten tenure, grad students who had languished on the job market for so long that they had been bumped off it by a younger, cheaper set, and others in similar situations like mine—used to meet in line at the Berkeley unemployment insurance office and commiserate about all the jobs, academic and otherwise, we were turned down for because we were overqualified. (You were unlikely to be hired for a nonacademic job because employers assumed that you would quit as soon as an academic job turned up—which they, in their unfamiliarity with the academic job market, supposed it quickly would.) All shared similar stories about the humiliations of academic unemployment: the way that all your positive accomplishments worked against you; the way unemployment became a self-fulfilling prophecy—"Well, if she hasn't gotten a job in all this time, there must be something wrong with her"; the failure of some departments to answer expensive application letters or, in some cases, even to notify you after an interview that you didn't get the job; the compulsion of some department chairs to add insult to injury; the arrogant claim that the job crisis just weeded out inferior candidates—coming from faculty who were lucky enough to have gotten tenure when times were good but who in some cases were less accomplished than those they now scorned; the anomaly of a profession that extols literature affirming human decency against Kafkaesque or Orwellian bureaucracies, but whose own institutional practices are as arbitrary, rigid, and inhumane as any satirized in such literature.

During this period, I sent out the following letter modeled on a typical rejection form, which I commend to today's applicants in the same situation:

> Dear Department Head:
>
> Please excuse this impersonal letter form, but I have received so many insulting responses from departments to my job application letter that it is impossible to answer each with the individual attention it deserves.
>
> Your response fell into one of the following categories:
> 1. You did not acknowledge or answer my application.
> 2. You stated that I did not meet your specifications for the position, which I did.
> 3. After having interviewed me, you failed to notify me that I would not be offered the position.
> 4. Your letter implied that I was not good enough for your department, or was otherwise gratuitously belittling.
> 5. Your letter lacked any expression of sympathy for the situation of highly qualified but unemployed Ph.D.'s.
>
> I wish you the best of luck in finding a candidate willing to subject herself or himself to your department's contempt for graduate students and junior faculty that was reflected in your reply or lack thereof.
>
> Yours sincerely,
> Any one of your applicants

I was eventually rescued from limbo through the good graces of Cal Poly, in San Luis Obispo, which in 1977 was the only university in the country that recognized that my record qualified me for an associate professorship, and that had the resources to come up with the extra funding to hire me at that rank, as a composition specialist. It could do so for two reasons. First, the school has a distinctive orientation emphasizing faculty achievement in teaching rather than research, and its curriculum is oriented to links between the classroom and the working world; thus it grants credit in hiring for both teaching and nonacademic experience such as mine in journalism and free-lance writing. Second, while liberal arts universities and departments were losing students and languishing financially during that period, Cal Poly's enrollment was booming because of its vocational orientation, with the spin-off of increasing need for composition classes.

The catch was that I was hired to teach four sections of Freshman English, technical and business writing, totaling twelve hours a week three quarters per year. No student assistance was then available—nor is it now—other than the option of using undergraduate readers to correct the mechanics of papers but not grade them; I rejected this option once I found that it took me more time than it saved, since most of the students hired knew little more than those they were grading, so I had to go over *their* corrections, correcting them.

These debilitating teaching conditions have, thank goodness, been alleviated somewhat over the subsequent years I have remained at Poly, as most three-hour courses have been increased to four hours, enabling faculty usually to meet their twelve-hour weekly load through only three courses rather than four (faculty at the research-oriented University of California campuses rarely teach more than one or two courses a term), and as increased general-education and breadth requirements have been mandated throughout the California State University system, creating more sections of literature courses and enabling professors like me who were hired to teach composition exclusively to shift into an even mix of literature and comp courses.

Even throughout that period of the most gruesome teaching loads, and even under the conditions of second-class citizenship that English and other liberal arts faculty are subjected to at Poly, whose administration and dominant technological faculties regard general education as having a marginal, service-course function at best, my position there—where I breezed through tenure review and promotion to full professor—was considered a plum by my former companions in the misery of unemployment or itinerant temporary employment. I too regard it as a plum in many ways, especially as Poly has progressed from being a provincial trade school into something more like a true university, admission to which is highly competitive due to its mix of technical and general education courses, its temperate year-round climate, and its pastoral setting in a valley near the ocean, midway between Los Angeles and San Francisco, sheltered from urban stresses.

I am often asked (and ask myself) what I, a notorious lefty, am doing teaching at California's most conservative public college. Taking account for an element of rationalizing the paucity of job opportunities elsewhere, I answer that this is exactly the kind of place where leftists should be teaching, instead of ensconcing themselves comfortably in the Ivy League and UC bastions of political correctness. Despite the constant sense of being like Sisyphus, waging the same battle every term to roll back the rock of student illiteracy, parochiality, and resistance to ideas challenging conservative orthodoxies, as Camus (1955) says, "The struggle itself toward the heights

is enough to fill a man's heart" (91). And the results are often surprisingly encouraging; students who know my reputation take my
courses as a novel departure from what they are accustomed to, and
many admit to seeing their life and careers quite differently afterward (if not immediately, a year or more later). I have even won two
awards for outstanding teaching.

Moreover, because the Poly student population has boomed while
English and other humanities majors in many more prestigious universities have declined (with a corresponding decline in faculty hiring), Poly has been able to build an excellent faculty in these fields,
precisely through recruiting (and rewarding with tenure and promotion) scholars primarily dedicated to teaching rather than to research
and publication, and through having the largesse not to discriminate
against those victims of the depressed job market nearing or past forty
without having gotten on or stayed on the tenure track. Those of us at
Poly and similar schools who have managed (at great sacrifice of time
in our private lives) to continue doing research and publishing have
the satisfaction of doing so out of commitment to projects we cared
strongly about, without the intimidation of publish-or-perish and the
backbiting competitiveness that bedevil faculties at research universities and their peers in national scholarly circles. Consequently, our
faculty has also managed to attain a spirit of true collegiality in commitment to teaching and a united front in face of the adversity toward
humanistic education in a technological school, without the rampant
egomania all too common among faculties in more prestigious universities.

Nearly thirty years of teaching primarily lower-division composition
and literature courses have made me steadily more exasperated with
the kind of theoretical concerns that dominate much graduate education and advanced scholarship—especially poststructuralist rumina-
tions about the biases of logocentrism, the indeterminacy of texts,
and the subjectivity of reader response—which seem to be formulated
in blithe ignorance of the fact that in most nonelite colleges today,
many undergraduates are prelogocentric, scarcely able to read or write
at all on the college level and too unfamiliar with the Western canon
to have been biased by it (indeed, resisting exposure to it or any general education as a distraction from vocational education).

As I get older, I get increasingly depressed at the sight of droves
of graduate students and junior faculty feverishly dashing around
MLA conventions jamming into sessions they hope will give them a
glimmer of understanding of the latest obscure theoretical oracle or
-ism. Meanwhile, now that I am finally on the receiving end of job
applications, I and other members of our hiring committee get equally depressed reading the hundreds of letters from graduates of the

top-ranked English departments eager to impress us with the theoretical sophistication of their dissertations but saying nothing about their qualifications to teach the undergraduate composition, critical thinking, or introductory literature courses that our job listing specified.

Shortly after I started to teach at Cal Poly in 1977, we hosted a national Association of Departments of English seminar, whose main constituency was administrators and teachers in undergraduate programs; our concerns were addressed helpfully in most of the sessions, but the keynote address was given by a famous literary theorist, on the latest trends in post-poststructuralist phenomenology. After the first twenty minutes of incomprehensibility, audience members were falling off their chairs like Harpo Marx in glassy-eyed stupefaction.

The saddest part of this whole story is that, with some notable and admirable exceptions, those at the upper levels in English have turned their backs not only on the rest of their own profession but on splendid opportunities for restoring English studies to a living social role by fostering basic critical literacy, as taught through both literature and composition. If those most influential in the profession continue to ignore the issues addressed here, they will not only be acting in bad faith ethically but will be isolating themselves ever further from a living role in American education and society, contributing to the stifling of future generations of literate children as their students and successors, and inviting the enmity of public officials who will make William J. Bennett and Lynne V. Cheney be remembered as cordial by comparison.

Works Cited

Camus, A. 1955. *The Myth of Sisyphus and Other Essays*. Trans. Justin O'Brien. New York: Vintage.

Morse, J. M. 1972. *The Irrelevant English Teacher*. Philadelphia: Temple University Press.

Shaughnessy, M. 1977. *Errors and Expectations: A Guide for the Teacher of Basic Writing*. New York: Oxford University Press.

Trillin, C. 1977. "U.S. Journal: Manhattan." *The New Yorker* (7 March): 89–96.

8

A Pedagogy of Respect
Teaching as an Ally of Working-Class College Students

Lawrence MacKenzie

If you burn your tongue in the kitchen, do you remember to tell your guests that the soup is hot?

Waiting out the ceremony on a high school stage forty years ago, I thought about how many tons of asparagus I had harvested. A student of lambtail docking, welding, rill irrigation, and Toggenburg goat rearing, I had no speech to make; I was on display because I had stunned my high school by winning a National Merit Scholarship, and Yakima Valley educators understood a windfall when they saw one. I remember estimating how many hundreds of bales of hay I had bucked in my teen years, and wondering what romantic or business-man had first convinced Americans they needed these weird caps and gowns. Being on stage felt phony to me. Since my picture had appeared on the front page of the local paper, I had been viewed in my high school with awkward amazement, then eagerly invited to join Demolay and other apparently prestigious clubs I had never heard of. Comment was made in town and school that I was a winner out of "nowhere," and promises were uttered that in the future, school officials would "scour the bushes" and "leave no stone unturned" to locate talent like mine, which was obviously "wasted" in the vo-ag classes and shops. I couldn't articulate why those comments rang so wrong, except that they seemed insulting to my peers in 4-H and FFA, and to my farmer/machinist father and farmer/housewife mother. I wanted to do something more independently meaningful than sit on that stage. I didn't feel so lonely as Sillitoe's long-distance runner, but neither I nor my dad and mom (in the audience dressed in their church-going garb) were sure why I was going to Reed College, or how in the world I would earn my bread after going there. Over the years, I've seen many shades of ambivalence about college in my own working-class students; my own remembered ambivalence helps me better notice theirs, and think how my teaching can respond to it.

In the mid-sixties I was working in an urban civil rights agency when I was invited to join the English department at the brand new Community College of Philadelphia. Looking back now at my teaching, I catalog not hay and asparagus, but concerns and teacherly questions. As a new college instructor in 1966, I asked "What are these students like and what should they be reading? What's so important about the five-hundred-word theme? Why are these students deferential and dutiful? And why don't they argue more, and ask more questions?" In the seventies I was happy when the students organized a successful sit-in to negotiate a permanent role in college governance, and I was active in the faculty's collective bargaining campaign. In the eighties I helped organize classroom observation exchanges, gained new appreciation for the excellent teaching being done at my college, and wondered how much of the low prestige of community colleges and their students stemmed from classism. I wondered why nearly two-thirds of my college's students were women, and why African American men, especially, were underrepresented. As my colleagues and I worked on building a more powerful curriculum, I met outside the college with other educators to dig up our poignant school memories to see how they were affecting our notions of teaching.

In the eighties and early nineties I paid more attention to education outside the college. I directed a college credit-bearing summer program for high school students. My wife and I studied schools and their workings with new care because our two sons, "ability grouped" differently, were having radically different school experiences. I became interested in high school tracking systems and was impressed by critiques from Jeannie Oakes, Jean Anyon, Michael Apple, and others. I tried to understand what the loss of industry meant to Philadelphia's working-class schools, and to my students. I worked on diversity issues as part of an Association of American Colleges and Universities project. Recently I've asked: "What does the working class mean to the diversity movement? Where does working-class estrangement from higher education come from, and what can college and university faculty do about it? How can we more fully acknowledge working-class students, and make them welcome and at home in the academy? Since the majority of my students are working-class women, what can I learn from them and from feminist pedagogy? If classist factors are at play that silence or undermine working-class students, how can we alter these factors? What role has classism played in shaping the traditional academic practices that I unthinkingly employ, and whose interests do they serve?" The broader question for me to ask over and over is this: "What gets in the way of my students' learning everything of value they possibly can?" Or turned differently, as John Smyth (1992) asks, "What constrains my view of what is possible in teaching?" (299).

Taking all of these questions seriously has led to my practicing what, silently until now, I've called a pedagogy of respect. By this phrase I mean not mere civility, but a program of collaborative pedagogy productive for nearly all students, but particularly aimed at contradicting the internalized classism that I perceive to be interfering with working-class students' power to learn. First-generation college attenders often start from a family and community base that gives them doubtful, neutral, or mixed messages with regard to college study and their chances of success in it. The confessional and analytic literature about working-class experiences in higher education describes alienation, embarrassment, self-doubt, intellectual excitement, struggle, compromise, and grieving (Ryan and Sackrey 1996; Tokarczyk and Fay 1993). It also points to institutions that are almost completely blind to working-class students, even while ignoring or tacitly silencing their voices. Working-class students are "defined out of existence" (Langston 1993, 70). I believe that the most valid pedagogy grows from the assumption that these students, in equal measure to others, are deserving of respect from the very start. Working-class students who feel respected by teachers and fellow students, especially in the classroom, learn better and think more powerfully than those who do not feel respected. However, on campuses where a big part of their identity has been "defined out of existence," working-class students are not likely to feel respected. Nor is respect likely to be communicated so long as, despite its promise, these students are alienated from higher education and so long as, in turn, most of higher education, expressing the classism of the larger society, is alienated from working-class people.

Do these generalizations, the questions I ask myself, and my teaching values and practices flow from my own early life, including my experiences in school? Indirectly. I was a rural working-class kid with roots in eastern Montana, growing up in eastern Washington. My machinist father was an active union member; my mother was a housewife who began attending college the same year that I did, on her way to becoming a schoolteacher. Until I was five years old, we lived in a red plywood trailer house built by my father; then we settled down in a rented government house. I liked school and was a big reader. My parents bought an encyclopedia—*The Book of Knowledge*—and a new Nash in 1949; I spent a lot of hours with the encyclopedia. My folks cashed in their war bonds to buy eleven acres of farmland in 1950, and for a couple of years we "pioneered"—hauling in water, using an outhouse, and reading by kerosene lamps. The house my folks constructed was made out of two frame cabins bought at a government auction. Over the next seven years my chores were tilling, irrigating, mowing, cow milking, and the like. Besides working alfalfa and asparagus, I raised rabbits, pigs, goats, and sheep. The junior high school I went to after we moved was a disappointment, but I kept reading.

The classist put-downs I heard in high school were the ones farm kids sometimes get, the middle-class town students teasing especially those of us who wore the blue corduroy jackets of the Future Farmers in the vocational agriculture program. There were some sturdy values around for me to learn—from scouting, 4-H (head, heart, hands, health), family, and some teachers. Mr. Engman, my algebra teacher, seemed more real to me because he also drove my school bus. My parents were fair-minded, compassionate people, though too quiet and passive in my young eyes. My pedagogy stems in part from their values. Influenced as a child by Bible stories (David and Goliath, the Good Samaritan) and tales of Robin Hood, by stories of persecution (of the Mormon pioneers on my mother's side, and of the European Jews I read about in library books), stories of the government's unjust war against the Nez Percé Indians (my first junior high school was named after Chief Joseph), stories about labor union struggles, questions about atomic weapons (my father worked at Hanford), and news created by McCarthyism, I developed a strong interest in social justice, an interest that has always shaped my teaching.

As a teenager who thrived on 4-H club and Future Farmers of America activities, on livestock shows and rodeos, I had thought I would find a way to attend Washington State College and maybe become a county agent. Instead, my magical scholarship took me to Reed College, where I arrived with three books: a Bible, *Ivanhoe,* and *Animal Farm.* Unlike Gregory Mantsios (1995), who credits an excellent college sociology course with changing his young working-class life, I managed to learn very little about social stratification or working-class history during my college years, despite Reed's radical reputation, and no big picture came into play to make sense of how my working-class tradition and academia could be related. Even in my senior year, when a Woodrow Wilson Fellowship panelist asked me if I considered the historian of the English novel Ian Watt (whose work I had discussed) a Marxist, I was hard-pressed to give a sensible answer. Nonetheless, I am largely grateful for my Reed experiences, which have influenced my views of adult learning. The intense, lively discussion-oriented classes in the humanities there, focused on interpreting primary texts, probably provided the earliest model for the classes I teach and how I teach them. Some of my Reed professors were excellent, playful, scholarly, challenging teachers, but I remember at least one prof whose challenges always seemed tinged with scorn; I remember his scorn more vividly than the arguments of Hegel and Hume. I learned most from teachers who became genuinely excited about the direction a discussion was going, whose style involved delving, vigorous inquiry and occasional celebration. One of these professors got me to fall in love with the works of Chaucer.

I was lucky. Though other sons and daughters of machinists have also won National Merit Scholarships, such educational trajectories have not been all that common for children of working-class parents. Why has that been so? Although softened by the rise of the community colleges, there remains a remarkable alienation between working-class Americans and higher education, especially the selective levels of it. This is a shame. Working-class college students in the United States are largely segregated, located disproportionately in commuter institutions that generally involve students more tenuously in academic culture. Dropout rates are higher in these institutions. There's no grand conspiracy to keep working-class students so segregated, but almost no one seems to see much wrong with this demographic pattern either. College costs and working-class perceptions about costs appear to drive the pattern (most of my students do not even consider trying to transfer to prestigious colleges because they assume they could not afford them). If I am even roughly right about these matters, they are a shame not only for millions of aspirants in the working class, climbing haltingly up the short ladders that American education seems to issue them, but for higher education itself, especially its more "selective" and elite strata, which go without hundreds of thousands of remarkable students and the fresh perspectives they are often capable of providing.

The pedagogy of respect that I advocate does not pretend to solve all of this malaise. I argue, however, that pedagogies that are organized around respect promise to be powerful. Respect is central to working-class education if for no other reason than that it contradicts the systemic, learning-disruptive disrespect addressed to poor and working-class people, particularly with regard to their intelligence. It is this relentless denigration that complicates the standard characterization of social class as an achieved rather than an ascriptive social trait such as race or sex. There is a somewhat paradoxical dynamic at work here: Class talk is sporadic and muted in our society, yet at the same time, classism itself operates freely as an essentialist myth serving as a tricky codicil to the American dream. Classism promotes the myth that working-class people are essentially and by nature less intelligent than professional or upper-middle-class people. It alleges that the limited brainpower, crude or at best bourgeois-derivative culture, barbarian language, authoritarian child-rearing practices, malleability, and simple morality of working-class people fit them naturally for subordinate positions. The myth stretches when necessary. Classist exceptionalism makes room in the dominant class for those whose mobility proves them only transiently and/or mistakenly located in the working class.

My writing students—and I'm thinking especially of students from the Community Women's Education Project (CWEP) in the old industrial neighborhood of Kensington, in Philadelphia—generally find it easier to locate injustice in the dynamics of racism and sexism than in issues of social class. Class issues are tough for these people, as for all Americans, to think and talk about. One of the reasons for this is a widespread belief in what we may call "the poetic justice of class." To believe in the most popular version of the American Dream is to believe also that the gods of social mobility are fair and just. It is a belief that class distinctions almost universally have been earned, and therefore that discrimination based on these distinctions, unlike race and gender distinctions, is a fair game. This latent, twistily Calvinistic social Darwinism naturalizes the class position of those kept outside higher education, or found almost exclusively in the nonselective institutions. How hegemonic these views are is demonstrated to me by how difficult it is for my adult working-class students to seriously question them. Most have gone through hard times; many see themselves as recovering from errors of judgment made in earlier life, and they have invested much hope in college's redemptive power. Social class talk smacks of unwelcome determinism and may seem to threaten the dreams that fuel the sacrifices they are making to attend college.

Nearly all of my students have grown up hearing messages belittling their intelligence or the intelligence of their people. Some have been slapped with the saying, "If you're so smart, why aren't you rich?" Drawing its power from the deep reservoirs of meritocratic myth, this oppressive trump card has been used to shut up and slow down any working-class person getting too "mouthy," too critical, too inventive. Working-class identity in America is viewed from the vantage point of the professional class as a dubious achievement, one

associated with poor performance in school. The poor and the working class are categorized not only by their subordinate range of less
self-directed occupations, but by their presumed lack of intelligence,
which is alleged to have led naturally to placement in such occupations. To a considerable extent, working-class people buy into this
view, confirming its hegemony. Many of my students have come
through remedial courses. Society's message to working-class students is in effect that nearly all of them are remedial: They must
remediate their family's history by remediating their own working-
class identity. From what I've seen, life for many poor and working-
class students is erosively perplexed by the clinging, deep-rooted suggestion that their class identity is a badge of cognitive failure, an
identity that an individual of sufficient merit can and should leave
behind—and that one's parents, if clever and enterprising enough,
and unless they are first-generation immigrants, should have already
left behind. The message is this: Working-class students must remediate their identities, and most of them will receive little or no respect
until they do.

Workers and working-class students do resist mental denigration.
The search for respect appears not only in the petulant "I don't get no
respect" of a comedian with a buffoonish working-class persona and
in the real or imagined "dissing" that can lead to death on an urban
street, but also subtly and poignantly in workplaces and schools
across the nation. As high technology becomes more important and
pervasive, most American workplaces have increasingly become sites
of knowledge struggle, complicated by hard feelings over the continued discounting of workers' minds, which has been conspicuous since
Taylorism began. A 1996 poll suggested that the majority of
American workers believe they are smarter than their bosses, and in
the mid-nineties *Dilbert* strips were being pinned up by technocratic
workers in white-collar cubicles everywhere. In the late Karen
Brodine's long poem, "Woman Sitting at the Machine, Thinking"
(1990), the typesetters and other workers are more thoughtful than the
suspicion-filled managers "barricaded / behind their big desks" could
ever imagine, "and because they must think we are stupid in order to
push us around, *they* become stupid" (98). Despite such analysis and
resistance by workers, deficit-oriented classism, always portraying
blue-collar workers and large numbers of white- and pink-collar
workers as the residual class (composed of people left over after the
smart ones have taken their rightful positions in the professional/man-
agerial stratum), prevails with deep hegemonic force.

Whether or not they think much about class prejudice, working-
class students are generally aware of class relations in terms of power.
They would not be surprised at Sandy Carter's (1979) idea that the

"particular ways that [professional/managerial types] dress, speak, write and live . . . contain within them the rituals of power and judgement," or that the class system simply parcels to "some the power to manage, teach, and plan while others remain the object of this activity" (111). Although working-class students can certainly get caught up in the joys of learning and can perceive some faculty as allies, they more generally see teachers and professors in terms of their power. Most tacitly treat professors as Management—as taskmasters and, through grades, as paymasters. The few undergraduates who are challenged to analyze social metaphors and models such as "ladders of mobility" and "the high school as shopping mall" may well see secondary and postsecondary educators as Hoopmasters. From this perspective, our roles as task assigners and guardians of knowledge are fused with our more powerful roles as social class sorters or social mobility gatekeepers. Armed with determination, but aware of their limited resources and power, thousands of working-class, first-generation college students have little confidence that they will excel or receive basic respect as they enter higher education. My students' papers about school memories help convince me that, because of their earlier experiences with teachers playing traditional judging and controlling roles, because of their own usual history of being grouped and ability sorted to dubious effect in the schools, and because of internalized classism, numbers of working-class people by the time they even consider attending college have developed modest-to-painful levels of discomfort, distrust, or even restrained hostility toward educators and their institutions.

You may object that you have not heard working-class students voice such anxiety or distrust, or voice resistance to disrespect. Except under unusual circumstances, these feelings and objections are not likely to be voiced, at least not to us. Consider audience reaction in 1996 to the initial episode of the televison sitcom "Pearl." When Rhea Perlman's character, longshoreman's widow and adult learner Pearl Caraldo, told off her arrogant humanities professor on the first day of class, the television audience celebrated not because this event was familiar or typical, but because it enacted a long-held desire of the classism-belittled. I suspect this kind of overt challenge to professorial condescension is exceedingly rare in real-life academia. The working class tends to be nearly invisible and almost mute there. We could ask, as with other closeted or muffled groups, "why we have created a system that privileges some and makes others invisible" (Tierney 1993, 61), but I less want to speculate on ideological motives for cranking up such a system than to explore mechanisms of its maintenance.

Factors in Working-Class Invisibility

Let's talk about six reasons why working-class invisibility and silence persist in academe.

Exclusion

In thousands of college and university classrooms, there are few or even no working-class students present; such students are sharply underrepresented in residential and elite higher education. Except to provide racial diversity, generally they are not recruited, and they avoid applying to elite schools, which they and their parents read as "not for them." As a result, when Jan Dizard (1991) teaches his Amherst sociology students about the stacked deck of the American class system, usually there are no working-class students in his classroom who can protest the "largely unstated collusion [of parents, schools, and employers] to keep losers losing," though there are plenty of unawarely elite students who become uncomfortable thinking that "the deck must also be stacked to keep winners winning" (152–153).

Paul Lauter (1995) has got it right when he says that "colleges and universities have replaced secondary schools as primary mechanisms for sorting people on the basis, mainly, of their class origins" (80). As the system works now, children from elite families flow to and through elite schools; graduates of elite boarding schools "are more than seven times as likely as are public school students to attend selective colleges" and disproportionately large percentages of private high school graduates help comprise the freshman classes at elite colleges—in 1982, for example, 40 percent at both Yale and Princeton (Persell et al. 1992, 216; see also Karabel and Astin 1975, and Kingston and Lewis 1990). Graduates of elite colleges seem to have enhanced access to the professions. "How to Succeed? Go to Wellesley" headlines a recent *New York Times* article that documents an aspect of this (Dobrzynski 1995). Meanwhile, most poor and working-class young people flow into the basic, general, or vocational tracks of public high schools to finish their relationship with formal schooling or, if luckier, go to college, more often than not attending community colleges and other nonelite colleges and universities. As Theodore Sizer (1984) says in *Horace's Compromise*, while schools rationalize that faltering students have different needs, "there is blatant class discrimination in how schools 'meet individual needs'" (233).

Elite colleges and universities could actively build transfer bridges to the working-class-based community colleges, but only a few of them have done this. This may be one reason why controversy exists about the effect of community college attendance on students' success at gaining the baccalaureate (see Dougherty 1987). Faculty of outstanding baccalaureate-granting institutions who wish to reach out to the working class should lobby and work to build vibrant "bridge" programs and respectful transfer agreements with community colleges, as well as engage actively in the recruitment of promising community college ransfer students. Such programs do exist. "Exploring Transfer," a program supported by the Association of American Colleges, the Ford Foundation, and other foundations, showed what could be done (Wechsler 1991). The model was established by LaGuardia Community College and Vassar College. Similar programs, such as those constructed by the Community College of Philadelphia and Bucknell University, and by Smith College and its several community college partners, have had some remarkable results. At least thirty Exploring Transfer alumni have graduated from Vassar with honors (Hungar 1995). For several summers the Student Transfer Enrichment Program (STEP) at Bucknell has recruited nontraditional students from my college, usually low-income, first-generation college attenders. Like Exploring Transfer, STEP features rigorous courses, teaching teams that link liberal arts college and community college faculty, strong engagement by students, and high rates of successful transfer by participants. In a national context, however, programs like these remain unusual, and miniscule. Some of the Exploring Transfer replication partnerships that started in the early nineties with Ford Foundation seed money are no longer running. Such programs should be proliferating and expanding, rather than disappearing.

Most of the major diversity efforts in colleges and universities neglect class as a lens for valuing on-campus diversity, except in the anthologies used in a few of the diversity courses. Working-class identity is rarely viewed as an aspect of cultural pluralism and is thus left out of the student head counts that give institutions their diversity scores. Why? Because non-middle-class identity is *supposed* to be invisible; it is viewed not as a cross-cultural asset but as a condition to be repaired. The myth of upward mobility dictates that working-class freshmen, even if they were identified as such, upon graduation would be defined as virtually working-class no more. Colleges and universities earn no diversity points for recruiting working-class students per se, and as David Karen (1991) points out, working-class students, unlike women and racial minorities, have never organized politically to challenge their relative exclusion from prestigious levels of American higher education. Some working-class minority students entered elite colleges in the early years of affirmative action, but it appears that most elite schools now tend to stick with middle- and upper-class Hispanic, Asian, and African American students. As a

Yale financial aid officer told *New York Times* reporter Crystal Nix (1986), "Our kinds of schools are not gambling as much on lower-income and lower-ability students" (24). Lower-ability, okay, but why lower-income? This spokesman was reflecting an elite school rejection of working-class minority students as risky precisely because of their *class*.

Anxiety and Distrust

Outside of television, how often is anyone imprudent enough to confide fear and distrust to the very ones feared and distrusted? I believe that a climate of class-based real or anticipated disrespect nourishes distrust. Though their sense of alienation may be too inchoate or embarrassing to tell anyone about, working-class students often act on it anyway by marginalizing themselves—sometimes by abandoning college itself after a short stay. The social class-based feelings of inferiority or alienation are often entangled with emotions based on ethnicity or gender. Looking back at her undergraduate years in Sacramento, at the institution where she now teaches, Olivia Castellano (1995) tells us, "I was so frightened by my white, male professors, especially in the English department—they looked so arrogant and were so ungiving of their knowledge—that I didn't have the nerve to major in English, though it was the major I really wanted" (307).

On campuses where working-class students are uncommon, they may be isolated from others by financial strictures that keep them from socializing (see bell hooks 1989, 1994), or by shyness and justified caution. When working-class students do reveal themselves, the result may be discouraging. Julie Olsen Edwards (1995) writes of telling her Mills College English Department head about how excited she was to watch the first installment of a two-part *Hamlet* on television. Edwards recalls confiding that she could "hardly wait to find out how the story ends." The professor is "amazed . . . [and] enthralled" at meeting such a naive student: "Mixed with surprise, her voice is tinged with shock, and pity, and worst of all, amusement," Edwards recalls. "I turn and walk away and am too embarrassed to watch the second half of the program" (353). As with some ethnic minority students, here a working-class student was greeted as an exotic creature. I entered college as a bewildered farm boy clutching a national scholarship. Two years later, I was struggling academically. When I confided to a dean how disoriented and ambivalent I felt coming from a rural working-class background to an elite liberal arts college, rather than offering encouragement, the dean urged me to consider quitting college and joining the Army. I could season myself there and find a

career, he said, as so many young men of my background had useful-
ly done in the past.

Hiding

Classism silences its targets in childhood and adolescence through
disparaging the intelligence of working-class students and instilling
subtle, sometimes crippling, shame; because of their checkered
confidence, working-class students may adopt a permanently tentative
stance. They may perceive that, like race and gender, class gives
"'authority' to some voices more than others" (hooks 1994, 185).
"Members of less privileged groups are often accustomed to silence
and avoidance as resistance strategies, unless they are in a safe setting
. . ." (Higginbotham 1996). Fearing embarrassment or "getting into
trouble," working-class students may censor themselves into silence
in order to approximate the version of middle-class decorum that college discourse seems to require, thus colluding with how "bourgeois
values overdetermine social behavior in the classroom and undermine
the democratic exchange of ideas" (hooks 1994, 179). Working-class
students may "lie low" and try just to get by with only passing grades
("I just wanna be average," Rose 1989), casually hiding out under
the ubiquitous, all-purpose middle-class identity. Even those who at
first resist conforming in clothing or other styles may finally, because
of their fear of being stigmatized, make elaborate arrangements to
appear middle class. Robert Granfield's 1991 study of law school students showed that, even if not adopted earlier, "making it by faking
it" social class strategies may emerge on the graduate level.

Denial of Disadvantage

One strand of research suggests that for some working-class students
a "denial of disadvantage" phenomenon may come into play. In this
scenario, individuals aware of belonging to an oppressed group view
themselves, *personally*, nonetheless, as immune to the effects of the
oppression. Working-class identity and the effects of classism can
thus be put aside through an act of private exceptionalism (Crosby et
al. 1989).

The Impoliteness of Class Talk

An oppressive requirement of being or appearing middle class is to
avoid social class talk; it is impolite or even rude to call attention to
social class identitities, social class advantage, etc. The upper bourgeois rules say that to speak of class is itself, conveniently, déclassé

(Mantsios 1992, 73, referring to research by Susan Ostrander). This norm affects faculty discourse as well as that of students. On many campuses, a question to another student or to a colleague such as "How do you think the working-class students among the freshmen are doing?" is likely to trigger a raised eyebrow, a shrug, confusion, or a graceful change of subject. Is the aversion to class talk also reinforced by faint ripples from fifties McCarthyism (Ehrenreich 1995)? The winning of the Cold War? Maybe so. Whenever anyone points to the obscene salaries of top CEOs and the smoldering despair of legions among America's working poor, a politician shushes this with the red-baiting alarm, "Class war! Class war!"

Since it is so clearly considered impolite and/or impolitic to discuss social class, except where it is on a sociology course's formal agenda, few college students bring up class perspectives in classroom discussion A remarkable real-life exception is bell hooks, and as an undergraduate at Stanford even she seems not to have brought up issues of bourgeois class bias until she took feminist courses that expressly permitted enough "voice" from students so that tackling neglected class issues seemed possible (hooks, 1994).

Messages from the Fate of Non-academic Staff

Don't have a flower on your desk. It's the badge of a secretary.
(Molloy 1977)

The relations that an urban university has with its African American, Hispanic, or other "minority" neighbors clearly mean something to the "minority" students who attend that university. I believe that similarly, though little acknowledged, class meanings are picked up by working-class students from their institutions' staff hierarchies. The makeup of the boards of trustees, the staff structures, and the treatment of nonacademic staff in the college or university repeatedly send big, semaphoric class messages to working-class students. One of the messages is that working-class people on campus are supposed to be silent, that they are the ones whose ideas do not count. Close to a million nonprofessional staff people work on college and university campuses in America, between 35 and 40 percent of all employees. They often provide much of the staff's racial diversity. Ironically, students enrolled in required diversity courses may sit highlighting passages in assigned articles about race, class, and gender, never thinking what might be learned from the groundskeepers at work outside the library window, the electricians remodeling the library's lighting, the heating engineers, the departmental secretaries, the security people, the computer technicians, or the vending machine restocker—learned from them, and from their relations or nonrelations with the teachers, researchers, deans, and trustees. The notion that a college or university represents an ideal community is almost always compromised by its own hierarchical structure, where faculty and upper-level administrators may happily treat clerks, secretaries, gardeners, mechanics, and technicians as inferiors, largely to be blanked out of the scene.

Working-class staff may believe in the academy as an ideal community, and may even think of themselves as community members. They may be disappointed. Kristin Kovacic's father was an electrician, fired with other staff three years before his planned retirement by a university whose "going corporate" plans included buying the "$1.9 million Sewickley estate for its new president, his wife, and their six horses." Kovacic, who graduated as valedictorian of her college, part of her father's university, writes: "My family felt, with great pride, a part of an educational community, until, without ceremony, Carnegie Mellon abandoned its role in it. Now, like too many other working-class families in Pittsburgh, we're left with the caution that it was foolish to have believed" (1995, 24). Kovacic's story will be dismissed by some as just another tale of union defeat in the eighties and nineties. But if a university acts in this way, how are working-class university students supposed to view its actions? For many, they must provide further motivation for students to hide class identity and be silent, hoping soon to reach relative safety in the upper half of the middle class.

Stories like this one have strong meaning for me, strengthening my commitment to let the values underlying my pedagogy of respect inform my actions in the educational community. I believe that genuine respect for working-class and other students goes hand in hand with respect for the clerks, secretaries, administrators, groundskeepers, maintenance workers, and food service workers who make the campus and its processes and systems physically possible. I agree with Michael Yates (1995), an economist at the University of Pittsburgh, who argues that working-class academics should reject elitism and condescension to students and staff, and should seek to view themselves as workers in alliance with other workers inside and outside the academy.

With one, some or all of these six factors at work, is it any wonder that working-class students largely remain invisible on many of our campuses, and that working-class issues go largely unacknowledged? "How are the working-class students on campus doing this year?" Class issues are so little heeded—there is such a lack of systematic attention to working-class students—that, in most cases, if students struggle or drop out, how can faculty or administrators concerned with retention even know if working-class educational issues have played a part?

The Denigration that Respect Has to Counter

Embracing a pedagogy of respect means believing in the intelligence of students, particularly working-class students. Conversations about promoting "diversity" and dealing with patterns of oppression such as racism, sexism, homophobia, classism, ageism, and ableism sometimes focus on issues such as which of the oppressions is more foundational, or how the oppressions interlock or magnify each other's effects. In almost every course I teach, I find it important to talk with the students about learning and about intelligence. I find it useful to focus on a common oppressive theme, the discounting of intelligence, the claim that "the Other" cannot think and learn. Insistence that the target group is dumb is an old strand in racism and sexism; students' remembered experiences readily are brought forward to attest to this. Of course, any societal oppressive pattern will justify itself by seeing the objects of oppression as faulty or diminished. "The Other" is "the lesser," and intellect is an obvious realm that the oppressive pattern can lie about. Intellectual dimunition of "the Other" is so pervasive that it is seldom acknowledged in public discourse, though educational theorists do engage in deficit talk and reformers employ deficit models. Nobody one day announces, "we've shrunk the Other"; instead, the shrinkage operates chronically and numbingly, without comic relief. It is well established by now that sexism has silenced girls in junior high school and driven most of them out of paths leading to careers in math, science, computer technology, and engineering. My female students usually have experienced this themselves, or have heard of the research. Students at the Community Women's Education Project know that sexism has pressed women to mute their intelligence in order not to "threaten" men or trigger male violence. Some of the women have experienced opposition to their attending college, e.g., opposition from male partners (Crutchley-Smith 1993).

My students and I talk about what happens when the intelligence of a belittled person is so obvious it cannot be denied. Sometimes it is celebrated, but evidence of strong intelligence in "the Other" is often interpreted away, recategorized. Just as white racism has twisted "white" the accomplishments and character of outstanding black people via exceptionalism, so also when women have shown intellectual success as mathematicians, scientists, and engineers, contortionist sexism has tried to twist that success into evidence of those women's masculinity. These and other mechanisms for hampering and discounting women's intelligence have been attacked and countered by feminists and their allies, for example, through pedagogy focused on helping women to find or shape their own academic voices.

As part of my pedagogic strategy, I usually tell my students that, from what I have observed, classism is even more stubbornly focused on the discounting of intelligence than are racism and sexism. The fact that large numbers of African Americans and Hispanics are poor and working class makes it all the easier for classism and white racism to be confounded. Classism, in denigrating the intelligence of its target group, reinforces racism and provides denigrative overkill. Because the dominant ideology of our society seems particularly to require the obfuscation of class and classism, it is no wonder that racism, sexism, and classism are often confounded, even by those on the receiving end of these oppressions. One form of resistance to professional elites and to the class-sorting machinery of schools is teens' scorning of the avid readers and science students—the "nerds." This gets confused with attempts to resist racism so that students of color sometimes are pressured by peers not to "act white" by studying hard or achieving academic success. And if the avid teenage scholar is female, anti-intellectualism becomes conflated with sexism. Olivia Castellano (1995) tells of the hounding boys she rejected who yelled, "So what do you plan to do for the rest of your life, fuck a book?" Meanwhile her Chicana classmates would attack her high grades: "What are you trying to do, be like the whites?" (306). Antiacademic attitudes may be meant as resistance to the social class machinery of schooling, but since a class framework and vocabulary are missing, the resistance is instead expressed in the language of race or sex, and absorbed into the machinations of racism and sexism.

I discuss such matters with my students. Working-class students can be moved by such accounts and discussions; they may decide not to be tricked out of enjoying and owning their own intelligence. They may permit themselves to celebrate their gains in learning.

A Pedagogy of Respect

Although, given that potent space in the front of a classroom, I have often donned the role of lecturer/intellectual acrobat, I find the best classroom discourse is deeply collaborative. My version of a pedagogy of respect calls for college students and teachers deliberately to call up past educational experiences, to reevaluate past pedagogy, and to treat proposed pedagogy as a matter for students to participate in shaping. This process helps acknowledge and perhaps put aside some of the educational baggage we at first bring to the classroom, and by getting us to pay attention to one another, or "engage in acts of recognition with one another" (hooks 1994, 186)—practice simple respect. I find the time taken to do this well worthwhile.

Hans Andersen's observant child, the one who punctured the delusion of a naked emperor, was one of my earliest working-class heroes. Like the emperor, undergraduate higher education clothes itself in the wisest distribution requirements and latest core curricula, and heads its own parade, trusting that everything important is covered. Despite all those elective introductory sociology courses across the country, and the standard sociology textbooks with their chapters on stratification, too often social class is *not* covered for students, especially in a way that makes sense of the educational experiences of working-class students. Remarkably, with exceptions like the diversity-oriented core course at SUNY Buffalo, most colleges and universities do not insist that *all students learn about social class phenomena and their effects, including their effects on higher education itself.* Undergraduates almost never study higher education, with its history, disciplines, codes, and myths; this subject is reserved instead for a few graduate students pursuing it as a specialty. This should change. I believe that all college and university students, but especially working-class students, should have the opportunity to use academic tools to examine higher education itself. Students who do conduct such an examination may decide that too much of the system is constructed not only of glass ceilings that limit women, ethnic minorities, and working-class people, but of similarly effective glass hallways, glass detours, and glass revolving doors. Hidden curricula and hidden agendas in all levels of education can and should be taken out from hiding and examined.

Such discussion, clearing the deck for whatever other learning is supposed to take place, can occur in almost any course. It should not be left to sociologists of education; there aren't very many of those, and few students meet them. The new attention paid to gender and race in general education is a good, but insufficient, thing. Not only can course readings and activities creatively take class issues into account, but the pedagogical actions and codes we employ can be examined for their social class assumptions and social class effects, and changed for the better. Let's examine what feminist and other pedagogical critics say about college teaching (e.g., Maher and Tetreault 1994). Let's do classroom research to see how our practices affect working-class and minority students, and if we don't like some of what our research reveals, let's change our teaching accordingly. I believe all college students should be provided with knowledge about the educational system they are involved with, about its mission, its unstated assumptions and expectations, its favorite processes, and its norms of language. *Empowerment* may have become a toothless buzzword to many, but issues of power and keys for entering academic discourse remain just as important for college students to research and study as they were before *political correctness* and *empowerment* buzzed by. As Lisa Delpit (1995) says of minority children in school, "if you are not already a participant in the culture of power, being told explicitly the rules of that culture makes acquiring power easier" (24–25). Similarly, Craig Nelson (1996) shows how important it is for teachers to step beyond traditional college teaching aimed at the well-attuned products of good prep schools and "to make the tacit disciplinary expectations explicit" by giving students "specific guidance in seeing and using the expectations: for example, study questions for reading assignments, detailed structure and guidelines for writing assignments" (1994, 50).

Working-class students especially, early in college study, must be offered a range of "big pictures" and tools for analyzing the systems and language of social domination, and they must be given as well an explicit introduction to ways of joining academic discourse. They are the students least likely to have had this sort of opportunity in their past schooling. They are the students for whom such tools may make the most immediate difference as they apply the tools to help shape their own academic success. Students readily understand the value of such tools as applicable cultural capital. Any friendly demystification of academia itself, along with its hierarchies, languages, and folkways, will be especially useful to nontraditional, especially working-class, students.

Of Ladders

My students are largely from working-class families; some of them say they are "just poor." For most of them, cautious, closely held dreams of upward mobility color the way they view their urban community college studies; they want to climb "the ladder of success." As part of my pedagogy, I sometimes find it useful to help students interrogate the ladder metaphor that so often conveys the dominant notions of upward mobility within the American dream. Americans are taught that education is the key to getting ahead, rising in the world, being successful. Just get on the educational ladder and climb. *The* educational ladder? Is there a single, common ladder? Or do some people enjoy escalators, some use stepladders, some look to steal a ladder, and some have no ladder at all?

Just climb. But the paths of upward social mobility are not always much like a ladder. For many, to borrow words from a Langston Hughes ([1959] 1972) poem, "Life . . . ain't no crystal stair." The ladder metaphor is attractive to us Americans because of our individualistic perspective. A ladder user climbs solo. This fits nicely with the American myth that success is essentially heroic, earned alone through solitary effort. (This is the very concept ridiculed by Abraham Lincoln and others in the grotesque image, "pull oneself up by one's bootstraps.") An alternate view portrays success as the product of ability catalyzed by inherited cultural capital that includes mobility know-how, marital partnerships, family efforts, access to networking, and community support. I ask students to talk about the stereotypical ladder to success and to compare it with what they know of real ladders, stairs, escalators—what they know of climbing. Some express a fear of heights; are they afraid of "higher" education? Earlier, we may have investigated other stereotypes we carry. In a classroom exercise, my students are surprised to find that their mental image of "an Indian" is almost always that of a male adult. Their stereotypical image of someone climbing a ladder is generally a male image too. Ironically, though the real ladder is often a blue-collar worker's tool, the metaphorical ladder signifies for many the transcending of one's working-class station.

My students and I can go further than this with our homely deconstruction of the ladder metaphor. Someone points out that in real life a ladder climber often needs a backup—a person to anchor the base of the ladder during the climb and to help reposition the ladder. We talk about the ways you're on your own in college, and the ways you can work with others for everyone's benefit. We talk about study groups, writing groups, and the work of Uri Treisman and his math students in California (see Nelson 1994), and at CWEP we talk about what McGrath and Van Buskirk (1996) call the "social and emotional capital" developed in CWEP's supportive environment. We find now-stereotypical ladder-of-opportunity rhetoric in Andrew Carnegie's famous essay "The Gospel of Wealth," first published in 1889, and fresher ladder talk in an excerpt from Stephen Covey's *Seven Habits of Highly Effective People* (1989). The students sometimes report feeling like eavesdroppers as they read these middle-class texts. They approve as Carnegie advocates philanthropy that will place people at the base of the ladder of opportunity, but admittedly, the allegorical image remains rather vague. In contrast, Covey asks his readers to think about *what wall they should lean their ladders against* (98). This notion of a strategic life—of ladders with context, of seeking to be very actively in charge of the direction of one's own attempted mobility—is a new one for many students. The American dream need not be so dreamy, the ladder metaphor so emptily rhetorical, a vague and placeless prop half-hidden in mobility mist.

A Final Lesson

One of the readings that students in my CWEP classes have argued and written about is Toni Cade Bambara's ([1972] 1995) short story, "The Lesson." In it, a college-educated African American neighbor,

Miss Moore, takes a group of reluctant children from African American working-class families on a puzzling field trip to the upscale toy store, F.A.O. Schwartz. Many of my students are tempted to explain Miss Moore's lesson as one about "the value of money" and the need to work hard and go to school so someday the kids will be wealthy enough to buy the outrageously expensive toys they see. As one student wrote, maybe the toy store experience can help the kids "push themselves to be more than a sanitation worker or nurse."

But other students point to key passages in the narrator's account, such as this one:

> So me and Sugar turn the corner to where the entrance is, but when we get there I kinda hang back. Not that I'm scared, what's there to be afraid of, just a toy store. But I feel funny, shame. But what I got to be shamed about? Got as much right to go in as anybody. But somehow I can't seem to get hold on the door. (486)

CWEP students, many of them mothers of young children, are sharp in their discussions of the crazy mechanism whereby a rich people's toy store could intimidate a bold girl like Sylvia. Why indeed should anyone be ashamed to enter such a place? A page later in the story, Sylvia reflects:

> I could see me askin my mother for a $35 birthday clown.
> "You wanna who that costs what?" she'd say, cockin her head to the side to get a better view of the hole in my head. Thirty-five dollars could buy new bunk beds for Junior and Gretchen's boy. Thirty-five dollars and the whole household could go visit Granddaddy Nelson in the country. Thirty-five dollars would pay for the rent and the piano bill too. Who are these people that spend that much for performing clowns and $1,000 for toy sailboats? What kinda work they do and how they live and how come we ain't in on it? Where we are is who we are, Miss Moore always pointin out. But it don't necessarily have to be that way. (487)

This passage, especially "Where we are is who we are," usually provokes some investigatory discussion of the whole social class system. Latent ideas about the poetic justice of class come into play. Some of my students say that no matter how unfair the system is, they have to keep trying, as if it were fair. "How come we ain't in on it?" sometimes leads to a consideration of what attending college classes at CWEP and an urban community college might come to mean, what the constraints on CWEP students look like in a time when scarce childcare support and radical welfare reform chill college plans and how naive or well-founded are students' strategies and hopes. When the fictional Miss Moore urges the neighborhood children to demand their piece of the American pie, one of my students argues that our society is one "where greed and power control how the pie is sliced." Even though Sylvia is portrayed by Bambara as a child who resents and resists Miss Moore, the final words of the story convince most of my students that Sylvia is going to get a lot out of her day's experience, through reflection, and when Sylvia says "ain't nobody gonna beat me at nuthin" (488), it's a sign she has a bright and intelligent future ahead of her.

When their arena of respect is most productive, it is my working-class students who are the intellectual acrobats, flying through the unfamiliar academic air. Their discussions and their writing demand critical, respectful attention. It's my job, sometimes, to anchor a rope ladder or to be one of the acrobatic catchers, helping students find a well-timed bar or hands to grasp, before they swing again into the work of interpretation, critique, and new thought.

Works Cited

Anyon, J. 1980. "Social Class and the Hidden Curriculum of Work." *Journal of Education* 162(1): 67–92.

Apple, M. W. 1979. *Ideology and Curriculum.* London: Routledge and Kegan Paul.

Bambara, T. C. [1972] 1995. "The Lesson." In *Rereading America: Cultural Contexts for Critical Thinking and Writing, 3d ed.* Ed. G. Colombo, R. Cullen, and B. Lisle, 482–488. New York: St. Martin's Press.

Bernstein, B. 1990. *The Structuring of Pedagogic Discourse. Volume IV: Class, Codes and Control.* London and New York: Routledge.

Bowles, S., and H. Gintis. 1972. "IQ in the Class Structure." *Social Policy* 3 (4–5): 65–95.

———. 1976. *Schooling in Capitalist America: Educational Reform and the Contradictions of Economic Life.* New York: Basic Books.

Brodine, K. 1990. "Woman Sitting at the Machine, Thinking." In *If I Had a Hammer: Women's Work in Poetry, Fiction, and Photographs*, ed. S. Martz, 94–99. Watsonville, CA: Papier-Mâché Press.

Carnegie, A. [1889] 1962. "The Gospel of Wealth." In *The Gospel of Wealth and Other Timely Essays,* ed. E. C. Kirkland, 14–49. Cambridge, MA: Belknap Press of Harvard University Press.

Carter, S. 1979. "Class Conflict: The Human Dimension." In *Between Labor and Capital,* ed. P. Walker, 97–119. Boston: South End.

Castellano, O. 1995. "Canto, Locura Y Poesia." In *Race, Class, and Gender: An Anthology, 2d ed.* Ed. M. L. Andersen and P. H. Collins, 304–313. Belmont, CA: Wadsworth.

Covey, S. R. 1989. *The Seven Habits of Highly Effective People.* New York: Simon & Schuster.

Crosby, F. J., A. Pufall, R. C. Snyder, M. O'Connell, and P. Whalen. 1989. "The Denial of Personal Disadvantage Among You, Me, and All the Other Ostriches." In *Gender and Thought: Psychological Perspectives,* ed. M. Crawford and M. Gentry, 79–99. New York: Springer-Verlag.

Crutchley-Smith, M. 1993. "Wake-Up Call." *Limited Edition: Student Writing and Photography '93.* 31–40. Philadelphia: Community College of Philadelphia.

Delpit, L. 1995. *Other People's Children: Cultural Conflict in the Classroom.* New York: The New Press.

Dizard, J. E. 1991. "Achieving Place: Teaching Social Stratification to Tomorrow's Elite." In *Teaching What We Do: Essays by Amherst College Faculty,* 145–162. Amherst, MA: Amherst College Press.

Dobrzynski, J. H. 1995. "How to Succeed? Go to Wellesley." *The New York Times,* 29 October, 3, 1.

Dougherty, K. 1987. "The Effects of Community Colleges: Aid or Hindrance to Socioeconomic Attainment?" *Sociology of Education* 60: 86–103.

Edwards, J. O. 1995. "Class Notes from the Lecture Hall." In *Liberating Memory: Our Work and Our Working-Class Consciousness,* ed. J. Zandy, 339–357. New Brunswick, NJ: Rutgers University Press.

Ehrenreich, Barbara. 1995. "Are You Middle Class?" In *Race, Class, and Gender: An Anthology. 2d ed.* Ed. M. L. Andersen and P. H. Collins, 120–123. Belmont, CA: Wadsworth.

———. 1989. *Fear of Falling: The Inner Life of the Middle Class.* New York: HarperCollins.

Fromm, E. 1961. *Marx's Concept of Man.* New York: Ungar.

Granfield, R. 1991. "Making It by Faking It: Working-Class Students in an Elite Academic Environment." *Journal of Contemporary Ethnography* 20 (3): 331–352.

Higginbotham, E. 1996. "Getting All Students to Listen: Analyzing and Coping with Student Resistance." *American Behavioral Scientist* 40 (2): 203–211. (Issue devoted to "Multiculturalism and Diversity in Higher Education," ed. J. Meacham.)

hooks, bell. 1994. *Teaching to Transgress: Education as the Practice of Freedom.* New York and London: Routledge.

———. 1989. "Keeping Close to Home: Class and Education." In *Talking Back: Thinking Feminist, Thinking Black.* Boston: South End.

Hughes, L. [1959] 1972. "Mother to Son." *Selected Poems.* New York: Alfred A. Knopf.

Hungar, J. Y. 1995. "Exploring Transfer: How a Program Helps Community College Students Achieve the Baccalaureate Goal." *Alliance* (Fall): 18–21.

Karabel, J. 1972. "Community College and Social Stratification: Submerged Class Conflict in American Higher Education." *Harvard Educational Review* 42 (4): 521–562.

Karabel J., and A. W. Astin. 1975. "Social Class, Academic Ability, and College 'Quality.'" *Social Forces* 53(3): 381–398.

Karen, D. 1991. "The Politics of Class, Race, and Gender: Access to Higher Education in the United States, 1960–1986." *American Journal of Education* (February): 208–233.

Kingston, P. W., and L. S. Lewis. 1990. "Undergraduates at Elite Institutions: The Best, the Brightest, and the Richest." In *The High-Status Track: Studies of Elite Schools and Stratification,* ed. P. W. Kingston and L. S. Lewis, 105–120. Albany: SUNY Press.

Kovacic, K. 1995. "'Proud to Work for the University.'" *Working-Class Studies,* a special issue of *Women's Studies Quarterly* 23 (1 & 2): 19–24.

Langston, D. 1993. "Who Am I Now? The Politics of Class Identity." In *Working-Class Women in the Academy: Laborers in the Knowledge Factory,* ed. M. M. Tokarczyk and E. A. Fay, 60–72. Amherst: University of Massachusetts Press.

Lauter, P. 1995. "'Political Correctness' and the Attack on American Colleges." In *Higher Education Under Fire: Politics, Economics, and the Crisis of the Humanities,* ed. M. Berube and C. Nelson, 73–90. New York and London: Routledge.

Maher, F., and M. K. T. Tetreault. 1994. *The Feminist Classroom.* New York: Basic Books/HarperCollins.

Mantsios, G. 1995. "Living and Learning: Some Reflections on Emergence from and Service to the Working-Class." In *Liberating Memory: Our Work and Our Working-Class Consciousness,* ed. J. Zandy, 120–248. New Brunswick, NJ: Rutgers University Press.

———. 1992. "Class in America: Myths and Realities." In *Rereading America, 2d ed.* Ed. G. Colombo, R. Cullen, and B. Lisle, 72–85. New York: St. Martin's Press.

McGrath, D., and B. Van Buskirk. 1996. "Social and Emotional Capital in Education: Cultures of Support for At Risk Students." *Journal of Developmental Education* 1 (1): 2–9.

Molloy, J. T. 1977. *The Woman's Dress for Success Book.* New York: Warner Books.

Nelson, C. E. 1996. "Student Diversity Requires Different Approaches to College Teaching, even in Math and Science." *American Behavioral Scientist* 40 (2): 165–175. (Issue devoted to "Multiculturalism and Diversity in Higher Education," ed. J. Meacham.)

———. 1994. "Critical Thinking and Collaborative Learning." *New Directions for Teaching and Learning* 59: 45–59.

Nix, C. 1986. "Inner City, Elite Campus: How Two Worlds Jar." *New York Times,* 3 January. 1, 26.

Oakes, J. 1985. *Keeping Track: How Schools Structure Inequality.* New Haven, CT: Yale University Press.

Persell, C. H., S. Catsamabis, and P. W. Cookson, Jr. 1992. "Differential Asset Conversion: Class and Gendered Pathways to Selective Colleges." *Sociology of Education* 65: 208–225.

Powell, A. G., E. Farrar, and D. K. Cohen. 1985. *The Shopping Mall High School: Winners and Losers in the Educational Marketplace.* Boston: Houghton Mifflin.

Rose, M. 1989. *Lives on the Boundary.* New York: Free Press.

Ryan, J., and C. Sackrey. [1984] 1996. *Strangers in Paradise: Academics from the Working Class.* Lanham, MD: University Press of America.

Sizer, T. 1984. *Horace's Compromise: The Dilemma of the American High School.* Boston: Houghton Mifflin.

Smyth, J. 1992. "Teachers' Work and the Politics of Reflection." *American Educational Research Journal,* 29 (2): 267–300.

Tierney, W. 1993. *Building Communities of Difference: Higher Education in the Twenty-First Century.* Westport, CT: Bergin & Garvey.

Tokarczyk, M., and E. A. Fay, eds. 1993. *Working-Class Women in the Academy: Laborers in the Knowledge Factory.* Amherst: University of Massachusetts Press.

Wechsler, H. 1991. *Meeting the Transfer Challenge: Five Partnerships and Their Model. The Report of the Vassar/AAC National Project on Community College Transfer.* Poughkeepsie, NY: Vassar College/The Association of American Colleges.

Yates, M. D. 1995. The Responsibilities of Working-Class Academics. Paper presented at Working-Class Lives/Working-Class Studies: An Interdisciplinary Conference, Youngstown State University, June 7–10.

9

Academic Life as Middle Ground
A Conversation
Christina Russell McDonald
and Robert L. McDonald

Rob

The incident that first made me conscious of how class issues had shaped my life, including my career choice, remains in my memory more as a sensation than a sequence of events.

I had made a quick trip home late during the second semester of my sophomore year of college. I remember the time of year, because I had recently changed my major from chemistry to English—to do what I had discovered I loved, not what I thought would guarantee me a high-dollar career—and with spring in the air, I was feeling pretty full of myself. We were sitting down to dinner ("supper" in my hometown), not more than a couple of hours after I had arrived, when I discovered an opportunity to exercise my new self-image. The particulars have faded, but my father, speaking as casually as he always has, said something that struck me as either incorrect or inelegant, and I decided to help him with his phrasing. The impulse was a mistaken one, as you might guess. Daddy glared across the table, boring in on me, and waited what seemed like a solid hot hour before he spoke, coolly and very deliberately: "Listen, boy. You're no English teacher yet; and when you do get to be one, just remember that this is my goddam house, and I frankly don't care if you don't like the way I talk. Can you understand *that*?" My mother and sister squirmed; I sat stunned, flushed bright pink, embarrassed and angry. It wasn't so much what my father had said, but his tone, which was firm and unaccommodating, that struck me. I contemplated it, replaying the whole scene over and over, on the drive back to school that very night; there was no way I could stay the weekend.

This incident (which my father and I have never discussed) is important because it marks the moment I remember understanding the necessary boundary between the life that produced me and the life I would pursue into my own, independent adulthood. The world I found at college, and decided to integrate myself into socially as well as professionally, was a world apart from the one my parents inhabited. Most of my relatives, on both sides, have lived within the twenty-mile radius of a very rural, farming-oriented South Carolina community for as long as anyone can remember. Work there is hard and regular, and concerns are local. Materially, we had a little more than some of our neighbors, but I grew up very much aware that all of it, our whole world, was earned on a time clock: my mother working as the long-time manager of a local drugstore, my father working a variety of jobs, most of them hard labor, from log truck driver to mechanic. Neither of my parents had followed the family tradition of farming.

In any event, theirs would not be my life—not because I was better than it, but because I never really accepted the prospect that it represented the most I could hope for. Down deep I knew that I was simply not capable of continuing that life, and education was a mechanism for discovering another one. I always knew this, and undoubtedly my parents did too. One thing I will never forget about my mother, in fact, was her constant admonition, "Get your education, no matter what." She had quit college after two years to marry my father, a Navy man, and while she didn't necessarily regret it, she had developed a profound understanding of the real cost of that decision. I saw the cost as well, and took her advice. The night of my failed visit home, I confronted the fact that the education I was "getting" was transforming me and emphasizing my incompatibility with the people and the place I call home.

Christina

As a new teaching assistant in my doctoral program, I attended a presemester workshop for writing instructors during which the director of composition explained the kind of students we could expect to meet in our classes. He characterized the university's "typical student" as an undergraduate who was affluent, well-dressed, accustomed to receiving good grades, and who drove the kind of car that cost more than he would earn in a year. Around the room, new and old instructors alike began nodding their heads knowingly, content that his description had provided them with the information they needed to understand their students. The subtext of the description seemed obvious. We would be teaching spoiled rich kids who are used to getting what they want without having to work too hard. Be prepared.

The director's description and the audience's response gave me pause, even as I laughed and nodded along with everyone else. Secretly, I recognized the students they were rolling their eyes at and cracking jokes about. Just two years earlier, I had been an undergraduate not unlike those I was about to teach: one who was from an upper-class family, who earned high grades easily, and who, in fact, drove a Mercedes 560 SL. Even as I tried not to, I must have looked like a spoiled rich kid—the very image I had been trying to avoid nearly all my life.

As a child, I learned quickly that kids reacted two ways to people like me who came from upper-class families. In elementary school, the "popular" middle-class kids dismissed me as a "rich bitch" when they discovered I lived in a wealthy neighborhood—reason enough not to bother to get to know me. At the other extreme, my older sister had a large group of friends in high school primarily because she generously took them out water skiing on our family's Ski Nautique, to lunch at the private beach club, and on summer trips to an island in the Bahamas where my family vacationed. It didn't take me long to notice that most of those "friends" cared more about how her money could entertain them than they cared about my sister. Given these experiences, I decided that the only way to force people to see *me* instead of my family's wealth was concealing my background, even lying about the neighborhood I lived in.

As an aspiring academic, then, the incident at the composition workshop served to confirm the impressions I had formed not only about the academic community, but also about middle-class people in general. Among them, my life as a member of the privileged class would be suspect. I would not be judged fairly if people knew the truth about my background before they had the chance to get to know me. So, there were some things that I would not tell my new colleagues in the profession. For example, they would not know—until now, I suppose—that in preparation for graduate school, I sold my Mercedes, put my Rolex watch in the vault, and boarded a private Lear jet with one suitcase and my cat, headed for a different life.

Two essentially different personalities from two very different backgrounds, we met in graduate school in the fall of 1989. The friendship (eventually leading to marriage) that developed during those frantic early days became for each of us an important middle ground: a

place where we felt safe lowering the masks we wore to conceal our
backgrounds from our new colleagues and a place where we continue
to help one another coax our personal and professional selves into a
more comfortable existence.

A Conversation

Christina

When I began teaching in 1990, my perspective on the college classroom was highly personal and distinctly upper class. In some ways,
the teacher I was that first semester was the most authentic version of
myself ever to enter the classroom. Having been exempted from
freshman composition in college, as a new teacher I was largely
unconcerned with the course as an institutional requirement. In my
mind, the purpose of the course was to help students achieve their
individual goals as developing writers, rather than to qualify them
for entrance into upper-level courses or to prepare them for a career.
High on an idea from my undergraduate experience that collaboration
was the best form of educational experience, I wrote a friendly syllabus, set reasonable (but not overly high) standards for the course
that assumed that the students were both responsible and intelligent,
and positioned myself as a friendly equal in the education of those
affluent undergraduates whom my director of composition had mentioned in that first workshop.

Looking back on this, I see that the kind of experience that I
intended this course to be, growing out of my perception of higher
education generally, was one that only someone from an upper-class
background can afford to hold. As a young woman from a wealthy
family, my education wasn't intended to "qualify" me for anything
more than being a well-rounded person. While it was important to my
father that each of his four children receive a fully funded college
education (mainly because he had only a high school diploma), he
sent his sons to college for the purpose of preparing them for professional careers, but sent his daughters for the sake of self-improve-
ment. My inability to agree with my parents on this point is likely the
source of my own professional aspirations. In fact, I still find myself
trying to prove to my father that women can be intelligent—that I
am intelligent.

Above all else, my parents' money has afforded me the luxury of
being able to choose those opportunities that I felt I wanted to pursue.
I can see now that their constant, unconditional financial support
acted as the safety net they intended, ensuring that life's necessities
would be provided so that I could concentrate on achieving whatever

I wanted for myself. But, in my mind, only my financial independence could legitimize my work. In order for the work I was doing to be real—more than just a method of improving myself or biding time until I received a proposal of marriage—I had to pay my own way. While I was working toward the Ph.D., for instance, I was thrilled to earn even the small salary I was paid as a teaching assistant because it meant, to me at least, that I was qualified in a way that my parents would be forced to recognize. In the world of business, after all, the dollar is the measure of your ability and, ultimately, your success. By this standard and by others, I have always been driven by the need to prove myself to my parents and, even now, to anyone who thinks that I'm not capable of something. But coming from a position of social and economic security, I seldom have worried that any opportunity wasn't mine for the taking. My desire to *prove* myself to be qualified is, I suspect, fundamentally different from your drive, Rob, to *earn* your qualification.

Rob

Yes, the idea of qualification is exactly it, exactly the impulse that motivated me as a student and continues to influence me as a professor. It has been mostly unconscious, but from the first time I had charge of a class my stance has been that of standard-bearer: one who views academic achievement as desirable for the position of access and respectability it can confer, and who believes that this is at least as attainable by hard work as by any native talent—something you can in fact "get," in my mother's words. This view has resulted in a fierce lack of tolerance for inattentive students who appear to be wasting their time or mine. Ten years in the classroom have softened me some, I think, but I have an elementally difficult time working with people, students or colleagues, whom I can't respect, and respect in my book is earned by demonstrated dedication to any task you are given. This is clearly a transference of the work ethic that pervaded my upbringing: You might imagine great (or simply different) things for yourself, but in the end you get only what you earn.

Professors who taught me during the first three or so semesters of my undergraduate career might chuckle at such an assertion. Admittedly, they got less than my best effort, as I gave academic work minimum attention while spending most of my time sampling the fruits of a social life of a kind and intensity that I could scarcely believe. What might be euphemistically called an opportunity to reassess this balance came during my sophomore year, when I learned that I had lost (by ten one-hundredths of a point) an academic scholarship that had covered half my tuition each semester. This was a moment of correction, a lesson about priorities that I would have to pay for, literally. It is bound up with the events that led to the change in major I mentioned in the beginning, and, hypocritical as this may be, it feeds my impatience with students who seem to take too long to appreciate college as the experience in foundation laying that I believe it can and should be. Let me put it like this: Diplomas typically announce that an education qualifies a person for certain "rights, privileges, and honors." I expect my students to be awake to the possibilities of coloring in these abstractions, and, from the very earliest moment, to assume an active role in making the experience mean something for the lives they envision for themselves. I think of my courses, any one of them, as providing material for this process, and I concentrate my attentions on those most involved with it. Though I'm hardly a pure romantic when it comes to questions of human possibility, I've often thought of making Emerson's "The American Scholar" (or maybe "Self-Reliance") the first reading in every course I teach, from composition to advanced literature seminars, to signal my expectations of an academically applied personal rigor. Other times, I feel like quoting Thoreau: "If you have built castles in the air," he wrote in his famous conclusion to *Walden,* "your work need not be lost; that is where they should be. Now put the foundations under them" ([1854] 1971, 324).

Christina

Though I still cling to it, my broader vision of a college education—that it is, and should be, *more* than just a rigorous academic experience—has gotten me into some trouble. At the end of my first semester in the classroom, a student offered favorable reviews of the course on an evaluation, but gently advised me to "toughen up a bit" so that students (like him) wouldn't be inclined to try to take advantage of me as a teacher in the future.

When you and I talked then about the student's comment, your advice was similar to the remarks you've made here. In essence, I needed to "get some standards." The following semester, I was the holy terror of standard-bearers. I imposed deadlines and doled out sanctions to all those who fell below the mark. I upheld standards for the sake of having them, most of which I didn't believe in or didn't care much about, but that I thought were necessary in the interest of students' "education." What I discovered, not surprisingly, was that the students hated me and I hated my role in the classroom.

That semester, I wasn't able to achieve the comfortable relationship that you seem able to cultivate with your students. You hold them to high standards, work them harder than they've ever been asked to work, and at the same time remain approachable, friendly, and supportive. All I seemed capable of was demanding that students perform at a higher level, and without my help. In my interpretation of the philosophy of individual responsibility and "personal rigor" that you advocate, I could not find a place for myself in the classroom, except in the limited capacity of goal setter and evaluator. Though I don't try to imitate your stance as a teacher quite so literally anymore, every time I write a syllabus I hear your voice reminding me of *both* my roles: as student ally and as standard-bearer. As I begin my fourth year of teaching, I am still searching for a relationship with students that is more honest.

Rob

And that is unquestionably where you have been my example: in cultivating a greater sensitivity to students as people. That statement might sound silly, too much like a tribute from a Hallmark card. But it really is the simplest way of expressing how your very genuine belief in every student's potential has tempered my no-mercy pedagogies. I remember the days, during my first couple of semesters in the classroom, when green ink was the emblem of my attention to students' "needs." I remember one poor fellow in particular, a Vietnam veteran in his late forties who was pursuing a degree under a special tuition waiver program offered by the university and the Department of Veterans' Affairs. He was very intelligent and, I thought, determined to use college as a gateway to a more stable economic condition. But in those days before everyone used a computer, the essays he typed for my EN 101 class were consistently flawed by one problem: To save his life, the man could not spell, even the commonest of words. Midway through the semester, after having noted the problem several times, I actually returned a six-page essay to him with 127 spelling errors all circled in green and with a single comment printed in fat green magic marker across the top of the first page, *"BUY A DICTIONARY! F."* He was badly shaken by that comment, by the judgment of him that it implied. After lunch, he showed up at my office to announce that he was, despite my opinion of his essays, working very hard to improve, and to ask—in a not altogether conciliatory manner—what the problem was, why I was being so harsh with him, what he could do to get along better in the class. For a moment I thought he might punch me, but he didn't, and summoning all my courage, I said firmly: *"I've already told you what you can do. You can buy a dictionary and learn to use it. "* He submitted a drop form that afternoon.

In retrospect, of course, I realize that this man probably had a common learning disability, one a little patience on my part and some help from a learning resources professional could have helped him begin to manage. He was one of a dozen or so casualties I can recall by name from those early years, when I had a much more difficult time admitting the basic humanness of the people lined up in rows in my classrooms. In all honesty, there was no meanness in my motives, no relish for exercising a newfound power to flunk those who couldn't cut it. And my manner in those days is more than just testimony to the fact that new TAs, perhaps especially those as zealous in their work as I was, need better supervision. It's a classic example of asserting my own work ethic as the universal by which all my students must succeed or fail, to the point of allowing that narrowness to obscure my ability to appreciate the difference between effort and ability and to view teaching as more than directing and evaluating. The man couldn't spell, so from my perspective his situation was very simple: He could take the initiative and correct the serious deficiency I had pointed out, or he could not expect to earn credit for the course. I hoped he would choose the former route, but I could not, and did not, feel it was my responsibility to do more than express his options. It is painful for me to remember having felt that way.

It's true what you say about that weird balance I've evolved for myself as a teacher since then. I'm more generous with my students now—not less demanding, just more forgiving as they stumble here and there. Because of my assumption that college is a developmental experience, one chosen for its accumulative value, I work very hard to deal with students as people who have made certain choices—to attend college, to select a major that would lead them to enroll in my class—and who must, as reasonable people participating in an elective experience, expect to be challenged in such a way that their effort can result in growth. An explicit statement to this effect appears on every syllabus that I generate. Interestingly, although the change began before, it has become increasingly pronounced in the four years I have been teaching at Virginia Military Institute (VMI), where so many of the students have backgrounds similar to mine and whose dreams are just as big. Among our peer institutions in this very status-conscious state, VMI is known as a "blue-collar" school, one that prides itself on taking fairly average young men (and beginning next year, women) and developing them—mind, body, and, most important, soul. Our graduates' remarkable success is attributed to the place's motto, which is inscribed over the main entrance into the barracks: Stonewall Jackson's apocryphal statement, "You may be whatever you resolve to be." Cadets are so inundated with variations of this theme that they can get virtually drunk on it over the course of four years, and even though it occasionally leads to an ugly kind of arrogance, it is one of the ideals of the place that I endorse unequivocally. I like the concept because, as I continually remind my classes, it places primary responsibility on them, implicating their entire educational experience in their ability to make themselves into whatever they can dream. Every class I teach heightens my awareness of my role in enabling my students' "resolutions," and sometimes helping them to refine them, even as I continue to hold them to what I see as appropriate standards.

Christina

I have seen evidence of the transformation you describe in all the materials you generate for your classes, and in the countless times we've talked about this, me wondering what I could do to enjoy the same kind of comfort, we have agreed that I just needed to give myself more time.

But now I'm convinced that our evolutions as teachers will not be the same. I cannot experience the richness of the relationships you have discovered with students who come from social and economic backgrounds that are similar to yours. I have taught students from upper-class backgrounds; most of the students I had as a teaching assistant came from lives nearly identical to mine. But I cannot draw on my life or myself as a source of insight into, or connection with, my students then or now because much of my energy is devoted to trying very hard to protect all that is personal. Despite my desire to define it differently, my part in the teacher-student equation is strictly professional. And I'm afraid that I come honestly by the rather formal, comfortably distanced relationship I form with students.

I was raised in a family of extremely private people—people who cultivate, and are most comfortable with, their public selves. I would be oversimplifying the matter if I said that the source of the need to project a controlled, capable public image was the desire to protect our family's good standing in business and social circles, though certainly this concern was part of it. But the need comes from a much more complicated place, one that has little to do with the upper-class life I've known. It is the paradoxical result, I believe, of my father's decidedly working-class roots.

At the age of twelve, he went to work to help support his mother and his two sisters when his father, an abusive alcoholic, began periodically disappearing to go on three- and four-month partying binges. There's little evidence, apart from a very few photographs and a fragmented story or two, of the life he spent growing up all over the South: Nashville, Tuscaloosa, Jacksonville, and other places that either I can't recall or have never been told about. Mostly, my father lives in the present moment, enjoying the upper-class life he began to build, as far as I can tell, when he married my mother. They met at an embassy party in Caracas, Venezuela. My father was working for the CIA and my mother was the daughter of a wealthy American family in the tobacco industry. I know little about how they went about making their life together once they were married. I have always assumed that the life they have now is the result of my mother's inheritance and my father's determination to create a better life for his own family than he had ever known.

But the history of our family is very sketchy. I'm not at all sure that my father would describe the events of his life the way I have here. I don't know for sure because the guiding principle in my family always has been never to reveal your weaknesses. For my father, his working-class background and his lack of formal education were weaknesses that would have jeopardized the opportunity he had to build the life and the business career that he envisioned. Growing up in a family where appearances were so highly valued, I came to understand the public guise as a way to conceal more than just your weaknesses; it was a way to protect yourself. After all, concealing the truth about my background has helped me move successfully in worlds, including academia, where people otherwise would have considered me an outsider. Consequently, I have kept all but a handful of people in my life at a comfortable distance. But since I began teaching, my private impulse to hold people at arm's length has come into conflict with my professional desire to give my best to students.

I have always wanted to be the kind of teacher that I admired during my own college career—the kind of teacher who cultivated learning environments in which both the academic and the personal had a place. I benefited from the interplay between literary ideas and individual experiences in classroom discussions so much, in fact, that I boldly suggested to one of my favorite professors that he allow for more spontaneous conversation, rather than more structured, facilitated discussions. Some of his most inspired moments as a teacher, I argued, occurred when he was willing to surrender his particular goals for the class meeting. In short, I told him he ought to come to class unprepared more often. In his own respectful, good-humored way, he tried to explain the tremendous risk I was asking him to take. He had a professional obligation to meet: Students expected him to teach them something. But more important, he couldn't walk into a classroom of twenty people, all looking to him for direction, with nothing to say. I understood his concerns, of course, but not nearly with as much insight as I am able to now. Each in our own way, we were trying to communicate the same lesson: Every day that we walk into the classroom, good teaching

results from the difficult, but perhaps necessary, mix of professional and personal risk.

Rob

I've watched you struggle with that battle almost since we met, and I
have to say it is one of the things about you that I understand intellectually—particularly now, after having talked about it relative to
your upbringing—but that I can't, somehow, accept as the inevitable
state of affairs for your life in the profession. I have told you before
about the physical change I can see come over you in almost any
kind of professional environment, especially those where you don't
know many of the people there, like a conference, or, I imagine, the
first day of a class—the unnaturally smooth movement, stiff posture,
scared smile. But this "public guise," as you call it, nowhere near
indicates the person that I know who got into teaching for a simple
reason, because you find *giving* a natural and rewarding condition.
Despite the legitimate business about being a woman and needing to
prove that you were capable of something other than life as a clubby
socialite, I can't figure out why all your accomplishments, so relatively early on, haven't permitted you the confidence to quit worrying
that students (or colleagues, for that matter) will sense some "weak-
ness" if they see you with your guard down.

I don't mean to suggest that I have never felt similarly conflicted on
the issue of persona, of course. Really, drawing that boundary between
my life in academia and the one where I was raised was a more complicated and awkward, and ultimately less successful, enterprise than I
think I indicated here. The problem is best expressed, perhaps, as a
matter of posture and taste. Not so much as an undergraduate, but by
the time I began my M.A. program, I began to emulate those who had
obviously achieved the life I wanted. I remember noticing that my
favorite professor, a native North Carolinian who had gone to UNC-
Chapel Hill, spoke with no accent whatsoever, and soon I was making
every public sentence I uttered an exercise in elocution, with particular
emphasis on filling out my -*ings* and not letting words like *pen* collapse
into *pin*. I started drinking tea—hot tea, that is—one day when that
same professor offered me a cup during a conference in his grandly lit,
book- and plant-filled office. I heard people talking about *Harper's*,
and so I tapped my small TA stipend to subscribe. The list goes on
and on, literally. It's not that I was being ingenuine, I think, just observing and sampling various models that the environment told me were
appropriate to my chosen profession and the life I thought it entailed.

The whole while, though, in my most perfectly honest moments, I
realized that academic culture was just plain at odds with most of

what I felt easy with. While traces of a distinct Southern accent remained, I grew quite adept at sounding like the highly literate people around me; the time a woman asked me if I came from the Midwest, I actually considered it a compliment. Away from academic crowds, or on ever more precious trips home, however, I felt as though someone had taken an overly tight belt off my speech as I let myself relax into saying, "Yes, I'd like some *ahse* [that's *ice*] in my tea!" I read *Harper's* because I enjoyed it, but I also liked the pedestrian *Time*. And while I was studying and enjoying the rarified worlds of Edith Wharton, Henry James, and even Kate Chopin, leisure reading led me to discover the Depression-era fiction of Erskine Caldwell, who wrote about a dehumanized and often depraved people not altogether unlike those I knew who lived in the rundown farmworkers' settlements all over my home county. Caldwell wrote about these people in a blunt, often brutally revealing way, unlike anything I had ever encountered, and I was brimming with enthusiasm to talk about the peculiar nature of his achievement. When I proposed both my M.A. thesis and Ph.D. dissertation on him, though, some faculty called the prospect "quaint," while others—privately, probably all of them, even those who served as my readers—balked and wondered if someone like Faulkner might not be a more appropriate subject for academic study. I resisted the advice to select something more conventionally academic, more acceptably canonical, and in fact wrote a dissertation about why Caldwell had nearly always been an outsider in discussions of Literature. Suddenly he wasn't just a writer I found interesting; he was someone I could sympathize with. I hadn't intended anything revolutionary, but it somehow became that, at least in my own mind.

Over time, I have gotten very comfortable with a persona, if you want to call it that, that incorporates and permits the expression of all the experiences that have contributed to my making. People have told me that my office is a particularly revealing example of this. Come there and you will find the space of what must look to some like the quarters of an academic schizophrenic: brilliantly colored posters of paintings by Matisse and Childe Hassam sharing the walls with autographed eight-by-ten photographs of Loretta Lynn and Buddy Ebsen (dressed as Jed Clampett); postcards from students who have gone to study at Oxford or in Scotland hanging on a board near a flyer for the 1st International Elvis Conference; public radio playing music that I love in the background throughout the day but that I publicly admit no interest in taking home with me. None of these is a more legitimate expression of who I am and what I appreciate than the other, and the days when I might feel the need to apologize for or explain any of it away have long since passed. (I still remember being a little unnerved when I told one of my professors that I was going to present part of my dissertation research at a popular culture conference. "*Popular culture*," he asked with a smirk. "Isn't that an oxymoron?") My colleagues are mostly amused by the colleague they hired in me, although I suspect that a handful might wonder about the wisdom of that decision. What I am trying to say is that I have somehow—maybe just by simple assertion—reached a comfort level in academia that has let this life feel more natural than I ever expected it might, and I think this has made me a better teacher. There is no pretense in my relationship with my students; we deal openly and bluntly on all points. Really, how could it be otherwise, with Jed Clampett hanging over my desk?

Christina

Your office is truly a menagerie. As your students marvel at the complexity of the contradictions that line your walls and bookshelves, my students seize whatever small opportunities there are in my office to discover something about me. They sometimes ask about the only two photographs that are on my desk: one of our dog, Gatsby, and the other one of us taken on our first Thanksgiving together. Other times, people in the department glance casually (and often furtively) around my office as if they're looking for clues. Recently, I accidentally left my keys sitting out on my desk and my department head, who had stopped in to talk about political wranglings in General Education, inquired about the Mercedes key ring I carry. Feeling unusually bold, I told him the truth: that I owned both the key ring *and* the car, and with that statement I stepped out of the "class closet" for the first time in my department. I was as surprised by the question as I was by my own honesty in answering.

Intentionally or unintentionally, my public guise as you described it—the stiff posture, the scared smile—usually prevents most personal inquiries. Though I think I'm concealing all signs of my "other life" by consciously tucking the key chain inside my desk drawer, or by wearing simple jewelry, or by dressing modestly, it is my formal demeanor, not my appearance, that helps keep my secret. My external disguise simply isn't as good as my often subconscious internal defense. Only on this occasion, my split-second decision to override my protective impulse and to test the truth on my colleague was the result of my growing need to reclaim a significant part of myself—the part cultivated by my family. Ever since we met, you have been trying to coax that side of me back into the present because, I guess, of your evolving belief in being honest about where you've come from and letting that figure into, not constrain, your life now. I have been able to share that aspect of myself with our friends and, as a result, have become increasingly frustrated by the sense that I must tuck it away again whenever I walk into the office.

Still, revealing my upper-class background openly is risky—riskier, I believe, than for those who reveal their working-class histories. As the essays in this collection demonstrate, what we have in common, regardless of where we come from, is that we all have suffered from a relative silence about the class issues that have divided our lives. But as we begin to talk about our personal histories, we must think carefully about the ways in which our stories might be received. Let's face it, the quintessential success stories in our culture are of those people who have climbed *up* the economic/social class ladder, not down. That I would choose a middle-class life and salary over an upper-class life supported by family money might earn some people's respect. But it is also just as likely to prompt others to resent me. After all, academia is no longer populated by the elite, privileged class. Today's middle-class academics exercise a similar kind of control over the profession (which succeeds in making individuals from working-class backgrounds feel unwelcome unless they adapt to the ways of "academic culture") but they no longer enjoy the luxury of upper-class status in society. The social, material, and financial resources that I retain through my family are available to only a very few in our profession.

As a result, whether we're trying to move up the ladder or down, we all feel the need to adapt to what we perceive are the ways of the middle-class in academia. Whereas you felt the need to adopt the language and interests of those in the profession, I was most aware of my need to adjust to the different protocols of the academic world. I knew how to operate within the professional world of business from watching my father, but none of the same rules seemed to apply in academia. For instance, the dress code was different. I learned this lesson the first time you asked me to teach one of your classes while you were away at a conference. When I arrived in the department, dressed professionally, I thought, another TA took one look at me and laughingly remarked that the outfit I was wearing made me look like a designer purse. Humiliated, I quickly abandoned the business world's "power suit" and went searching for more middle-of-the-road fashion, what I have come to call my "teaching clothes."

The more I adapted to "academic culture," the more I began to reject openly what I perceived to be the values of people at home. I began referring to my hometown on the southwest coast of Florida as "the land of the beautiful people," where everyone has deeply tanned and tightly toned bodies, lives in houses with perfectly manicured lawns, and drives sparkling-clean, expensive automobiles with moon roofs. When I arrived home for Christmas that first year, I felt more strongly than ever before that I didn't fit in. Tired and pale from too many hours spent in front of a blue computer screen, I looked like a hard-working graduate student, not like the active, athletic person I had been throughout high school and college. Strangely, I wasn't upset by the difference because I had always quietly felt as if I belonged elsewhere, in a culture that valued less physical, less material things. As an academic, I thought I could assume a more comfortable, less self-conscious existence. The same standard is applied in academia, though, even if it is defined differently.

Despite my best efforts to adopt the ways of academic culture, I constantly stood out. I was in a state of limbo, floating between two worlds without feeling as if I really belonged in either. I was no longer like the people I'd grown up with; I didn't care about the same things, aspire to the same lifestyle, or feel good about myself in their world. But I was not like the other graduate students either; I didn't live like them, dress like them, or understand my students or the classroom as they did. I remember explaining my confusion in a letter to one of my most supportive undergraduate professors, trying to find out if there was any hope of integrating myself into either of these two worlds. His advice, in this instance, was simple: My parents, like his, would never fully understand why I chose this career, so I shouldn't expect them to; and even if my background separated me from my colleagues in the profession, perhaps my difference in perspective was one of the best things I had to offer to my students.

I had forgotten his advice until now.

Works Cited

Thoreau, H. D. [1854] 1971. *Walden*. Princeton: Princeton University Press.

10

Seeing Different
A Reflection on Narrative and Talk About Social Class

John McMillan

I

Not long ago, I read a short paper at a CCCCs workshop on class (McMillan 1997). What I tried to convey in that little essay was that our conceptions of our own social class are, at least in part, the by-products of the stories we tell ourselves about where we come from. Not only of the places in which we lived and worked, but also of that collective body of the experiences and interpretations by which we know our people. I said it this way:

> There are silos in the suburbs. There are church pews from tiny Pennsylvania Baptist churches in the office buildings of the city. Pre-dawn milkings and prayer meetings give shape to our days. . . . There are silos in the suburbs; they're in my classroom too.

This essay is an attempt to extend this notion a bit further.

I'd like to begin to consider the implications of the idea that story, richly defined, is central not only to the construction of our class identities, but that it is central to all epistemological activity. More specifically, I'd like to consider how the function of story or narrative in the construction of one's class identity might serve as a model for the consideration of the function of story in epistemology more generally.

My interest in this idea stems from my concern that conventional educational practice, in the words of Grant Wiggins (1993), often risks "letting students believe that authoritative answers matter more than inquiry," resulting in a situation where "we may well end up convincing students that 'knowledge' is something other than the result of personal inquiries built upon questions such as theirs" (43–44). My hope is that a reconception of the role of story or narrative in epistemology might help reduce this risk, that it might assist us as teachers in our efforts to help students become more critical, and creative, readers and writers.

II

In his essay "The Teaching of Science as Enquiry" Joseph Schwab (1962) criticizes what he calls the "rhetoric of conclusions," where

> the current and temporary constructions of scientific knowledge are conveyed as empirical, literal, and irrevocable . . . which imposes this false impression of literal and irrevocable truth us[ing] a variety of devices. With respect to the initiating phase of inquiry, the invention of guiding principles, the commonest device is massive silence. (25)

Schwab adds that "Almost as common as massive silence is the device of converting principles from conceptual to existential status. Sometimes, they are flatly treated as factual, as when Mendel is said to have *discovered* the gene or Bernard to have *discovered* homeostasis" (25).

Read Schwab's remarks through Mary Paumier Jones's notion that "narrative [can be] seen as the usual way stories are told, metaphor as a little story about how something unknown is like something known, and theory as a kind of story or paradigm to explain what is generalizable and universal about the historical and particular phenomena we observe" (657), and I think we've got the makings of a pretty good explanation for what's *not* happening in schools today. It's an authority problem: Answers are derived from certain authoritative sources. Classrooms are set up to protect certain kinds of authority. Knowledge is disconnected from personal inquiry. The stories that are theory and methodology and metaphor are converted, as Schwab said, "from conceptual to existential status."

This kind of practice has everything to do with talk about class. Talk about class has everything to do with changing this kind of practice.

I suspect that one of the reasons we haven't until recently talked about class much in the academy is because it is difficult, if not impossible, to be abstract about it. To talk about our own social class is to tell stories, so that it becomes apparent that the two are inseparable—no stories, no class talk. This makes me apprehensive about the sort of posturing that prevents us from talking about something as central to our lives as our social class. It makes me want to give serious attention to questions I have seldom, if ever, heard raised in my academic career, questions such as "Why do we read stories?" "Why do we ask students to write narratives?" "What is it that leads us to value exposition over narration?"

I suspect that we have often treated narrative, in the writing classroom at least, in a sort of mindless manner. We ask students to write narratives early in a semester in order to get them writing so that we can move on to more "serious" expository endeavors. We either imply or directly state that narrative is "natural" or "easy" or "not serious." Because we aren't sure why narratives are important, not in any holistic and practical sense anyway, we fail to ask questions about the need for stories, those we deem "literature" as well as those by which we know ourselves. We fail to explain to students, and perhaps to ourselves, why stories are imperative for our own survival, for the survival of cultures, for the survival of the land. In this failure, we belittle narrative form. The fact that we so casually use narrative as "set up" for the "more serious" business of argumentative analytical prose seems to me to be evidence of this bias. We write narratives so that we can leave them behind in the name of more "important" work.

But stories are the important work, and I contend that class talk may offer us a fresh way to think about all this. For example, to speak casually about class as a sort of distinguishable attribute of ourselves is to ignore the ambiguity and slipperiness of class. When you talk about class, you are rendering and weaving together narratives—you are telling stories. You are labeling and placing yourself alongside other similar stories. In many ways it's a matching game. I know my social class by and through the stories I know, tell, and have been told. It is a process of definition that deals in specifics and episodes; its currency is particulars.

Hence, it seems to me that implicit within any request or attempt to write narratives is the belief that the experience that one is rendering can be alternately rendered in a number of other ways (Bruner 1994, 36). This would mean that the story or stories I respond with when my colleague asks me about my own social class are merely one telling. And it is a telling that, at least momentarily, "fits" with other tales I might have also told. In this way then my social class, as I know it, is the product of particular tellings that fit within a number of master narratives by which I view my life. And while I might have many master narratives jockeying about for positions (what Jim Corder [1985] has called "contending narratives"), what remains the same is this sort-of process, a kind of jigsaw puzzle in which stories are determined as "worth telling" according to how they fit with the narrative that happens to be foremost in my mind at that time. Another way: It is a group dance of some sort. And how I step and twirl, and how others step and twirl, determines whose hand I touch, determines what I tell and how I tell it, determines what difference the telling makes.

Puzzle Pieces and Pirouettes: An Interlude

It was lying there on the east side of the barn. I had to fall against the corrugated barn siding to pick it up. It had been there a long time: Grip, lift, fall against the barn, heave. It was red. There was a blue one not much further away, but its engine was missing as were most of its other components—brake levers, seat, kickstand. I liked the color blue better. When we added oil and gas, lubed up the chain, replaced the spark plug, and put air in the tires, my dad gave it a kick and it started. I remember riding all over my grandparents' lot, from the edge of the fields out back to the road west of the house, blowing oil all over the place, marking my path like Hansel and Gretel in the forest. But it ran. When we loaded it up in the back of our blue Oldsmobile station wagon to take it back to my home in New York, we laid plastic down, wrapped it up like in a cocoon.

It had a short life in the city. For while it ran strong at my grandparents' farm, I have no memory of it in my neighborhood. It took a couple more years of pitching papers—and a violation of my mother's wishes—to acquire the next one. It cost three hundred dollars; I bought it from my best friend when I was a freshman in high school. I rode it last summer, twelve years after the purchase, at my folks' new old house in the country. It sits in their barn next to the woodpile. An oil leak here, a stripped bolt there; the same hand that breaks it, fixes it; getting broken and getting fixed.

My father was raised on a farm in Ohio; my mother was the oldest daughter of a Baptist minister who, over the course of her growing up, pastored congregations in rural parts of New York, Pennsylvania, and Ohio—places called Black Creek, Wellsville, Pavillion.

From what I can make of it, it went like this: When my father graduated from high school, he wanted to go to college. No one else in the family had ever considered such a thing. A few of them were even opposed to it. He enrolled at Ohio State in Columbus, paid his way working as an R.A. during semesters and by raking asphalt in the summers. Got a job at Kodak upon graduation. They funded his MBA. I know less about my mother. The oldest daughter in a family of seven children, after a year of business school in Olean, New York, she went to work as a secretary at Kodak. They met and married; I was born three years later.

I grew up in a suburb in upstate New York. I lived in the same house until I left for college. When my brother was born, rather than moving to a bigger house, my parents decided to add on. With the help of relatives (my mother's father built a fieldstone fireplace in the new addition, peppering it with "stones from the holy land," I was told, gathered from a recent trip), they built the addition off the back and cut out of the attic a room for my sister. My brother moved into her old room, downstairs, next to mine.

I started delivering penny papers door to door when I was eleven. You could work that young if you had a permit, signed by your parents. I graduated to the city paper a couple of years later and remember something of the excitement I had at the prospects of a real job where I collected money and got Christmas tips, where someone actually read what I was delivering. Eventually I passed the route off to my little brother. Later, in high school, I could be found working at the local pizza joint six days a week.

I went to a private college in Texas. It was cheaper than going to a private school in the Northeast. My parents paid. The summer before my sophomore year I bought a car, a new Honda Civic. I took a loan out from my folks and paid them back before I graduated. I didn't really need to, I guess, but I worked during school as well, minimum-wage stuff mostly—an after-school daycare job, a stint as a tutor. For a while, I tried to live off of my earnings. It didn't work out so well. I ended up calling home and while my parents wondered why I hadn't asked earlier, those calls made me kind of uneasy.

If you were to ask me about my own social class, you would hear in reply some variation of these stories. You would witness a compilation, from which you could, perhaps, formulate an explanation, spin out a theory about my class status; but for the efficiency of your hypothesis you would blur my edge—you would be messing with my shape. For it could be said that when we speak of our social class, and when we speak of our social class influencing our teaching, we are crafting distinct shapes; we are stacking narratives upon narratives. And these shapes, over time, become familiar to me. And I know myself by these shapes and, as I mentioned before, when I see similar shapes in books, in speeches, in other stories, I gravitate toward these. In fact, I ache for them, like I ached for home when I was nineteen and two thousand miles from anything familiar. Sometimes I wonder if what we absolutely hold in common is that we are all storytellers—that when we are faced with questions about our social class we turn to stories of a farm, a job, a school, a parent, a house. We are all of us also listeners. We all need a place.

But if we all have a need to be "placed," albeit ever so briefly, in terms of class, we also need this kind of placing in other "areas" as well—areas such as ethnicity, gender, sexuality. How do these identities "mean"? How do we know ourselves according to these terms?

It seems useful to say that they have been "unstoried." The fact that "whiteness" remains a largely uninterrogated construct is a prime example of this. My contention is that class talk can help us begin to "restory" some of these places, by forcing us to see their constructed-ness. And this process of "restorying" is an invitation to converse, to think critically, and to inquire.

What better way to begin to rethink the place of stories than to talk about things that inevitably force you to deal in specific inci-dents and their renderings? What better way to begin to rethink the importance of narrative than to confront a construct such as class—a construct that plays a paramount role in determining our beliefs, our actions, our selves—that forces you to deal in specifics, that prevents detachment, that shatters illusions of the possibility of authoritative naming?

Class is a reality, like race is a reality. Classism is a reality, like racism is a reality. People can be reductive, mindless, and cruel, and I wonder if this is largely because we're in such a hurry to be some-where else that we forget to be where we are (we love our abstractions because they make us go fast?). And thus beginneth the stories of selves and others, of success and standards, of damnations and salva-tions. We are alchemists conjuring up realities, and these realities have real implications. The most negative of these implications grow from what is perhaps our most powerful story, the one that tells that some of our stories are not stories, that some of our constructs are not constructs, that some knowledge is free of human touch, fitting per-fectly in the lap of language. And when this story gets enough assent, we come to see in a new way. Rose-colored glasses. Power to the particular people. Eradicate all signs in the name of grand designs.

III

I am trying to think about the relationship between narrative and social class. I have suggested that we only know our social class by the stories we tell ourselves about ourselves and about our families, our places, our jobs, and so on. But on some level this seems like an unnecessary thing to say, if only because it seems appropriate to say that all knowledge of ourselves is the stories we tell ourselves about ourselves. So what's the point?

One point is that "dominant" cultural values (we often attempt to designate these values when we say that they grow from a "white," "male," and "middle-class" agenda) are open to critique. Let me illus-trate: It has been said[1] that in the West we have a habit of (1) being busy; (2) living in the future at the expense of living in the present; (3) constructing dualities, such as asserting, and pitting, the mind versus the body. We arrive at a place where we can critique these habits only when we can see them. And, as one who has arguably grown up "white," "male," and "middle class" in America, the only way I have a chance at seeing the stories that have defined my life *as* stories is to expose myself to other people's stories.

The question is, how do we begin to make arguments on behalf of communities and cultures that do not enjoy the kinds of access to power that certain other communities and cultures have in our society? And how does one keep a desire for those "other" people's access distinct from, thereby avoiding the veneration and replication of, the values those "other" cultures adhere to? Consider these remarks by James Baldwin (1962):

> How can one respect, let alone adopt, the values of a people who do not, on any level whatever, live the way they say they do, or the way they say they should? I cannot accept that the four-hundred-year tra-vail of the American Negro should result in his attainment of the present level of the American civilization. I am far from convinced that being released from the African witch doctor was worthwhile if I am now—in order to support the moral contradiction and the spir-itual aridity of my life—expected to become dependent on the American psychiatrist. It is a bargain I refuse. The only thing white people have that black people need, or should want, is power—and no one holds power forever. White people cannot, in the generality, be taken as models of how to live. Rather, the white man is himself in sore need of new standards. (129–130)

At the most recent CCCCs meeting, I was struck by a certain kind of prejudice that I found particularly troubling. When it was time for comments and questions at a session pertaining to issues of social class, one audience member pointed out that while we need to talk about issues specific to the working class, it is perhaps just as important to remember to think more broadly about the effects that any class experience has on an individual in the academy. He pro-ceeded to tell a story of a particular student he once worked with. This student was very wealthy, and was acutely aware of "not fit-ting" in an academic world imbued with other values. The student went out of the way to efface, though unsuccessfully, her class roots, so that she might exist more comfortably in that different kind of class environment that is the academy.

At that point in the tale where he mentioned the acute dis-ease and even embarrassment that student felt in regards to her class ori-gins, a mock pity erupted around the room. We laughed at the dis-comfort of the rich kid. I wonder why.

It seems to me that implicit within that ripple of snickering were certain beliefs about class, specifically, here, the "upper class." And I wonder if our snickering didn't belie a certain kind of envy—a certain kind of illusion. It goes something like this: We envy their cash, while despising their souls. Rich people deserve no pity, because their wealth gives them power, gives them access to vacations and therapy and BMWs and . . . But while cash does enable such things, I wonder if it doesn't also induce certain kinds of blindness, as Jesus was perhaps suggesting in his story of the rich man, the camel, and the needle. I think this is close to what Baldwin was getting at. Let's listen to him again, this time a clip from his letter to his nephew, also James, "My Dungeon Shook":

> Please try to be clear, dear James, through the storm which rages about your youthful head today, about the reality that lies behind the words *acceptance* and *integration*. There is not reason for you to try to become like white people and there is no basis whatever for their impertinent assumption that *they* must accept *you*. The really terrible thing, old buddy, is that *you* must accept *them*. And I mean that very seriously. You must accept them and accept them with love. For these innocent people have no other hope. They are, in effect, still trapped in a history which they do not understand; and until they understand it, they cannot be released from it. (19)

Baldwin is sensitive to the previously mentioned paradox. For does he not imply that on some level the "powerful" are to be pitied; and that unless the "powerless" can transform their anger into a certain kind of acceptance, "with love," the "powerless" risk adopting the self-destructive habits and desires of the "powerful"? But I contend that if we can stand to listen, in the manner that the Zen master Thich Nhat Hanh suggests that we listen to our anger[2], our snickering can begin to save us. For, as Baldwin suggests, prejudice in any form imprisons and oppresses the racist or the sexist or the classist perhaps in even deeper ways than those they lash out against.

bell hooks (1994) writes that

> Progressive, holistic education, "engaged pedagogy" is more demanding than conventional critical or feminist pedagogy. For, unlike these two teaching practices, it emphasizes well-being. That means that teachers must be actively committed to a process of self-actualization that promotes their own well-being if they are to teach in a manner that empowers students. (15)

With hooks' definition of pedagogy in mind, the question "How do we liberate the oppressed?" becomes synonymous with "How do we liberate everyone?" In this way, the issue of how to make arguments on behalf of those who do not have access to certain important kinds of power is inspired by the desire to work for the liberation, the "self-actualization(?)" of *all*.

IV

In conclusion, I'd like to offer up three contentions in an effort to summarize and focus the ideas in this paper so that their usefulness might be more easily considered.

Contention #1: Class talk is overtly "storied." Wayne Booth (1996) has suggested recently that authoritative discourse derives its power from its ability to collapse "narrative audience" and "authorial audience."[3]; that is, it could be said that its status as "authoritative" comes from its ability to unstory itself, its erasing and effacing of the personal narratives that precede it. I want to say that class talk resists this erasing—which is precisely why I like class talk. It feels more honest. The personal narratives of class are written in permanent ink. To unstory class is to cease to talk about class.

Contention #2: Class talk is not unique in its being "storied." All knowledge is "storied," it's just that we can't always see that.

Contention #3: Class talk, heavily storied as it is, has the potential to teach us how to consider the storiedness of other constructs—such as race, ethnicity, and gender, for example. Using class talk as a model, perhaps we can begin to see more easily the "storiedness" or "constructedness" of other aspects of our identities. For to see these aspects as constructions is the first step toward inquiry and rerendering, those practices that are central to any resistance against that kind of authoritativeness that sustains those "isms" that wreak havoc on all of us.

We need to generate practices and pedagogies of reading and writing that guard against the promotion of the kinds of authoritativeness that prevent inquiry into the construction of identities, methodologies, and principles. By using it as an example of the way in which it might be said that knowledge is "storied," I think class talk can help us begin to do this.

Notes

1. A few of the places I have encountered such critiques are the writings of Thich Nhat Hanh (1991) and Kathleen Norris (1993, 1996). Both write from contemplative traditions: Hanh, from Zen Buddhism; Norris, from her participation in the Benedictine monastic tradition.

2. In his essay "Mindfulness of Anger" in *Peace Is Every Step*, Hanh (1991) employs the analogy of an organic gardener. He says, "We need the insight and non-dual vision of the organic gardener with regard to our anger. We need not be afraid of it or reject it. . . . We need anger in the way the organic gardener needs compost." Hanh says that we need to "observe" and "accept" our anger; my suggestion that we "listen to our anger" is intended in the spirit of this advice.

3. Booth says that the "authorial audience is a constructed 'person' who is in a sense extracted from the flesh-and-blood person, someone who is sufficiently sophisticated to savor the complexity of half joining, or becoming, a narrative audience taking the events as real occurrences" (249). He says that in what he calls "an orthodox interpretive tradition," we are "trained to believe in the literal and unchanging truth of the stories [the Bible tells]. In short, there was a certainty that there was no essential difference between the narrative audience and the authorial audience" (238).

Works Cited

Baldwin, J. 1962. *The Fire Next Time.* New York: Laurel.

Booth, W. 1996. "Where Is the Authorial Audience in Biblical Narrative—and in Other 'Authoritative' Texts?" *Narrative* 4: 235–253.

Bruner, J. 1994. "Life as Narrative." In *The Need for Story*, ed. A. Haas Dyson and C. Genishi, 28–37. Urbana, IL: National Council of Teachers of English.

Corder, J. 1985. "Argument as Emergence, Rhetoric as Love." *Rhetoric Review* 4: 16–32.

Hahn, N. 1991. *Peace Is Every Step: The Path of Mindfulness in Everyday Life.* New York: Bantam.

hooks, b. 1994. *Teaching to Transgress: Education as the Practice of Freedom.* New York and London: Routledge.

Jones, M. P. 1996. "The Storytelling Animal." *The Georgia Review* 50: 649–666.

McMillan, J. 1997. "Silos in the Suburbs." *Journal of Basic Writing* 16(1).

Norris, K. 1996. *The Cloister Walk.* New York: Riverdale.

———. 1993. *Dakota.* Boston: Houghton Mifflin.

Schwab, J. J. 1962. "The Teaching of Science as Enquiry." In *The Teaching of Science*, 1–104. Cambridge, MA: Harvard University Press.

Wiggins, G. 1993. *Assessing Student Performance: Exploring the Purpose and Limits of Testing.* San Francisco: Jossey-Bass.

11

Color and Class

Cecilia Rodríguez Milanés

For Academics Like Us
. . .
It is fascinating to see the ways erasure of the body connects
to the erasure of class differences, and more importantly, the
erasure of the role of university settings as sites for the
reproduction of a privileged class of values, of elitism.

—bell hooks

Inescapable Markers

The experience of growing up in a blue-collar, ethnic, and urban
neighborhood continues shaping my world view because contact with
and affinity for cultures, languages, and ethnicities guides my pedagogy, my research, my critical and creative writing.[1] There is not a
single aspect of my work that isn't influenced by class or color; the
ramifications of gender are as conspicuous but it is important to note
that these three are not equally divisible denominators.[2] How my
color, gender, or class status are interpreted varies with the inter-
preters—the beholder betrays his expectations and assumptions in his
"othering" of me as a woman. In fact, by the end of my first year as a
full-time tenure-track academic, I wrote "Juggling on an Uneven
Playing Field" (Rodríguez Milanés 1998) to address sexist barriers to
competently satisfying my job's requirements and fulfilling my familial obligations; the entire manuscript remains too dangerous for me to
share with more than a few women.[3] Most of my teaching has been in
a second-tier state school serving a population of more than ninety
percent white, working-class students, the majority of whom have

never met a Latino/a. Situating myself in the classroom and carving out a space for myself in academe require my coming out, narrating myself into existence since so few of us are in tenure-track positions in higher education.[4]

I was born in the United States in 1960 to working-class immigrants (they were exiles, actually—all economic and political conditions leading to an immigration of desperation is an exile). If my parents were European immigrants I might not be contributing to this volume; I might have negotiated my way up and through academia and been more established and assimilated, at the very least, acculturated. But my mother and father came from Cuba, a troublesome thorn in the American government's side and an enigmatic island to most; my parents still speak only in Spanish to me, and their English, used when there is no option, is heavily accented and frequently the cause for North American contempt. If they were of the middle to upper middle class, their accents would be forgiven by America— think of how many foreign-born professors are well ensconced in academia, even when their American-born students find it hard to understand their English. Maybe if my folks had arrived ten years before my birth and better acclimated themselves, our situation would be different; I might have gone away to college (rather than commuting and working), read books for pleasure as a child (not just for homework), channeled my creative energies in constructive ways (instead of vandalism). With more experience, my parents might have made the inroads I am now forging for my daughter; at the very least, she will have more informed options. Unfamiliarity with the culture, non-Anglo ancestry, little to no literacy preparation before schooling, and more were and are circumstances mitigating against acculturation into academia. Working-class people cannot afford to be nonconformists—class status works against differences, but when you are physically and linguistically different from "middle" America, you have more strikes against you; yet many of us rebel anyway, becoming filmmakers, artists, musicians, or writers despite the odds.

I am light-skinned, young, and female. Sometimes it's easier for me to negotiate in society than it is for my brother, who is darker, bearded, and big. Females in mainstream society continue to be viewed and represented as commodities; it's easy to dismiss young women, especially seemingly young white women. As objects, they can be categorized into two groups—those prized and worthy of possession and exploitation because of their beauty (always measured by a Western European or Scandinavian standard) or those unworthy and erasable, always described as undesirable, the unlucky ones, but also to be exploited. My brother is hard to miss; he looks like a threat to most mainstream people, a big brown man is too close connota-

tively to a big black man, a sexual and physical threat. One of the prevailing cultural associations for Latinos includes the Valentino stereotype of the Latin lover and the darker the male, the more the type of
the black stud comes into play so that my brother's body intimidates
much more profoundly than just any big, burly white man would. If
his presence is emphatically visible, so is my presence apt to elicit
erasure or invisibility.

Our family's search for upward mobility resulted in our move into
a small house in a suburb of an upper- to middle-class community. I
was a good student at the academically enhanced high school that all
the "rich kids" attended, and when it came time for sending transcripts
off to college, my guidance counselor was taken aback: "You're going
to college?" I had taken both the PSATs and the SATs, and signed up
for and succeeded in college prep courses, yet he was so genuinely surprised he continued, "Oh, you must be going to *community* college."
This advisor had no expectation that a working-class Latina would
aspire to much more; he never advised me on any matters—academic
or social. The only reason I knew he was assigned to me was because I
had to forge his signature when I doctored the attendance number on
report cards. At that high school, no one had ever informed me about
the college resource room, where university catalogs, brochures, and
scholarship opportunities were available for any student beyond
sophomore year. Even as a naive seventeen-year-old, this experience
taught me that the dominant culture was not obliged to reward academic achievement or merit, especially from my kind. I could be rendered invisible or erasable without much thought. I completed my secondary studies a semester early because I could not stand to be within
the walls of an institution that was so oblivious to me. Think of how
easy it is for disenchanted people to drop out; Latino high school students drop out at the highest rates nationwide—the average is 50 percent. So while I strive to be visible, therein lies another danger, exoti-
cization. If Latinos are Don Juans, Casanovas, or Valentinos, Latinas
have another representation besides the highly sexualized, wildly passionate creature—the meek, primitive, and noble servant. In mainstream circles, my presence evokes a range of troubling responses;
whether seen as a spicy number or erased as an unworthy pretender, I
learned to be myself, with or without makeup, perfume, heels, and
cleavage if I felt like it. In Latino communities, acknowledgment may
come in the form of the *piropo* (a flirtatious gesture or statement meant
and accepted as a celebration of femaleness), which always disarms
and reminds me that while the dominant society inflicts and infects its
designs on us, cultural identity balances and combats these ills.

One of the most transformative lessons I gleaned in graduate
school was the significance of one's class status on the use of and

facility in grammar. My family didn't have books or magazines at home and didn't speak mainstream English, so I couldn't easily replicate or use standard American grammar. It was liberating to learn that I wasn't linguistically retarded. We not only didn't speak standard English, we spoke an unprivileged, despised tongue, Spanish, which about twenty-five million Americans speak. Roseann Dueñas Gonzalez (1996) and others have spoken about the threat some monolingual folks feel facing this growing demographic;[5] and it is ironic that one mark of elite status, the ability to speak several languages, works in reverse for working-class people, who are not entitled to have more than one language. It must only be the master's tongue, jammed into our mouths, suffocating our native tongue. Cut it out and conform, or run for the border. I learned to speak unaccented English.

Coming to work in the academy as a working-class individual means not knowing how to negotiate up front all you need to, so you don't get stuck with the crappy teaching load, unventilated office, lower starting salary, no explanation of the ground rules, or game strategies for surviving your first year. You don't know about grants, fellowships, faculty exchange programs, postdoctoral awards, or seminars because these are perks that insiders don't like to share—especially when you are the competition (and if you happen to be a woman and/or a person of color, you are even more of a threat because of your supposed "entitlements"). If you are a working-class man, you might be privy to some of the "good old boys" knowledge, racquetball breaks, locker-room exchanges, and e-mail confidences; as a working-class woman, I wasn't a country club member, hadn't belonged to any sorority, and wasn't trained to "work" social ties to my advantage. I grasped for infinitesimal, nonconsequential bits of information—getting stationery, office supplies, a filing cabinet, or forms for reimbursement (while the well-informed/prepared, middle-class colleague negotiates a semester off in another country, a quarter release for writing, honorarium for visiting speakers who are friends . . .).

Out of the loop of information and mentoring, working-class people of color are still known to survive, but at what cost? For me it began when I was asked to teach a compressed graduate seminar during the first summer semester in 1991.[6] Like others, I was enticed into the field by the attractiveness of the academic calendar year; my summers off would allow me the freedom to write, relax, research, be with my family. But then I thought, we could use the money (that bottom line informs all decisions for the economically underprivileged), so I agreed. It took six weeks to prepare for it and five weeks to teach it. Because I left town immediately upon turning in my grades, and only because I had already prearranged travel months before, I was spared from the continuous flow of students to my office asking for guidance on exam reading lists and students lining up readers for their dissertations (though prior to the term I had already agreed to serve on two dissertation committees). The following year I was asked to teach in the second summer session, and because students knew I was around during the first part of the summer, I was bombarded with requests. The third summer replicated the pattern of intense preparation,[7] condensed teaching, punctuated by student entreaties and framed by exhaustion. Had I been in the loop of information, perhaps I would not have taken on that first graduate summer course so soon after my first full year of teaching, but economic necessity, and eagerness to participate in graduate education prompted my decision.

Working-class academics struggle against assumptions about our qualifications, confront others who feel we have no right to be in the academy, and are consistently caught up in a battle to prove ourselves worthy, to show our loyalty, never letting our guard down for a second. There are additional pressures, however, related to ethnic affiliation. Burnout is normal for teachers, but scholars of color work under additional constraints that often compel us *not* to say "No." For example, I wonder how many of my mainstream colleagues have loaned out money to students of color? "No" could mean another Latino dropping out of school. How many colleagues have felt compelled to take them into their homes, perhaps feeding, or sheltering, students and/or their children? As advisor to the campus Latino student group, I have done all these things and more. "No" would mean turning my back on cultural values that helped me become the professor.

In working-class families of color, there may be one member who is an academic, perhaps even a financially secure, tenured full professor who is related to someone doing time. One may be an agile public speaker, an esteemed writing instructor, and a dedicated teacher of literacy, but also the child of an illiterate parent. I would argue that the "accomplished" academic of color, even when both parents attended college and perhaps finished college or some postgraduate schooling, still maintains a consciousness about materiality that is based on consistently seeing people of color, our relatives, in servile, demeaning jobs all around. Witnessing the marginalization and often brutalization of our folks on a daily basis (cataloged by even the most mainstream media, even when we're not reading between the lines), has a pronounced way of grounding our professional lives and responsibilities. How can I tell you what it is for me to see students of color, often recipients of some more open access policy in the institution, prove time and time again that, like me, they (1) have to work twice or three times as hard as the "other" students because we have to prove ourselves worthy; (2) become overburdened with obligations related to our "color" status—for example, the need arises for a representative student/faculty of color at this function, on that committee, within task forces, on trouble-shooting panels, and so on; and (3) are under- or overqualified for said position/role—either we come with more preparation or inappropriate preparation and the powers think themselves generous (when "we" really know that this is so "they" can say, "You see, we give those folks of color a chance but they couldn't cut it," or, my favorite, "It's hard to keep good faculty of color at this predominantly white institution because the community is so white").

At my university, for example, the administration expects that a third of its African American first-year students will drop out before the spring term. It is economically advantageous to the university for these students to drop out—they are obligated to sign an academic yearlong contract for housing that is paid up front and is nonrefundable. Even for students who may not be paying for their classes directly out of their pockets because of financial aid (and more than 90 percent of the whole student body receives some form of assistance), college often creates additional hardships for their families of color. Being away at college does not defray the cost of the son not being home working full- or part-time, helping to contribute to the household income, or of the daughter's spending money somewhere else for lodging, food, clothes, or books she wouldn't need at home. If the student is the only fluent speaker of Standard American English, the family loses its translator, the child who helps resolve the family's "paper" problems relating to contact and interaction with government agencies, utility companies, lawyers, bosses, and so on.

If the student of color makes it through undergraduate school and even manages to get a M.A., she finds it impossible to leave a "career" job, often the most recent hire and in a precariously unstable position, to devote all energies toward doctoral work, no matter how promising. Giving up a steady income with benefits for grad school poverty would plunge the student and her family into financial distress, the likes of which higher education was supposed to spare them. But if she makes it, survives grad school, and gets a position in higher education, she must learn to socialize with academic colleagues since lack of networks across the university leads to lack of advocates and allies. She must be able to discern when it is appropriate to ask the question that is received as blunt; tact becomes a plaguing four-letter word. When experiencing discomfort among what she may perceive to be the "refined" but what really is middle- and upper-middle-class privilege and rearing, she becomes obsequious, submissive, and silent (that unruly tongue now tamed). If her colleagues speak in another language, even if it's her own, she refuses to participate in order to give them rein to posture, since they probably would misunderstand her native pronunciation anyway. Their clothes—timeless, expensive garments symbolic of status—trigger awe and envy. Their good skin and teeth (regardless of skin color), make the working-class academic embarrassed and self-conscious—generations of good nutrition and health care will get that for her progeny, too.

Color and class work against my assimilation into academe. I may resist the markers but I cannot escape them. I've come to incorporate discussion of identity into the classroom as necessary for transformative education, a vision that curtails the "othering" of others.

Color and Class Inflected Pedagogy

> When our lived experience of theorizing is fundamentally linked to processes of self-recovery, of collective liberation, no gap exists between theory and practice. (hooks 1994)

When one's social class and color are self-consciously—though critically—acknowledged, teaching is energized by resistance, risk taking, and dialogue.[8] By focussing on narrative and autobiographies of literacy when I teach, I ask students to unravel the facade of education as an equally serving public endeavor.[9] As they tell the stories of how they came to be readers and writers, my questions (in conferencing or commentary on their texts) about family involvement and educational preparation contextualize literacy and academic achievement or lack thereof. I make myself vulnerable in sharing my own literacy narratives, and I have found this sharing to be imperative to education as the practice of freedom. As bell hooks (1994) states:

> When professors bring narratives of their experiences into classroom discussions it eliminates the possibility that we can function as all-knowing, silent interrogators . . . linking confessional narratives to academic discussions so as to show how experience can illuminate and enhance our understanding of academic material. . . . Progressive professors working to transform the curriculum so that it does not reflect biases or reinforce systems of domination are most often the individuals willing to take the risk that engaged pedagogy requires and to make their teaching a site of resistance. (21)

Progressive teachers stand the chance that their democratic, facilitative pedagogy is read by students, colleagues, and administrators as ineffectual and permissive. Practicing student-centered dialogic pedagogy is especially wrought with difficulties when the teacher is "colored." For women it is even more complicated because our antiauthoritarian stance is read as nonauthoritative; flexibility is interpreted as lack of organization; sensitivity is assessed as flightiness; and our radical approach is critiqued as nothing more than whining. Any professor who values students' opinions, contributions, and work is suspect, but more deliberately so if she has a "foreign" name, is young and more overtly "other" than themselves. The costs can be discouraging and demoralizing—denied tenure, inability to achieve promotion, rejection of grants or sabbatical requests . . .

The echoes of class and color haunt every commentary I write on students' papers; the oral tradition I come from makes me more attentive to the sound of the writing than to its textuality. Scribbling "awkward" next to the sentence that doesn't sound correct is more natural to me than detailing the grammatical sins the student has committed to paper. I avoid changing perfectly good English into other perfectly good English because it's more important to me that students own their language and claim authority in their writing than having them speak/write like me. It may be blasphemous to admit that I never use an English grammar handbook in composition courses, but it's true; my experience in grammar school, high school, and college taught me that mechanical errors in my writing were to be expected and borne as a symbol of shame despite workbook after workbook, exercise after exercise, lecture after lecture (all that penance hasn't converted the masses). Once I understood that grammatical errors were manifestations of my underpreparation for literacy, I reconsidered the errors to be what they were: technical mistakes (and *not* morally egregious behaviors). These days I model for the students that I never trust my own proofreading skills and depend on others whose first language is Standard American English for their ability to catch the grammatical sins I commit (though now I am without remorse). In addition to sharing early rough drafts and late polished drafts of my own papers, I tell stories about publisher rejections of award-winning writing,[10] point to the once neglected, now acclaimed work of writers long gone; and describe the editorial, review, and copyediting processes to let students in on some of the real nitty-gritty of publishing. Above all, I want students to realize that professional writers, even accomplished and articulate ones, have to revise and re-vision.[11]

It is an arduous and perhaps impossible exercise to attempt a discussion of color without addressing the issue of class and the reverse. Even if there are times when I am wearing the right clothes and saying the appropriate things with authority, class status still lurks beneath the surface, and race remains an obsessively evaluated and estimated marker.

When it seems to me that students accept me as I am, a teacher, not simply nor extraordinarily a teacher of color, that they understand me and I understand them, and that all is well, there will be a student like Phil. He had been a somewhat quiet though very competent introductory creative writing student; his efforts were consistent and displayed an admirable knack for simple, solid lines expressing his Pittsburgh working-class origins and touches of the influence of urban culture. His class oral presentation on beat poets revealed his awareness of and debt to black culture in that writing. The next semester he signed up for a writing-intensive African American literature class I teach. Again, he was diligent and applied himself, though perhaps he was more reticent in class participation because this time the enrollment consisted of more than one-third African American students (a highly disproportionate number), the preponderance of whom were not English majors as Phil was. He was talkative in conference, but in class he seemed intimidated, as if he feared saying something offensive (he admitted in conference that he had not had much contact with African Americans on campus or at home). He was appreciative of the literature, and when it came time for the first paper, an open topic/genre writing of the students' choice, he decided to work on his creative writing, trying his hand at a science fiction piece. Being the writing teacher I am, I encouraged his efforts, though he knew that I was neither a big fan of, nor very well read in, sci-fi. I collected drafts and read Phil's paper last, because I knew it'd be a treat.

It wasn't, however. Aside from forgivable technical flaws, the world view expressed in his alternative life on another planet was troubling, holding that evil was not only a matter of fact and expected in humans/humanoids, it was also acceptable to eradicate those deemed evil because they were unreformable. The moral of the story was that some folks are bound to be evil, from birth, so we should just lock them up and throw away the key or better yet, exterminate them. I don't hold this world view and, as a teacher of color, I know it is antithetical to my role in the classroom—if I didn't feel that racist, sexist, fascist people were capable of transformation, I would have quit long ago. So I tried to problematize and not usurp Phil's paper, commenting on his content, drawing connections to civil rights struggles, and finally asking open-ended questions in order to give him room to rethink his work. At the end of his story, when the world he created is a sterile and barren place (all the evil has been eradicated but "unfortunately" so has humanity), I posed the question: I don't understand how this is utopic.

When revisions came back, I saved Phil's paper for last, hoping that being the good writer and thoughtful student of literature he is, there would be real revision. Not so, and I was a bit put off by having almost exactly the same paper turned in. He had attended to mechanical errors and decorative flourishes, and I found the ending to be even more emphatic about his alternative world as utopic and inevitable. When I reviewed the first draft with my comments in the margins (which is always turned in with revisions), I noticed that he had responded to my questions in a hostile way in pencil. I know all about getting one's feelings hurt when others critique, even constructively, one's writing, and we believe we're misread; I sensed it in Phil's marginal comments addressing me. When I got to the end, to my question of not understanding how this world was utopic, he simply answered that it was "because you're a stupid cuban."

My blood rushed. I blinked, almost not believing my eyes. Deeply disappointed, having my whole attitude about this "good" student suddenly come crashing down on my head, I thought about how I would attend to this racism. (Inside me there was a struggle for dominance. The cynic in me was gloating: *You see? They can't really "get it"; they can never understand the depth of their racism; you're fooling yourself to think these white kids are capable of transformation.* The optimist was placating: *Aw, come on. You don't like his story and he's hurt; he wants to hurt you back. He can't really mean it; this is his second class with you.*) Pushing my warring psyche back into my working-class "take care of business" mode, I decided that Phil and I needed to have a conversation at once and, amazingly, he answered the phone on the first ring and was able to come and see me immediately. He even sounded chipper, eager to talk about his writing. As I hung up I thought, surely he has no recollection of writing that accursed line.

Phil came in smiling, happy to see me. I told him I was glad he could come in on such short notice and that we had two things to talk about, both related to his paper. As I asked him to sit he said he was pleased about the way his story turned out.

We began the conference; for the next ten to fifteen minutes we focussed on the characters, their motivation, and other adjustments he had made in his revising process. Then we hit on epistemology.

I reminded him of what I had said earlier about my not being his ideal audience since I didn't read a lot of science fiction but, even more important, I didn't have the same idea about utopia. I told him that I didn't believe that evil is predetermined or innate and that if he felt this vision of life, one without humanity, is utopic, I would respect it though I couldn't share it. So, I admitted that I would probably never fully appreciate his short story, though I knew he had received positive responses from classmates in workshop. "You can't expect to reach all audiences all the time," I said, one writer to another.

He understood, was glad he had attempted a genre he hadn't before, and thought we were done for the day. His revision was graded and he seemed satisfied.

I moved to the second order of business as I took up his draft copy, flipped back to his last page and pointed to his epithet. I said "What am I to make of this?" *Because you're a stupid cuban.*

He blinked. It seemed like he almost couldn't believe it either. His face turned bright red (the cynic inside snickered: *Guess blood does what it must do*). After an awkward moment or two, he began to ramble, and I let him. He said that it was "stupid" over and over again, that he loved the class, that he was always praising me to others; he was both animated and sluggish.

I simply said, "And this is how you repay me?"

He continued making excuses: that he didn't mean it, couldn't remember writing it, that it was so stupid.

This last word still on his lips, I began, "No, Phil, if you had just written 'because you're stupid,' it would be stupid. No, Phil, this is racist; you have implicated my ethnicity, my ancestry, my people." I was very calm and spoke without my voice wavering. I let that sink in for a moment, then I said, "Tell me how you feel right now."

He revealed his guilt, shame, remorse, and then anger. The longer he talked, the more agitated he became.

I responded with more calm, "I felt pretty bad too when I read this. I was angry at you and angry that I believed you knew better. But this bad feeling is yours, Phil, not mine."

"Here," I handed him back his paper, "this is yours, take it back. Take it in your hands and feel it, feel what racism feels like, own it because it is yours."

He took it back, crushing the sheets in his hands.

He seemed distraught, and before I could feel sorry for him, I continued, "This betrayal leads me to distrust you. How can I believe your comments in class or on papers as honest? I don't know how you can really understand the literature and the struggle of people of color. But I'm not going to fail you, Phil, and I'm not going to the department chair or dean because I want, *I need* to be rid of this today. I don't want this negativity in my life for another moment. In giving you this paper back, I am done with it. And I don't want you to think that I will be vindictive or spiteful, either, though it'd be really easy to do that. No, Phil, that's not me. I want to teach the class as I have been teaching, and I want you to know that I will not single you out or be harsh in any way."

He said he knew I wouldn't and that he was very sorry.

I said I knew he was and that the next time he thought about doing or saying or writing something like this again, he'd remember today. He started to say that he'd never do it again but I cut him off, saying that maybe he would and maybe he wouldn't; maybe it was a test for both of us.

His eyes were watery and even though I felt sorry for him, I felt good about how I had handled this. About whether he came back to class or not—he was so undone—I was a little worried. He needed to think; I needed to be free of his slur. And I was free.

The next time I entered the African American literature class it was with a pronounced sense of the differences between white working-class people and colored working-class folks. Early in my career I had believed we could never see eye to eye, but the students taught me that our economic situations allowed us a sense of familiarity that comes from viscerally knowing what the banker, landlord, boss, or supervisor can do to you and yours. After three or four years, finding that common ground, a mutual vocabulary of assorted experiences and expectations, I finally felt comfortable with all of my students. The experience with Phil shook me.

There is a happy ending to this story, though there isn't always. A few weeks later, the class was discussing the collected poems of Ishmael Reed, a writer whom Phil read carefully, and it was one of those times when the material exactly fulfilled the teaching moment's exigencies—Reed, admitted and avowed trickster, satirist, activist, and accomplished writer in several genres—would teach Phil what I couldn't. In Phil's class writings, I discerned a gradual progression in Phil's identification with the yeah-we-expect-you-to-be-evil mode to the later, we-can't-always-expect-the-worst-first mode revealed in Reed's poems. After some time, evaluating his writing, assessing his group interaction and oral participation, I was heartened. I collected an informal ink-shedding writing from the group on Reed's short untitled "law isn't all" piece about there not being anything on the driver's test about not hitting dogs. Phil wrote that people wouldn't naturally want to hit and run over the dog and extended his discussion to admit that people wouldn't normally be cruel to one another—that we are driven to it by our experiences. I smiled this time. My faith was renewed; this time we were able to meet each other again, eye to eye. He as a young, white, working-class man, and I as an older, working-class Latina. We recognized our differences and departures, and in struggling through our conflict, we were moved to change. Recalling bell hooks's words, I see now we should not fear the conflicts; if challenges are lovingly met and struggled through not as combatants but as beloved beings, we can arc toward liberation and transformation.

Notes

1. In Rodríguez Milanés 1996, I describe how race, culture, and ethnicity are intertwined in the term *color* for me and postulate how these emerge in boundary crossing, hybrid texts, and identity.

2. The black feminist/womanist theory of bell hooks forms the foundation for my work, especially her discussions of mainstream feminism's privileged erasure of race/class differences. See 75–76 and 101–108 in *Outlaw Culture* (hooks 1994a).

3. A version of this was part of my June 1996 National Women's Studies Association Roundtable discussion, an excerpt of which will appear in *The Family Track* (1998), edited by Diana Hume George and the late Constance Coiner (she and her daughter Ana died in TWA's flight 800).

4. The recent PBS special "Shattering the Silences: Minority Professors Break into the Ivory Tower" profiled eight scholars of color. The web site on the program (http://www.pbs.org/shattering/theprogram.html) notes that in 1993, persons of color represented only 12.2 percent of all full-time faculty and 9.2 percent of full professors.

5. See Dueñas Gonzalez (1996). In addition, the "English Only and Colonialism Revisited" session at the 1997 CCCC where panelists, including Geneva Smitherman, Victor Villanueva, Gail Okawa, and Raúl Sánchez, treated the responsibility of literacy education in ever more linguistically diverse populations. The work of Mary Louise Pratt (1996) also confirms mainstream reactionary responses to the diversification of the population.

6. Indiana University of Pennsylvania has a highly visible summer graduate program designed to facilitate graduate education for teachers who want to earn terminal degrees without having to give up their jobs. The bulk of the course work can be completed during three summers (two five-week terms offered back to back).

7. Teaching mostly writing courses virtually eliminates my chances of reading anything other than student writing during the academic year, hence the need for such intense preparation for summer graduate teaching.

8. See also Rodríguez Milanés 1991.

9. In Rodríguez Milanés 1992, I describe the course outline, readings, and strategies I used in first-year composition courses when I started teaching as an assistant professor.

10. For example, William Kennedy's *Ironweed* was submitted to seventeen publishers before it was published and later received a Pulitzer prize.

11. See Rodríguez Milanés 1996 for specific writing classroom strategies.

Works Cited

George, D. H., and C. Coiner, eds. 1998. *The Family Track: Keeping Your Faculties While You Mentor, Nurture, Teach, and Serve.* Urbana and Chicago: University of Illinois Press.

Gonzalez, R. D. 1996. "Notes from the Arizona Underground." *NCTE Latino Caucus Newsletter* 2(1).

hooks, b. 1994a. *Outlaw Culture: Resisting Representations.* New York and London: Routledge.

————. 1994b. *Teaching to Transgress: Education as the Practice of Freedom.* New York and London: Routledge.

Pratt, M. L. 1996. "Daring to Dream: Re-Visioning Culture and Citizenship." In *Critical Theory and the Teaching of Literature: Politics, Curriculum, Pedagogy,* ed. J. F. Slevin and A. Young, 3–20. Urbana, IL: National Council of Teachers of English.

Reed, I. 1989. *New and Collected Poems.* New York: Atheneum Press.

Rodríguez Milanés, C. 1998. "Juggling on an Uneven Playing Field." Excerpted in *The Family Track*, ed. D. H. George and C. Coiner. Urbana and Chicago: University of Illinois Press.

————. 1997. "Crosstalk: Teachers, Texts, Readers and Writers." In *Writing in Multicultural Settings*, ed. C. Severino et al. xxx. New York: Modern Language Association.

————. 1996. "Where Narrative, Autobiography, Color and Feminism Converge." *English in Texas* 2.27 (Winter): 17–28.

————. 1992. Literacy to the Literate. Paper presented at CCCC.

————. 1991. "Risks, Resistance and Rewards: One Teacher's Story." In *Composition and Resistance,* ed. C. M. Hurlbert and M. Blitz, 115–24. Portsmouth, NH: Boynton/Cook.

Shattering the Silences: Minority Professors Break into the Ivory Tower. 1997. PBS. WPSU, State College. 24 January.

Villanueva, V. 1993. *Bootstraps: From an Academic of Color.* Urbana, IL: National Council of Teachers of English.

12

Intersections of Race and Class in the Academy

Beverly J. Moss

Maintaining connections with family and community across class boundaries demands more than just summary recall of where one's roots are, where one comes from. It requires knowing, naming, and being ever-mindful of those aspects of one's past that have enabled and do enable one's self-development in the present, that sustain and support, that enrich.

bell hooks, *Talking Back*

While bell hooks's statement challenges each of us to think about our own self-development, it makes me think first about my role as a teacher-scholar and what I bring from my background, particularly my class background, to that role; second, about what aspects of my students' pasts have "enabled and do enable their self-development"; and third, about how teachers can make use of our diverse and/or common experiences to enrich classroom experiences.

When I agreed to write this essay on the role of social class in my teaching, I had imagined I could do so with the usual degree of difficulty I have when I write—nothing more, nothing less. Of course that "nothing more, nothing less" is filled with hidden meanings. My usual degree of difficulty emerges whenever I think about writing for anyone other than myself. I immediately become concerned with how my peers will judge my work. Will they discover that I don't belong in the academy, that somehow, I'm not good enough? Some will argue that this lack of self-confidence is class related; others will

157

argue that it is gender related; still others will argue that it is race related. And there is probably another group who will argue that my writing anxiety cannot be traced to any one cause. There may be some degree of accuracy in each argument. Yet, this writing task brought on more difficulty than usual. In thinking about the issues involved in examining the relationship between class and teaching, and particularly in thinking about the relationship of my social class to my teaching, my struggle to write intensified. As I turned hooks's statement over and over in my head, thought about who I am as a teacher-scholar (it's of no use to me to separate the two), my place in the academy, and my students' places in the academy, I found myself struggling not just to write but to define class in relation to my experience. How can I discuss the influence of social class on teaching, I wondered, if I can't even define and/or categorize class?

Part of what has led to this struggle is my inability to separate class from a constellation of other features such as race, gender, region, age, and religion (among others). Also contributing to the struggle over defining class, however, is my experience of growing up in a household where class boundaries were more fluid than they seemingly were for others. I've never known how to answer the class question when it is directed at me. Most around me would say that I'm firmly positioned in the black middle class (which is quite different from the white middle class) by virtue of my level of education and status as a professional. On some level, I accept that. But what does it mean to be a member of the black middle class and an academic, given that race, income, gender, and other factors play major roles in separating the black and white middle classes?

Being a member of the black middle class may, in fact, give one more options about where one lives, what schools one's children can attend, what cars one can buy, and the level of education one can attain, but it does not ensure equal treatment with that of middle-class whites. While the 1970s saw a growth in the black middle-class and a narrowing of the gap between black and white middle-class incomes, the late 1980s and 1990s have seen that trend reversed. Marc Breslow (1995), a senior editor at *Dollars & Sense* magazine, cites a study by economists Bound and Freeman that shows that "from 1974 [to] 1977 young black college graduates actually earned slightly more on average, than white graduates, but in 1989 they earned 17% less than whites . . . belying the notion that it is only those with little education who have faced problems in the modern U.S. economy" (11). Breslow also points to a study by the Federal Reserve Bank of Boston that showed that "even when blacks and whites were equally credit worthy (in terms of credit history, income, and size of loan applied for), blacks were 56% more likely to be turned down for mortgages than were whites" (39). It is statistics like these that help to explain the anger of members of the black middle class as highlighted in Ellis Cose's (1993) *The Rage of a Privileged Class*, a book in which Cose presents his readers with one case after another of middle-class blacks who, despite their high educational achievements and their middle-class occupations, have hit the glass ceiling in their jobs, earn less money than the white counterparts whom they've trained, experience housing discrimination or police harassment, or have been followed in department stores because of their race. One of the newest sayings among middle-class blacks, particularly black men, is that they were stopped by the police for "BWD—black while driving." There are numerous instances of police stopping blacks because they are driving expensive cars, which many police suspect the drivers have gotten through illegal means.

I often wonder if my white colleagues, especially the men, are questioned as many times as I am about whether I have a Ph.D., or whether their authority is challenged by their students as much as mine is, or if their students seem as surprised to see them walk into the classroom on the first day as many of mine are when I walk in. I wonder if they were told by "well-meaning" colleagues, just after a positive tenure decision, "I'm so proud of you" or "I thought we'd have to go in and fight for you, but you'd done all the work," as I was told. Neither of those statements did I find comforting. One was paternalistic and the other was filled with assumptions about my ability to be a productive, quality scholar. It is these scenarios/realities that indicate, for me, the gap between the black and white middle classes in our society.

Those who know my family and community background would probably hesitate to place me "firmly" in the black middle class. Neither of my parents has a college degree; their parents picked cotton, worked as sharecroppers, domestics, and janitors; most of my aunts, uncles and cousins—almost all of whom still live in the same small, rural town where I was born—would be labeled as working-class African Americans, some living below the poverty level. Like their parents, my parents also picked cotton, worked as janitors and domestics. But I never heard my parents describe that time in their life as being "poor." In fact, that was not a concept that my family (extended and immediate) began to apply to anyone in the family until the last ten years.

When I was five, my family moved from that small, rural town to a large city thirty miles away. When I was twelve, we moved from a small frame house into a partial brick split-level home in what would probably be considered a lower-middle-class black neighborhood. When I was in high school, my mother moved into a management position at the bank where she had been working for almost ten years. Though she moved into this management position, her pay was still much lower than that of my father, who was working on the loading dock at a trucking company. In this, she was not unusual. Black men who held blue-collar jobs often made more money than did black women in the limited number of white-collar jobs that were open to them (Giddings 1984, 7). And with the exception of an aunt living in New Jersey, I was the first member of the family to go away to college, a private black women's college at that. And now, though I work at a large, predominantly white institution and interact professionally and socially with white colleagues, I continue to attend a predominantly African American church and live in a predominantly African American community, described by a friend as "lower middle class that might go either way," meaning that within two blocks on my street one can drive by small two-story frame homes with well-kept lawns, low-income apartment complexes, and absentee-landlord-owned low-income duplexes. Even in my current neighborhood, the class boundaries are fluid, not distinct.

I recognized early on that because of a variety of events in my life—the combination of my parents' jobs, my not having siblings, our relocation from the rural area to the city, and further, our relocation into the new house—I was privileged in ways that my relatives were not. I don't ever recall not knowing that I wanted to go to college. I always wanted to play school when I was a child while my cousins and friends wanted to ride bikes. My parents, especially my mother, always encouraged my interest in furthering my education. Like many African American parents, my parents valued education for their child. They wanted me to have more than they did. bell hooks (1989) and Richard Rodriguez (1982) describe the conflict emanating from their families' support for and simultaneous suspicion of academic institutions of higher learning as instruments that can lead toward freedom and a "better" life while, at the same time, pulling them away from their roots and leading them to be ashamed of their pasts; my family never showed such ambivalence toward my goals. I don't think they inherently trusted the institutions so much as they trusted me to take away what was valuable from the institutions and to dismiss what was not valuable—like any notions that my education and profession would demand that I isolate myself from my family and community. Richard Rodriguez would not gain any sympathy or understanding in my family (nor should he). They trusted me to "remember where I came from and be proud of it." And where I came from was a place of fluid or blurred—not distinct—class boundaries.

What these memories point to, for me, is that class, already a complex concept, is made even more complex when one is, as I am, an African American woman academic from the South who has one parent who has always held blue-collar jobs and one parent who has moved from blue-collar to white-collar jobs and, in fact, has been in a white-collar job for the past twenty years. The complexity intensifies when one considers that I grew up in a relatively large city, the largest in my home state, yet continued to go to a rural church some thirty miles away with my extended family who lived in this rural area, and that I have maintained close ties to my extended family although my academic career has taken me away from this setting into what hooks might term "new class environments."

What Do I Bring to the Classroom?

It was as I tried to examine my life—present and past—that I recognized the growing complexity of class and the growing impossibility of the task ahead of me, examining the relationship between social class and teaching, as long as I tried to isolate class from the rest of my background. African American women do not have the luxury of focusing on class only, when, every day, our race and gender are placed in positions of prominence. For me, race, gender, and class, along with other characteristics, are aspects of my being that enrich me. It is that broader background that has led me to be the teacher-scholar that I am, and it is in that context that I will focus on the impact of my background on my pedagogy and scholarship.

While we academics are encouraged to think of ourselves as middle class with middle-class values (though many in the humanities do not have middle-class incomes), African American academics often find ourselves as misfits in the academy. Though we may "talk the talk" and/or "walk the walk," for many of us, neither the talk nor the walk is comfortable or comforting, nor are many members of the academy whom we meet along the way neighborly. As a way of fitting in, many of us find ourselves "wearing masks," as Paul Laurence Dunbar (1972) so eloquently describes in his poem "We Wear the Mask," and trying to erase any racial, ethnic, gender, or class markers that point to our differences. Many of us try to fit into two worlds, wearing a mask in the office, in the classroom, at conferences, and in publications, and taking it off in the privacy of our homes or when we're with our "friends from home." An alternative that I prefer to this trying-to-erase-all-markers approach, one that many of us strive for through our scholarship and pedagogy, is to stretch the boundaries of the academy by making space for or establishing a different path to walk for others who are not the norm in the academy, a space that would eliminate the necessity for a mask. Thus our scholarship and pedagogy become demonstrations of this alternative. I have been fortunate in that I have had mentors, black and white women, who have fought to make the academy more accessible and welcoming to underrepresented groups and who have supported me in my attempts to stretch the boundaries of pedagogy and scholarship.

I speak of scholarship and teaching together because how and why I do both come from the same source and are inextricably linked. In the scholarship that I do, mainly through ethnographic means, I seek to make my scholarly life and where I come from compatible; I seek a way for the public and the private to enrich each other. I seek a way to establish my place in the academy without giving up myself. While these are not always easy goals for me, neither are they impossible goals. It is my background as a southern African American woman who has experienced the fluidity of class lines within family and community that has contributed greatly to my journey to examine the literacies that nonmainstream (mainly nonwhite middle-class) people practice in their home communities. I have been mostly concerned with the nature of literacies in African American community institutions outside the academy, such as African American churches.[1]

In that work, I have been struck by how rich are the literacy and language practices of people who have repeatedly been failed by our schools, while being cast as the ones who have failed. The rhetorically complex structures and styles of African American worship services signal a kind of literacy practice that many African American students are familiar with and that may be an asset in the classroom. How best can I make use of such literacy practices in my courses? This question has led me to consider how we, in the academy, can value and build on those literacies that students bring into the classroom rather than demean them, as often happens to students of color and students from working-class backgrounds. Of course, what is probably obvious is my assumption that we all have multiple literacies rather than a single literacy. Even the notion of a single academic literacy is more myth than reality, though that myth is still a very powerful one. An important part of my pedagogy begins with recognizing that just as I, and many like me, have found the walk and the talk of the academy to be uncomfortable, so, too, do many of our students. In the past fourteen years, I have taught at two unique institutions, one a large urban commuter university where almost all the students were the first in their families ever to attend college and where most lived in racially and ethnically segregated communities. By two in the afternoon, the campus was empty and most of the students were on their way to their jobs. The second institution, where I now teach, is a large state university where students come from all over the state and from diverse class backgrounds, meaning that a large portion of these students come from small farm towns and working-class communities. Too few are African American, Latino/a, or Native American. I am much more likely to have white students from diverse class backgrounds in my courses than I am to have students from racially diverse backgrounds.

Though my students may not initially think so, my background provides a foundation for me to see the diversity within seemingly homogenous classes and to begin to find out about their literacy backgrounds. I do not ask my students to leave their pasts behind, to erase racial, class, ethnic, and gender markers. In many ways, that would be stripping them of what bell hooks reminds us may be sustaining, supporting, and enriching many of them. Equally important, however, I do not ask them to wear the banners for their race, class, ethnic group, or gender. My path into the academy also provides me with a perspective from which to question long held racist, sexist, and classist assumptions and practices that have traditionally been perpetuated by the academy. I question those practices through assignments that ask students, and consequently the academy, to expand their definition of what counts as literacy, what counts as text, what counts as scholarship—ultimately, what counts as valuable. For example, I send students, graduate and undergraduate, out to various sites and communities (courtrooms, swim teams, religious organizations, preschool classes, and military organizations, among others) to do fieldwork investigating literacy and language practices. I use gospel music and blues as examples of literacy events in my second-level writing course on "African American Voices in American Literature." Fieldwork and gospel music in writing courses are considered by many to be too nontraditional. But for me, it is an attempt to help students value nonacademic community texts, and to get them to question the limitations of canonical notions of texts. This attempt is not necessarily welcomed by privileged students nor, surprisingly, by marginalized students. Many students think that the traditional or the canonical is the only avenue of study that is legitimate and that will ensure their success. Often I run into working-class white students who are nervous about questioning the very institution in which they are striving so hard to succeed and from which they seek approval, and often they are the ones most challenged by finding an African American woman in front of the class.

Many students, including students of color, look to the academy as their ticket to a better life financially than the ones their parents have. Their parents look to academic institutions in the same way. These students look to professors to prepare them to become part of the American middle class or upper class. They have long-held ideas about how this middle class talks, dresses, and eats; what they read; where they live; and what kinds of cars they drive. These ideas are often at odds with where the students themselves come from. And the reality is not as straightforward as their dreams. Many want to be Forrest Gump, thinking that loving one's country, God, and mother; working hard; and never questioning authority, especially academic institutions of higher learning, will lead to success. They do not want to acknowledge that racism, sexism, classism, homophobia, and other societal ills might alter their dreams.

Yet, I see no need to dissuade them from their goals and dreams, and I resent those who try to do so. It has become popular for many academics, in the name of questioning the academy, to tell students that their goals of financial success are not worthy. In their ardor or zeal, these academics don't necessarily value what students bring into the classroom. Who are we to determine what a worthy goal is for our students? One of my arguments with critical pedagogues is that too often they want to "empower" students, as if they have the power to give. It has not escaped my notice that most critical or radical pedagogues place themselves in the position of setting the agenda for the disempowered, thus reinforcing the very hierarchy they are encouraging students to question. Most of these scholars are operating from positions of privilege to begin with. Setting the agendas for their "uninformed" students does not threaten that privilege at all. Michael Holzman (1991) reminds us that

> the behavior of many critics who write about education is congruent with the existing structure, no matter what they write in opposition to it. Whatever they say, and whatever their intentions, the effect of their writing and speeches is to position themselves as liberators, as more or less charismatic leaders, and it seems that charismatic leaders are always in opposition to the liberation of those-to-be-led. (304)

My goal is to value what students know when they come into the academy, build on that knowledge by exposing them to multiple literacies, traditional and nontraditional, and challenge these students to blur the boundary lines that keep some out and others in. As educators, we can provide an opportunity for students to gain tools that they can use to empower themselves. Whether they use those tools to do so—to challenge boundaries or question traditional academic values—is up to the students. Of course, this might make some students nervous because it is not necessarily what they expect. Just when they think they have the rules down, they run into someone who says "Let's make some new ones; let's redefine what it means to do research; let's turn basic writers into ethnographers and send them to national conferences to discuss their work; let's negotiate the syllabus for this class." I, too, have asked if the powers that be were changing the rules of the game just as I had my foot in the door.

When I want to challenge traditions of the academy, some students and colleagues believe that I am trying to change the rules of the game. They're right, I am. I realized early on that the rules were arbitrary and that I was not always invited to the game. Changing the rules of the game, maybe even changing the game, is another step toward blurring the boundaries in ways that may allow for easier movement along and across them.

Teaching Biases in the Academy

Changing the rules goes beyond what one does in the classroom with one's own students; it also means rethinking who our teachers are and how we train them. For the past several decades, we have heard a consistent call for a more diverse teaching pool in elementary and secondary schools and a more diverse professoriate in colleges and universities. I second that call. It will only benefit students and teachers on every level and from every background to interact with as diverse a teaching staff as possible. However, those benefits are limited if we continue to produce teachers who reinforce problematic societal structures, who continue to value only one kind of literacy and demean others. As long as we continue to turn out professors who silently (and sometimes not so silently) assume that all minority students will be underprepared for college and graduate school, that most students from working-class backgrounds will encounter difficulty understanding Shakespeare, and that students from privileged backgrounds are well prepared when they enter the academy, then our system is doomed to repeat its mistakes.

Of concern to me are the number of colleagues and graduate students who are willing to talk theoretically about issues of race, gender, and class—to write articles and books with these golden words in the title—but virtually ignore how these concepts work in their own classrooms. Even more troublesome is the attitude that many graduate students new to teaching bring into teacher-training courses, particularly those courses that ask new teachers to think about how issues of race, class, gender, sexual orientation, and other axes of difference impact one's teaching. I've taught several teacher- and tutor-training courses. A growing number of students in those courses have a blatant disdain for teacher-training courses and resent having to think about teaching when they could be taking another critical theory seminar. Their assumption is that if they know their subject, classical rhetoric or Milton, then they will be good teachers—a not-so-uncommon attitude among faculty in most disciplines. Many who hold such attitudes almost always blame the students who don't do well in a course rather than examine their own pedagogies. These are generally the teachers who ask me, "What do I do with those students? Can I send them to a basic writing class?" Most often, "those students" are from marginalized backgrounds. Holzman (1991) argues that the education system is in fact succeeding if it fails to engage and educate a particular group of people. Society is then assured of an underclass, which ensures the place of the dominant class. It just happens that, in this country, the underclass is usually tied to a particular race.

Another prominent attitude in my institution among new teachers is that because we are a large land-grant institution, our students are not as smart as the students at private institutions. If they were smart enough, they would have gone to one of the smaller, more expensive, private colleges in the state. This attitude is so obviously tied to a class bias. Many of us have come to equate an expensive education with a good education. Attitudes such as these signal a need for more focus on teacher training with more emphasis on how to value all of our students.

Given the many predictions that in the twenty-first century our schools will be heavily populated with more and more students from diverse racial, ethnic, class, and, hence, language backgrounds, teacher-training programs in education schools and in English departments need to provide future educators with more of a background in how language works. In particular, I see a need for more focus in English departments and English education programs on multiple literacies and language awareness. In a basic survey of language awareness of high school teachers conducted in 1996, Jacqueline Jones Royster (1997) found that most teachers who come through English or English education departments have inadequate formal training in how the English language works, have little knowledge of the variations of English from one community to another and of language variety's relationship to cultural differences, and have not been trained in how to discover and use as resources the community language practices that their students bring to school. Particularly interesting in Royster's survey is that almost all of the respondents were teaching in non-middle-class, nontraditional classrooms throughout the country. As Royster indicates, they are good teachers who want to do good, but their lack of training in language awareness may create barriers when, in fact, these teachers want to cross barriers.

At the same time that I call for more of an emphasis on teacher training, I am aware that many teachers feel beseiged. Recently, I've spoken to groups of graduate students in both education departments and in English departments in two different state universities. Most of the education students were already teaching in public or parochial schools, and the English graduate students were teaching writing at the college level. What struck me about my interactions with both groups was that they asked the same questions: "How and why should teachers learn about all the different language communities that their students might possibly come from? Why can't we just teach English?" Although I am always surprised by those questions no matter how many times I hear them, the questions come out of genuine frustration and an equally genuine lack of understanding about how language works, about the relationship between language and culture. More teacher training in language awareness, in language varieties, in how the English language works might eliminate the need to ask those questions. Better teacher training for K–12 teachers and for college teachers might lead to more pedagogically sound practices that invite students from all backgrounds to feel as if they belong in the academy rather than practices that reflect the biases of the academy.

Talking the Talk of the Academy

An important aspect of the impact of race, gender, and class on my teaching has much to do with speaking the language of the academy. As I discussed earlier, walking the walk and talking the talk are often uncomfortable. And even more often, for African American academics (and other groups as well), speaking the language of the academy distances us from the majority of our people because we are encouraged to dismiss them as an important audience. We are made to feel that the language and literacy of our pasts, our home communities, our families, are not acceptable. Even worse, we are made to feel as if "our people" are not valued enough to be engaged in scholarly debate. bell hooks (1989) suggests that,

> the use of a language and style of presentation that alienates most folks who are not also academically trained reinforces the notion that the academic world is separate from real life, that everyday world where we constantly adjust our language and behavior to meet diverse needs. The academic setting is separate only when we work to make it so. It is a false dichotomy which suggests that academics and/or intellectuals can only speak to one another, that we cannot hope to speak with the masses. What is true is that we make choices, that we choose our audiences, that we choose voices to hear and voices to silence. If I do not speak in a language that can be understood, then there is little chance for dialogue. (78)

One of my most disturbing moments in graduate school occurred when my professor in a critical theory course wrote on my final paper that my "language was not sophisticated enough to handle the sophisticated ideas of critical theory." As a twenty-two-year-old graduate student, I understood that he was trying to tell me that I did not belong in graduate school, that people like me were not smart enough. I understood that I was the only person of color in his class (and in the entire graduate program) and that he never spoke to me the entire semester. I understood that I was not an acceptable audience in his class. And because I had imagined my audience for the paper I wrote in his class to be people like me, I was an unacceptable audience for this academic exercise. As I went further in the profession, I began to understand that this professor was appalled by my attempt to discuss Hegel and Heidegger in a language other than academic theory-babble. And finally, I understood that in my own naive way, I was trying to cross a line or blur a boundary; some would consider it a class line, some a color line, some even a gender line, perhaps all three. I am no longer naive about my attempts to cross those lines now.

I am perfectly clear that my attempts to interweave public and private, personal and theoretical, are also attempts to unlock the gates to nonacademics. I also understand the risk that I will be judged as lacking by various colleagues in the academy who place themselves in a position to judge. I heed hooks' (1989) call and her warning:

> Combining personal with critical analysis and theoretical perspectives can engage listeners who might otherwise feel estranged, alienated. . . . Speaking about one's personal experience or speaking [writing] with simple language is often considered by academics and/or intellectuals (irrespective of their political inclinations) to be a sign of intellectual weakness or even anti-intellectualism. (77)

On the contrary, I find that trying to write to multiple audiences and using inclusive rather than exclusive language is much more intellectually challenging than writing to a narrowly defined group of academics in my field. I feel an obligation to write in such a way that I invite people from a variety of backgrounds to come along with me on my scholarly journeys and make a few detours of their own. I don't want to be the only one from my community on the journey. I don't want my classroom to be a place that is welcoming only to those from privileged backgrounds. Our classrooms become hostile places that reinforce already existing hierarchical structures if we do not create spaces where students from diverse backgrounds can engage each other, including the teacher.

Notes

1. For a more detailed description of this topic, see Beverly J. Moss, *A Community Text Arises* (forthcoming).

Works Cited

Breslow, M. 1995. "The Racial Divide Widens: Why African-American Workers Have Lost Ground." *Dollars & Sense*. (197): 8–11, 38–39.

Cose, E. 1993. *The Rage of a Privileged Class*. New York: HarperPerennial.

Dunbar, P. L. 1972. "We Wear the Mask." In *Black Writers of America*, ed. Richard Barksdale and Kenneth Kinnamon, 352. New York: Macmillan.

Giddings, P. 1984. *When and Where I Enter: The Impact of Black Women on Race and Sex in America*. New York: Bantam.

Holzman, M. 1991. "Observations on Literacy: Gender, Race, and Class." In *The Politics of Writing Instruction: Postsecondary*, ed. R. Bullock and J. Trimbur, 297–304. Portsmouth, NH: Boynton/Cook.

hooks, b. 1989. *Talking Back: Thinking Feminist, Thinking Black*. Boston: South End.

Moss, B. Forthcoming. *A Community Text Arises: Literate Texts and Literacy Traditions in African American Churches*. Cresskill, NJ: Hampton.

Rodriguez, R. 1982. *Hunger of Memory: The Education of Richard Rodriguez*. New York: Bantam.

Royster, J. J. 1997. "Teaching Away from Home: Language and Literacy in the Language Arts Classroom." In *Bread Loaf Rural Teacher Network*. Middlebury, VT: Bread Loaf School of English.

13

Notes from Another Underground
Working-Class Agency and the
Educational Process

Kevin Railey

Where to begin? How does my class origin affect my life in the academy? The times I have paused to consider this question I usually have not been able to draw any lines: It has affected everything! Wanting to escape the physical labor of working-class life drove me to college in the first place. There, however, I rejected the cool, analytical manipulation of language into rhetorically sound arguments that my professors generally wanted, and I embraced writing about the relationship between my life and the ideas in the books I was reading. I wanted to record what I saw and felt, what raced through the stream-of-consciousness in my head. I identified with writers, not with critics or the professors who taught me. I admired the writers' rebellion, their emphasis on real life; I wanted to make my life a work of art. I emphatically did not identify with the notion that one went to college to gain qualifications to acquire a high-paying job. So, though somehow I was rejecting my vision of working-class life, I was also always associated with that life in definite ways. I find myself today in a similar situation: both rejecting and identifying with my working-class background; rebelling from certain aspects of academic life while being proud of my Ph.D. and my tenured position. But I have also achieved a balance. Rather than feeling nowhere at home, I often feel everywhere at home.[1]

As any respectable academic would, when I began thinking about this essay I sought books and articles discussing the relationship between working-class culture and academic culture. What struck me over and over again were the feelings of anger, frustration, and guilt that many working-class academics focused on in their essays.[2] Many of these writers confessed to feeling, on one hand, that the academy had oppressed them somehow, that their voices were not given respect and attention, and on the other hand, that their lives as academics had unfairly separated them from their working-class origins, families, worlds. Though in many ways I identified with discussions about dual estrangement and with a certain frustration with the elitism of the academy, in general I was amazed by this outpouring of angst. Though I have working-class "credentials" and still think Marxism is the best master narrative out there, I can't identify with the angst. Though sensitive to concerns about social justice, I find the claim that people are victims because they are working class to be almost insulting. Working-class individuals, myself included, are not just cannon fodder for the middle class. Working-class people have subjective agency that directs their energy to attain ends not always compatible with the larger system in which they are placed. Despite a structured society that offers more cultural capital to those in the middle-class, working-class individuals can and do exercise power. Working-class people, academics included, do not NEED to internalize middle-class values and standards and suffer the psychic pain caused by this internalization. What I want to explore here are the ways I have exercised my own power, my own agency—as a student, an academic, and a teacher.

Paul Willis (1977), for one, has convincingly revealed that people in a working-class culture are not simply acted upon by a middle-class world. Definite values and attitudes work to shape the working class, and many of these work in such a way to cause a rebellion, in boys especially, against some of the standard features of school culture. The most basic feature of this school culture is the simple exchange between teacher and student: The teacher promises knowledge, that which offers qualifications and entrance into a comfortable middle-class life, and the student offers cooperation—to respect and maintain the teacher's position of authority. Students generally abide by this unstated agreement because they identify with what the teacher's position promises. In the case of working-class boys, however, there is no identification with the promise for the future. Their interests lie in finding what is relevant and important to them NOW; therefore, the bargain seems worthless and indeed even a little silly. For them, the usual teacher has very little authority.

Though it is sometimes hard for me to admit, I was this kind of student, though one who generally received good grades. I found it very easy to outwit high school teachers concerned only with authority, and since almost all classes were knowledge-based, factual, I really didn't need the teacher. (I could read and memorize anything.) I was not rejecting the knowledge about my world that school offered; I was rejecting the attitudes of teachers who discounted me. Those teachers who expected me to respond, to think, to relate what I was learning to my life were exactly the kind of teacher I respected, precisely because they included me in their vision of school. This overall process did not change much in college. I was not there to get a good education in order to get a good job; I was there to read, to think about my life and life in general, and to explore the possibilities as much as possible. I loved teachers who expected journals from me, who encouraged and valued discussion. I gave them more than they usually expected, pages and pages of ideas. I read and worked and stayed up nights thinking about what it all meant. With other teachers, however, I struggled: I couldn't tolerate lectures about what was in the textbook, and I didn't see the point in analyzing how literature was constructed with artifice, formal structures, and intent; I was very bad at close readings and literary analysis. Those teachers who expected only these tasks seemed pompous to me, the bearers of arcane knowledge, holders of secrets that they refused to share. They made me mad, and I dropped their classes.

At the time I saw this behavior as the justified rejection of "bad" teachers, but I see it now as a form of class *resentment*. This behavior was a kind of working-class survival technique on my part. I rejected these teachers, ultimately, because they rejected me. Though I did not know it consciously, I felt it, and I wouldn't stand for it. These teachers were, in fact, the holders of arcane knowledge, the possessors of cultural capital, and they were masters at the symbolic manipulation of language. They had the credentials. As Willis (1977) and Kurt Spellmeyer (1996) have discussed, academic specialists acquire their status and position by using a discourse separate from the real life of most people; their prestige is based on familiarity and facility with "theory," which offers them the status of specialists (Spellmeyer 1996). In a way, my professors were purposely speaking over my head: That was their job as they saw it. They were not talking to me. If I felt as if I did not belong in those classes, and I did feel that way, it was because those professors didn't want my life in their classroom; they wanted me to be different. Thinking reasonably at a great distance from sensations and emotions is precisely the lesson indirectly taught by higher education, but, true to my working-class culture, which refuses to turn life into a text, I refused to learn this lesson. I wanted my intelligence to be respected and given credit on its own terms. At the time, who would have suspected that I would become a professor myself one day?

My professors then did not have unfair expectations of their students. They simply expected their students to demonstrate that they too possessed skills and knowledge, that they too could manipulate symbolic language and reveal they belonged in the middle, successful class. What they expected remained a mystery to me, however. I had no idea how to produce what it was they wanted simply because no one had ever taught me how to perform these tasks. I had never been trained to look at literature analytically, and there was nothing in my background that even vaguely expected me to look at life in abstract and analytical ways. I was at a complete loss simply because I was from the working class, whose culture is lived experience and narratives of personal lives—the face-to-face meeting of people in a family and the stories we tell. Implicit in my confrontations with these professors was indeed class conflict—as many cultural studies–influenced educators now claim. But, unlike someone like Richard Rodriguez (1982), whose process led him to become alienated from his private, working-class world in order to identify with the public world of school, I refused to reject my private world, my private self.[3] I did not become a scholarship boy, primarily because, like many working-class kids, I had an attitude. My professors, thus, were not simply rejecting me; I rejected them. I felt my thinking was important, and I wouldn't tolerate their judgments.

Yet I also would not tolerate failure, because school offered me more than working in a factory (which I tried). Thus, like others in a counter-school culture, I became adept at managing the formal system, at limiting its demands on me, and at shaping and managing my own education. I did this through choosing certain professors, establishing independent studies, writing a lot, and having my own writing count for other, more formal assignments.[4] After graduating and recognizing that I would not escape the world of work entirely, I came to see how those analytical skills could enable me to acquire a kind of work I would enjoy—at least most of the time. I set out to develop those skills and abilities, teaching myself through reading—and trial and error—how to analyze literature in formal ways and how to create logical and rhetorical arguments for my ideas. Am I proud that I achieved that success in graduate school and beyond? Yes. Is that pride based somewhat on an implicit identification with the values of a class that rejects other values than the ones I hold? Yes. Does it matter? No. Life isn't perfect. The balance, in fact, has become extremely important and has been directly responsible for my being able to feel everywhere at home. More important, though I have come to have success in a middle-class profession, I never feel as if the profession controls my decisions. I still manipulate the system. I knew what I wanted, and I got it. I knew there would be costs, and I was willing to pay them. But finally, the process did not tear me up or separate me completely from the world I came from. Education means (should mean) radical self-re-formation—that is its price and its promise—but it does not mean being unable to talk to those I love. I would not have behaved in any other way, and these experiences have led to my strongest attitudes about teaching.

In retrospect, I understand why my own professors expected certain kinds of thinking and writing. On one level, those ways were all they knew, and, on another level, they were what made people successful in the world. What I can't understand, though, even today from this emotional distance, is why these professors never TAUGHT students how to perform the tasks expected of them. Classes in which professors reject that function simply replicate class structure; they reward middle-class students who already have the skills to be successful, and they punish other students who do not. They ultimately teach nothing, I would say, because "a knowledge made for others is no knowledge at all" (Spellmeyer 1996, 904). In my classes now, I refuse to travel down this path. When I see that feeling of loss on my students' faces, and I do, I cannot forget the feeling and deny my responsibility to them. I want to teach them how to perform in order to be successful, teach them the ways no one ever taught me. So, all of my classes make known the assumptions about literature that have guided the formation of the canon, the assumptions and principles by which the so-called experts have been guided.[5] All of my classes involve students in processes that force them to investigate the various structural elements of literature, how they hold together, and how they lead readers to ponder aspects of life. Students cannot escape my classes without being exposed to the processes of analyzing literature or without being given tools to help them engage productively in those processes.

These processes help students in other classes because they take some of the mystery away from what other professors expect. These other professors understand why I engage students in these ways, and they see what I do as a kind of service. Yet, this step cannot be all. I would be denying my own process of education as well as my working-class cultural world if I engaged students only in these processes. As my own education revealed in gory detail, signification itself—naming that which we know—cannot occur without an experiential anchoring. In order to learn at all and to grow, students need to start where they themselves are in relation to a text, an idea, a class. They need to fill that space between them and a text with their own words, their own reactions, their own guts if you will. For me to step into that space and to fill it for the student would be an exercise of my expertise, my "superior" knowledge. I could define my job in that way, many do, but it would also be an attempt, however implicit, to reject the student's subjectivity. Do I do it at times? Sure. We all have to "prove" our expertise in certain places and at certain times. But my pedagogy actively seeks to involve students in responding to literature in ways that span a spectrum from the personal to the analytical and formal. I want my students to respond to literature on a deeply personal level. I want them to write journals like the ones I used to write—engaged, thoughtful, meandering, personal, and nearly profound. I also want them to respond in analytical, interpretive ways, to see literature as constructed via various formal patterns, and I want them to formulate ideas about what makes good literature. I want them to bring their intelligence to bear on their personal experience, to consider and complicate it in order to develop an attitude to bring to the analytical tasks required of them.

Because of these goals, I utilize in all of my classes the theory and pedagogy of reader-response. This approach is defined in various ways and is often misunderstood, but I see it as a developmental approach rooted in students' personal responses to literature. These responses have to be articulated in order for students to choose or to identify with a particular theoretical or analytical approach to a text. Whether students see texts, eventually, through feminist, Marxist, or liberal humanist eyes has much to do with their preliminary personal response, and reader-response is the only approach that allows for and encourages a developmental process in which students can move from an articulated personal response to a theoretical interpretation. This process occurs according to students' own perspectives, their own set of values, and my task is to give them the tools, and offer them the guidance to move from one task to the other.[6] By moving students to consider the personal realm seriously, I encourage them to see their lifeworlds as important and to relate them to the lifeworld described in the literature. Moving to the topical realm students investigate how their personal worlds have been shaped by the social, cultural, and historical forces around them. With this work behind them students can approach formal analysis without feeling they have to regurgitate the teacher's view. They can hold onto their "selves," as they have understood them at the time.

Reader-response also opens the possibility for students to realize that there are various ways to read; that their insights may be valid but are not simply right. This approach encourages the development of self-knowledge along with the articulation of literary interpretation. Encouraging a range of responses to literature, from the personal to the topical, through the interpretive and formal, helps involve students in processes that encourage radical self-re-formation through awareness and articulation. And these are essential to the educational process. Teaching is a self-defeating act unless those involved find ways to expand their lifeworlds. This notion seems to me to be a particuarly working-class one about education—certainly I could not have become educated in any other way—and I think all teaching should be influenced by this philosophy.

Easy enough to do, right? Not always. I often put my own position as the holder of cultural capital on the line in this process, and this risk becomes exaggerated depending on where I teach. Despite my own class background, and despite where one teaches, the usual attitude toward teachers resembles that articulated in the basic bargain I discussed previously: Teachers are there to help students "get ahead." When, as a professor, you require students to write in personal forms in order to help them engage with literature, you are not necessarily involving them in a process that will help them develop those symbolic manipulation skills necessary to be successful. Students often, indirectly or directly, know this, and they wonder why you ask them to respond in these ways. They think, perhaps, that you don't know much more than they do, and they question your degree, where you got it, and/or why this school hired you anyway. Thus, to teach in this way becomes a very political act. While teaching at a very expensive private college, I often encountered students who resisted writing in a personal mode. They saw this mode as silly, babyish, and below them, and they couldn't understand why it was part of a college course. These students were not very good at responding in this mode either. They had been astutely trained in the abstract reasoning skills necessary for entrance and acceptance into the middle class, and they blamed me for assigning what they considered to be silly work. To my mind, they were not concerned with education as self-re-formation, with "real" learning. They wanted grades and qualifications, and their middle-class definitions of teaching and learning affected the way in which I was perceived. My very status as a professor was questioned because I was not abiding by the illusion maintained in the basic bargain of middle-class school culture.

While teaching at a primarily working-class state college, I find the general attitudes of the students different, but what defines status generally remains the same. Students here, for the most part, are happy for the opportunities to write in a personal mode in which they relate their life to what they read, but they see these tasks as easy and don't respect them much. They are, however, mystified by the analytical writing assignments. They need time and many opportunities to revise, to discuss what the expectations for these assignments are. To get these students to be successful at the analytical tasks requires much more than my own professors were willing to offer to me. It takes starting where the students are and moving them step by step to where they need to be in terms of skills and abilities. It takes time—time in class, time in the office—and it takes the willingness not to lecture, not to reveal to them over and over again why I am the professor with the Ph.D. and they are mere students. This kind of teaching is not what offers one prestige in the academy. When professors choose to do it, and I do, they make a political choice, denying or defying the elitist standards of our middle-class profession.

I work also with an English education program, training people how to teach. I chose this job, this place, and I love it, but when I tell that to some people who have jobs at major universities, who teach mostly graduate students and who have stronger publishing records than mine, I feel as if I am making a major confession. I'm not supposed to love it, it seems. Even people in my own department cannot identify with teaching teachers, with worrying about how to teach. They are concerned with the books, with the ideas. In each instance I have been placed in a position of low prestige to some extent by the elitist values of higher education—with that assertion I would have to agree. But I have also purposely chosen these paths and these ways to teach as a form of commitment to what I see as a kind of working-class culture within the academy. I have clearly exercised my subjective agency in choosing this particluar job and these particular activities.

And, you know, I can't help it: I like teaching. For me, the activity of teaching is immersion in material reality. Teaching in ways that engage students and myself in processes of exchange and mutual dialogue resists the abstract activities so valued and prioritized by the academy in general. Teaching, for me, is unalienated labor; it is process and engagement, rapport and communication. Writing and publishing are lonelier activities; their end products represent reified labor, the commodification of my thinking processes. I can do them; I do perform them. But I love to teach. That love places me on the nonprestigious track. I go to NCTE conferences, not MLA.

As Susan Miller (1991) has articulated wonderfully for us, teaching is the manual labor of our profession. Its association with manual labor places it below the other labor for which professors receive praise. This separation fits perfectly with the split between the middle class and the working class. The most salient feature of the middle class, its greatest defining characteristic, is mental labor, and it separates itself from the working class by separating mental from manual labor. Many professors, wanting to separate themselves from their secondary school colleagues, claim they only teach by necessity; they would prefer not to teach at all. Many secondary school personnel separate themselves from college and university professors by claiming that professors spend too much time with theory, and not enough

time thinking about real kids with real problems. The working-class
concern for the pragmatic and with application gets revealed here. I
find, however, that I do not accept this dichotomy, this conflict. I
don't want to separate the two; I never have. I see that many of my
choices have actively sought to keep the theoretical and the pragmatic alive and well for me. I am not at all surprised that I teach at a state
college, with primarily first-generation college students, many of
whom want to teach. I am not surprised that I continue to try to write
and publish, to root my signification in the experiential and have it
heard by a wider audience than the personal and the local. I don't
prioritize these two activities the way that many in the academic
world do, but I want to do both. I am not overly impressed when I
publish an article or finish a book manuscript—not any more so than
when a student writes a touching thank-you note or when my sister-
in-law gives birth or when my brother builds an addition to his house.
In keeping with my working-class roots, I don't believe my job
defines all of me. The important part of teaching for me relates directly to how I have always conceived of education—the ways that
words, reading, talking, and thinking enable us to transform ourselves. That notion itself does not belong to any class. Books, education, have always been part of my life; now they are part of my life
and my work.

As philosophers such as Susan Bordo (1989, 1993) have discussed, middle-class social power often operates by colonizing the
self, first evacuating and then reconstructing it. Spellmeyer (1996)
has linked certain kinds of teaching to this social and cultural process.
In retrospect I can see clearly how my own educational process
attempted to resist precisely this kind of evacuation. I refused to
sacrifice my working-class culture, my ideas and feelings, and mean-
dered my way to find means to be successful despite refusing total
indoctrination. For me as an educator, and I think for all of us, there
are lessons in this story. Working-class culture—and pedagogies
respectful of the personal and the narrative (as well as the analytical
and abstract)—can offer the roots of resistance to this kind of evacuation. Ideology can be resisted through the chaos of subjectivity, and
students and teachers alike can develop their own narratives from that
chaos. We, as professors, do not have to be complicitous in the colonization of our students' minds by filling them with our own expertise. Working-class educators need to think about the power of working-class culture, not its victimization. As Janet Zandy (1994) seeks to
explore, working-class consciousness does definitely act in the world.
To pursue the ways in which it does act might help lead us back to the
pursuit of wholeness in our lives, to a place where we do not internalize bizarre and inane elitist value systems. Rebellious working-

class kids are right: There is no reason to respect authority figures simply because they are in positions of authority. There is no reason for working-class academics to feel stigmatized by a value system that we do not see as valid. There is no reason to compare ourselves to others in academia. As I used to tell my brother, when certain people don't like you, take it as a good sign; you don't want them to like you anyway. In academia, teaching, or at least teaching in particular ways, is the manifestation of working-class culture. We must relish it. Teaching has become less valued precisely because it is the activity least able to be commodified, because it resists regulation and measurement. Educational institutions will always be middle class, let's not kid ourselves, but we can exercise our own subjective agency in our teaching. We too can manipulate the system for ends and goals not always compatible with those of a middle class value system. Let's do it.

To return to my place of origin, this educational process was and is a clear choice on my part. My choices did not lead me to the highest place of prestige within the American academy. That does at times bother me on an abstract, egotistical level. But the choice itself rarely bothers me on a day-to-day level because I like what I do, and I like where I teach. When I sit down and think about it, I don't want to be teaching in some high-powered graduate program or sitting alone in my study almost all of the time crunching out the next book. Yes, I want to learn and grow and always be developing as a person, a teacher, a professor. But I want to continue to move along these roads remembering my roots, my earliest educational experiences. I want to respect my students enough to allow them to start where they are and resist claiming that students these days just are not as bright as students used to be. My getting older and wiser should not be the excuse for rejecting my students and erasing their lives. My students are me.

Notes

1. The phrase "nowhere at home" is from Overall 1995.

2. I refer mostly to Dews and Law 1995.

3. In this book Rodriguez talks at length about how he moved from a working-class world to the public world of the middle class. He identifies himself with Richard Hoggart's scholarship boy as Hoggart describes him in *The Uses of Literacy*.

4. Willis (1977) discusses the ways in which working-class kids learn to manage the system to achieve their own ends. Their biggest goal is usually the freedom to run and live their lives in ways they choose without being hassled by authority figures and the system.

5. These are the assumptions that I share with my classes:

- The rule of significance: A literary work expresses a significant attitude about people and the world.
- The convention of metaphorical coherence: Metaphors should always be consistent.
- The convention of genre: Genres offer stable sets of norms with which to evaluate and label works.
- The rule of totality: Works should be understood to be coherent on as many levels as possible.
- The convention of thematic unity: Semantic and figurative oppositions should be made to fit into symmetrical binary patterns.
- A code of poetic tradition: This tradition provides a stock of symbols and types with agreed upon meanings and helps us recognize some object as poetry.

Students begin to see how and why their professors talk about literature in the ways they do when they come to understand these assumptions.

6. Most people automatically think that personal responses are easy, simple in fact, and they avoid or discourage them. But personal responses can be as complicated and intricate as any other kind of response. I do not see the relationship between the personal and the interpretive/formal as a hierarchical one. They exist on a spectrum.

Works Cited

Bordo, S. 1993. *Unbearable Weight: Feminism, Western Culture, and the Body*. Berkeley: University of California Press.

―――. 1989. "The Body and the Reproduction of Feminity: A Feminist Appropriation of Foucault." In *Gender/Body/Knowledge: Feminist Reconstructions of Being and Knowing*, ed. A. M. Jaggar and S. P. Bordo, 13–33. New Brunswick, NJ: Rutgers University Press.

Dews, C. L. B., and Law, C. L. 1995. *This Fine Place So Far from Home: Voices of Academics from the Working-Class*.

Hoggart. R. 1957. *The Uses of Literacy*. London: Chatto and Windus.

Miller, S. 1991. *Textual Carnivals: The Politics of Composition*. Carbondale: Southern Illinois University Press.

Overall, C. 1995. "Nowhere at Home: Toward a Phenomenology of Working-Class Consciousness." In Dews and Law, 209–220.

Rodriguez, R. 1982. *Hunger of Memory: The Education of Richard Rodriguez*. New York: Bantam.

Ryan, J., and Sackrey, C. 1996. *Strangers in Paradise: Academics from the Working-Class*. New York: University Press of America.

Spellmeyer, K. 1996. "After Theory: From Textuality to Attunement with the World." *College English* 58 (8): 893–913.

Willis, P. 1977. *Learning to Labor: How Working Class Kids Get Working Class Jobs*. New York: Columbia University Press.

Zandy, J., ed. 1994. *Liberating Memory: Our Work and Our Working-Class Consciousness*. New Brunswick, NJ: Rutgers University Press.

14

Living on the Border
Ethotic Conflict and the Satiric Impulse

Carol Reeves

Crowded in a dark amphitheater, they wait for class to begin. Miranda has heard rumors about this class—how impossibly esoteric the lectures, how difficult the exams, how persnickety the grading standards. But she is optimistic today because she has come to the city from a small village and is ready to enter this strange new world. As she surveys her peers, who are either sleeping or drinking Stay-awake and popping IQ-enhancers, screens magically surround her. Music plays. The Grand Canyon looms to her left, Jupiter on her right. A face appears on the front screen, so huge she can see inside the nostrils. "Good morning, class. I'm professor Carl Roganne. To obtain your copy of the course syllabus use the number 8590 and your password. If you need to speak with a person about your work, the program to access is ACT-Human-speak." Dumbfounded, Miranda asks a sleepy young woman sitting next to her, "Don't they have real people teaching at the university any more?" The woman rolls her eyes, "Where are *you* from?" and nudges a man next to her. "Didya hear what she asked? 'How come there aren't any real people teaching any more?'" They both laugh. Soon muffled titters can be heard as Miranda's question circulates through the crowd.

In his tiny cubicle, Malone Mavers works steadily and persistently on his latest article—his twentieth this year—to *Minutiae: A Journal for the Marginal* via

Academnet. Since leaving his small village many years ago, Malone has lived in a series of cubicles like this one, its walls covered with shelves stuffed not with books but with optical disks containing the contents of hundreds of recent academic journals that specialize in the rise and fall of the comma in the first ten years of the printing press. Malone had intended to read through these journals before he began his study, to make sure his claim was, if not original, at least "differently figured" from other contributions. Unfortunately, he just doesn't have the time. If he wants to keep his job here, he must produce thirty articles by the end of the year. Sometimes he wonders if anyone ever reads them. Sometimes, he feels lonely.

Satire may be our best weapon against the subjugating and alienating power of our academic institutions if only because it embraces the irony inherent in the act of resisting what ultimately subjugates us. To satirize is to be at once an insider and an outsider, to have both the insider's knowledge of the institutional conventions one is satirizing and the outsider's skepticism. Recent cultural criticism of institutions does not suggest satire as an agent of change, however. Mary Douglas (1986) argues that institutions "systematically direct individual memory and channel our perceptions . . ." and that our only "hope of intellectual independence is to resist" (92). But if our perceptions—including our concepts of independence and intellect—are directed and channeled by the institutions we inhabit, then how is resistance possible? Douglas is more concerned with "discovering how the institutional grip is laid upon our mind" (92) than in identifying the tools of resistance.

In his critique of academic institutions, David Damrosch (1995) doesn't push for outright resistance but rather for more diversity in the academic gene pool: "For the better part of a century, we have been selecting for certain kinds of alienation and aggression on campus" (9). He asks that we "reconsider the sorts of academic personality we encourage—and even create—through our extended rituals of training and acculturation" (9). While Douglas calls for wholesale resistance, Damrosch calls for the blending of diverse voices, including that of the "intellectually sociable" individual who hasn't yet conformed to the institutional principles of alienation and aggression, which, Damrosch believes, are "historically outmoded and intellectually counterproductive" (14).

However, neither Douglas nor Damrosch seems to understand the inexorably ironic position of those with the diverse voices whose very existence at the university is, at times, a form of resistance in itself.

And neither of their solutions is automatically possible for those of us who inhabit the borderland between the academy and our social class culture because we are forever moving *between* cultures, inhabiting a space where resisting the academy and blending into it are often done simultaneously—to our advantage as well as disadvantage. Even if outright resistance were possible, it might be more easily accomplished by those who are, because of their social class, more entitled culturally, more thoroughly academic insiders, secure in their belonging and intimately acquainted with the institution's modes and values. However, they may lack the skepticism necessary to reassess the norms that they have lived with comfortably for most of their lives. While Damrosch's solution of blending diverse voices is laudable, who is willing to *listen* to those diverse voices? I have not noticed any active interest in my voice, in my perspective as a cultural outsider—a "provincial," as my provost has called me, not unkindly, during a performance review. It is I who must blend into the academy, not the other way around.

To be at once an insider and an outsider, to resist while fitting in, is to inhabit that ironic negative space underlying the satiric voice. Satire is merely the controlled, polished, intentional product of that state of being. Escaping the poststructuralist loop in which the notion of ideological and linguistic subjugation calls into question the notion of ideological and linguistic resistance, the satiric impulse originates in the bipolar voice of the insider who is also the outsider, the reformer who is also the company person. For example, Jonathan Swift's outsider perspective was the engine of his scathing attack on the institutions that were exploiting the powerless, an attack made possible by his insider knowledge of those institutions. Another border dweller is P.J. O'Rourke, a liberal in his years at the *National Lampoon* but now a conservative who has never fit entirely into the conservative agenda and sometimes sounds like a liberal in his condemnation of particular conservative positions. Writers for the San Francisco–based *Diseased Pariah News* (Thorne and Shearer 1990), a satirical magazine for HIV-positive people, declare in the first issue that their purpose is to carve out a place for those HIV-positive folks who have never quite found community among the angry Act-Up crowd or the touchy-feely New-Age self-healing crowd and have had their fill of drug trials and doctor-patient relations and funeral directors. They satirize all the various corners of the AIDS epidemic they have inhabited as insiders with the outsider's ambivalence and skepticism.

I have inhabited that negative ironic space of the insider/outsider in unconscious as well as consciously intentional ways at the university. My unconscious response to the cultural conflict that has boiled inside me has been to alternate *between* resisting and joining the academy through two conflicting ethical appeals, one I reserved for the public and one I reserved for the page. In public, I have been the daughter of the West Texas flatlands where I was acculturated toward community and taught to avoid aggression, self-assertion, and direct confrontation—to self-efface, if necessary, in order to suspend the physical alienation and build the social harmony so crucial to cooperative ventures. Off the page, in the classroom and across campus, I am one of those "social intellectuals" that Damrosch proposes as fresh genetic material for the academy. I have unconsciously employed my public ethos to resist the academy, to contest the posturing and the threatening behaviors that were anathema to the values of my home. On the page, however, where I learned very early that I could be aggressive, assertive, and directly confrontational, I am the daughter of the academy, the professor. While my public ethos became the vehicle for what occurs rarely in the academy—playful discourse, self-effacement—writing became a vehicle for what never occurred in the talk of those around me back home: direct argument and self-assertion.

Nowhere has this ethotic conflict[1] been more conspicuous than in the classroom, where I have been the funny flatlander in person and the punctilious professor in my written comments on students' papers, unconsciously creating an odd mix of levity and antipathy. While I challenged the academy in the classroom by resisting the combative forms of communication and the authority students probably expected from me, in my comments on their writing, I affirmed the aggressive and alienating modes that I dispelled in the classroom. This *unconscious* playing out of my ethotic conflict disabled my teaching by confusing and angering students.

On the other hand, I made a more *conscious*—and effective— effort to help students, many of whom were from backgrounds similar to mine, blend into and, at the same time, resist the academy: to challenge, to critique, to argue through indirect means, through the double-voiced levity and antipathy of the satirist. Once I recognized my midwestern students' passivity, their reluctance to argue openly, or to criticize anyone—including each other, me, or the institution itself— as a cultural roadblock, I turned to formal satiric writing assignments that ask students to criticize and argue indirectly, as a way to encourage them to enter the academy as empowered citizens with the freedom and the knowledge both to join and to resist the academy.

The Unconscious Ethotic Conflict: The Flatlander in the Classroom/The Professor on the Page

While the values of academic culture, as David Damrosch (1995) points out, "foster—and reward—alienation and aggression at all levels of academic life" (6), my social class culture of origin fostered and rewarded nonaggressive behaviors calculated to increase comfort and familiarity among those who must depend on one another. I inherited the flatlander ethos from people who settled the West Texas plains, who were among the first to break up the miles of bluestem grasses to plant wheat and cotton, the first to plunge wells down through the thick, loamy soil to the underground ocean in the Ogalalla formation. The social organization was nonhierarchical, partly because the first settlers had migrated from southern and eastern states, where they had sometimes existed near the bottom of well-defined social hierarchies and partly because preagribusiness farming communities depended on harmonious participation from everyone. To increase comfort, one avoided communication behaviors that tended to create discomfort—*overt* self-assertion, *open* confrontation. The more accomplished one was, the more modest and self-effacing one was expected to be. Self-assertion, disagreement, and criticism were indirect, delivered through irony or humor or mock self-effacement or elaborate disclaimers, all of which, if used appropriately, can attenuate the perception of connection and reduce the perception of arrogance so that one's intended point might be accepted, like a bitter pill coated with jam. (Sometimes, the bitterness seeps through the jam, of course, which explains the acerbic tone of Molly Ivins's writing as well as the quips of the former Texas governor Ann Richards. For example, in a gubernatorial debate with Clayton Williams, Ann Richards referred to Williams's famous dismissal of rape victims— "They oughtta just lay back and enjoy it"—by explaining at the beginning of the debate that she was going to avoid any mudslinging but that she would have some clear evidence against her opponent. Then she looked over at Williams and said, "And when I lay out this evidence, Claytie, I want you to just lie back and enjoy it." Even "Claytie" had to chuckle sheepishly.)

The humorous, indirect attack allows all parties to escape the consequences of misunderstanding. Just in case you have misunderstood the other person's position or that person has misunderstood yours— and it is always likely that people who live many dusty miles apart do misunderstand one another—you can shuck it all off with a laugh. For the sake of community, the harvest, the co-op, the history of family connection, you simply never challenged anyone unless you had the skills of the *eron,* the ironist who can clothe his or her position or criticism in irony, allowing what Kierkegaard (1965) called "negative freedom," for "it is by irony that the subject emancipates himself from the constraint imposed by the continuity of life" (273). The constraints of community within some cultures prevent outright critique, so the *eron* manages to critique indirectly. For example, my father's neighbor had a habit of neglecting to plow his fields to keep the top-soil from blowing in the high winds. The result was sand blowing from his field, across the road, into our house and yard, creating not only a "dirt-out" for us but a loss of good topsoil for our neighbor, whose farming practices tended to work against the conservation efforts of my dad and the other farmers in the community. All criticism of this farmer would be playful, leveled through joking and iron-ic remarks so subtle that any stranger to the community would miss the intent. For example, during a game of canasta with this neighbor and his wife, my dad would say with a wide grin: "Sorry about the dust everywhere; we've just been bathed in Harvey's entire field." Harvey would grin sheepishly, understanding that although his neigh-bor was not happy with the unplowed field, there was no real hostili-ty between them.

Mine is certainly not the only culture that has developed joking rituals to accommodate both social critique and social harmony. On the Aegean island of Fourni, inhabitants are generally pacifists who suppress hostilities through joking to keep peace with neighbors and family members. Established as a colony for fugitives from the law and from prosecution in the Ottoman Occupation forces in the 1840s, Fourni has a history of antagonism among its inhabitants, who learned to criticize indirectly, to diffuse open confrontation, through what Dimitriou-Kotsoni (1995) called "institutionalized joking" (36). Institutionalized joking—recognized teasing relationships, patterned irony, and innuendo—is subversive, functioning as a way to assert domination or criticism of an individual or the society without dis-rupting social harmony. Such joking indicates a society without hier-archy, for as Dimitriou-Kotsoni explains, "In a hierarchical relation-ship there is no room for joking" (44–45). Moreover, "the less hierar-chical a society is, the more widespread the occurrence of joking pat-terns may be, because the less hierarchical a society is the more it allows for negotiation of the power relations and for flexibility" (45).

In my culture, social symmetry is often maintained by joking rit-uals that deliver the intended message while deflecting hostility that will lead to years of silence. Unfortunately, within institutions such as the college classroom or the workplace, with their more hierarchical social situations, the friendly, sometimes barbed irony, the indirect, self-effacing use of humor to soften the edges of conflict and formal power, may be interpreted by those expecting hierarchies to be assert-ed and maintained, or those accustomed to directness, as confusing or, worse, dissembling.

My classroom demeanor has been folksy and informal, funny and elliptical, eliciting very high marks on student evaluations for "respects students" and "stimulates good discussion." In my first

years as an assistant professor, I was unconsciously and automatically disposed against hierarchy and my own domination in the classroom setting, always working unconsciously to increase comfort levels and always unconscious of how these tendencies diminished my
authority. To offset tension and insecurity that I sensed among students, especially first-semester freshmen, I employed the flatlander
behaviors that reduced me to their level. Spontaneously, I would tell
funny anecdotes that related only indirectly to the day's topic and
that sometimes focused on my mistakes rather than accomplishments,
as an example of how one negotiates around one's weaknesses. Often
the more confidence I had in my knowledge and expertise, the more I
effaced that knowledge and expertise. My subtext seems to have
always been "If I can do this, you can, too." Unfortunately, only the
more mature, older students understood my objective in telling such
stories. One student, Julie, who was my age, who was from a background similar to mine, and who eventually became a friend,
explained,

> You always made me feel I could be successful, that what you
> achieved was possible for me because you equalized the distance
> between us. My other professors only made me feel in awe of them,
> but you made me aware of my own strengths. But I think younger
> students misunderstood you. They expected you to be like the other
> professors.

She was right. Students were not always satisfied even while they
might have enjoyed my class. While my early student evaluations
were never terrible, they were never stellar. I received consistently
high ratings on questions dealing with my concern and respect for
students, but there were entirely too many comments like these:

> Dr. Reeves does not act like a professor. I don't think she is ready to
> be a professor.

> Dr. Reeves is well-degreed but not well-educated.

I believe these comments reflected students' disappointment in my
failure to "seem" professorial and my failure to make them feel just a
smidgen of discomfort. Neglecting to challenge students in the way
they had come to expect, my challenges were often too indirect for
them to notice. If students offered half-baked responses in discussion, responses they and I knew were half-baked, I felt satisfied that I
had created a climate in which students felt comfortable offering half-
baked responses. Or, attempting to encourage the student toward a
fuller understanding, I would offer playful, humorous nudges whose
critical intent was often lost in the wave of laughter I created. Once,
on a midterm evaluation of my teaching, a young woman wrote, "You

make class fun, but you never pounce on the stupid ideas; all ideas seem equally relevant which is very confusing. Tell us when we've presented a stupid point!" Indeed, in his review of my teaching performance, my department chair once noted my tendency to "back off from challenging students, to give up an opportunity for substantive debate way too early so that students remain comfortable in their ignorance."

Coming at the end of classes for which I had worked arduously to create challenging and interesting assignments and had used what I considered my best personal resources to create a harmonious classroom environment, such comments demoralized and depressed me. While I knew I had a command of the material I was teaching, that I had been well educated and well prepared for my teaching responsibilities, I began to think I had made a terrible mistake in becoming an academic. I simply did not fit in. I told a woman conducting interviews with assistant professors around the country that "it is becoming more and more clear to me that my most important strengths as a human being are getting me nowhere in the classroom."

Noting my ethos, several concerned colleagues, in sincere attempts to advise me, criticized my passivity and my tendency to self-efface in public. One friend and colleague, with a public style that can be imperious and aggressive during debates, advised me after a meeting: "Carol, you've got to stop that self-deprecating way of yours. You'll get nowhere with it." And another colleague, on a conference panel with me, told me after our panel that my little jokes on myself, told before my talk, "are typical you, but you should really learn to stop that; it makes you look less serious and respectable."

Yet, where those colleagues saw my failure to command respect, my audience often saw someone who would not make them feel threatened, someone who invited participation. In particular contexts, when audience participation is absolutely necessary, a nonthreatening public persona will draw out the collective. This style has served me well in my role as director of a writing-across-the-curriculum program because it stimulated open exchange among people who had little confidence in their ability to teach writing. I discovered that my humor and self-effacement were powerful tools that put everyone at ease, that allowed a remarkable entrance into serious discussions, a way to tap the turbulence—the criticism of a writing requirement above the freshman level, the suspicion that the "English department was shirking its duties to teach writing," and so on—and allow it to escape without much incident. In the end, I believe this ethos encouraged faculty to feel confident in themselves, to take risks in their teaching, and to report both their successes and failures to me and to

the others. I was only the expert in the shadows of their attempts—
someone who sent them articles to read, who asked good questions,
who made everyone comfortable and sociable, who made good discussion possible. The flatlander ethos served to create solidarity
among faculty who had always been divided by disciplinary boundaries and by a pervasive lack of dialogue about teaching.

Within the institutional hierarchy, Writing Across the Curriculum
(WAC) programs are themselves "outsider," second-class enterprises
behind honors, core humanities, and other university programs whose
cultural entitlement derives from particular elitist class assumptions as
well as traditional knowledge domains. As sly instigators of reform—
in promoting writing to learn as a framework for more global pedagogical transformation—WAC programs are built upon a skepticism
of the received values of elitist academic culture: that intelligence is
academic talent (either you've got it or you don't, and no teaching
trick is going to make a dumb kid bright); that teaching is merely common sense; that student learning and teacher knowledge are highly
correlated. However, without acknowledging those values, in some
way, or without taking on insider status, no WAC program can accomplish reform. Successful WAC programs become institutionalized, but
they maintain their integrity by reforming from the inside out.

Similarly, to be a successful class outsider is to reform from the
inside out, to *consciously* inhabit the class consciousness and cultural
rhetoric of the other in order to accommodate as well as to resist and
reform. However, I was unconsciously resisting and accommodating
academic culture in ways that worked against my success. In my
despair, I had not pinpointed the real source of my problem, which
wasn't my strengths themselves but the way they were working at
cross-purposes. Diametrically opposed, my public, folksy ethos and
my academic, on-the-page ethos were creating misunderstanding and
blocking my efforts to teach well.

While off the page, I have been more often a flatlander; on the
page, particularly in commentary on student papers, I have been more
often a professor with a direct, assertive, and, at times, acerbic voice.
Long ago, writing introduced me to an intellectual life and to my
aggressive, argumentative self. Because no one I knew wrote anything other than letters, writing allowed me to develop an on-the-
page assertiveness that prepared me for academic success. Because I
had no fear of someone standing there, expecting me to concede and
connect, I could be entirely direct and aggressive on the page. I could
play the game of argument and analysis and scholarship—and they
always seemed like games to me because I had learned them outside
of my essential home, my essential cultural self—with impunity and
to great personal satisfaction. As a child, I wrote arguments against

the teachings of my church—where you were not supposed to argue, especially if you were a girl; against the racists in our community; against the raucous boys on the bus who grabbed my diary and read it out loud. But I never shared that writing with anyone, and it wasn't until much later, in high school, that English teachers noticed I could write. And it was through my writing, rather than my speaking, that I eventually became an academic.

In my teaching, I did, in fact, pounce on students' weak ideas and weak writing, but only on the page, where I was liberated from their physical presence and from my ingrained public ethos. While in my comments I tried to be kind, encouraging, and positive, I was more often unrelentingly academic and analytical, pointing out faulty reasoning and faulty writing in a direct, authoritative, commanding style that contradicted my folksy, informal classroom tone. The following are excerpted examples:

> Surely you could have extended your thinking beyond the obvious here, especially given our class discussions that have covered so many different perspectives. Where have you been? In la la land?

> This is simply unacceptable. You keep making the same point in every paragraph without moving beyond the obvious. And your only bit of evidence lies at the bottom of page three.

> Foucault has ruined your style. You've become turgid and unreadable. Just look at your syntax in the paragraph I marked. It's like a parody of Foucault!

> You aren't backing up these assertions with evidence from the text. How do you know that Pearl was taking her anger at her husband out on her children? Where is the evidence?

Here, on the page, I was challenging the student, being "the professor"—lecturing, judging, asserting my expertise—with a tone that I would have never used in class or in conferences. While I also commended students for what they did well, and while I took great care to remind, respond, teach, argue with students—that is, to establish a challenging intellectual relationship with them on the page that might not have been present in the classroom—I am certain that I caused more harm than good. After reading my teaching evaluations for one semester and noting the frequency of comments about how "critical" and "demanding" and "demoralizing" they found me (while they also gave me high marks for "treats student with respect" and "stimulates good discussion"), *I* felt demoralized. After all, I took such pains to be kind and understanding! I shared my problem with another colleague.

After examining a stack of papers I had graded, she remarked that my comments were thorough and conscientious, the sort of commentary she viewed as necessary and effective and what she tried to employ in her own teaching. So why had a student run to her advisor in tears after reading my comments on her paper, complaining, "I just can't satisfy Dr. Reeves!"? Why was my colleague commending my work while my students complained? One possible explanation is that even if she did employ this sort of critical style—she never showed me papers she had graded, but I took her at her word—her classroom style is formal and authoritative, evoking the professorial ethos of expertise. Her in-class and on-the-page styles were complementary, while my styles were directly opposed. If students didn't see me as the authoritative professor in the classroom, as some of them indicated in comments on teaching evaluations, then how could they allow me to be the authoritative professor on the page?

Why wasn't this obvious to me at the time? Why was I so oblivious to the source of the irony—that students would laugh with me in the classroom but vent their animosity and distrust later, in their comments on course evaluations? My reluctance to challenge in person, coupled with a happy willingness to challenge on the page, created a mixture of levity, confusion, and animosity.

We all have different ethotic styles we reserve for different occasions, for public speaking, for different kinds of writing, but my two distinct styles represented a strange bipolarity resulting from my *unconscious* attempts at diaspora, at uniting the best of my past with the best of my present life, to create and enjoy connection within an atmosphere of judgment and competition, to establish social symmetry where hierarchy is expected and, sometimes, enjoyed, and to accomplish all of the above by deflating students' perceptions of my own hierarchical position. This was my way of resisting academic hierarchy and merging my divergent voice, like a weed, into the academic field. But while the flatlander ethos creates comfort, warmth, and solidarity, which are essential for eliciting open-hearted discussion, self-revelation, and genuine exchange in the classroom, it detracts from the ethos of academic expertise and authority, which often creates boundaries and distance that are essential in most situations for establishing respect. While my flatlander ethos detracted from the public style expected of a professor, the assertive style I had saved for the page at times conflicted with what students had come to expect from me in person. It was as if I had become two very distinct persons who seemed to be at war with one another.

For too long, the explanation of my failure to achieve the success in the classroom that I thought all my hard work deserved escaped me. Then I experienced one of those crystallizing moments when the shock of self-recognition is dizzying. It happened while I watched another young academic, whose nasal lilt placed her origins somewhere near Amarillo, Texas, give a conference paper. After the first panelist completed a dry, abstruse paper, this young woman stood up and told a funny story about herself, about how she had missed her flight and arrived just a few minutes before the panel began and how she was "not sure if I've brought my conference paper or a student's research paper in this briefcase. So this could be either what you came to hear, or it could be a paper on the pros and cons of airline deregulation." The comment wasn't especially funny, but her thick accent and her body emphasis produced a few chuckles and a palpable sigh of relief from the audience who had just sat through a very tedious paper. Yet some people exchanged skeptical glances. I was embarrassed for her. Next to the deadly serious, exquisitely elutriated scholarly persona of the person sitting next to her, she seemed unprofessional. She had liberated the audience from academic formality and allowed them to breathe—she had given them permission to laugh and relax—but in so doing, she had lowered perceptions of her own expertise and authority despite her own exquisitely elutriated scholarly *paper*, the product of maniacal overpreparation. I saw myself in her and suddenly understood the source of my despair. Like her, I was caught between two cultures, between two ethotic modes, not quite an insider, not quite an outsider, and my response had been an odd mingling of what I must have assumed were the strengths I'd taken from both modes.

Overcorrection of what the outsider perceives as behaviors that are alien to the insider culture is a likely response to the recognition of ethotic conflict. A colleague and friend in another department confided to me that he is from a background similar to mine and has experienced the same ethotic confusion I describe here. His response was to thoroughly hide his culture of origin in his demeanor and play within the rules of the academic game—and he understands quite well that it is a "game," a cultural rhetoric and not an essential truth he has adopted. Yet he often feels dissatisfied and lonely, no longer fitting into his culture of origin but never quite satisfied with his position in the academy, no matter how many books he writes. Even so, it is not surprising, given what I have already said about satire, that my colleague's primary research topic is Molière.

After discovering my own ethotic conflict, I went through a brief period of overcorrection that, thankfully, has begun to resolve itself. In the classroom, I worked so hard to be serious that I was, in fact, soporific. I turned to lecture, planning thirty- and forty-minute talks after which students were so enervated that they couldn't participate in discussion. Trying to avoid the irrelevant anecdote or self-disparaging humor that I had employed so spontaneously before, I controlled my use of humor to the point that I bored myself.

Conscious Ethotic Conflict:
Satire and Student Activism

My own ethotic conflict has become an engine of purpose in the classroom, where I have exploited my own tendency to assert my mem-
bership in the academy on the page while making fun of that mem-
bership off the page. I employ satiric assignments to "academize" my
own ethotic tendencies toward indirection and humor as well as to
acculturate students, to grant them the power to critique aspects of
academic culture that they feel are most oppressive while also practicing the voices of the academy. Like me, most of my students at
Butler are also caught between cultures, not quite insiders, not quite
outsiders, and my job, I have always felt, is to help them learn what I
had learned—to use writing to play the game of argument and analysis. But I also want these polite midwesterners to learn how to consciously employ the tools of indirection—irony and humor—as vehicles of social critique.

As they become insiders, our students may very well want to satirize the conventions they are learning, conventions that are not at
all playful or ironic. When students satirize academic discourse conventions, they demonstrate sensitivity to what Cathy Popkin (1992)
calls the "ubiquitous academic 'of course,'" a rhetorical posturing
that "admits no uncertainty, invites no discussion; it invokes only to
dismiss from debate or explanation; . . . it silences both forceful dissent and timid questions" (173–74). One pharmacy major chose the
writing in math textbooks as his satiric victim, explaining to me that
although he felt comfortable with mathematics, he often noticed that
the textbook writing is both arrogant and patronizing. In the introduction to his burlesque, the phrases "everyone knows" and "it is
obvious" and the omission of important information reveal his sensitivity to the "of course" posturing:

> Everyone knows that when baking chocolate chip cookies, one must
> have something in which to bake them. Thus, after many computa-
> tions which we will omit here but can be read at leisure in the
> Appendix 32b in the back of the cookbook, we find that the ideal
> area of the baking apparatus, commonly called a cookie sheet, is 82
> inches squared. Therefore, it is obvious that the dimensions of the
> ideal sheet should be 9.055 inches by 9.055 inches in order to pro-
> duce the maximum amount of cookies in one baking as is proved by
> Theorem 53c on page 236.

Many students choose to parody their professors' "voices"
either in the classroom or on the page. In her parody of a "major"
writing project in "Business Seminar," the "Five-Year Plan," in
which students are to create a five-year plan of their lives, a business

major captures a tone that is condescending and patronizing as it aims—or pretends—to be caring. In her "professor's instructions" are the following:

> The path you choose for yourself is the most important decision you will make in life (after deciding to attend Butler University with advantages like no place else. . . .). We want students to really look deep into their inner selves to find their goals and path choices. You will map out the next five years of your confusing yet enjoyable life. This is quite a scary process and requires much thought. But we, the professors, know that the students of Butler University, with advantages like no place else, are of the caliber to tackle this assignment and make the school proud to have them as students.

In the rest of the piece, the student gives "the professor's" example of what a good five-year plan would look like, revealing an uncanny ability to capture and ridicule the tedious and patronizing habits she notices in the classroom.

Since I encourage students to parody me, I have been forced to see myself in the satiric mirror. As an English professor, I have that annoying habit of analysis that often seems tedious to students and that parody captures to humorous effect. Here, in an excerpt from her "How to Analyze a Text," one student gets back at me:

> Find the deeper meaning underlying the surface of the piece. You can NEVER take a piece at face value. Again, you must dig. You cannot fully appreciate a text unless you understand its complete, deep meaning. You must pick, pick, pick! If you cannot find a meaning at first, dig deeper.

A taciturn, farmer's daughter from a rural Indiana community, this student would have never openly complained about the analytical approach I was asking her to take toward her favorite literature, but this exercise allowed her to make her point and helped me understand why she always had a pained expression during discussion and why my students needed me to justify the intellectual work I was expecting them to do. And as someone who can certainly take a joke, I wasn't offended.

Encouraging the indirect, satirical attack enables students to voice what is really bothering them without fear of retaliation. Many students decide to satirize a required core course that has become a sacred cow to the faculty who teach it but sometimes a dead cow to the students who must take it. Students sometimes perceive the educational philosophy of this course, Change and Tradition, as breadth rather than depth; in one semester, students are exposed to several different cultures—ancient Greece, Victorian England, and Spain, for example—and faculty are rarely specialists in any of these areas, although they do engage in preparatory workshops. In a parody of a Change and Tradition course syllabus, one student offered as one goal "to give students an opportunity to listen and interact with professors who have little or no knowledge of the topics covered in class," and offered as one learning objective "to teach students to read entire novels in two days and write papers on subjects totally unrelated to the novels." Another student wrote a faux letter to the editor by the late Sam Walton of Wal-Mart fame, whom she imagined had just been named as the new Change and Tradition director:

> Why am I so thrilled to direct this program? What could have motivated a dead billionaire out of the grave? Let me just say this; it stands for everything I have built my past life upon: Take the most intricate and wonderful items, the most diverse and thought-provoking works of cultures that have taken thousands of years to develop, and cram it down the throats of students in three weeks!

Sam was going to change the course title to "Spare Change for Traditions Program" and narrow it down to "the time it takes to cook a pop tart." This student's sophistication in using irony would likely have gone unnoticed if he had not been given this opportunity. Even though irony is a master trope, signaling both cognitive and rhetorical astuteness when used correctly, it is also, as Lori Chamberlain (1989) has said, subversive, invoking "notions of hierarchy and subordination, judgment and perhaps even moral superiority" (29). As a result, we don't often encourage students to be intentionally ironic. Liberated from fear of retaliation, these student satirists could consciously imitate and critique, resist, and join the academy. Usually mute and reluctant to participate in aggressive oral debate or to openly contest the ways in which the institution subjugates them, these students employed satire to become insiders who could talk the talk while remaining skeptical class outsiders who were not yet ready to walk the walk.

The class outsider can be plagued by the ethotic conflict, the unconscious stylistic move toward both accommodation and resistance. To inhabit that ironic negative space is to be always negotiating the class terrain with its border conflicts and its tacit roadblocks, always searching for a way to blend into that scene while also protecting and savoring an identity that just might, ironically, become the force of resistance to and reform of that terrain. Because it is the conscious manifestation of the insider/outsider opposition, satire can serve as a useful vehicle for controlling ethotic conflict, negotiating the terrain, and, thereby, planting the seeds of reform.

Note

1. Readers may wish to refer to Brinton 1986 for more on ethotic arguments.

Works Cited

Brinton, A. 1986. "Ethotic Argument." *History of Philosophy Quarterly* 3(3): 245–258.

Chamberlain, L. 1989. "Bombs and Other Exciting Devices, or the Problem of Teaching Irony." *College English* 51 (1): 29–40.

Damrosch, D. 1995. *We Scholars: Changing the Culture of the University.* Cambridge, MA: Harvard University Press.

Douglas, M. 1986. *How Institutions Think.* Syracuse, NY: Syracuse University Press.

Dimitriou-Kotsoni, S. 1995. "Dramatization and De-Dramatization: Conflict and Joking in an Aegean Island." *Journal of Mediterranean Studies* 5 (1): 33–49.

Kierkegaard, S. 1965. *The Concept of Irony*, trans. Lee M. Capel. New York: Harper and Row.

Popkin, C. 1992. "A Plea to the Wielders of Academic Dis(of)course." *College English* 54 (2): 173–181.

Thorne, B., and T. Shearer. 1990. *Diseased Pariah News #1.* San Francisco: Thorne Publishing.

15

Rising and Converging
Race and Class in the South

Hephzibah Roskelly

"White people know a great deal about how racism works," says
Christine Sleeter (1994) in a recent article on teaching multiculturalism: "We have observed White people intimately all our lives" (7). Of
course, white people know much about race and racism from their
own cultural and ethnic experience. Yet in teaching and in other
aspects of academic life, race and racism continue to be matters that
white university professors and the students in their literature and
writing courses avoid, except in the most abstract, and therefore safe,
ways. They disavow the racist label themselves, they make racism
into a historical artifact, and they ignore their own racial and ethnic
identities. But the primary way that white students and their teachers
ignore what they know about how racism works is by claiming class
instead of race as the real discriminator in society and culture.

In a workshop I gave two years ago on the issue of racism, writing,
and the uses of diversity, the group of all white (save one) male and
female English professors participated by thinking and writing about
issues of oppression and how the dynamics of disenfranchisement
worked out in personal, social, and cultural ways. They made lists of
how dominant groups reacted to their nondominant opposite—male to
female, heterosexual to homosexual, educated to illiterate, married to
single—and considered how these attitudes reflected institutional rules
and cultural values. The discussion was lively and thoughtful, and the
lists helped participants move into the sensitive area of white/black
relations. And then one teacher said, "Isn't all this talk of race really a
matter of class?" I looked around the room at the nodding heads, the
suddenly relieved faces. They *wanted* to believe that racism and race

itself was really "a matter of class." They were willing—happy—to begin a discussion of how class, which they left undefined, determines individuals' futures and beliefs, of how little race matters in the equation of opportunity and attitudes of the majority culture.

Class and race are so interwoven in this culture that it's difficult—maybe especially in the South where I grew up and teach—to tease them apart. But unless we explore how and why they're connected we risk continuing to see class in only its most shallow, undefined ways and continuing to ignore race and the ugly spectre of racism that undermines much of our work as teachers of literacy. As southerners have always known, in legend at least, telling a story is the best, sometimes the only, way to explain things that are vexed or complicated. In this essay, I want to tell several southern stories in order to explain the complicated connection between race and class that matters to me as a teacher and writer, to my students in a large southern state university, and to the ethical dimensions of the work we accomplish together.

Flannery O'Connor tells lots of stories about the race/class conundrum. A white southerner of what a southerner might call "genteel upbringing," a woman whom Alice Walker (1981) surprised herself by calling "a lady" in her essay on O'Connor's work, O'Connor knew how deeply embedded and intermingled race and class are in the culture. O'Connor remains one of the few white American writers to grapple with what Toni Morrison (1992) calls "the Africanist presence" in American culture. Morrison's study, *Playing in the Dark: Whiteness and the Literary Imagination,* is a discussion of the effect of a totally racialized culture on American writing in the nineteenth and twentieth centuries. Her premise is that the central cultural and literary traditions of mainstream American writing—including individualism, opportunity, and duality—are responses to the racial *other* and the threat that this other poses to the social order. It is a slim, but sweeping, book, suggesting how deep and powerful the metaphors for blackness and difference are in the work of writers from Melville to Faulkner, and implying that few writers have confronted race or the *other* directly at all. O'Connor is one of the few who have.[1]

"Everything That Rises Must Converge," one of O'Connor's most clear assertions of the race and class problem, is set in the civil rights era South, where tensions arise when events force the main character, an older, white woman of genteel class, to recognize that neither class nor race determines how people will, or can, act. When African Americans ride the bus like their white counterparts, when they shop in the same stores and bring home the same hats as their white female employers, then as the woman's son says, "You haven't the foggiest idea where you stand now or who you are" (1962, 407).

"Knowing who you are" is the key to knowing how to behave. The mother in "Everything That Rises . . ." is certain about what to wear to town, how to sit on a bus, how to talk to black children and their mothers, because, as she reminds her son, "your great-grandfather was a former governor of this state . . . your grandmother was a Godhigh" (404). She is also clear about the fact that any African American female—even one riding the same bus or wearing the same expensive hat—has no such heritage and therefore no such claim on the kind of genteel behavior she herself exhibits. For the mother, who counts on class and racial distinctions, the shock of the distinctions' suddenly being erased, as the black mother wearing the same hat reacts angrily to her ladylike offer of a penny to her small son, causes her literally to lose her identity. She crumbles and falls to the sidewalk at the end of the story, "retreated in her mind to a time more congenial to her desires," as Alice Walker (1991) describes the ending to her own mother (51).

Walker's essay on O'Connor is her attempt to come to terms with race and class, and she makes a visit to her childhood home, just down the road from O'Connor's, where she admits: "I have come to this vacant house to learn something about myself in relation to Flannery O'Connor, and will learn it whether anyone is home or not" (57). Walker uses O'Connor's story to tell hers more fully. Both their stories help me tell my own, like theirs a story of how deeply connected and divided the races are in the South by class and color, of how painful and how necessary the telling of the story is.

Like some of my colleagues and like many more of my students, my class background is mixed. My father was born the twelfth child of tenant farmers on a sandy tract of land in northern Florida; my mother was born the second of four children of a doctor in an airy, verandaed house in New Orleans. The difference in their class status made for clear divergences in every cultural facet of their southern lives but one: They were divided by religion, politics, education, art; their unconscious assumptions about race connected them.

My mother's family had a cook and a man who did the gardening, and some of my earliest memories are of moments where I see myself following one or another of these two around, listening to their talk, asking questions, no doubt getting in their way. There is little or no overt racial hostility or even demonstration of condescension in these memories. What's significant, now that I look back, is that I didn't question, and clearly was taught not to question, the differences between us, the fact that Emma, my grandmother's cook, was never asked to stay to dinner, the fact that Noel, the gardener, never sat in the parlor with my Aunt Effie to discuss what to plant in the fall. The careful alignment of position took place in a context of both racial and class-bound privilege that seemed so smooth that it felt benign.

But one memory of my visits to New Orleans reminds me that the lessons I learned were not at all innocent. Emma had a daughter, Marie, who was about the same age as I was, and for years we played together when my family came to New Orleans on vacation. One day, laughing and tussling together on the sofa, we were abruptly rebuffed by a friend of my grandmother's who walked into the room and pulled me up straight while admonishing me to "act like a lady." There were no other discussions that I was privy to, but Marie stopped coming to visit, and we lost touch.

Historian W. J. Cash points out in *The Mind of the South* (1941) that southerners did not view their world primarily in terms of class: "He [the Southerner] never got around to being, before all else, a member of a caste . . ." (35). But the emphasis on codes of behavior, "acting like a lady," as well as the obsession with genealogy and family connections in the South demonstrate how bound together class and culture have been. For southerners of the urban and relatively wealthy class, those who would have been planters or their overseers in antebellum days, knowing the past is like knowing a religion. And as Cash says, that class set itself "sharply apart from the common people, still pretty often lumped together as the poor whites, not only by economic condition but also by the far vaster gulf of a different blood and a different (and long and solidly established) heritage" (4). This story, a denial of history, of course, has been a powerful fiction for southerners of upper and lower class and for African Americans as well.

Yet even among the "poor whites" who were excluded from the genteel southerner's idea of personal identity, pride in knowing who you were and knowing how to behave were deeply embedded. Given the exploitation of these poor white yeoman farmers who worked for meager compensation for landowners who resented and feared them, it seems amazing that there was—and remains—so little obvious class hatred. Cash argues that the southerner's habit of claiming kinship, even distant, was enough to mitigate class anger. Added to that, of course, was the way that class hatred directed itself against the northern intruder and against the freed slave. "If he had no worth-while interest at stake in slavery, if his real interest ran the other way about, he did nevertheless have that, to him, dear treasure of his superiority as a white man, which had been conferred on him by slavery; and so was as determined to keep the black man in chains, saw in the offensive of the Yankee as great a danger to himself, as the angriest planter" (66).

The intimacy between black and white was quite different for the rural southerner than for the urban one. In the city, the employer-servant relationship determined a kind of close knowledge, but the relationship between the two, as between my grandmother and her cook, was patently unequal and based on clear recognition of class difference. But among the large group of poor white families who tenanted on farms across the South, the distinctions were much less overt. After slavery had ended, the sharecropping system in the rural South put everybody in the fields, both poor white and black, men, women and children, since a family's labor figured in the amount of land they might rent and in their income.

Jack Kirby (1987) writes about the poor Southern farmer after the Civil War in *Rural Worlds Lost*: "So free women and children marched off to chop and pick cotton and to weed and pull corn and tobacco as before. Large families remained as economically important as ever too; for theoretically, the larger the labor force, the more production, the more earnings and security. And as the row-crop South expanded, life and labor for white families came increasingly to resemble the sort of freedom blacks had found" (155). Which, of course, was little freedom at all.

My father's family were sharecroppers, tenants on several farms in northern Florida during the twenties and thirties. They lived on a farm outside White Springs for several years in the early thirties. On the next farm over lived a black family, with thirteen children just like my father's. They farmed next to one another, often sending children to help on one plot of land or another when the crops came in and required lots of hands. My father used to tell me how the two groups of children played among the tobacco rows and rode together on the wagon into town to sell feed corn.

As adults, my father and two of his siblings bought part of the farm they had tenanted, and discovered that Ponce Martin, one of the children on the next farm, had come back to Florida and bought the farm where his family had sharecropped. As a child, I would sit on the porch with my father and his brothers and listen to their stories. Ponce was often there too, but he never sat on the porch with us. Standing at the bottom of the steps and leaning on the rail, he'd sometimes accept a glass of iced tea, and he'd talk about the mules and the weather and the evils of various farm programs, but the racial barrier held, and I wasn't encouraged to question it. After my father died, I made a visit to the farm and talked to Ponce, who told me how my father used to walk over to his family's house carrying food that my grandmother knew his family needed. "I'm black and you're white," Ponce said, "but I loved your daddy."

The relationship between my father and Ponce reminds me of the one V. S. Naipaul (1989) describes in his ethnographic study *A Turn in the South*. Naipaul talks with the son of a poor white farmer who remembers the African American children who lived near him on the farm where he grew up: "It wasn't something you discussed—black people didn't marry or date white people. They worked with them on farms. In the fields there was equality. We were even playmates. When we were small we played with black children. But at a certain point you knew that they were black—the time you started school. You accepted that" (253).

I listen to all these stories, and I hear my own again in their words. When I asked participants in the workshop on race to write about their earliest memory of encountering someone from another race they wrote stories very much like the ones I've told here, stories about visiting a friend's home, playing on the basketball court, sitting on a stoop and talking. Many of their stories ended with phrases like "I don't know what happened to John." "Maybe she moved." The conclusions were all indecisive, vague. They were like Ponce's wistful comment to me, like my memory of losing the friendship of Marie. They were all filled with loss.

It seems to me that recognition of that loss is the beginning point for a discussion of race and class in educational contexts. And that recognition comes when students and their teachers are encouraged to tell and hear their stories of race and class in their classrooms, encouraged to read others' stories and to make new meaning out of them both. The story is crucial to coming to understanding, to what Paulo Freire (1987) calls *conscientization*, or belief suffused with action, and as we write stories and listen to them we learn some truths that help us link them and thus tell our own more honestly. Following are some maxims, and classroom stories illustrating them, that may help guide the lessons we make for our classes to help us confront together issues of race and class.

Maxims and Stories

Everybody is Ethnic

Ethnicity is not a choice, nor confined to one group. Classrooms must avoid labels that make "ethnic literature" a code for work by nonwhites and that suggest that ethnicity has nothing to do with power or class consciousness. I teach a course for undergraduates preparing to teach high school English. In this class, few of the overwhelmingly large percentage of white students in the class could even name their ethnicities and were clearly confused by the question I asked about their ethnic groups. A recognition of the plain fact that every person is ethnic means as well an understanding of how privileged ethnicity confers class status. Peggy McIntosh's (1986) classic essay on "White Privilege: Male Privilege" describes this status as "unearned assets which I can count on cashing in each day, but about which I was 'meant' to remain oblivious" (1). Recognizing ethnic and class background means confronting it directly, choosing not to remain oblivious. It means having students see that their English/Irish/Scots background (the ethnicity of many of my students) often provides privileges that other ethnicities—less white, less European, less dominant—do not.

Race Matters; Class Matters

Teachers and students must leave behind their comfortable and wrongheaded assertions that racism is dead, or at least confined to the isolated and the ignorant. They must abandon as well the even more entrenched notion that class doesn't matter. The American educational system presumes an equality of action, that the desire to learn unites all students, that even with differences, we are all committed to improvement, to "getting ahead," which suggests that even if Americans understand class, they don't accept class as a barrier. As bell hooks (1995) notes, "Class is rarely talked about in the U.S.; nowhere is there a more intense silence about the reality of class differences than in educational settings" (177). Sleeter (1994) points out how much what she calls the "ideology of individualism" prevents teachers and students from examining the institutional and social controls we persist as seeing as class and color free. When I asked students in a first-year composition class this semester about their own class within the class system in the United States, all twenty-five students wrote that they are "middle class" or that there is no class system in this country. Yet in a journal entry later the same week a student spoke of her grandmother's poverty and the fact that her mother was the first in the family to graduate from high school. Students are conditioned to see themselves as free agents even when their own experience denies that vision. Students reading Mike Rose's (1990) study of literacy, *Lives on the Boundary,* with its often explicit reminders of class structures in educational practice, were able to find links on their own between the experiences they wrote about and those Rose describes in terms of class and schooling.

Silence Is Not Golden

Recently, a group of white students approached their history professor at my university to complain about the emphasis on slavery and the Civil War in his American history course. They were afraid that their African American peers were uncomfortable with the topic, they said. Why such emphasis on something that was so painful? It might make black students resentful. It might make them *discover* racism. Their perception is not uncommon, that talking about painful topics such as race and class in school will exacerbate problems or begin them. hooks remembers her college experience with regard to discussions of class: "During my college years, it was tacitly assumed that we all agreed that class should not be talked about, that there would be no critique of the bourgeois class biases shaping and informing the pedagogical process (as well as social etiquette) in the classroom" (178). The oblivion and evasions that McIntosh and Sleeter criticize are part of the tacit agreement to remain silent about issues that might provoke anger or despair. Teachers must learn to help students share their fears about painful topics of race and class in safe ways. The history professor asked students to write about their discomfort with his discussion of slavery, using their responses to confront issues of race in current history.

Talk Is Not Cheap

Cornel West's *Race Matters* (1994) is a story of class as well as race, a powerful commentary on the status of relations in this country, and a document about change. The anecdote that begins the book is about the hope that class status can mitigate race. West is keeping an appointment with a photographer who will shoot the cover of his book, and West cannot get a cab in central New York City to pick him up. His angry frustration becomes part of his rationale for writing. My students' reactions to this story are often unsympathetic, even suspicious. "I've waited a long time for a cab myself in New York" or, "Aren't most of the cab drivers black anyway?" they say. Many of these responses come from first-generation college students, with parents or grandparents who did not finish high school, who worked on farms and later in mills. In other words, these are the children of a working class that itself has seen few privileges accrue to it. When I ask them to write about their reactions, they often bring up instances of their own experience with neglect or discrimination, their doubts about West's need to talk about his feelings. Yet when confronted with how they've used writing to make sense of their reactions, they find a reason for West's story. The mediating power of words comes home to them. This power of words is in fact the lesson of all these classroom examples, the point of the maxims. To speak and listen and to write helps break the repressive silence that hooks claims is "the most oppressive aspect of middle class life" (180).

Breaking the Silence

What follows is an excerpt from graffiti on the women's restroom wall at my university that shows how students are breaking the

repressive silence on race—and on class—that their university
maintains.

> Fuck the KKK and they momas
> *Their* (Hello—spelling!)
> Merely a syntax variation of dialect. No spelling or usage errors. I can
>   do without the profanity though
> Mommas, mamas, race is not an issue it's an excuse.
> To abuse people.
> Humankind.
> Don't worry. The African American race is outpopulating Caucasians.
>   By 2014 whites will be the minority.
> So will blacks! The Mexican American population will within 15–20
>   years outnumber us all.
> And we'll all be starving. Overpopulation is not an answer to
>   anyone's problems—the earth needs fewer to feed and house,
>   not more.
> I can't believe so many people are making race an issue. We are all
>   humans.
> Over 200 years of slavery and racial discrimination make it an issue.
> I haven't done shit to you.
> Get over it!!!

The five- or six-way conversation continues with writers talking about
their personal and class backgrounds: "I am a white middle class
Christian female who treats everybody equally," and responders who
talk about welfare myths: "Think of the fact that black women on
welfare are being blamed for this country's economic crisis, when
the majority are white." Two of the last sentences read: "You're dis-
criminating against black people by saying they aren't as capable as
white people of getting ahead," and "No, she's saying the world, the
reality that black people are relegated to is not equal to the world of
white people."

This graffiti is powerful testimony to the need for real talk about
race and class. The issues are ongoing in students' experience despite
determined efforts to make classrooms neutral spaces where race and
class do not matter. The dialogue here shows that classrooms cannot
be neutral spaces, and that people need to find ways to talk about
issues that so deeply affect their own lives. It also shows how
beneficial talk can be. This is mediated dialogue, with comments that
soften, critique, agree, rethink positions that each writer separately
holds but that change as they write and read. What we write helps us
find where we converge as well as where we differ. Writing helps us
make new connections, write new stories by allowing us to use our
own backgrounds to make the educational experience become "liber-

atory" in Freire's (1987) term, an "invitation to make visible the languages, dreams, values, and encounters that constitute the lives of those whose histories are often actively silenced" (21).

"It was not a story to pass on," the narrator in Toni Morrison's *Beloved* (1988) says at the end of the novel. Beloved's story, of oppression and slavery and death, is so harsh that "remembering seemed unwise." The characters in the story want to erase the pain that speaking out brings. "So they forgot her. Like an unpleasant dream during a troubling sleep" (175). But Morrison's message is that the pain of the story is precisely why it must be passed on, for the painful is also true. The troubling dream returns and will as long as silence keeps oppression alive. Issues of race and class continue to haunt and confound this culture as we attempt to move beyond old habits without first confronting them, just as the ghost of Beloved haunted all those who refused to tell her tragic story and theirs.

The women writing on the restroom wall are choosing to escape their silence, if not yet in their classrooms, at least anonymously in their institution. They rise and converge on that wall, not because they have one story to tell but because they have many. In Alice Walker's essay, after she has related the plot of "Everything That Rises Must Converge" to her mother, her mother asks, "What did the black woman do after she knocked the white woman down and walked away?" She answers, "O'Connor chose not to say, and that is why, although this is a good story, it is, to me, only half a story. You might know the other half" (40). Writing teaches us that we do know the other half of the story, the story that one answers to the question of another on the bathroom wall, the story that connects a grandmother's hope for her children and class structures, the story that tells what happened to a childhood friend of another race. As we write these stories, we can finally begin to act on the belief that the lessons about race and class and culture, the stories of loss, can connect us, perhaps begin to heal us. They are not stories to be passed on. And so they must be.

Notes

1. There is a growing body of scholarship dealing with race and culture and on connections to literary theory. For good beginning discussions, see particularly Appiah 1992; Fields 1990; and Michaels 1995.

Works Cited

Appiah, A. 1992. *In My Father's House: Africa in the Philosophy of Culture.* New York: Oxford.

Cash, W. J. 1941. *The Mind of the South.* New York: Knopf.

Fields, B. 1990. "Slavery, Race and Ideology in the United States of America." In *New Left Review* (May).

Freire, P., and D. Macedo. 1987. *Literacy: Reading the Word and the World.* South Hadley, MA: Bergin Garvey.

hooks, b. 1994. *Teaching to Transgress.* New York: Routledge.

Kirby, J. T. 1987. *Rural Worlds Lost: The American South 1920–1960.* Baton Rouge: Louisiana State University Press.

McIntosh, P. 1986. "White Privilege: Male Privilege." Wellesley College Center for Research on Women, Working Paper 189: 1–19.

Michaels, W. B. 1995. *Our America: Nativism, Modernism and Pluralism.* Durham, NC: Duke University Press.

Morrison, T. 1992 *Playing in the Dark: Whiteness and the Literary Imagination.* Cambridge, MA: Harvard University Press.

————. 1988. *Beloved.* New York: New American Library.

Naipaul, V. S. 1989. *A Turn in the South.* New York: Knopf.

O'Connor, F. 1962. "Everything That Rises Must Converge." In *The Complete Stories.* New York: Farrar, Straus, and Giroux.

Rose, M. 1990. *Lives on the Boundary.* New York: Penguin.

Sleeter, C. 1994. "White Racism." *Multicultural Education* 2 (2): 5–9.

Walker, A. 1981. *In Search of Our Mothers' Gardens.* New York: Harcourt Brace.

West, C. 1994. *Race Matters.* New York: Random House.

16

Teaching "The Renaissance" *Queer Consciousness and Class Dysphoria*

Alan Shepard

Some of the most assiduous class climbers are university professors.

P. Fussell, *Class*

We are accustomed by now to think of literature as optional.

M. Nussbaum, *Poetic Justice*

Where he can, he tends to pump iron textually.

F. Spufford, writing of Derek Jarman

In American higher education, social class is an almost invisible force field. In its quiet way, it profoundly shapes why and how we study for a degree or teach a particular subject. Yet universities market themselves as unproblematically democratic spaces, in which individual talent and effort are all. This is an attractive fantasy, and not only to the young. More than we usually care to admit, however, our families' histories, finances, and reading habits as well as our ancestors' notions about occupations, income, and educational achievement have established certain expectations in us before we ever matriculate.

We have been coached to pretend otherwise. I first became conscious of that while studying abroad on an American program at Cambridge University in 1982. I had been drawn to apply to the program by a mixture of admirable intellectual urges and not-so-noble class desires, reasons I could not then have put into words. As a visiting student from the American Midwest, I was unprepared for the blunt attention to social class that I saw at Cambridge. It may have surprised me to learn that degrees were rated by the faculty as first, second, or third class; in the United States we pretend that a B.A. is a B.A., while keeping the very open secret that a 2.0 GPA on a degree from an admired institution is worth more than a 4.0 degree from one that is scorned or merely ignored. It mildly surprised me to find that the printed schedule of lectures by the Cambridge faculty paid careful attention to the degrees and honors held by so-and-so, M.A., D.Phil., O.B.E. It surprised me a great deal to find lawn signs in the manicured gardens of some of the colleges that read, "Only those who hold the degree of M.A. may walk on the lawn." Aimed at tourists—or so I hoped—the signs shamelessly affirmed that at the heart of class privilege is the restraint of other people's literal as well as figurative mobility.

Only after returning from England did I begin to see how our culture of higher education at times disguises class privilege and always holds open the idea of rising by merit, in order to perpetuate a myth that may be peculiarly American. At St. Olaf College in Minnesota, then my home institution, the lawns were for everyone. It was a social error to address any faculty member as Doctor. For reasons of Lutheran humility or in imitation of the Ivy League (it was never clear), all were Ms. or Mrs. or Mr., including one of my first-year English teachers, a fresh Harvard Ph.D. whose credentials amazed me, who made a point of saying that we must not call him "Doctor."

Pretending that we Americans live in a fundamentally equitable society in which class boundaries may be surmounted by hard work is one of our oldest customs; in 1832 Frances Trollope noted our "fable of equality" (Fussell 1983, 17). With respect to higher education, the fable has seldom been more strong. In 1997 the president of the United States set a goal of providing a college education to every high school graduate. Probably it was an impossible goal, more difficult to engineer than sending someone to the moon. Yet it embodies our fantasy that education alone will raise the impoverished up out of misery. As bell hooks (1994) observes in the course of discussing students' passivity toward the ill effects of class barriers in their own classrooms, "From grade school on, we are all encouraged to cross the threshold of the classroom believing we are entering a democratic space—a free zone where the desire to study and learn makes us all equal" (177).

The fiction of infinite possibility about which hooks is writing is narrated most explicitly when students cross what is for most of them the final academic threshold—the commencement platform. "Graduation," with its subtle connotations of being ranked (graduated), of one's class rank and GPA being forever fixed in a computer database somewhere, is one of the few public rituals still intact in America in the late, late twentieth century. The geography of commencement reveals a lot about our culture's priorities—on most campuses, the basketball arena is the only space that has been built large enough to seat everyone who has come to see the spectacle. In these arenas, or, if you will, these theaters-in-the-round, universities still stage a quaint, even affected ritual. While there is something otherworldly about all of those black gowns, worn as if in tribute to the thousand-year-old monastic roots of university instruction, the exotic otherworldliness contrasts ironically with the pragmatic choices made by most of our students to attain degrees in vocationally marketable subjects such as accounting or fashion design or computer science. During the ceremony, the gowns overwhelm most signs of the differences among us; only academic rank is inscribed onto the costumes, academia's parting shot at students who have been examined and graded and ranked for some seventeen or eighteen years when they finally reach the platform. Thus a B.B.A. in finance is not visually distinct from a B.A. in English, though their starting salaries will surely not be the same, nor is a scion of wealthy West Texas ranchers distinguishable from a first-generation college graduate, unless the shoes give it away as the graduate crosses the platform. Cowboy boots, wingtips, soiled Nikes, fire-engine red flats, black pumps—under the gowns, the shoes hint at the function of education in the graduate's social class status.

Before crossing the platform, students are invariably asked to endure a pep talk, in which their growth as thinkers and social beings is reduced to a few clichés and their bright futures as leaders of society are extrapolated. Students are no more fooled by these portents of Piconean invincibility[1] than they are by the single-use academic gowns, made of paper dyed black, that some universities (not TCU, I am happy to say) dress them in for the occasion. We know they are not fooled because of the irreverent antics that carnivalize the ritual. I've seen an entire class of law students throw dollar bills into the air; kayaks, surgical gloves, snakes, and booze make annual appearances at the commencement ceremonies of the University of Virginia, where I did a Ph.D. The whistles, horns, and shouts at commencements everywhere help to keep that public rhetoric of reaching for the stars from getting out of hand.

In the pages to come, I write about the largely intellectual tensions between my students and me that arise when I talk about the mechanisms and effects of class in my courses in early modern literature. In those courses I find that while students are more or less eager to talk about matters of race or nation or gender or religion, or at least resigned to doing so, they are baffled by, or resistant to, talking about class. On that vexed topic my own background produces what I have come to see as a productive estrangement. The gay son of farmers, I was raised on family farms and in small towns in Iowa and Minnesota with middle-class financial stability but with working-class respect for all physical labor.[2] My family is skeptical about intellectual labor for its own sake and about "culture," equated with the opera, the symphony, the art gallery, in which they profess no curiosity. Education is admired when it leads to better pay. It is important in my family to wear learning lightly, and to retain the humility of country people when a job takes us to the city. To adopt the self-promoting arrogance of urban dwellers in the fast lane is to become a "citiot." The neologism is my father's favorite for knocking city slickers who bring their fast ways to the country. He seems not to recognize that his delight in the word is akin to my own love of words and of their power to make reality. In spite of successful, often simultaneous careers in corporate America and on the farm, my father remains daunted by the sheer idea of university education. A high school graduate, smart and shrewd, he still equates a university degree with intelligence, sometimes unconsciously, in spite of what experience has taught him. It is an equation I am mindful of deliberately contesting whenever it appears in any form in my classroom.

A refugee from small midwestern towns, I have embraced attitudes about education that once puzzled my family. At times, especially in the first years of my Ph.D. work, the bonds between us were strained by my immersion in the culture of academe, which is to them a foreign place, and by my coming out as a gay man, which they understood, I think, as a sign of intellectual freedom gone awry. Ironically, my parents had steered me toward academia. From childhood, I was said to be destined for college. As did Allan Bérubé's parents, my own purchased—for me—a set of the *Encyclopedia Britannica* from a "door-to-door salesman who worked the trailer park," well before they were able to afford it or I was able to read it (Bérubé 1997, 52). Yet because we have never talked much about the books I teach or the essays I write, they do not know how deeply their own values, and particularly their deconstructive views of class privilege and authority, have shaped my scholarship and my commitments and habits as a teacher.

Principally I teach British literature written in the sixteenth, seventeenth, and eighteenth centuries, much of which, it may be said, is obsessed with social class. From Thomas More's ambiguously heretical treatise *Utopia* (1516), in which hereditary class privilege is replaced by a system of merit; to my favorite Jacobean comedy, Francis Beaumont and John Fletcher's *The Knight of the Burning Pestle* (1613?), a hilari-

ous play rife with anxieties about the social-climbing merchant class
and the disintegration of a chivalric England that in any case had largely existed in the pages of romances; to Aphra Behn's *The Widow
Ranter* (pub. 1690), a tragicomedy about the ignomy of an English
adventurer who goes to Virginia to seek his fortune—in these and hundreds, perhaps thousands, of other texts, social class is a ubiquitous
theme. And in more than a few such texts, aristocratic privilege is fighting for its life. More and more, this is being recognized by scholars.
Indeed, the subject of class in the early modern period has received a
great deal of new attention in recent years, spurred on by developments
in new historicism and cultural materialism.[3]

Specialists in the field are more likely now to say "early modern"
than "Renaissance," as the focus of scholarship continues to be dilat-
ed to include freshly recovered voices beyond those long heard from
as part of the canon. Some scholars deem it almost offensive to continue to identify our corner of the discipline of English studies by the
French noun used for centuries to name an epoch in which a tiny elite
lived "the good life" on the backs of millions. This shift of focus is
both celebrated and helped along by remarkable books such as Carlo
Ginzburg's *The Cheese and the Worms* ([1976] 1983).[4]

A historian, Ginzburg has reconstructed efforts by the Inquisition
in Italy in the late sixteenth and early seventeenth centuries to silence
a dissident Friulian miller nicknamed Menocchio, whose theorizing of
the origins of the cosmos, on the basis of wide but untutored reading,
had mocked Roman Catholic teachings even more than did Galileo's.
Ginzburg's account is often the first assigned reading of the semester
in my Renaissance Literature and the "New" Science course. For all
of its fascinating particulars, some of which astound students,
Menocchio's story of resistance unto death is also a lean allegory of
the slow disintegration of elite authority, including the power of
Roman Catholic prelates. More than I have expected, students are
frequently outraged by the injustices done to Menocchio and to
Galileo, whose trial transcripts we read later. In those eruptions of
productive outrage in the classroom, I am able to help students to see
clearly how the relative cost of resisting authority depends so greatly
on one's class status, which is not to be calculated simply upon
wealth. According to Ginzburg, Menocchio's status as an independent
and socially prominent miller made him more dangerous than an ordinary peasant (120): He was executed by Inquisitors before July, 1601.
Galileo, son of a court musician with noble ancestors, who knew
"how to present himself as a *gentiluomo*" (Biagioli [1993] 1994, 114),
who spoke the courtier's tongue, was also shown the instruments of
torture by Catholic Inquisitors, but suffered only house arrest after
being convicted of heresy in 1633.

Had literary and historical scholarship not already taken the direction it had by the time I reached graduate school in 1984, I might not have chosen Renaissance literature as my field of special interest, for most of the canonical texts in the field immerse readers in aristocratic culture. While few of us have grown up as aristocrats (I've met only one Renaissance specialist who is also an Italian countess), one needn't have been born at court to have been invested at an early age with a sense of cultural and economic entitlement. Such privilege is often signified by one's early acquaintance with high art. *The Faerie Queene* and *Hamlet* are magnificent texts, yet they are written in what is still, to my eyes and ears, something of a foreign language.

It is no coincidence, then, that my teaching and research interests have emphasized the heretical impulses of the less canonical and non-canonical texts of the period: I give courses in Renaissance witch literature alongside those in Shakespeare; in science and literature courses, I delight in pairing astronomy treatises with John Donne's "The First Anniversary," in which the poet and Dean of St. Paul's famously worries about the displacement of poets and poetry in the new world order. And in my own scholarship I have written about William Harvey's treatise on circulation, where a centuries-old tradition of worshipping Galen and Aristotle is carefully set aside; and texts relating to the Mary Toft rabbit-pregnancy hoax in the early eighteenth century, in which members of the Royal College of Physicians, so keen to shine in the limelight, are gulled by a cunning country woman eager for publicity.

I have been most intrigued by military conduct books produced by ordinary soldiers (rather than commissioned aristocrats) in England between ca. 1560 and 1600. Aimed at the crown, these treatises by commoners offer advice to Queen Elizabeth on military affairs. More often than not, their authors are to be found collaborating with the elite by invoking aristocratic exempla in their books, in order—paradoxically—to justify their own hegemony as a fourth estate of commoners that is crucial to a strong defense, particularly against Spain. I have been reading these hawkish military conduct books in relation to Christopher Marlowe's plays. While Marlowe is famous for creating bloodthirsty soldiers on stage, it is possible to hear under the din of war rhetoric in his plays a series of small, persistent rejoinders, in which dissent against martial law is claimed to be heroic if also usually futile.

My project is personally resonant, as is perhaps the case with many intellectual projects in the arts and sciences. The playwright, a shoemaker's son who was said to have been what we would call "gay," specialized in dramas saturated with fantasies of being able to disrupt elite systems of power, as when Faustus crashes a papal banquet at the Vatican, and of social climbing as a principal mode of creating such disruptions: Tamburlaine the Great sheds his shepherd's weeds for battle armor to begin getting an empire in the face of inherited royal prerogative, the social-climbing earl of Gaveston worms his way into wanton King Edward's heart. In other words, I have chosen to focus my scholarship on the plays of a social climber who invented such figures for the stage—where the very activity of actors getting into disguise is bound up with the fantasy of escaping the boundaries of one's lot in life. Plays and *playing*, the word for acting in the early modern period, open up to ordinary people all sorts of opportunities to reinvent themselves and to pretend out loud, as it were, that the world is different than it actually is. As has been said of Ben Jonson's *The Alchemist*, that brilliant farce about the criminal side of social climbing in London, in the theater it is not precious metals, but people's lives, that are being transmuted.

When I began to work on Marlowe's plays in the late 1980s, gay and lesbian studies were still in their professional infancy. Although Alan Bray's signal work *Homosexuality in Renaissance England* ([1982] 1995) was in print, we did not yet have that first wave of influential books on early modern gay and lesbian subjects, the likes of which now include Gregory Bredbeck's *Sodomy and Interpretation: Marlowe to Milton* (1991), Bruce Smith's *Homosexual Desire in Shakespeare's England: A Cultural Poetics* (1991), and Jonathan Goldberg's *Sodometries: Renaissance Texts, Modern Sexualities* (1992) and *Queering the Renaissance* (1994).[5] There was as yet no queer theory to read of; and in the graduate English program at Virginia in the late 1980s, the topic of homosexuality in literature was still mostly ignored.

Yet as a graduate student at Virginia, being gay proved to be less of a liability than being a first-generation college graduate. Renaissance studies is a field demanding of its students, for example, proficiency in Latin and French, at the least, for admission to the inner circle, but no one advises farm boys to study foreign languages, especially not the outrageously overworked academic counselors in public high schools, for the possibility that we might grow up to do early modern studies is scarcely to be imagined, much less hoped for. Pierre Bourdieu ([1965] 1994) has coined the phrase "scholastic mortality" to describe the fate of first-generation university students in France who cannot assimilate the lexicon of the academy quickly enough to survive—for as Bourdieu recognizes, success in the academy depends at least as much upon picking up the lingo and the ways of thinking as upon native intelligence.

Although I am less self-conscious about my class origins now that I have learned enough of the educated middle-class graces to pass in the company I usually keep, my sense of being conspicuous has shown up at odd moments. As a Ph.D. student, I was once asked to fetch Stephen Orgel from the Charlottesville airport as he arrived to give a lecture at Virginia; the plum task fell to me in part because, like Orgel, I was "out." While I drove south on U.S. 29, he peppered me with wonderful questions about my work on Marlowe. But I could concentrate only on imagining his reaction to my shabby decade-old car; I regretted having to use it to collect a man so learned—and so well paid by Stanford. Those sensations I read then as more evidence that, whatever my past or future scholarly achievements, I was likely to remain something of an outsider gazing in upon elite culture, be it that of early modern England or modern academia.

I asked Orgel what in retrospect strikes me as too obvious a question: To what extent had his celebrated work on Renaissance masques early in his career provided him, as a gay man, a venue for thinking about disguised desire? I did not confess then that class anxieties had tempered me against the pleasures of masques. Although I have had some success recently in teaching Ben Jonson's *Pleasure Reconciled to Virtue* and *The Masque of Queens* in my Witch Lit course, the masque, as a form, invites spectators to indulge in the pleasures of artifice and luxury. It would seem that my Anabaptist heritage has genetically selected me to resist those pleasures, to see them as extravagant and wasteful. For seventeenth-century aristocrats, to be sure, those vices were part of the great pleasure of participating in masques.

It is no comfort to me, either, that Jonson anticipates my displeasure. He sneers at those of us who have common blood in his stage directions for *The Masque of Queens* (acted 1609). There he predicts our dissatisfaction with the artificial spectacle he has composed. There "men" with "enquiring eyes" and "quick ears" are distinguished from those "sluggish ones of porters and mechanics that must be bored through at every act with narrations" (323). Jonson understands that the success of *The Masque of Queens* will depend on the class status of its spectators. Jonson flatters his patrons by naturalizing keen powers of observation and quick wits as the province of the well-to-do, who can afford his art. "Porters and mechanics" are unlikely to commission or attend a masque in a private theater, except in a service capacity, so they are cursed with dull wits that keep them from appreciating the exquisite art he has made. Since the porters would be hovering at the beck and call of the principal spectators, however, the playwright's vulnerability to the taste of a certain class is limited. By this definition of an audience fit though few, only the occupations of the underlings are even named; the rich have leisure. The rich are gifted with keen senses and refined judgment; porters and mechanics are said to be burdened with brains that must be "bored through," as if writing an entertainment for the rabble is, for Jonson, like drilling through oak.

Rather than teaching masques, I prefer to teach more gritty literature. In part, gritty texts seem less like works of "art" lost in an ethereal aesthetic realm and more like cultural artifacts that may be made relevant to contemporary concerns in ways that will be understood by students who have little time for "art." This obviously artificial and problematic distinction between art and artifact plays well in Texas, where I now teach. There is something intrinsically bizarre about keeping alive in the cultural memory sixteenth- and seventeenth-century English texts in modern Texas, where Anglophilia stops at Shakespeare and where, on the frontier, geography sometimes makes my subject seem even more arcane than it did in Charlottesville. Yet there are uncanny parallels between England and Texas: As England was four centuries ago, Texas in the nineties is hawkish, hypernationalistic, xenophobic, puritanical, and yet fond of the veneer of civility that is lent by "culture." I notice, for example, that Fort Worth marks its very impressive collection of art museums with street signs that read *Cultural District.*

Beyond obvious historical and technological differences between early modern London and modern Fort Worth, however, is a less visible difference—in England, social climbing was usually regarded as a horrific threat to the nation's well-being, even by those such as Ben Jonson who were eagerly engaged in improving their fortunes. In Texas, as you may well guess, the opposite is true. Texas is obsessed with money, which is equated here with social class. Social climbing is a patriotic sport. This value sometimes colors students' responses to class issues in early modern texts in peculiar ways.

Three summers ago, thinking about this essay, I chose to begin an introductory fiction course with *Robinson Crusoe.* It was wildly popular, in ways I had not anticipated. Most of the students, including seven college football players, strongly identified with Crusoe for being as plucky as they are. For them Crusoe represented a maverick adventurer whose restless travels fly in the face of consecrated cultural privilege. His resistance to the emasculating constraints of civil society affirmed for them a nostalgic attraction to the Huck Finn life as a solitary wanderer or with a buddy, unfettered by the complications of networked communities, where class status is often a barrier to the self-actualization that Crusoe pursues. The hero's resistance to class privilege frames his subsequent adventures, in which he simultaneously rebels against privilege, yet works feverishly to reproduce for himself what he has surrendered. When the novel opens, Crusoe's father, well-to-do but not rich, urges his son to settle for the financial security of the middle station into which he has been born. It is a station that will free him, as Crusoe knows, from the "necessity of seeking my bread" (Defoe [1719] 1980, 11). This opportunity to inherit a life of leisure, what the father poetically glosses as choosing to live "in easy circumstances sliding gently through the world" (11), does not appeal to Crusoe, however. And although in telling his story retrospectively he admits that as a youth he had been "obstinately deaf" to the offer (13), there is little evidence that Crusoe's occasional moments of self-recrimination, which occur only when he is in a tight spot, ought to be taken as sincere.

Without such youthful obstinance from the protagonist, of course, there would be no story. But in the classroom, as we began to explore the implications of the frame for interpreting Crusoe's mock-heroic misadventures, students grew uneasy about the weight I wanted to give to Defoe's exploration of class privilege that is initiated by tension between the father's advice and the son's various mishaps and victories. Students preferred to take Crusoe's wanderlust at face value as an element of *bildungsroman* or as an expression of a native trait in the Crusoe family character: Before the story begins, we are told early on, the elder son has run off to war in the Low Countries and been killed; and the grieving father is himself an immigrant to England who has made his fortune by taking risks. But these interpretive choices do not fully account for Crusoe's obsession with making adventures to foreign lands bear him fruit in the form of capital gains. Crusoe is perversely eager to risk his life on the high seas or in dangerous liaisons and confrontations with locals in order to amass gold and silver and real estate. His is a fantasy of the entrepeneur who wants to believe he is created *sui generis*.

Surely this fantasy of self-creation is as attractive to contemporary Americans as to early eighteenth-century Britons such as Defoe. In part it is so because it helps to legitimate a national myth that promises material prosperity as the reward for hard work, self-reliance, and acquiescence to a capitalist system that makes wealth on the backs of the poor; and of course the system principally makes new wealth for those who are already privileged.

Crusoe suggests that one's class status is virtually fixed at birth. Privilege is expressed as economic or biological inevitability, thus requiring little moral reflection. So Crusoe is able to sell Xury, a young Moor who has helped him escape pirates, to the captain of a Portuguese slave-trading ship. And later, in spite of his warm feelings for Friday, who is ever loyal, Crusoe treats him as an inferior for decades without concern, except when other men do likewise. As Crusoe is wrapping up his tale, Friday expediently vanishes from the narrative. His departure warrants even less notice than Xury's had.

Yet none of this caused my students to ask if Crusoe's moral code is troubled.

Whether or not Defoe invites us to read from an ironic stance, the gaps between Crusoe's self-understanding and his actions do comment ironically on the power of class privilege alongside the privileges of racial and religious hegemony.[6] From his first voyage Crusoe laments the isolation produced by privilege: "having money in my pocket and good clothes upon my back, I would always go on board [a ship] in the habit of a gentleman; and so I neither had any business in the ship, or learned to do any" (22). He is freed from the burden of class privilege only when he constitutes a society of one, shipwrecked (almost) alone on an island, for then is gold worth less than a knife; there, skill and imagination, and not hereditary privilege, keep him on top. On the thirteenth day of being cast ashore, Crusoe returns to the carcass of his ship a twelfth time to retrieve food and supplies. Now discovering a locker of European and Brazilian coins on this visit, he recoils from filthy lucre in mock horror: "I smiled to myself at the sight of this money. 'O drug!' said I aloud, 'what art thou good for? Thou art not worth to me, no, not the taking off of the ground; one of those knives is worth all this heap; I have no manner of use for thee; e'en remain where thou art and go to the bottom as a creature whose life is not worth saving'" (61). But instantly he thinks again, and totes the cache to his island in a piece of canvas sail.

As my students and I savored this comic moment, we smiled back at Crusoe, admitting with Defoe that money is sometimes an irresistibly intoxicating "drug." When I pressed them to account for the hyperbole of Crusoe's initial aversion to the gold and jewels, however, they balked. Unfamiliar with the *contemptus mundi* tradition, they were nevertheless reluctant to read Crusoe's hyperbole as religious enthusiasm, much less as devotional platitude. Even less willing were they to understand it as a frank confession of what really drives his insatiable appetite for entrepeneurial adventure. To read the episode in this way would, in their eyes, have tainted Crusoe's professed separation from the material culture of an England he had rejected when first setting forth. So while they were willing to accept that Crusoe's adventures might contain within them Defoe's critique of such vexed matters as European contact with Africa or Christian contact with Islam or even the lack of contact between men and women, even as the discussion was concluded they were reluctant to concede that matters of class might be at the heart of Crusoe's puerile religious sentiments or his distress at the sight of money or his magnetic attraction to the profits to be reaped in foreign parts.

In an effort to help students see how the adventure *topos* in *Crusoe* elides fundamental assumptions about gender and class privilege, I included as one topic for the first essay this question: "What do we learn by observing that Crusoe's principal emotional ties are with men, especially with Friday?" Needless to say, none of the male students chose to write on that topic. In discussions they had been highly resistant to reading the dynamics of material wealth and homosocial bonding, or of the historical organization of male sexuality, while women in the course were eager to read the tale as valorizing in a pernicious way their own subordination when their exclusion was impossible, as in the mother's presence early in the novel or the fact that Crusoe takes a wife in order to reproduce at the novel's end. I broached these topics midway through the discussion, after several mimetic moments in which I performed an act of close reading in the classroom and asked them to do likewise for a second moment or episode in Defoe's text. As I said some of these words aloud— *homosocial*, etc.—I experienced a subtle but nonetheless swift reversal in my stock as a teacher.

Having started the course by talking of adventure, I had felt earlier that I had won the cooperation and perhaps even the interest of the male students in the room but had left many of the women wishing they had taken a different course. Once the discussion turned to matters of homosocial bonding and the liminality of women in the adventure *topos*, however, these gendered loyalties reversed themselves. I "lost" some of the male students with marginal reading and writing skills, whose enthusiasm for *Robinson Crusoe* had temporarily boosted their always tenuous commitment to a summer school course for nonmajors. When I introduced the idea of *homosocial bonding* to describe some of the phenomena of relations between Crusoe and Friday, I sensed that in these students' eyes I instantly surrendered my epistemological privilege as a "straight" white male reader of literary texts;[7] I could no longer be trusted to unlock adventure stories in a way that would pay the genre homage, or that would reify what young men, many of them groomed in Texas, already believed to be true about the nature of buddy relationships.

Advocates of gay and lesbian teachers sometimes claim that sexual orientation is irrelevant. This line of defense was used to combat an episode of overt discrimination involving a head teacher in east London in 1994. When Jane Brown, a lesbian English teacher, refused to accept a number of subsidized theater tickets to *Romeo and Juliet* because some of her students would not have been able to pay for them, and then was quoted in the press as describing the play privately as a "heterosexual love story" (which it is), a political storm ensued that nearly cost Brown her job. In *Over the Rainbow: Money, Class, and Homophobia*, Nicola Field (1995) elevates Jane Brown to the status of a proletarian lesbian saint who was also nearly martyred by a 1988 law that forbids any local authority, including teachers, from promoting homosexuality. Field remarks approvingly that "supporters of Jane Brown all agreed that a person's sexuality had nothing whatsoever to do with their ability to teach" (156). While I am obviously not in favor of sacking gay and lesbian teachers, neither would I want to see sexual orientation discounted as irrelevant to a gay or lesbian teacher's sensibility. I would wager that it has everything to do with how one teaches: In the classroom, one chooses to pass or not; to name or not name homosexuality when it is in a text or a biography; to ignore or affirm those students who in any way fall outside the narrow definitions of what is "normal" in American culture; to challenge or accept students' assumptions about ubiquitous and compulsory heterosexuality; to push or not push students to "see the familiar in new ways" (Bérubé 1997, 63). For teachers who are gay or lesbian, as for other teachers, these questions are always with us, and not always easily answered. When I need courage to bring up queer matters in a classroom, it helps me to recall my own unfortunate undergraduate experience of giving an oral report on the speculations about Henry James's homosexuality by literary critics in the early 1980s. My report was answered with a stunned smile from the instructor and silence from other students. In another course, this one a seminar in James's novels being led by a hip, young professor, we did not speak of new work then being done on James's fiction and sexuality. The cost of such silence is regrettable, and unnecessary.

In teaching *Robinson Crusoe* or almost any literary text, it is easier to adopt a new-critical perspective—not easier in preparing for classroom contact, necessarily, but in avoiding being estranged from students, however productive that intellectual alienation might be for them and me. Students do not enjoy learning, for instance, that seventeenth-century editors of Shakespeare's sonnets changed pronouns to protect the Bard from any accusations of being a sodomite or a pederast, accusations the editors obviously considered to follow from the evidence in the poems. Students do not enjoy learning that contemporary critics often interpret Antonio's personally dangerous affection for Bassanio in *The Merchant of Venice* as having homosexual overtones; in studying act 5 of the play, where Bassanio and Portia wed, students are more pleased to hear about the happy-ending formula of Elizabethan comedy than the exclusion of Antonio, for whom there seems to be no place in the next generation. Purely formal readings of literary texts seldom threaten students' assumptions about life, or my epistemological privilege as an interpreter who deserves their trust, or my authority as a professor worthy of their respect. Yet as with many university teachers of my age who have come of age intellectually by reading political criticism, I have been trained to contextualize literary texts in historical and sociopolitical terms, and to believe in the merits of doing so. For me, part of that merit lies in making early modern literature, and the act of studying it, deeply relevant to the present.

One very good recent defense of the value of reading literature has come from the philosopher Martha Nussbaum. In *Poetic Justice: The Literary Imagination and Public Life* (1995), Nussbaum maintains that contact with literature enlarges our capacity to empathize with those who occupy subject positions substantially different from our own, and further, that literature gives us pleasure in the very act of engaging those differences. In that way, she says, literature is uniquely able to break through our self-protecting stratagems, so that we may grow as moral beings, and so that our society may grow with us. Whatever the limitations of Nussbaum's examples (she relies on Victorian novels to make her case, a limit that I confess does not trouble me), the argument is a shrewd effort to resuscitate a commitment to literary study on the part of the tax-paying public, whose fiscal and political conservatism has had devastating effects on the budgets of English departments, just as those same departments have seemed less and less able to articulate the civic value of what we teach students to know.

I admire Nussbaum's argument. Nevertheless, it is occasionally difficult to reproduce her thesis under classroom conditions. Undergraduates's empathy develops most readily, in my experience, when a text makes *visible differences, such as race or nationality, invisible*. Thus when the white English writer Aphra Behn praises the black king-made-slave Oroonoko by observing that in spite of his Ghanian heritage, his French education has moved him from savagery to civility, as is registered in his French physiognomy, students are attracted to Behn's erasure of the visible markers of race and ethnicity; they want to sympathize with Oroonoko as a human being who in his general humanity deserves a better life. Such a position allows students to condemn slavery without contemplating the economics of slave trading or the ethnocentrism of Europeans, whose contact with various African nations only intensified their righteousness as slave traders. As *Oroonoko* progresses and Behn deconstructs her own first images of a noble hero, as Oroonoko comes to murder his pregnant wife Imoinda in order to escape the bondage of shame, my students part company with Behn's admiration of her protagonist. They have not, perhaps they cannot, close the gap between Oroonoko's subject position as a deposed king forced into slavery and their own horror of uxoricide. Yet it is a teacher's job to complicate students's mimetic impulses, to explore distances between our own historical circumstances and other times and places. When a writer insists upon making *visible what is customarily invisible or coded*, as with sexual orientation or social class, students are even less inclined to reach out toward the difference spoken of in the literary text; they often react as if they have been fooled by the irruption of that difference.

For proof that empathy is strongest when students are able to see themselves in a character or text that does not surprise them by bringing out an *invisible* difference, I would compare my experiences in teaching two Marlowe tragedies, *Doctor Faustus* and *Edward II*. *Faustus* teaches itself. It appears frequently on undergraduate syllabi and in major anthologies of English lit. Students are rightly fascinated by the doctor's bargain with Mephistopheles for twenty-four years of immediate gratification; it is a deal close to the hearts of the college-aged. Even those students who are ready to condemn the character for blasphemy take seriously the play's criticisms of ecclesiastical abuses of authority in the episode at the Vatican, for example, or its hero's delight in the possibilities of disguise, as when, with Mephistopheles's help, Faustus makes himself invisible at the Vatican and the court of Charles V. In both of those scenes, Faustus mocks the bearers of elite authority and class privilege, boxing the Pope's ears in one case and growing cuckold's horns on a knight in service to the Holy Roman Empire in a second case. It may matter more than is recognized that, as *Faustus* opens, the Chorus notes that he is from "parents base of stock" (1 Chorus 11); class hostility may well be at the heart of Faustus's rebellion. Yet students who delight in that rebellion cite the universal appeal of defying authority. As one first-year student wrote to me this semester, "there's a little Faustus in us all."

No student of mine has ever said that of *Edward II*. Satanic rebellion is one thing. Sodomy is quite another. When I teach Marlowe's tragedy of the fourteenth-century "homosexual" English king deposed for neglecting his throne and other disputed causes, students readily side with his estranged, murderous queen, Isabella, and only a little less enthusiastically with her lover, the earl of Mortimer, who arranges the deaths of the king's lover, Gaveston, and then of the king himself. In the classroom, I show how the rationalizations of murder expressed by Edward's enemies are made ambiguous in the play. I show them how the play explores the inextricable links between queer consciousness and class dysphoria. I ask them to see how it complicates the predestined conclusions of its historical and tragic genres: The complications reveal themselves in the class anxieties voiced by the peers of the realm. Their fears, especially of mutability, press them to fratricide of a fellow peer and then to regicide.

In high school English courses, students have been trained to spot a tragic flaw from afar, and they relish the apparent boldness of the evidence early in Marlowe's play that Edward II is unnaturally seduced by another man; in students' eyes, the fact that the bait by which Gaveston expects to reel in Edward is some pretty, artful, cross-dressing boys—this only compounds the crime. In helping students to complicate their model of tragedy beyond the concept of a tragic flaw, I show them how *Edward II* dramatizes the cost of social absolutism, in which the empowered members of a community commit murder to protect their ideological convictions and class privileges. Students tour a number of scenes in the play that illustrate the aristocrats's anxiety that their privileges are only as secure as the court and kingdom are unchanging.

The tour concludes by analyzing a revealing speech by Roger, the Younger Mortimer, as he explains why he hates Edward II so much. In this early speech Mortimer is still cautious enough to triangulate his fury toward Gaveston, the "night growne mushrump" who is "so baselie borne" (1.4.284, 403). Bathetically, Mortimer fumes over Gaveston's wardrobe and presumptuous conduct at court:

> He weares a lords revenewe on his back,
> And *Midas* like he jets it in the court,
> With base outlandish cullions at his heeles,
> Whose proud fantastic liveries make such show,
> As if that *Proteus* god of shapes appearde.
> I have not seene a dapper jack so briske,
> He weares a short Italian hooded cloake
> Larded with pearle, and in his tuskan cap
> A jewell of more value then the crowne. (1.4.407–415)

Mortimer's colorful attack reveals more about his own habits of mind than it does Gaveston's. It displays an impressive array of prejudices against actors, men-about-town, the nouveau riche, courtiers, and Italians. As a French subject at the English court, the "homosexual" in a heterosexual universe, the aesthete amidst more pragmatic barons, who prefer war to music, Gaveston is obviously a locus of "difference." So is sexual hostility figured here as class hostility, or vice versa? As Mortimer has just claimed that Gaveston's sexuality, if kept private, is not at issue, I think it is fair to say that Gaveston's greatest threat is to the stability of the class system (see 1.4.389–402).

The mere allusion to "*Proteus* god of shapes" opens up a Pandora's box of Elizabethan anxieties about mutability of the social order and human identity. In Machiavellian fashion, wearing an "Italian hooded cloake," Gaveston works to invent himself anew for every occasion at court, and his machinations have infested the court with servants in "liveries," a mock-heroic retinue that makes class a specific category among the already competitive courtiers. In Mortimer's characterization of Gaveston's antics, his own flatterers are reduced to their lowest anatomical denominator: They are "cullions," or, in its Old French derivation, "testicles," a term of abuse that is uncannily appropriate for these French invaders whose access to the court, Mortimer implies, is driven by the king's desire for genital self-gratification.

Moreover, the contemptuous Mortimer, the keen observer of Gaveston's costumes, particularly resents being made the object of the gaze by this French Proteus and England's mesmerized monarch. As his complaint continues:

> Whiles other walke below, the king and he
> From out a window, laugh at such as we,
> And floute our traine, and jest at our attire:
> Unckle, tis this that makes me impatient. 1.4.416–419

Are we really to believe, I ask my students, that Mortimer suffers from some sartorial distress? That he plays the straight man who is anxious not to be outdressed by the queer Gaveston? Hardly. Mortimer cannot bear that the favorite and the king are less than perfectly sober about their images as men, or that they mock men who strut about the grounds below the royal portal.

Mortimer's hostility toward Gaveston's costumes and behavior is an attack against the theatricalization of identity, or the performativity of social status; as Laura Levine (1994) observes of the antitheatrical tracts that suffused London in the 1580s and 1590s, as Marlowe wrote his tragedies, antitheatricalists who attacked the theaters as sites of civic and moral disorder had come to "fear that action is constitutive" (36). Mortimer likewise. He would prefer to quell Gaveston and Edward's public performances of supposedly careless infatuation. Mortimer favors a bewitching return to an atmosphere that celebrates the absolutism of identity and class status. This return would effectively disguise his own ambitions as a social climber who is willing not merely to mock his fellow barons (one complaint against Gaveston), but to have them murdered, surely a greater offense.

As a companion piece to Marlowe's play, Derek Jarman's 1992 film *Edward II* sharpens Marlowe's critique of the hostility of the English Establishment toward class difference and sexual difference. These criticisms are explicitly embodied in Gaveston, whom Jarman, in an interview, has described as "sexuality and class merged" (O'Pray 1991, 9). In teaching the film to a group of eight honors students a year ago as part of a course that moved from Vergil's *Aeneid* to Bobbie Ann Mason's *In Country* and back to *Edward II*, I experienced again the limits of Nussbaum's thesis about the empathy that art cultivates. I think I lost the students's good will during the film's second scene. There, with the opening credits having just rolled, the exiled Gaveston responds to a letter from Edward inviting him to be repatriated now that Edward's father is dead. In the foreground of the scene, on a large bed, Gaveston and another male lover dress themselves; in the background, but also on the bed, two naked musclemen continue with what is apparently an orgy-in-progress. "What art thou?" asks Gaveston. "A sailor." "A sailor." Their presence confirms Jarman's Marlovian urge to deconstruct the ideal of the soldier. As Jarman had quipped in that interview, "If we must have troops, let's have them in bed" (O'Pray 1991, 8). What we have in this scene is Jarman gleefully satisfying a stereotype of gay men as obsessed with transient sexual encounters with multiple anonymous partners, and obsessed too with fantasies of having Navy men in bed. These fantasies are treated to a mix of Gaveston's own class hostility and homophobia. "I have no war," he tells his sailors. "There are hospitals for men like you," he continues, throwing money at them. In Marlowe, Gaveston's dismissal of soldiers begging for succor calls forth the shameful treatment of veterans who returned from service in the Low Countries only to find that Elizabeth's government was prepared to ignore the economic, familial, and physical problems that resulted from their military service in the first place. Aristocrats leading foreign campaigns had smooth reentries; common veterans often did not. In the film, Jarman intensifies Marlowe's oblique criticism of the abandonment of soldiers along class lines. The filmic Gaveston is not simply full of loathing for the aristocracy—"farewell base stooping to the lordly peers," he snarls, taking a line straight from the play; he is more contemptuous of commoners, as if his own liminality has shrunk rather than enlarged his capacity for sympathy with others who are outside the charmed circle of power. To the sailors on the bed he mutters his own slur against the rabble: "As for the multitude, that are but sparks, / Rak'd up in embers of their poverty—fuck 'em."

Although I had prepared my honors students intellectually for Jarman's film, perhaps no amount of talk would have readied them for the celluloid images of graphic homosexual acts, including simulated sodomy. I would guess that none had seen those before. The few male students averted their eyes. Most of the women gazed intently at the TV screen; I'm not sure why. Once the film had run its course, no one wanted to talk about it. At the time, I chalked up the silence to embarrassment, disgust, or both. But I may have had it wrong, as a colleague recently suggested. It may well have been that these students needed more time to digest what they had seen. Jarman's critique of the motives and effects of the Establishment's bloody attacks against characters whose queer consciousness threatens the security of the privileged class is dense and at times contradictory. Or, it may have been that the students were alienated after all. It's difficult to know. I would like to think that in that silence, my students and I experienced one of those not-so-rare episodes of productive estrangement. For a while, I hope, the politics of class and sexuality became intensely apparent.

Notes

1. One of the most prominent Renaissance statements about the infinitude of human potential is the humanist Pico della Mirandola's "Oration on the Dignity of Man" ([1486] 1948).

2. For an excellent, extended discussion of the effects of growing up homosexual on an Iowa farm, see Willow 1997.

3. Sometimes cultural studies critics write as if they have invented the sociohistorical study of literature, which of course is not so. Among the more influential books in early modern studies from the 1930s and beyond we might include Mohl 1933; Thrupp 1948; White 1944; and Wright 1935. Books on a more recent list might include collections of essays such as Burt and Archer 1994; Hendricks and Parker 1994; Turner 1993; and Veeser 1989. A list of pertinent monographs might include Amussen 1988; Kegl 1994; and Jardine 1996.

4. See Ginzburg's defense of scholarly interest in nonelite culture (xiv).

5. Stephen Orgel (1995) offers a compelling tour of changes in the discipline of early modern studies in "Teaching the Postmodern Renaissance."

6. Writing of Moll Flanders's revulsion to being in service, her apparent fate as a parish orphan, John Richetti (1987) observes that Defoe considers her a "character worth writing about" in part because she "undermines the hierarchical inevitability summed up in 'service'"; "service as such excludes the singularity of personality that defines an authenticity (in fact a class privilege) we now identify as novelistic" (85). But the circumstances of service are fundamentally different in *Robinson Crusoe* precisely because the hero's contact with "foreigners" subordinates English assumptions about class to those about race and nationality. Defoe does not allow characters such as Xury and Friday to enjoy the "singularity of personality" he gives to Crusoe, who retains his class privilege while having it virtually obscured.

7. See the classic account in Sedgwick (1985). In *Saint Foucault*, David Halperin argues that the act of claiming a gay identity "operates as an instant disqualification . . . and grants everyone else an absolute epistemological privilege over you." Halperin is cited by Donald Morton (1996), who protests that gay and lesbian solidarity is presently being disrupted "*along class lines*" by a "romanticized" commercialism of middle-class lesbigay culture, where it is common to imagine that one may "*spend*" one's way "out of subjection" and into respectability (479, 472, 473; original emphasis).

Works Cited

Amussen, S. 1988. *An Ordered Society: Gender and Class in Early Modern England.* Oxford: Basil Blackwell.

Beaumont, F., and J. Fletcher. [1613] 1967. *The Knight of the Burning Pestle,* ed. J. Doebler. Lincoln: University of Nebraska Press.

Behn, A. [1690] 1992. *Oroonoko, The Rover and Other Works,* ed. J. Todd. New York: Penguin.

Bérubé, A. 1997. "Intellectual Desire." In *Queerly Classed: Gay Men and Lesbians Write About Class,* ed. S. Raffo, 43–66. Boston: South End.

Biagioli, M. [1993] 1994. *Galileo, Courtier: The Practice of Science in the Culture of Absolutism.* Chicago: University of Chicago Press.

Bourdieu, P., J. C. Passeron, and M. de Saint Martin. [1965] 1994. "Students and the Language of Teaching." In *Academic Discourse: Linguistic Misunderstanding and Professorial Power,* ed. P. Bourdieu, J. C. Passeron, and M. de Saint Martin. Trans. R. Teese, 35–79. Stanford: Stanford University Press.

Bray, A. [1982] 1995. *Homosexuality in Renaissance England.* 2d ed. New York: Columbia University Press.

Bredbeck, G. 1991. *Sodomy and Interpretation: Marlowe to Milton.* Ithaca, NY: Cornell University Press.

Burt, R., and J. M. Archer, eds. 1994. *Enclosure Acts: Sexuality, Property, and Culture in Early Modern England.* Ithaca, NY: Cornell University Press.

Cassirer, E., P. O. Kristeller, and J. H. Randall, eds. 1948. *The Renaissance Philosophy of Man.* Trans. E. L. Forbes. Chicago: University of Chicago Press.

Defoe, D. [1719] 1980. *Robinson Crusoe.* New York: Penguin.

della Mirandola, P. [1486] 1948. "Oration on the Dignity of Man." In *The Renaissance Philosophy of Man,* ed. E. Cassirer, P. O. Kristeller, and J. H. Randall. Trans. E. L. Forbes, 213–254. Chicago: University of Chicago Press.

Field, N. 1995. *Over the Rainbow: Money, Class and Homophobia.* London: Pluto.

Fussell, P. 1983. *Class: A Guide Through the American Status System.* New York: Summit.

Ginzburg, C. [1976] 1983. *The Cheese and the Worms: The Cosmos of a Sixteenth-Century Miller.* Trans. J. and A. Tedeschi. Harmondsworth, England: Penguin.

Goldberg, J. 1992. *Sodometries: Renaissance Texts, Modern Sexualities.* Stanford, CA: Stanford University Press.

———, ed. 1994. *Queering the Renaissance.* Durham, NC: Duke University Press.

Hendricks, M., and P. Parker, eds. 1994. *Women, "Race," and Writing in the Early Modern Period*. New York: Routledge.

hooks, b. 1994. *Teaching to Transgress: Education as the Practice of Freedom*. New York: Routledge.

Jardine, L. 1996. *Worldly Goods: A New History of the Renaissance*. New York: Doubleday.

Jarman, D. 1992. *Edward II*. Produced S. Clark-Hall and A. Root. Directed D. Jarman and K. Butler. Screenplay D. Jarman, S. McBride, and K. Butler. Color. 92 min. London: The Sales Company.

Jonson, B. [1609] 1979. *The Masque of Queens*. In *Ben Jonson's Plays and Masques*, ed. R. Adams, 321–340. Norton Critical Edition. New York: Norton.

———. [1618] 1979. *Pleasure Reconciled to Virtue*. In *Ben Jonson's Plays and Masques,* ed. R. Adams, 364–372. New York: Norton.

Kegl, R. 1994. *The Rhetoric of Concealment: Figuring Gender and Class in Renaissance Literature*. Ithaca, NY: Cornell University Press.

Levine, L. 1994. *Men in Women's Clothing: Anti-theatricality and Effeminization, 1579–1642*. Cambridge, UK: Cambridge University Press.

Marlowe, C. 1981. *The Plays of Christopher Marlowe*, ed. F. Bowers. 2d ed. 2 vols. Cambridge, UK: Cambridge University Press.

Mohl, R. 1933. *The Three Estates in Medieval and Renaissance Literature*. New York: Columbia University Press.

More, T. [1516] 1991. *Utopia,* ed. R. Adams. 2d ed. Norton Critical Edition. New York: Norton.

Morton, D. 1996. "The Class Politics of Queer Theory," *College English* 58 (4): 471–482.

Nussbaum, M. 1995. *Poetic Justice: The Literary Imagination and Public Life*. Boston: Beacon.

O'Pray, M. 1991. "Damning Desire." An Interview with Derek Jarman. *Sight and Sound* 1:6 (October): 8–11.

Orgel, S. 1995. "Teaching the Postmodern Renaissance." In *Professions of Desire: Lesbian and Gay Studies in Literature*, ed. G. Haggerty and B. Zimmerman, 60–71. New York: Modern Language Association.

Richetti, J. 1987. "Representing an Under Class: Servants and Proletarians in Fielding and Smollett." In *The New Eighteenth Century: Theory, Politics, English Literature*, ed. F. Nussbaum and L. Brown, 84–98. New York: Methuen.

Sedgwick, E. 1985. *Between Men: English Literature and Male Homosocial Desire*. New York: Columbia University Press.

Shepard, A. 1995. "The Literature of a Medical Hoax: The Case of Mary Toft, 'The Pretended Rabbet-Breeder' (1726)." *Eighteenth-Century Life* 19 (2): 59–77.

————. 1996. "'O seditious Citizen of the Physicall Common-Wealth!':
   Harvey's Royalism and His Autopsy of Old Parr." *University of Toronto
   Quarterly* 65 (3): 482–505.

Smith, B. 1991. *Homosexual Desire in Shakespeare's England.* Chicago:
   University of Chicago Press.

Spufford, F. 1991. "Blank Verse and Body Fluids." Review of D. Jarman's
   film *Edward II. Times Literary Supplement* 15 November, 19.

Thrupp, S. 1948. *The Merchant Class of Medieval London.* Chicago:
   University of Chicago Press.

Turner, J., ed. 1993. *Sexuality and Gender in Early Modern Europe:
   Institutions, Texts, Images.* Cambridge, UK: Cambridge University Press.

Veeser, H. A., ed. 1989. *The New Historicism.* New York: Routledge.

White, H. C. 1944. *Social Criticism in Popular Religious Literature of the
   Sixteenth Century.* New York: Macmillan.

Willow, M. 1997. "Class Struggles." In *Queerly Classed: Gay Men and
   Lesbians Write About Class*, ed. S. Raffo, 105–117. Boston: South End.

Wright, L. B. 1935. *Middle Class Culture in Elizabethan England.* Chapel
   Hill: University of North Carolina Press.

17

Passing
A Family Dissemblance

Patricia A. Sullivan

I

You're telling the story of your life
for once, a tremor breaks the surface of your words.
Adrienne Rich, "Twenty-One Love Poems" (XVIII)

When I was in graduate school, a friend and I were unpacking boxes of books for a new professor who was teaching a class. We chatted and laughed as my friend handed one book after another to me to plant neatly and alphabetically in rows on the professor's office bookshelves. Then my friend stopped and drew upright all of a sudden, and grew silent. And then she spoke again, looking me directly in the eye. "Can I ask you a question?" she said. "Have you lived a charmed life? You look as if you've led a charmed life."

Four years ago, I received a letter from a part-time writing instructor in the composition program I direct. His letter concerned the status and salaries of adjunct teachers on our staff, and it included these lines: "You have spent so long being a self-confident success that you don't know what it's like to be utterly wracked with self-doubt like our instructors are. You don't know how hard it is to teach, to write, even to speak up at staff meetings without an ounce of self-confidence or the slightest hint of self-esteem backing you up."

These comments, addressed to me seven years apart, are frozen in

I wish to acknowledge and to thank from my heart Stephen Barrett, whose courage, kindness, wisdom, and learning enabled me to write this essay. I am grateful, too, to Cinthia Gannett, who helped me revise an early rough draft, and to Carol Sullivan and Maureen Sullivan, who said the difficult and right things at the moments I most needed to hear them.

memory. Each time my reaction was the same: stunned silence, disbelief, and then anger—an anger that has never quite gone away. I begin
with these comments because if I can make sense of them and of my
reaction, then maybe I can write this essay. If I can figure out how two
people I regarded as friends could know me so little, could mistake me
so completely, then maybe I can come to an understanding about relations of social class in academe—an understanding I have always post-
poned, have consciously and deliberately deferred, until now.

Whatever reason each person had for attributing to me a life and
self I couldn't recognize, I have to grant in retrospect that neither
expressed a willful misperception so much as stated the obvious:
They put into words a self that I project. I had never told either friend,
nor anyone else I have ever worked or studied with in academe for
that matter, the social and familial circumstances of my life. In trying
now to take measure of that silence—now, as I am about to break it—
I am stalled by a wave of fear. There is a voice inside that has been
there as long as I can remember, and it says that it isn't right to speak
of private matters, family matters, money matters. That there will be
hell to pay. That it is far safer to "pass," to keep projecting a self
who has made it, than to disclose the conditions of getting here. But
then that figure of self-confident success, she of "the charmed life,"
rises in memory to taunt me again. And will again and again. And so
she must be reckoned with.

And so. I am the fifth child of nine of a lower-middle-class family. My father was in the Navy for twenty-two years, and took odd
jobs the year he retired, including the night shift at a 7-Eleven, until
he was eventually offered a job as an accountant for the civil service.
He held this position for fifteen years until he died, at age fifty-seven,
of a heart attack. My mother was a teacher in a country schoolhouse
in Kansas when she met and married my father. She stayed at home
raising her children until the youngest turned five, then took a job as a
nurse's aide in a local hospital. Most recently she worked as a clerk
for the IRS; she retired in 1997, at age seventy.

We lived in middle-class neighborhoods all my life, in a two-
bedroom house in Lincoln, Nebraska, until just after the sixth child
was born, and in a duplex in Denver the year my father retired from
the Navy, when there were eight children. (Four of us, aged ten to
seventeen, lived in an apartment above the rest of the family because
my father could not afford rent for a single house large enough for us
all.) I never thought of my family as poor, only as having no money
for the sorts of things our friends had. The poor, to my mind, were
those people who had less than they needed to thrive. We had what
we needed: clothes, a house, and food and medical care subsidized by
the federal government. Our circumstances were modest but as a

function of family size and not income alone. As a child I sometimes wished I was one of only two or three kids so that we could have and do what our neighbors did: own our "own" toys and clothes, join the scouts, go on vacations. And I still recall the wonderful, physical sense of freedom I felt when, for the first time in my life, I had my own room and slept in a bed alone; I was a senior in high school. But looking back, I would not describe my childhood as deprived, much less as oppressive. Though we personally knew few families less well off than we were, at church and at school we were constantly reminded of the less fortunate on this earth and asked to give our prayers and pennies so that they might have enough food to eat.

As the middle child of this large family, the experiences I recall are very likely different from those who came first and last. I grew up during our family's leanest years financially (and, in a sense, I was a cause of them). So when I speak in terms of "us" and "our," I can't claim to be speaking for my eight siblings—my six sisters and two brothers. And in truth, my older and younger siblings by virtue of birth order and my brothers by virtue of gender had possessions and opportunities the three of us in the middle—all girls— didn't have. But though I can't speak *for* eight of us, I have to note a certain psychological reality that may strike some readers as curious: I tend to speak and write and act *as* a group. I tend to think in terms of "we" and "us" and "ours" even when I use the word *I*. Having lived for the first sixteen years of my life, morning through night, in the continual, physical presence of others, my abiding sense of self is a sort of collective subjectivity. In body and mind, I have experienced life as a "we" from the moment I was born—a way of being or state of mind that, I have to suspect, will not be all that peculiar to readers from large families.

If our material circumstances were a product of family size, they and our family's size were also a function of religion: our parents' traditional and fundamental Roman Catholicism. All nine of us children received a Catholic-school education through grade twelve. (My two oldest sisters also went to a small, Catholic college.) My mother was adamant on this point, no matter how often and how ardently my father, also Catholic, protested that we couldn't afford it. For my mother, a Catholic education—its theological training, the spiritual values it would instill, the rewards it would reap for us in the next world—was worth any and every sacrifice it demanded of us here on earth.

My mother came from a large, extended family of farmers and educators. Her parents divorced when she was four, and her mother abandoned her. Her father was a journeyman plumber and a professional wrestler; he traveled most of her life so she was raised at various times by one of her twelve aunts and uncles, all devout Catholics who frowned deeply on their brother's errant lifestyle. Lacking parents who cared for her and any stability or consistency in her life other than the Church, my mother held fast to three things: her marriage; a traditional, conservative notion of family; and old-school Catholicism.

I mention these things with my friends' comments, their perceptions of my charmed life, still, I hope, in my readers' minds. My mother clung to her marriage though my father beat her and us—her, several times in full view of her children; me, so forcefully once that I was lifted off my feet and sent flying across the living room. Now in my forties, I still dream of sisters and brothers being slapped and spanked and shoved, of me watching through a window, helpless to intervene, to call an adult to help, to stop the violence. My father's anger was chronic, his temper volatile, his ruptures into violence utterly unpredictable. I tried but failed to figure out what would set him off, and I could not as a child and still cannot as an adult fathom why a father would want to harm his children. For the longest time, nearly through high school, I thought that that's how men—how fathers—just were. When close friends in high school told me they loved their fathers, that their fathers never laid hands on them but to express affection, I thought I was hearing stories of exception. Of sheer, blessed luck: accidents of fate that simply weren't mine.

My mother's desire to raise as many children as God might give her (and so, perhaps, atone for the sins of her parents), her expressed belief that God would never send her more than He would provide for, and her unflappable faith in His superior wisdom and goodness became the sustaining fiction of our lives, even if some of us already had an inkling that we were nursing that fiction for our mother's and our own psychic survival. But that fiction was eroded each time my father yelled or struck out, and died for me altogether when, in the eighth grade, I witnessed a fierce argument between my father and mother about her pregnancy with her ninth child. He blamed her and the Church for the pregnancy, and screamed that he couldn't possibly afford another mouth to feed, that they had "too many already." He pointed in my direction as I sat doing my homework at the dining room table. My mother's eyes darted at me for half a second, then back at his: "Well you're responsible for this too, you know." She cradled her belly with one hand and lifted the other to point to me, then let it flop down again at her side. Then she began to cry—deep, choking sobs that my father couldn't bear to hear. He left the room. And left me there, trying to think of what I could say or do that would comfort her.

No child should ever hear such an exchange, perhaps, but it clarified for me, at thirteen, the difference between the material and the spiritual, between brute reality and misplaced hope. Delivered with the heat of existential truth, my parents' message conveyed to me who I was (an economic burden, an accident of religious piety) and ultimately foretold and foreclosed my future. (It said: You will have to earn the very space in which you live and move. It, and you, are not a given, much less a gift.)

My family's Catholicism, as both theology and lived ideology, was what I came to think of as fundamentalist. For what always mattered, finally, was moral principle over actual deed, the punitive God of the Old Testament over the merciful and forgiving Christ of the New, the next world over this one, the eternal soul over the yearning body. In a home cluttered with yearning bodies, all competing for attention and affection but entitled in their very being to nothing, in a home where no look or word or smile was safe, self-discipline—suppressed desire—became key to survival. Some of us learned to stop wanting: If we didn't want what we couldn't have, we could stave off disappointment and hurt. Barring that, we made a pretense of not wanting—feigning indifference when desire arose, or just after, when disappointment came. In this way, we conditioned ourselves, our very bodies, to expect and to survive the shock of the real.

Like the night when I was a senior in high school, getting ready to go to bed, and my father came to my room to announce that he was "not paying one thin dime" for my college education. His explanation was that I had chosen to go to the "radical" state university and major in liberal arts when I could have accepted the scholarship the local business school offered. I could have studied something practical, something that would earn me a living, and lived at home for free. But since I had chosen to go to the university, I'd have to find my own way to get there. "You're on your own, sister," he said. And he slammed the door behind him.

Years later I would understand that my father was telling me the money had run out. He couldn't put a fifth child through college and feed the four still at home. But what I heard then was the earlier rage all over again—not at something I had done or had chosen but for existing at all. For being his child. For being one child too many. I remember making a conscious decision not to cry and to show my parents that they didn't matter, no matter what it took. *I'll be fine on my own, thanks. You don't need me? Well, I don't need you either. I'll be just fine. You'll see.* I can recognize it now, that same old survival trick learned almost from infancy. Don't want what you can't have, and you'll always be safe. Cut off need before it starts, and life is in your control.

That summer, at seventeen, I worked sixteen-hour shifts, six days a week, in the dishroom at a resort in the Wyoming mountains, the only job I could find. I made $1.60 an hour. For two and a half

months I took speed to stay awake and to keep hunger away. The day
I glimpsed my body in a mirror as I stepped into a shower between
shifts and saw a skeleton peering back, I literally gasped, and then
stared . . . and stared, unable to believe that it was my own eyes, in
those hollows, looking back. I tiptoed into the warm rush of water and
pulled the shower curtain behind me, scared to touch sponge to any
bone, even lightly, lest it shatter. I quit taking speed. But I continued
to do dishes, morning through night, to make money for college.

As a college freshman, I lived in the cheapest dorm—the "ghetto"
as we called it—and chose a five-day meal plan to save every dollar I
could. Friends would smuggle rolls and fruit from the dorm cafeteria
so I could eat on weekends. My roommate shared her car, gym shoes,
shampoo and toothpaste, Gen Ed textbooks, money from home. I survived with a little help from my friends, including the occasional
numb euphoria of drugs, without a dime from my parents, and earned
As and Bs for the year. But I was filled with self-loathing and shame.
I couldn't justify my existence, let alone my presence in college. In
college. The very idea meant so much to me, I hated my presumption
for wanting, thinking, I could be a part of it. I dropped out of school
after my first year and moved to California to work, to live near a
much-loved sister, and to "find myself."

Where I most often found myself when I wasn't working was in
philosophy courses at U.C. Berkeley— "auditing" large classes where
I could be anonymous but do the reading, even pass in essay exams in
bluebooks. A student I befriended in one class, a young black man
who always saved a seat for me, with whom I traded whispered conversations about assigned readings, and to whom I eventually
confided that I was an impostor, not a real student, took me aside
after class one day and told me directly that I belonged in school if
anyone did, that I belonged more than anyone he knew. He said he
was on to my gig, that he knew all about passing, and that I had to
stop playing at what I was supposed to be doing. *Get your ass back in
school real time*, he said.

If this man hadn't literally taken me by the shoulders and faced
me down, I'm not sure I would have found my way back. But I took
his unlikely friendship, his sympathy and caring that wanted nothing
back, as a sign. And that fall, I returned to the university I'd left.

To make it through my sophomore year, I waitressed in the summer, moved into a small apartment, hitchhiked or walked to school,
applied for and received $30.00 a month in food stamps, bought no
clothes or shoes—and paid my full tuition. I could finesse the clothes
and the hitchhiking when I had to, but the food stamps were a particular source of shame. I told only one friend I was on the dole—my
roommate from freshman year. I changed my major from English to

philosophy and threw myself into its truth-sayers, paradoxes, and conundrums: Plato, Aristotle, Maimonides, Boethius, William of Occam, Augustine, Aquinas, Descartes, Locke, and Hume, truth vs. appearance, mind vs. body, free will vs. determinism, empiricism vs. idealism. The philosophy department awarded me a tuition scholarship for my junior and senior years and gave me a work-study position in the department library where I spent most of each day the next two years, reading, studying, smoking to stave off hunger, writing papers. (I continued to waitress the summers in between school years, doing double shifts whenever my employers would let me.)

I want to say that I loved my life during these years. I want to say this to someone and be believed, to at least suspend disbelief for a short while. Because I really did love my life. I loved that my body didn't matter—that I could go for hours reading and puzzling over Fichte, Hegel, Schopenhauer, Marx, Wittgenstein, Husserl, Whitehead, Anscombe, and Russell, without eating or feeling hungry. That I could be the only female in a class and go unnoticed on that account. That I could be heard and respected on the basis of my mind. That philosophy allowed "me" to disappear into the intellectual work at hand, and that my professors, male and female, valued and honored that work, the labor itself and not (at least never expressly) the laborer. I want to say that I loved my life precisely because my body and looks and situation didn't matter. That philosophy—a life of mind, of reading and writing, something I could do well—gave me a reason to live at a time in my life and under circumstances when a reason to live, when rationality itself, was especially hard to come by.

But of course bodies do matter. I know that now, now that I'm writing this essay and am in a position to reflect, to dislodge story and truth from their safe nest in my unconscious. I know now the lengths I went to suppress my body's hunger, to conceal its attractiveness, and to present a self who was the picture of studiousness. I lived a life of mind, excelled at it, and the rewards came: I received tuition scholarships, was elected to Phi Beta Kappa, was awarded the senior prize in philosophy, and graduated magna cum laude. I was alive, I was safe, and I was a star—but only because I inhabited a metaphysical world light years from home. Analytical philosophy was as far from *home* and all it represented as any discipline I might have studied. But the physical world my major so effectively allowed me to escape and deny was inscribing itself all along. On the day of my college graduation, which I "chose" not to attend (I couldn't afford to rent a cap and gown) and which my parents took no notice of, I weighed just over one hundred pounds. I'm 5'6".

If someone learns to survive in the ways and for the duration I have, perhaps she takes on an aura of success to that person who sees only the effect, not the process. Perhaps her very person, which can never be too rich or too thin by a certain privileged standard, signals self-confidence, self-control, a mastery of circumstances to someone who is "master" by birthright, for whom survival is a simple given. Perhaps she really is the embodiment of self-confident success to someone who doesn't instinctively know how to act, what to do, when the world or one of its institutions threatens that safe sense of self, the gratification of basic need, to which one has always felt entitled. My friend in graduate school could not possibly have known what went into the charmed life she beheld—that it was the function of a series of careful calculations: one meal a day is plenty; foregoing six meals = a textbook for next term; first sell the books you love and the rest will be easy; walking will get you anywhere you need to go; water will suffice; a sweater worn daily can become your signature outfit; pot is cheaper than health insurance. My colleague in the writing program I now direct couldn't possibly know, from the conviction and passion and joy with which I talk about composition to other teachers of writing, whence that "self-confident success" came. That it was salvaged from a wreck, that it is one of the few true miracles of my life. It wasn't supposed to *be*. But somehow, inexplicably, it is.

II

The story of our lives becomes our lives. (Rich 1978)

The unkindest cut of all was not the instructor's remark that mistook the visible, outward sign of success for the personal history and inner life it concealed, but the charge that followed it: that I can no longer "identify" with the adjunct writing teachers on my staff who are struggling to make ends meet on inadequate wages, whose self-esteem is affected on a daily basis by the low esteem in which they are held by tenured faculty in our department. Not only was I accorded a life I didn't live, I was inserted into a syllogism with an utterly damning conclusion: Faculty with Ph.D.s, tenure, and middle-class salaries (the "haves") are oblivious to colleagues who do not have these things (the "have-nots"). I am a tenured member of our faculty. Ergo.

An irony is that I received the instructor's letter as I was drafting a proposal to our college dean to raise instructors' salaries, to improve their benefits, and to make their positions "permanent"—renewable every three years on the basis of a strong record of teaching. As director of our composition program, I lobbied hard for these gains, arguing that a stable core of professional writing teachers was crucial to the long-range effectiveness of our program given the large number of

graduate teaching assistants we employ. The final proposal we submitted grew out of a yearlong series of meetings among the adjunct
writing instructors on our staff. I was invited to attend after a few, initial, "closed" meetings. Our conversations were frank, difficult, often
anguished and bitter, often full of recrimination, always exhausting.
The despair in the room was palpable. But the meetings were also
productive—they resulted in consensus and action—and were eventually successful. We got the gains we sought.

The gains we sought. There is that "we" again. Groupthink. A
"we" at least one instructor felt I had no right to use because I am not a
member of the class of people it names. I do not suffer the conditions
that demarcate that class—material, financial, political, psychological—and that bind together the women and men within it. I can advocate *for* but cannot speak *as* . . . I am an outsider, privileged in ways
they will never be, and it is disingenuous of me to speak and act or
even assume that I am one of them because, in fact, I am not. Am I?

Class, as Paul Fussell has pointed out, is America's dirty little
secret. Sex has nothing on class in America: We are far less squeamish talking and hearing about "the act" than we are about class. And
academe certainly has nothing on the rest of America: Class is academe's dirty little secret, its last taboo, that about which we dare not
speak. Class almost never appears in the disciplined, sanctioned discourses of the academy but as that category of social analysis "studied" by sociologists. When class is spoken of at all, it hitches itself to
gender and race, is subdivided into the familiar triumvirate of income,
education and occupation, and is analyzed as a composite of vari-
ables such as religion, age, ethnicity, nationality, local habits, linguistic practices, and community mores. Thanks to a growing body of
work in cultural studies, women's studies, anthropology, and education, "class" has more recently begun to take on a human face, or
more accurately, faces and bodies of every conceivable shape and
color and age and desire and circumstance and relation to other bodies, born and unborn. Qualitative methods in the social sciences (case
studies, oral histories, ethnographies) have joined narrative, interpretive, and critical practices in the humanistic disciplines to provide us
increasingly with biographical and autobiographical accounts of lived
experience. But many quarters of the academy still cast a suspicious
eye on the personal as a form of inquiry, regarding it as too subjective. Not even *The Uses of Literacy*, Richard Hoggart's (1958)
ground-breaking and intensely personal account of the working class
in Britain, would have been published, much less have found an academic audience, had Hoggart written only about himself, had he written only of what life was like for him—had he merely written a personal story.

Not long ago, an older colleague from another department joked about the sandwich trays spread before a small group of us at a university committee meeting. "I'm still tempted," he chuckled, "to load my pockets with food when the rest of you aren't lookin' and take it home to my children, like my parents did during the Depression." The remark was funny on several counts: We all recognized that "hereditary" gesture, learned in the body, that never goes away; this man couldn't possibly have had children still at home; the bread and ham splayed before us couldn't have set a salivary gland going with a hacksaw. But what made me laugh, out loud, was the "when the rest of you aren't lookin' " part. The man was breaking a taboo and he knew it. We were hearing what we were and are forbidden to "see," to acknowledge. The man's joke was uncanny, in the Freudian sense. But what struck me as uncanny in a far more personal vein was that this was the first time in my academic life I had ever heard a professor tell of growing up poor. The good professor had let us in on a dirty little secret.

What would happen if this professor wrote his story down and offered it to an academic public—to readers of a journal or to the colleagues he passes in the hall—as a way to understand microbiology: one student and scholar's passion for microbes? Again, he would have broken a taboo—the academic, scholarly, scientific, epistemological, professional injunction against telling personal stories. Only he would have broken—and this is my point—the same taboo. For class and lived experience, lived experience and the personal, are one and the same thing. As a rule, we allow ourselves to contemplate class in the academy only insofar as it is, in fact, an act of contemplation we are doing—the studied pursuit of knowledge, truth, and reasonable certainty by reflection, observation, and research. And the object of such contemplation must include at least one person, and preferably a group or community of persons, other than the perceiving/emoting/speaking/writing subject. Otherwise we grow suspicious about the seriousness of the work we are reading. All our well-trained defenses come into play.

But what are we defending ourselves against? Is our prevailing anxiety about narrative in the academy—the "personal essay" in composition, the case study in social science, the first-person account wherever it appears—really about narrative's status as knowledge, its reliability, its representativeness, its applicability to other cases? Or do we fear what the personal might be about? What an *I* might have to tell us if granted the same epistemological standing as an *it* or a *them*? Don't we fear at some level what the personal might commit us to if we allow a self to speak in a genre other than fiction? Haven't we consigned class, on the one hand, to the disciplined, contemplative discourses of philosophy and social science (and to their applied or service branches—education, public policy, social work), and on the other hand to the private, individual psyche (from which it can speak uncensored only in private conversation or a therapist's office) because only in these two realms is it safe? At a safe remove from deliberate, systematic action?

When Gayatri Spivak (1988) asks whether the subaltern can speak, she is asking whether marginalized members of a culture can be heard by the dominant culture, can be effectual within that culture's discourse, given that that culture and its discourse are the effects of relations of power that determine who and what constitute (count as) proper subjects. Can the subaltern speak, say, if the subaltern is an adjunct writing instructor in an English department, in a culture and discourse that valorizes the personal so long as it is fictional and past, at a safe remove from the real, living, embodied conditions of its teachers and students? Richard Hoggart (1972) has noted that most literary criticism is written in a style that seems intimate but that in fact distances: "It becomes an invisible but impenetrable film; it separates both the writer and the reader from the shock of the experience being written about" (38). The tones used in literary criticism, he says, "neuter or reduce experience . . . cut it down, thin it out" so that it fits our assumptions about "the limits of the permissible, emotionally" (38). If the speaking subjects who count in an English department are its professors, and the subjects legitimately spoken about are those found in texts—their emotional power attributable at best to their verisimilitude—how is the writing instructor without status, without power, to be heard when she speaks of the material conditions of her life? How can she speak and be heard when she herself embodies academe's dirty little secret?

We know that academe reflects, in its own hierarchical structure and meritocratic system of rewards, the class arrangements and market conditions of the larger society in a capitalist culture. Part-time, adjunct, nontenurable writing teachers are the equivalent of society's working class: They are perceived by management as unskilled and interchangeable; they work for minimum wages, often without benefits and protections; they are hired and let go at the whims of an ever-fluctuating economy. For every administrator, teacher, and student who protests the essential injustice of the system, for every resolution passed, article written, and convention convened, a far greater number of academics stand opposed to change because the very hierarchy and inequity of the system serve their self-interests. All are competing for a finite pool of dollars. A system of distribution in line with their progressive social beliefs but that would take away dollars from their research and travel budgets is not in their own interests. And so they turn a blind eye and a deaf ear. And instructors are well aware of this. The issue is not so much sociopolitical as psychopolitical. The instructor encounters a system that depends on her labor but to which she does not "belong." Evidence everywhere tells her that she is an impostor, not a "real" academic. No matter how hard, how long, how well she prepares and teaches, she remains invisible to those empowered to see—to confer recognition. She is passing—taking on the gestures, signs, and practices of those who legitimately belong. But in a liminal state and with a self-consciousness that can only, in time, inflict a deep wound to the psyche.

I have said that I lobbied for our instructors' improved status and salaries by arguing that such gains were for the intrinsic good of our composition program—our curriculum and students. And I said that I spoke as an advocate for, but not as a member of, the class of teachers for whom that argument was made. But in each case I dissemble (and thus bear a "passing" resemblance to my father, who concealed in his own display of self-righteousness the real reason he could not send me to college). The real story, what really happened, is this: During the long course of meetings we—the instructors and I—held, what I initially heard were the demands of a disenfranchised group: claims being staked on the basis of experience, commitment, expertise, and labor. Then, at some point, the question that could not be asked was asked: What would happen if the instructors' claims weren't met? The silence in the room answered it: Nothing. The teachers thought of themselves as invisible to the powers that be and hence expendable, interchangeable, easily replaceable—their experience, commitment, and expertise for nought. This perception jarred with my sense of reality, my experiences in "our" program and department, and I said so. I was immediately assailed for my naiveté. For weeks afterward I was politely but decisively taken to task, instructed in the ways academe "really" works, given a good dressing down (as in the letter from my colleague). I heard stories of invisibility, of silencing, of professional disrespect, of outright cruelty. My defenses were working overtime: I wanted to deny or defuse every problem I could ("There's another way of interpreting that"; "He said that? Well, consider the source!") and solve every one left over ("I'll handle it"). But the stories continued—personal, devastating stories. One teacher could not afford the airfare to a grandchild's funeral. Another had not bought any but secondhand clothing and household goods in years. A single mother made a practice of "fasting" twice a week so her children could eat. A thirty-five-year-old still could not afford to have a child (she had no medical benefits or maternity leave). Class began speaking itself in the only register it can be heard in academe—the personal. The limits of the permissible, emotionally, were breached. I was hearing what I had desperately wanted not to hear, what my position and status, my sense of earned entitlement, had kept safely at bay.

I was hearing the stories of my life.

I would very much like to bring this part of my essay to a close by finding or creating closure. I wish that a simple reiteration of my thesis would do: that our academic surveillance at the borders of the emotionally permissible is entwined with our anxieties about class. That these anxieties run deep, so deep that they remain hidden and disguised even to a self whom life has prepared for the shock of the real. So deep that even the editors of this book, on social class, on our lives and teaching, felt they needed to tell authors to tell more than personal stories. Yet the personal is the only way in which class can speak itself in the academy and be heard. Class will remain suppressed, and whole classes of humans oppressed, so long as personal accounts of lived experience are devalued as knowledge.

But neither my story nor my theory is finished. In fact the hardest part remains.

For now, while I can no longer help but identify with the teachers on my staff, women and men who are experiencing conditions of life I know in the marrow, how are they to identify with me? How can class, once seen, acknowledged, (re)cognized, be bridged? Surely one answer lies in reciprocity: Surely the personal story, a life told, must be reciprocated in kind. Otherwise it will merely reinscribe the relations of power from which it was wrested. It is not enough, in other words, for me to listen to the personal, to forge a silent connection, nor even to act on the understanding such stories afford. I need to speak back, to say "I am not who you think I am. I am not the Other, I am *you*." But how does a professor speak of hunger, of shame, of passing, of a father's slap, of a spirituality disowned, of desperation, of a life salvaged, when she is speaking now from the other side? From the perspective of history? From a distance as safe (and safely removed, if emotionally evocative) as a literary text? To recast Spivak's question, can the "dominant" speak personally? And if she does, can she be heard? Spivak doesn't say. Nor, right now, can I.

Perhaps the dominant, the "upper" class, is locked into its own sphere of silence, whatever other spheres its individual members have inhabited, whatever conditions they have personally overcome, denied, or continue to live in secret. Perhaps it is the fate of privilege in any form—in *any*—to be misheard, misread, taken and mistaken for the Other. Perhaps nothing I say or do will matter, finally, when it is my very presence that chafes, when it is all that I re-present, that scrapes against bone.

I can live with that. I've survived worse.

III

Close between grief and anger, a space opens . . . (Rich 1978)

I have been teaching college writing courses for sixteen years, as a graduate teaching assistant, as an instructor, as an assistant professor, and now as an associate professor of English. From the first course I taught to the present day, I've remained a strong proponent of the conferencing method. I find I can learn more about a student's background, needs, strengths, fears, and abilities and adapt my course to the manifestly different learners within it by meeting students individually in weekly or biweekly conferences than from any other method I might use. To remain committed to the conferencing method is to remain resolutely open-minded: able and willing to concede the force of my own history, experience, and knowledge to the greater force and need of learners who embody, narrate, represent—and thereby stand to teach me—difference.

That said, I have to confess that if there is a student who evokes a kind of visceral antipathy in me, it is the one who takes higher education as a simple birthright, who has a free ride with respect to tuition and board (all amenities paid) courtesy of his or her parents, and who bears a sense of privilege—of uncontested entitlement—in his or her very carriage and demeanor. Such students are glibly certain of their future prospects and seem to regard both the writing classroom and college life in general as a kind of personal playing field or a spotlit stage whose center they occupy. Such students never think to ask if they are imposing on my time when they drop by my office to talk nor to apologize when they call me at home. My time, my life, are considered theirs for the asking. If I have to miss a prearranged appointment or hand papers back later than I planned, I become insufferable in such students' eyes . . . Good help is so very hard to find these days.

And if, at the other end of the spectrum, there is a student who evokes my unsolicited empathy, it is that student who resembles the student I was—trying desperately to pass, to act like he or she belongs, to stay in school no matter what the cost. These students approach my office apologetically, even at their own assigned conference time, as if presuming upon a space that isn't theirs. They wouldn't dream of calling me at home. Such students almost never miss class, are always attentive (if visibly tired) when there, and are usually quiet—absorbing but seldom contributing to class discussion. Unlike their privileged counterparts, these students quietly blend in, calling the least possible attention to themselves.

Though aware that I have created caricatures, at best, I am necessarily portraying these two kinds of students as opposites and as types for now. For each type in fact poses a very different set of pedagogical challenges in the writing courses I teach, and each of these challenges calls for a solution as different in kind as the emotional responses evoked by the actual students I have known and taught. I will discuss each of these challenges, and the "solutions" at which I've arrived, in turn.

The first student, owing perhaps to a prep school background, the advantages of world travel, and/or the social connections and communities he or she inhabits before arriving at college, already possesses many of the verbal skills I am trying to teach in a first-year course. The student's first drafts reflect a lexical and syntactic sophistication other students' essays do not approximate even after multiple revisions. The student is able to produce a nearly flawless paper stylistically and grammatically. On a surface level, the paper is nothing if not reader-friendly. But in nearly every case, the polished, highly literate writing I receive from such students is bereft of substance. Such students tend to write essays that reaffirm their privileged experience and view of the natural order of things and occasionally their narcissism. They write about problems that annoy them and sometimes find writing itself tedious and annoying. But in place of the question, conflict, or issue that calls for essaying and reflection—that typically gives rise to writing in the first place—the reader finds a deft exercise in ego gratification and spleen-venting. The reader can find no trace of a tension or exigence that signals the presence of a rhetorical situation, in Lloyd Bitzer's (1968) famous formulation.

Let me offer two quick examples. In response to an assignment to write about a significant, transformative personal experience, one student wrote in vivid, descriptive detail about the "annoying" hurricane that ended her summer on the Cape. When another student in workshop asked whether anyone was hurt or their houses damaged in the hurricane, the writer pondered the question, blinking a few times, then answered: "I don't know . . . but that's not, you know, what my paper's about." Another student, a business major whose father is an executive at a Fortune 500 company, chose to investigate unemployment for his research essay. He concluded, after eight pages of library research and fieldwork—including interviews of employment counselors at three agencies—that if "able bodied men" really wanted to work, they could: "There are plenty jobs out there," he wrote. But some men "refuse to work at a place like McDonald's because they think it's beneath them. So their families go on welfare and we taxpayers are left footing the bill. Why? Because these men don't really want to work, not when Uncle Sam is there, ready to bail them out."

I would speculate, following James Moffett (1968), that students who have lived lives of material comfort, sheltered from everyday problems of sustenance and safety, are unable to problematize or abstract from experience in the way that students who experience everyday life as conflictual do. The stylistically adroit but vacuous essays this student writes reflects an internalized sense of how the world is. The world outside, and hence inside, are one and the same: the only life-world the student has known. But my hypothesis and my ability to respond, professionally, as a writing teacher are mediated by my gut reaction to the student. When I read such essays or meet with the student in conference, I want to say to the writer what I imagine his or her classmates are thinking: Get a life.

But of course the student *has* a life . . . the very sort of life, give or take a few ideologies, I might wish for my own daughter. The sort of life I never had.

And so there is, most certainly but quite personally, a class in this text. For if it is not class that makes me want to dismiss both the writing and the writer as trivial, unimportant—as undeserving of serious attention and a share of my energy— what is it? If I read an essay that is competent, even sophisticated, in all matters but substance, from where does my sense of what counts as "real"— as substantive—come if not from my own life? My sense of life as a struggle, materially and intellectually?

But to acknowledge my visceral response to such students is one thing, to act on it quite another. In the past I have bracketed my emotional response and applied those teaching strategies, made those calls of judgment, that my professional studies and experience have availed me of. For example, I have asked a student to try rewriting a piece from the perspective of the Other he hasn't considered or whom he has resolutely opposed in his essay. And I have given tailor-made readings to a student in conference that disturb and complicate her ingrained sense of the natural order of things. But I usually get platitudes back where learning should be: Well acquainted with and conversant in the discourses that open doors, the student simply writes what he or she thinks I want to hear. Cumulatively, over the years, these students and their pseudo-revisions have taught me a much needed lesson about my own ineffectuality.

Fortunately, these students' classmates have taught me that I have been the problem, the main obstacle to learning, all along. When the student writer who perceives and styles life's problems (from soiled prom dress and fraternity beer bust to hurricane and unemployment) as an "annoyance" confronts peers in collaborative workshops who encounter the very use of the word *annoyance*, not to mention the concept and worldview it implies, for the first time in their lives, the resulting negotiations of perception and reality are more than I can singly ask for, more than I, as teacher, can possibly effect. The writer's self-absorbed story or screed is infected by alternate realities—lived experiences and worldviews—voiced by those who matter most. I now leave it to other students to ask the salient question—to speak and enact the personal, to pose the problem and thus create the rhetorical situation—that I can't. The writer is no longer trying to placate me but rather is immersed in a discourse situation from which she must extricate herself, traversing a path to and from the other en route to making meaning of a personal event or social issue.

The second student presents a more formidable problem if only because he or she is far less visible, as a student and as a writer, than the first— by the student's own deliberate design. I almost never know anything about this student's background and day-to-day circumstances until late in the semester, until *I've* raised the subject, heeding the familiar, telltale signs: interest, desire, motivation, and intellectual presence all countered by bouts of physical fatigue; a seemingly intuitive appreciation of otherness and contingency in readings and writing; a quality of mind in the content of the writing that indicates there is more going on than the writer has chosen to disclose; even a detail as small as the same clothes worn to class every day. These students don't want to let me or anyone know they're working twenty to thirty hours a week, that they're paying all or part of their tuition and board, that their parents can't or won't help financially, for fear I or someone will think less of them, that I won't regard them in the same terms, by the same standards, on the same plane, as those they think "naturally" belong in college. When I do ask a personal, pointed question about the student's background and circumstances, it is always because the student has begun to miss class, to request extensions of due dates, or to inquire about getting an incomplete—and the reasons he or she has offered are veiled in the most general and oblique terms: "There are things I need to take care of"; "I have to straighten out some things"; "I'll get the work done but I have to do some other stuff first." Having hidden so much of my own background from my professors, having resorted to this same language when I've begged financial counselors for aid while simultaneously trying to protect my own parents from scrutiny and criticism, I well know what is materially happening behind such significations of language. I recognize the signs. I know that what distinguishes this student's use of those vague "things and stuff" so many of our students resort to when they want out of an assignment or due date is that telling *I* in the subject position. This student is not offering an excuse. He isn't casting himself as the victim of circumstances beyond his control but as the agent of actions he still needs to perform. He is bearing a weight he is long used to. And now he is in an institution as seemingly impervious to whatever personal story and circumstance he might convey as any other he and his family have encountered.

Again, let me offer two examples. In a second-year writing course, I had a bright and serious student, an English major, who sometimes fell asleep in class. He increasingly handed in work late, always begging for a few more days, and when he did hand it in, it was not up to the quality he had earlier proved himself more than capable of writing. At midterm, I received a second course roster that confirmed student enrollment in the course. His name wasn't on it. I asked him to talk to me after class. At first he merely related the fact that he still owed three hundred dollars on his tuition bill so the registrar refused to grant him official status. Then he said he had taken a second job to try to earn the money, but he kept falling short because he had rent and other bills to pay, and now the registrar was telling him time was running out. When I asked whether his parents could help him out, he started crying. His mother was seriously ill. His father thought English was a frivolous major and college itself a luxury, and had cut off all financial support. "I want more than anything to stay," he said. "I'm working two jobs, I never sleep anymore, I hardly ever get time to eat, I never go out. I know I haven't been the greatest student in this class, but I will get the money if you'll just give me a little more time. I'm good for it, I swear. Just please don't drop me from this class. Just please don't." I assured him he could stay, told him that I had been where he is, and offered to call the registrar on his behalf. I told him that I believed him, that I knew beyond a shadow of a doubt that he was good for the money. And I wrote him a check for three hundred dollatrs. (Fourteen months later, he paid it back.)

Another student in an honors section of first-year composition was the sharpest reader and most gifted writer I have ever had. For one assignment—to explore media(ted) literacies—he wrote about a sailing magazine that continued to come to the previous tenant of an apartment he now shared with four other men, all in their late teens and twenties, all ethnically and politically diverse, all of them in working-class jobs, he the lone student. As he leafed through and decoded the magazine's pages in his essay, speculating about the original subscriber from its articles, pictures, and ads and interpreting "sailing culture" through the ironic lens of the magazine's now-actual (but utterly unlikely) readers and their circumstances, he noted the single appearance of a black person in the magazine—in an ad for linens in the back; a smiling woman in a white maid's uniform stood on a dock, a cluster of crisp white towels folded over her outstretched arm, bidding the reader/sailing aficionado "a clean and worry free voyage." The student happened to be watching TV as he read the magazine, and every channel was filled with the aftermath of the Simpson verdict, which had been handed down that afternoon. He interlaced his essay with televised, talking-head pronouncements of justice served or justice denied, and he ended with a description of the black maid in the ad, now implicitly conflated with—or complicit with—the African American women on the jury.

No reader, certainly no white reader, could come away from this student's essay without their own sense of justice deeply and profoundly disturbed. I doubt I will ever again receive a piece of writing from a student like that essay, and that essay was on a par with everything else this student had written in my course toward his final portfolio. And then he disappeared. Stopped coming to class.

When two weeks passed, I called his apartment and left a message. He returned my call. His father had been laid off, he had had to increase his hours working at a discount clothing store to thirty-five hours a week, he was supporting his family now, he didn't own a car and so had to take a bus to work and back—carving into his day—he was exhausted. He simply couldn't stay in school.

"You have to," I pleaded. "Say the word and I will do everything I can to get you a tuition waiver, a scholarship. What do you need to stay? How can I help?"

He laughed—at himself, at his hopeless predicament—his self-effacing wit and sense of the absurd intact. "I can't stay in school, Pat," he said. "I want to—you have no idea how much—but I can't. Thank you so much for calling, for everything, but I just can't. I'm really sorry."

I told him I would give him an incomplete in the course. I called and wrote to him, explaining that if he just completed the final writing project in the class, and handed in his portfolio, he would pass. With an A. He said he'd try. When the registrar sent me a form letter three months later, asking me to submit a change of grade or simply let the grade revert to F, I called him again, at his apartment, at his parents' house, leaving him messages to submit something, anything, lest he fail the course.

He never called back. He didn't send a paper, a portfolio.

He got an F. My best student in sixteen years failed my course.

In one recurrent fantasy, a man now in his thirties or forties wins the Pulitzer Prize for nonfiction, and he laughs when he recalls for his interviewer and the public the F he received in freshman composition years ago. I laugh with him, like everyone else, only my joy is like the rapture of saints—giddy, transcendent, beyond the reach of the rational, beyond the limits of the permissible, emotionally.

If I didn't indulge this fantasy from time to time, I think I would go crazy.

And so I arrive, on the one hand, at a solution to the personal that is not personal at all but social: I offer up the elite to the masses, the narcissist to the Other, the student who knows only one kind of

life to the contingencies of living—and the possibilities for learning—embodied and voiced by diverse peers. And I arrive on the other
hand at a solution that is so personal, so idiosyncratic, so pitched
from and to individual circumstance, that it is no solution at all. I can
never truly "reach" those like me, do anything for them that would
offset or defray their need before the fact because then they would
have to admit and forsake the mask, to stand out, to declare that they
are other than what they are. They can't "pass" if someone is on to
them. And that need to pass is far stronger than most of us know,
stronger than many of us can begin to understand. It subsumes everything, including the utterly consequential and utterly trivial matter of
passing a course. And so I am left reacting to, not acting upon, another's crisis. Bound by my own understanding of and identification with
a student's hierarchy of needs, I remedy an injustice here and grieve
an injustice there, failing throughout to address (much less redress)
the structure of class relationships indigenous to the academy—an
institution to which I now "belong."

"What is 'remembered' in the body," Elaine Scarry (1985) writes,
"is well remembered" (109). I think of the bodies in my classroom,
some strutting into class, staking out their space and birthright; others
finding a way to become the self scripted for them over the decades;
and still others there by a miracle they know can be undone at any
moment but there nonetheless, laying tentative stake to a claim that
will never be safely theirs, that they can never own, that may still be
yanked away whatever they do, however good they are. If I am on the
lookout for the latter, if my sympathies and energy are too liberally
directed there, perhaps I can be forgiven. It's personal, you see; it
keeps coming back to that. If an older sister hadn't inexplicably loved
and nurtured her sister all these years, if an unlikely friend in
Berkeley hadn't taken hold of me twenty years ago and told me I
belonged, if some unnamed but still cherished professors hadn't cared
about who I was though I tried to stay hidden, I wouldn't be here. I
wouldn't be writing this essay. An essay, alas, that still resists closure.

I cannot bring this essay to a satisfying end, to reach a conclusion
that will slake anyone's thirst for a good story, sate their need for
practical advice, or offer the promise of a viable theory. Least of all
can I now turn to theory—one that might place class in clearer perspective. For it is theory's nature, for better and for worse, to put
individual selves under erasure. And I have been laboring hard in this
essay—indeed against my own lived history and professional inclina-
tion—to write bodily about class, to keep selves in the foreground,
lest class disappear once again into the rhetoric that has always concealed and contained it. So I must finish by sharing yet one more personal revelation: I have discovered my aim in writing this essay by

writing it. And it is as simple and profound as my hope for this book itself: that my fellow contributors and I (that collective "we" I carry inside like family) might draw into a clearing those who have been too long invisible to academe. That through our stories of teaching, of learning, of writing, and of listening, our presence in academe will matter to more than those few individuals we have had the good fortune to meet. That our writing will thus do important work in this world. That, all told, even the most uncharmed lives will be found compelling.

Works Cited

Bitzer, L. 1968. "The Rhetorical Situation." *Philosophy and Rhetoric* 1 (Winter): 1–14.

Fussell, P. 1984. *Class*. New York: Ballantine.

Hoggart, R. 1972. *On Culture and Communication*. New York: Oxford University Press.

———. 1958. *The Uses of Literacy*. New York: Oxford University Press.

Moffett, J. 1968. *Teaching the Universe of Discourse*. Boston: Houghton Mifflin.

Rich, A. 1978. "Twenty-One Love Poems" (XVIII). *The Dream of a Common Language*. New York: Norton.

Scarry, E. 1985. *The Body in Pain*. New York: Oxford University Press.

Spivak, G. 1988. "Can the Subaltern Speak?" In *Marxism and the Interpretation of Culture*, ed. Cary Nelson and Leonard Grossberg, 217–313. Urbana: University of Illinois Press.

18

Halfway Back Home

Gary Tate

Memories that Continue to Haunt Me

My mother sobbing—I am six or seven—because she could not afford to buy a hat to wear to church on Easter Sunday. At the time, my father, who had quit school after the seventh grade to go to work, was making fifteen dollars a week working in a pool hall. The scene, as I recall it, took place in the tiny dining room where I slept at night on a cot until I was eleven or twelve.

My mother reading—I am older now—but unwilling to go to the public library to check out books for fear of seeing someone "important," a fear she carried with her to her grave. So I was sent to the library for my first introduction to discourse analysis. Because she loved only novels that were more conversational than descriptive, I soon learned to scan the books I checked out to make certain that there were few long, solid blocks of type and that there were many short lines in quotation marks.

My father kneeling—I am in college now—on the bright green grass in front of the sorority house, a bejeweled and high-heeled sorority board matron standing over him, giving instructions. Two or three months after I left home for college, my parents sold their home— my home—bought a trailer, and headed west. Thus I had no home to return to, but I followed my parents and ended up in graduate school at the university where my father cleaned sorority houses in the summer and did dormitory maintenance work the rest of the year. He never complained, never seemed to hear the matron's condescending tone that made me want to snarl back. But I didn't, out of respect for a man whom I never knew well but came to respect and admire. This scene has stayed with me all these years as a painful symbol of power and willing subservience. It was at moments like this one that

I began to see the gulf that was widening between my parents, leading their quiet, often fearful lives—and me, growing educated and arrogant.

My father coming to me one December—I am still in graduate school—to borrow money to buy my mother a coat for Christmas. I still feel with incredible vividness the embarrassment I felt as I sat opposite him in my tiny apartment, but I can only guess at the emotional price my father must have paid as he sought to find money for the present. I quickly agreed to lend him the money and he promised to pay me back. The incident was never mentioned again.

My cousin preparing food—I am now sixty-five—in her small kitchen after the graveside service for my mother. A day for memories. The food—sliced meats and cheese, potato salad, Jello—reminds me of a lunch I served to a colleague, Ivy League through and through, my second year of teaching. He arrived late, after "lingering too long over the sherry" at a christening at the Episcopal church down the street. He sat down at the table, looked at the food, smiled broadly, and exclaimed, "How midwestern!" At my cousin's house there were no such exclamations, only silent men, sitting stiffly in the parlor, several of them missing fingers from farm accidents, and busy women in the kitchen. Distant cousins, half-remembered faces and names, reminders of how far I had grown away from my beginnings, how much I had changed, how much I had denied.

Tales of Denial

I remember the joy I felt as I left the small farming community in northeastern Kansas and headed off to college, located, ironically, in another small farming community, but away from much I had come to dislike. And here were the books I had learned to love, a by-product of my trips to the public library for my mother. More important, here were people willing to talk about these books and about music, and art, and politics, and the theater. But I also found that in many ways I did not belong, for here were people, even in this tiny church-related college in the middle of Kansas, who had not only read widely, but had lived in Paris, had heard Flagstaad sing Isolde. I loved it, yet I could not overcome my feelings of incompetence, my sense that I did not really belong. Ashamed of my parents, I was mortified when they appeared in their new house trailer to spend a few days before "heading west." When my roommate asked to meet them, I told him they were "Holy Rollers" and would pray over him and try to convert him. He insisted, and the visit went well, but I was jubilant the day they finally left town.

My rituals of denial continued through graduate school and into my teaching career, where they assumed many forms. I have tended, until very recently, not to sympathize with students who have trouble overcoming the odds of a deck stacked against them. I had overcome great odds. Why shouldn't they? I have also tried to prove that I belonged by adopting the highest possible standards. The better the college, the higher my standards—read "degree of insecurity." During one two-year period at a good liberal arts college, I taught 179 students. In that two-year period, I gave two A's. During the first five minutes of the first graduate course I ever taught, I kicked one student out of class for whispering to her neighbor while I was talking. And the story continued. I scorned the use of popular culture in the classroom—"Go to the movies on your own time." I lectured on the latest composition theories while penalizing first-year college writers for the slightest deviations from Edited American English. And I turned from the study of Renaissance literature to composition studies for reasons I still do not clearly understand. All I know is that the descent from what has long been considered the pinnacle of English studies—the Renaissance—to the basement of the English department somehow seemed right, comfortable, meaningful. Although I didn't realize it at the time, this was my first small step toward an acceptance of who I was and where I came from, an acceptance that was not to be complete, or nearly complete, for another thirty years.

The scorn I felt for my past, my parents, my students was nothing compared to the scorn I felt for myself, which explains, in part at least, my final act of denial: a turn to drugs. An eighteen-year addiction to painkillers killed some of the pain I felt—some of the time. It also nearly destroyed my career and my life. Some fifteen years after freeing myself from this addiction, I think I understand a part of what happened. It involves storytelling.

The Stories We Tell Ourselves

In her brilliant book *Landscape for a Good Woman*, Carolyn Kay Steedman (1987) argues that it is not so much what has actually happened to us in the past that matters as it is the stories we tell ourselves (and others) about what has happened. More than any other insight I have encountered in years, Steedman's formulation has helped me to understand my past and, consequently, my present. The stories I have told myself about my past have, until recently, always involved an only child, lonely, out of place, introspective. A child and, later, an adult who did not "fit in" because of personal weaknesses and failures. My seeming inability to write as well as my colleagues, my dry mouth when attempting to read convention papers, my fear of speaking at meetings of the college or university faculty, all of these, I told myself, were the results of personal shortcomings. I alone was to blame for who I was. Never once did the thought of social class as an ingredient in my life enter my thinking. It was all ME. My failures, my weaknesses, my fault.

In 1993, at the annual meeting of the Conference on College Composition and Communication in Nashville, Erika Lindemann and I debated the merits of using literature in first-year writing classes. She argued that literature should not be used because the primary goal of the course should be to help students write more effectively in their other college classes—in other words, to teach them to write academic discourse. In my defense of literature in the course, I mentioned, in passing, that I had always been personally uncomfortable with academic discourse. It seemed at the time an observation that I had added to my talk merely to achieve a more personal tone, to establish some kind of rapport with some members of the audience. But the comment stayed with me, and I began to think about not only my negative feelings about academic discourse, but about my feelings of discomfort in the academy. I'm not certain when it happened, but at some point it occurred to me that social class might be involved. This was a new idea. Having been interested in gender issues for several years, I knew something about hierarchies, oppression, and so forth, but interestingly enough, in all my reading of feminist writers, I do not recall finding a discussion of social class. In any case, this idea took root and I began to talk a bit about it to some of my colleagues, but I was still vague and directionless in my thinking until I found, on a dusty lower shelf in Foyle's bookstore in London, a copy of *Strangers in Paradise* (Ryan and Sackrey 1996), a collection of essays by working-class academics. To put it simply, I found myself in that book. As I read account after account of the pain and discomfort and anger of these authors as they had tried to negotiate the rituals and traditions of the academy, it was as if my entire previous life changed in front of me. "Yes!" "Yes!" I kept saying to myself. "I am here, in this book, on almost every page."

I gradually began to tell myself different stories about my past, stories that did not exclude social class, stories that involved more than a single, lonely, incompetent person attempting to achieve more than he was capable of achieving. The stories I now told had the same cast of characters, the same narrative outlines, but they meant something entirely different. No longer did I understand my Ivy League colleague to be commenting on my deficiencies as a luncheon host. *He* might have meant it to mean that, but now I understood and accepted the class (and regional) snobbery underlying the comment. My struggle to write academic discourse did not disappear, but now I viewed it as an opportunity to write other kinds of prose, simpler, more direct, more informal, more personal, a prose that will not satisfy all needs but that has seemed to touch more people than the halting academic prose I had previously attempted. No longer did my working-class directness worry me. The academy *needs* it, I now told myself. The academy needs people who will attempt to tell the truth, briefly, simply, directly. At a recent national meeting, when I said in a paper that, in recent years, "I had become more and more impatient with journal articles and conference papers that take what is often a fine idea and bury it in an overelaborated dunghill of jargon and needless extension," the audience of fifty or sixty people broke into applause. That had never happened to me before—I had never observed it happening in any meeting—and I took it as a small sign that plain, direct speaking and writing are not always scorned in the academic world, but are, indeed, sometimes welcomed.

And so I began revising or reinterpreting the stories of my life. At the same time, because my life has been spent with books, I began to read more widely about social class.

A Bibliographical Interlude

If it can be said that *Strangers in Paradise* served as a catalyst for my thinking about social class, it was, nevertheless, a book that made me uncomfortable because of the negative feelings, the real anger that comes through in many of the essays. I can understand this anger, but I have spent most of my academic career arguing that anger, cynicism, bitterness are destructive unless somehow converted into action, into work. I bore graduate students—future teachers—with my constant lectures on the need for optimism—about their students, about their work, about themselves. I do this because I have spent forty years in five colleges watching many colleagues become increasingly bitter and cynical about their work, their students, their worlds. To see such people, desperate to retire, to escape, one would never believe that they had had the privilege of spending their careers reading, and writing, and talking to young people about the writing, the books, the ideas they had—at some point in their lives—loved. In any case, it was this familiar bitterness that I felt in *Strangers in Paradise*, a bitterness unrelieved by any sense that there are working-class attributes that can be used in the academy, that are needed in the academy. And so it was with relief that I turned to other books.

A book equally realistic but much more optimistic about the possibility of making productive use of a working-class background in the academy is *This Fine Place So Far from Home* (Dews and Law 1995). In this collection of twenty-four essays by academics from the working class, I found and underlined scores of passages that suggest that there is more for the working-class academic to do than complain. Here are some of those passages:

> I am seeking ways to keep the language of the working class in academia, not just in my office with my working-class office mate, to nurture its own kind of vitality and rawness and directness, its tendency to ask "Why?" even as it says "Ah, what the fuck." I would like my colleagues to listen for the narratives embedded in their own writing, to feel the power of that movement forward just as they feel the power of the turning concept, the academic idea. And I would like my colleagues to turn my language over in their mouths with the same respect that my father and I turned over the items on those flea market tables. (25)

> I can never escape from my class background, and there's nothing quite like the hallowed, upper-class halls of academe to remind me of it. As a journalist, I was a professional outsider, observing and criticizing. As an academic, however, I must now be an insider, functioning within a system designed by and for the elite. I know all too well the system's effect on me; the question is whether I can affect the system. (40)

> I will probably always be most comfortable on the margins. (85)

> Shortly thereafter, I took back my own name . . . and set out to discover how to integrate my working-class past with my middle-class present. (99)

> I want to suggest that we can't afford to get sick like the governess [in Henry James's *The Turn of the Screw*] on realizing how the middle class uses the working class as a screen for what's most aberrant about itself; we can't afford to work our psyches into a permanent grimace because of the lack of fit of working-class face to middle-class mask. Instead, we need to tell the things we see as what we know: a knowledge that is just as valid as any and possibly more instructive than most. (131)

> A working-class person's daily thoughts, a shoemaker's poetry, may be just the resources higher education needs to divine itself, to plumb the depths of its mechanisms of exclusion, its refusals to know or to find marginal knowledge(s), in the best sense of the word, useful. (136)

> It is only through my studies and my increased understanding of marginalized populations that I have been able to come full circle and integrate the changes in my own life. There was a time when I had to take the cloak of my education on and off frequently, always trying to fit in. It is only in the last few years that I can leave it on all the time and still be myself; it is only in the last few years that I can truly accept and speak of my own history. For now, I truly understand the pervasive effects of being marginalized. I realize that my

own pretense was an effort to fit into the dominant discourse when I
felt I needed to. (295)

I do not want to lose the connection I have to my past. I do not want
to forget that the person who worked in that factory and the person I
am now are the same. (306)

Pleased as I was to find this more positive spirit among working-
class academics, it was not until I encountered Janet Zandy's
Liberating Memory (1995) that I began to sense some of the possibilities of turning the hopes expressed by the writers I have quoted into
important cultural work. Zandy's anthology contains plenty of talk
about working-class problems, but it also contains the poetry, the
photographs, the stories that have resulted from the contributors'
determination to do more than complain, their determination to use
their working-class memories and lives as inspiration for important
work. It was this book, more than any other, that showed me the possibilities of moving beyond complaint and denial into the use of
memory, in Zandy's words "not . . . as weepy nostalgia, but memory
as lever, a physical force—rough and beautiful—that multiplies our
power to act in the world" (xi). Thus the question I now faced was
how to turn my rediscovered past, the past I had worked so long to
deny, into something worthwhile in the academy.

Is There a Working-Class Pedagogy?

I think not. Just as there is no single feminist pedagogy, no single critical pedagogy, so there is, I would argue, no single working-class
pedagogy. Working-class lives are too various, too much intertwined
with gender and race and region and age, to inspire a single way of
teaching. The everyday details of our teaching will always be profoundly divergent. On the other hand, it may be possible to discover
commonalities—at a fairly high level of abstraction—that unite those
committed to incorporating their working-class values into their
teaching. It is not my goal, in this essay, to search out those values. I
am not yet ready for such an endeavor. The best I can do now, in this
early stage of "coming to class," is to speak of my own attempts to
cease denying my past, my own attempts to make use of this past in
my pedagogical work.

I have always felt more at home with graduate students than with
undergraduates, especially the privileged undergraduates that I have
taught for so many years. After my first dismal attempts to exert my
power over graduate students, I gradually began to relax, to create
cordial professional and sometimes personal relationships. These
were my kind of people: dedicated, eager, and—I now realize—often

working class. Undergraduates are an entirely different story. I have, more often than not, met them in required courses where many of them did not particularly want to be. And most of them are definitely not working class. (As I walked into my composition class last month, the day after spring break ended, one student was asking another, "How *was* Paris?") I have not found it easy. But as I have come to terms with my own past, so different from theirs, I am beginning to understand that just below the surface of most (all?) of us there exists a life not often viewed by others. Just as I, for decades, have done my best to hide portions of my life, so, too, I now realize, do my students. Privileged they may be, economically, culturally, but immune to life's blows they are not, even though on the surface they appear to have it all. As I, remembering my own past, have tried to see my undergraduate students more clearly, more sympathetically, I find lives that are scarred by drugs, divorce, alcohol, death. In the small composition class I just mentioned, one student has had to face, in recent months, the deaths of two close friends, another has spent the semester trying in vain to convince his alcoholic mother to seek treatment—she is dying of liver disease—and a third young woman's brother has just died of AIDS. And so, I am attempting to use the strength that a better understanding of my past has given me not as a barrier between myself and my students, but as a means to understand them more compassionately—and thus, hopefully—to teach them more effectively, more imaginatively.

As I try, not always successfully, to relax in my relationships with students, both in and out of the classroom, I find that my teaching has improved. I am less inclined to use the textbook, the syllabus, the content of the course as barriers to protect me from my students. Gone, most of the time at least, is the aloofness, and the dry, critical humor that had come to form the basis of my pedagogy. Gone also— again, most of the time—are the syllabi, the assignments, the lectures prepared more with the discipline than the students in mind. In a recent writing class, I distributed the first day a syllabus containing impossible assignments and expectations: twelve long, documented papers, *one* absence allowed, etc. The class read the syllabus and sat in profound silence. "Any questions?" I asked. Silence. "Does all this seem reasonable?" Finally, a tired voice asked, "Would it matter if it didn't?" I smiled and they began to stir. "Since the title of our text is *Negotiating Difference*, I suppose we could begin with the syllabus." "Really?" asked a suspicious student. (At that moment, I despaired about the servile attitudes that we are teaching our students.) I told them, "I'm going to my office. When you have a proposal for a revised syllabus, come get me." And I walked out. One hour later— the class met once a week for three hours—a student appeared at my office door. "We're ready." I returned to the classroom and to a chalk-board covered with notes, numbers, outlines, and other signs of a lively class discussion. One student then read to me their counterpro-posal, a wonderfully sensible yet demanding set of course require-ments that were to become our guides for the rest of the semester, a semester in which the students found themselves with enough sense of agency to ask, on several occasions, "Could we negotiate that?"

My newfound confidence has also enabled me to hand over to students some of the control that I formerly clutched to myself as a shield against those who would find out that I didn't belong in the academy. One more brief example. As most teachers know, the first day of class is the most important day of the semester, the day when, more often than not, the whole course and tone of the semester is established. (The writing class I just described was a joy to teach the entire semester, a result, in part at least, of that first day of real nego-tiation.) Consequently, I have begun talking with students on the first day of class using only notes prepared by students the last time I offered the course. In other words, a major part of almost every final examination I now construct is an invitation to students to prepare lecture notes for my use on the first day when I again offer the course. "You know better than I what I might have said that would have been helpful the first day of the semester—about the course, about me, about the material to be covered, the approach taken, etc., etc." Students respond with eagerness and imagination to this invitation—in classes as different as "Working-Class Literature" and "Linguistics." And when I use their notes the next time I teach the course, I say, "This is what your fellow students from last year thought you needed to hear." And they listen. And I learn.

Finally, I have begun to understand that effective teaching involves not only the knowledge that gives the course its title, but also the lives of the students who sit before (or around, or with) me. I have begun asking myself and my students what I take to be working-class questions: What is the point of all this? How does it relate to us? To our lives, as we are living them today? I ask these questions whether I am talking to future teachers about the English language, or to graduate students about composition theory, or to privileged under-graduates about a working-class poem or novel. And I am amazed that so few of them have ever been asked these questions before. It has been assumed, apparently, that knowledge and skills are impor-tant for their own sake, and that students have nothing important to say about relations between what they are learning and the lives they are living. Today. Not "down the road," not in that "future" that we invoke when trying to convince young people of the value of learning. Just as my students were surprised that I was willing to negotiate the course requirements, so my students are surprised when asked how they *really* feel about a poem, a story, a writing assignment, how it relates to their lives, how it interests them or bores them—and why. But once they realize that I take their responses seriously, no matter how negative, they begin to see some value in what we are doing. This desire for value for their money is a profoundly working-class desire, a desire that I am beginning to respect more each day, because even though I no longer belong to the working class from which I came—I have read too much, traveled too much, learned too much, earned too much—I continue to carry within me at least some of the working-class values and manners and beliefs that I learned as a child. They will always be a part of me, no matter how many times I deny them, how many drugs I take, how many books I read. The difference is that now, at long last, as I am nearing retirement, I feel the need not to deny, but to celebrate and to use those values and beliefs. Thus, although I can never return to the working-class home I left long ago, I can, if I am lucky, get halfway back home.

Works Cited

Dews, C. L. B., and C. L. Law, eds. 1995. *This Fine Place So Far From Home: Voices of Academics from the Working Class.* Philadelphia: Temple University Press.

Ryan, J., and C. Sackrey, eds. 1996. *Strangers in Paradise: Academics from the Working Class.* Lanham, MD: University Press of America, Inc.

Steedman, C. 1987. *Landscape for a Good Woman.* New Brunswick, NJ: Rutgers University Press.

Zandy, J. 1995. *Liberating Memory: Our Work and Our Working-Class Consciousness.* New Brunswick, NJ: Rutgers University Press.

19

An Introduction to Social Scientific Discussions on Class

Victor Villanueva

I

When the grocery checker who had been my student threw me the keys to his new BMW, I knew he was financially better-off than I was at the time. And I knew that in some ways he was the middle class and I was not. Yet I knew there were ways that I was more the middle class than he could be. I was a graduate student.

Mami and Dad live in a mobile home. It's nice, a comfortable place. Paid for. It provides comfort during an old age that tends to include little more than a social security check for economic security. It's small payment for all those years at hard labor, those years of helping to make others wealthy. Dad's childhood was spent, in part, sweeping the sidewalks and the walkways leading to the university professors' houses. He talks still of MissMachín (one word, always one word), the professor's wife, herself a teacher at the *Universidád de Puerto Rico*. She treated him with respect. His father, my grandfather, was their gardener. Dad was always uncomplicatedly the working class. Mom was raised by a foster-mother who was a live-in maid for the local priest. It was a position of some prestige. Yet it was a position of servitude. Mom's ways of being, her ways of seeing the world, are so clearly of the middle class, maybe even a minor aristocracy. Yet when was she ever other than poor? Dad continues to dress up, proud of his physique (looking fifties in his mid-seventies). Mom dresses down, since she can no longer buy "good" clothes, still working part-time when she can to get some material thing or other that will make her "later years" more comfortable. Class is complicated.

A quarter century ago I began nibbling at that dangling college-career carrot. This year, through a number of flukes and a number of hard-gained successes, we bought our first house. My boss smiles at me and says, "A house. How boozhwah!" She's happy for us. Joking. I like her. But what a funny notion of class: the bourgeoisie, me? Not even close. Nor is she.

II

Class is a complicated matter. Perhaps the only social matters more complicated than class are ideology and hegemony, since they provide the glue that maintains funny perceptions of class. Maybe more than anything else, class is a perception, a way of seeing. But we also know that class is material, a matter of economics. Confusing stuff. Hard to get a handle on. All of this is surely new for us in rhetoric and in composition. Our discussions of class are few, which is not to say that we aren't conscious of class. In our workplaces, we're careful to include the poor in our list of Others. In our conversations we've tossed about Basil Bernstein's linguistic concerns with class, though always somehow in terms of them and not in terms of us (Tuman 1988; Villanueva 1994). We are conscious of class but less of class consciousness. We seem never to talk in terms of *it*, of what it is we mean when we say "class." Descriptions of class will slip and slide: matters of money, somehow attached to gender, matters of culture or color, the where we came from, the something we can never stop being. We'll nod with understanding, even those of us who have never known poverty, real poverty, outside of some discomfort during graduate school. We'll agree to all of the manifestations of class—money and gender and race and ways of being—because they all somehow apply.

Meanwhile, those who think of themselves as followers of Marx in one sense or another will speak of capitalist classes and ruling classes, ways of underscoring that class is a matter of power and economics. Those who follow Weber will speak of privileged classes, those with the money, and as a separate thing, the political elite, those with political power. Me? I'm one who believes that those who hold political office are subject to ideology as much as anyone, no great controllers, really; that those who are our "rulers" don't rule; that somehow, in ways I surely don't understand, capital does rule the day.

What I want to do here is to highlight some of the conversations that appear outside of our disciplinary concerns. I want to look to some of the discussion that has been taking place outside of the rhetorical and the literary. And that means no Bourdieu or Foucault or any of the other critical theorists we are fond of. It seems to me that now that we in composition studies in particular have ventured into the political, we really should look to others who have held long discussions on these matters of concern to us, those within the social sciences. This, then, will have to be decidedly selective, broad, and theoretical. I leave the stories that comprise the rest of the book to provide the particularities, examples of the class system at work. What I'll provide is a brief review of the foundations of these discussions—Marx and Weber—and a glimpse at some of the discussions that have developed since, if not to define *class*, at least to know the kinds of things thought about when thinking about class.

III

Class—an inherited rank in a stratified society, a matter of who is propertied and who is not, not much different from our common understanding of caste. Static. Born into. The way of Athens. The way of Rome. Wage labor: a futuristic notion of Plato's *Republic*. Or maybe older. Immanuel Wallerstein (1991) figures capitalism and thereby class distinctions to go back five centuries, with what he believes (along with others) is the real birth of a capitalist world economy, long before industrialization. But it's the industrial capitalism of Western Europe in the eighteenth century that begins the *conceptualization* of class, a setting down of what class *is*. It is the reorganization of society that coincided with or was caused by this newer form of capitalism that created a newer level of awareness among the people of Europe. What came was the generalized realization that reorganizations not only can happen but do. There came the realization that birth ascription need not be the sole determining factor in class positions. But there also came, more and more, the realization that ability alone (no matter what the ideology claims) is not sufficient to class change. The first to bring these realizations to light (or to print), then, becomes Karl Marx.

What Marx did was to devise historical materialism, a look at economic conditions that give rise to changes in social structures. The particular time he was most drawn to was his own.

What Marx sees is the coming to power of the bourgeoisie. In the system prior to industrial capitalism, that bourgeoisie would consist of merchants, the middle class, the founders of America, where the middle became the top but held on to the ideology of the middle. It was they who had the economic power with which to rally others with the promise of change. Merchants could have a Boston Tea Party and introduce coffee (with all that that implies in terms of who exploited South Asia and who exploited South America). With this change Marx sees the simplification of the class system, a change that he believes would eventually lead to a polarization of the classes. This is one of the messages of the *Communist Manifesto*:

> Our epoch, the epoch of the bourgeoisie, possesses . . . this distinctive feature: it has simplified the class antagonisms: Society as a whole is more and more splitting up into two great hostile camps, into two great classes directly facing each other: Bourgeoisie and Proletariat. (Marx [1848] 1978b, 474)

The bourgeoisie has not only simplified class systems, according to Marx; it has simplified the ideologies of rule (my language, not his). The bourgeoisie removed the "power" of the aristocracy:

> The bourgeoisie, wherever it has got the upper hand, has put an end to all feudal, patriarchal, idyllic relations. It has pitilessly torn asunder the motley feudal ties that bound man to his "natural superiors," and has left remaining no other nexus between man and man than naked self-interest, than callous "cash payment." . . . It has resolved personal worth into exchange value, and in place of the indefeasible chartered freedoms, has set up that single, unconscionable freedom—Free Trade. In one word for exploitation, veiled by religious and political illusions, it has substituted naked, shameless, direct, brutal exploitation.
>
> The bourgeoisie has stripped of its halo every occupation hitherto honoured and looked up to with reverent awe. It has converted the physician, the lawyer, the priest, the poet, the man of science, into its wage-labourers. (475–76)

Marx, we have to know when we wait for payday, is right. But what he says is hard to take down. Intellectuals as wage-laborers? Hard to take. So we don't. While Marx built a theory of class struggle based on the realization of the exploitation necessary to the well-being of the bourgeoisie, he missed the real essential—that just knowing we're being exploited is not the same as acting on that knowledge. For Marx ideology was a veil of ignorance, "hegemony of the spirit," in his words, a trick of the mind played by intellectuals in the service of the ruling class (1978a, 174–175). The material vs. the ideal, for Marx; real vs. veil, science vs. ideology. But Gramsci (1971) shows that hegemony is consensual, that we know we're exploited, that we know that someone else profits from our labors (Villanueva 1992). And everyone in academics, it seems, has recognized the ideological in the scientific. We now speak of scientism. And history has proved Marx wrong. Twentieth-century revolutions toward socialism have failed, have given way to capitalism. We haven't split into two classes.

Then again, Trotsky (1945) did say that if the Soviet Union he saw didn't change its bureaucratic ways, the Soviet Union would more likely succumb to capitalism than develop into the socialism it desired. And Max Weber (1905–1910), about the same time, figured that the bureaucratic was the great institution for the growth of capitalism. A distrust of socialism, the accuracy of what would come to pass, the downright pragmatism brought folks concerned with class to Weber.

Perhaps the special appeal that Weber enjoys is that he doesn't distill all group relations to class relations. That rings true to us. For Weber there is class stratification and there are other forms of stratification, like social status or ethnicities. For Weber, class concerns our chances in the market. Class, for Weber (1958), is

> the typical chance for a supply of goods, external living conditions, and personal life experiences, in so far as this chance is determined by the amount and kind of power, or lack of such, to dispose of goods or skills for the sake of income in a given economic order. (181)

Those who have this power are the propertied and those who control "monopolistic qualifications and skills" (Weber 1968, 303). Their opposites are those without property and the skilled, semiskilled, and unskilled workers. So far, there isn't much difference from Marx. But Weber also includes those in the middle, such as bureaucrats and highly skilled technicians. Altogether, these propertied, unpropertied, and middles are social classes—the working class, the petty bourgeoisie, the intelligentsia without property, technicians, and the privileged through property and education (1968, 305). We like him all right. He credits the paid intellectual as something more than a wage earner, at least when he describes social classes.

When Weber is centered on class without the adjective *social*, he returns to economics. Class is tied to economics. But class interests need not be. In Marxian terms—class status does not make for class consciousness. He's right, we know. Hard for the doctoral candidates, say, to join forces with the building maintenance crew (from an equal footing, that is, as opposed to a charitable or moralistic stance)—even when both earn the same income (or the grad student earns a bit less). Education is status, even impoverished education is status. It rings true. In like manner, we know that racism and sexism apply even to the wealthy (Villanueva 1996b), so it must be apart from the economy.

Or maybe we can look at this differently. Consider a part of Gramsci's (1971) explanation of hegemony. With Gramsci, hegemony is not only domination with a consensual dimension, it is a complex interweaving of belief systems, beliefs from the way things are, might be, and the way things were, what he calls *sedimentations* (20). The educated were traditionally those who could afford to be educated. The highly educated were those who could afford the leisure simply to read and to hold discussion over their reading. The intelligentsia came from the leisure class (or from the economically pro-vided—the clergy). Racism is an outgrowth, even an aberration, a deviant growth arising from economic exploitation, a product of, still attached to, and nevertheless different from class. Those still subject to race prejudice are the previously owned, either through slavery or through colonialism (Villanueva 1996a). Here's Erik Olin Wright (1985) on the matter:

> Class structures constitute the central organizing principles of soci-eties in the sense of shaping the range of possible variations of the state, ethnic relations, gender relations, etc. (31)

We can say that social systems are divorced from economic systems only in a sense. Erik Olin Wright (1994) in terms of sexism and Etienne Balibar (1991) in terms of racism both note that neither can be reduced to class, nor that the elimination of either gender or race discrimination would lead to a classless society. But neither are they unrelated. Inequality in the workplace links race and gender and other forms of discrimination to class. Balibar mentions immigration and race as conflating the two. Not the same but surely related, class and other social forms. So there is sense to Weber, but not as substantive-ly separate from Marx.

IV

Maybe the way to getting at who is the working class is to look more closely at who is this middle class that we aspire to, that has us deny our working-class backgrounds, that has us deny our working-class situation still. Nicos Poulantzas (1978) describes the middle class as a new petty bourgeoisie, a kind of update of Weber's contention that the proletariat would move more and more to a class that fills the space the petty bourgeoisie would leave behind. Or, better, that the petty bourgeoisie would be eaten up by bigger economic fish while the rise of bureaucracy would make for a new class of white-collar workers. What Poulantzas does with this is not to say that there is a class displacement but that the middle class joins with the petty bour-geoisie, given their similar ideological predispositions. For instance, the petty bourgeoisie and the middle class, says Poulantzas, display similarly firm beliefs in the sanctity of individualism, liberalism, rather than a collective sense. The middle, then, joins the petty bour-geoisie in disparaging workers because they are lazy, unwilling to pick themselves up by their bootstraps. Poulantzas also sees the mid-dle class as occupying basically the same position as the petty bour-geoisie in the structure itself, a position between the bourgeoisie and the proletariat. Both are structurally in the middle.

Alvin Gouldner (1979) sees intellectuals as the ruling class of statist governments (as in the former Soviet Union) and a specialized class within capitalist governments, a class, he says, that could almost rival the position held by the bourgeoisie. According to Gouldner, those with special technical skills or special knowledge are members of a "new class" that has control over "cultural capital." In other words, Gouldner holds to a Marxian perception of the bourgeoisie as those who control the means of production within a society; that being the case, if the new means of productions are primarily technological or matters of what has come to be called a service society, those with technical expertise or special knowledge of how these services operate must be the possessors of those means. Better still: To own knowledge in an economy run by specialized kinds of knowledge is to rule. Barbara and John Ehrenreich (1978) give considerably less power to this "new class," this middle of our time, what they term the "professional-managerial class." They argue that the middle provides the function of reproducing capitalist class relations because of their commonalities with both workers and capitalists. Within every neo-Marxian view there is a Weberian one trying to come out (a paraphrase of Wallerstein 1991). In all of the current discussion on the new class, it seems to me, there is a struggling to salvage the integrity of the intellectual within the current system— the siren song of Michel Foucault (at least in how he tends to be read)—knowledge/power.

Erik Olin Wright's (1985) depiction of class is at once the most pragmatic yet face-saving for intellectuals. Wright presents a theory of "contradictory locations," in which managers and bureaucrats comprise a central position of being both exploiter and exploited, having allegiances to both the proletariat and the bourgeoisie, having elements in common with both. As Wright sees it, particular classes move within certain "locations" within the overall class structure— the ups and downs of income, the place to which you "make it," even though you still have very little real power in a larger sense. There is a great deal of latitude within the structure, as long as the centers of power remain unthreatened. Gramsci (1971) would add that this room for movement allows for consensus, the necessary ingredient for maintaining cultural hegemony. Paulo Freire's (1982) *conscientização* represents the traditionally excluded's ability to recognize this power relationship. According to Wright (1985),

> The claim that class structures define the qualitative lines of demarcation in trajectories of social change is, typically, combined with a closely related proposition—namely, that class struggles are the central mechanism for moving from one class structure to another. If the map of history is defined by class structures the motor of history is

class struggle. Those in possession of power recognize that to maintain power they must reproduce the class system, even make major concessions to public will in order to avoid basic change. (32–33)

This is Gramsci's notion of revolution/restoration, concessions granted to maintain consensus—here applied to discussions of class.

Wright notes that there is a range of movement the entire citizenry can enjoy within the structure; but the structure is such that the range is limited. America, for instance, tolerates dissent, even encourages it; but at a certain point Black Panther Bobby Seale found himself bound and gagged, literally, in the courts intended to protect individual freedoms. The classes within the structure are engaged in antagonistic relationships; they are not merely coexistent like *pluralism* or *relativism* would suggest. The antagonism is a product of exploitation, the exploitative relations resulting from the ways of accumulation.

Although this reads like basic Marxism, Wright moves away from the mechanistic conception of exploitation. Exploitation remains parasitic in a contemporary rendering, but the host is not sacrificed completely. What I mean is that in contemporary capitalism, the bourgeoisie does not profit solely by using the proletariat to the point of turning them into paupers. In global capitalism there are many middles (with many more paupers than in America). There are those few who are neither exploited nor exploiters—artisans working for no one but the market, employing no one but themselves. But the numbers of those are decidedly few, their economic strength tending to be slight. And there are those who might well be exploited but gain such benefits in the exploitative relationship that they become more the objects of envy than pity. These are the highly skilled wage earners, like professionals and high-level managers, who often exploit the skills of those below them, technicians of various sorts, yet who remain exploited in the sense that they must nevertheless receive pay from another rather than accumulate capital without having to labor themselves.

Profit is the key, ideology is the door, to maintaining the good will of the exploited. Those who can afford to can buy into the class that holds power, through capital investments, stocks, property, and the like. This middle class gets to feel like the bourgeoisie. The difference, however, is that the bourgeoisie, according to Wallerstein (1991), gain their wealth solely on the work of others. They themselves produce nothing except capital, capital they then invest for the main purpose of accumulating further capital. Those investments for that college fund for the kids or for comfort in retirement do not count as truly of the bourgeoisie. That paycheck, no matter how large, that was earned at the cost of bringing the office home or never quite getting home does not count as surplus value. The middle class gets to live relatively well. But the middle class has no real power, whatever its knowledge.

Gramsci says we know of this exploitation, really. Ideology acknowledges the exploitation, stating that without the capitalists we could not enjoy the comforts to be had in this "exploitation." Ideology also acknowledges inequality, arguing that the underprivileged would be worse off were it not for the benefits of the privileged who take risks through international investments. Exploitation is acknowledged and concomitantly denied by avowing a general welfare.

V

Where this leads is to class consciousness and the formation of what Gramsci has called "new intellectuals." Class consciousness might be a term with a long history, beginning with Marx, elaborated upon by Karl Kautsky, popularized by Georg Lukács's *History and Class Consciousness* (1971), but unlike Lukács' definition of the term as an ascribed consciousness, an ignorance of real class interests, Erik Olin Wright (1985) applies a Gramscian twist. In an essentially Gramscian fashion, Wright distinguishes between class consciousness and class formation. He writes,

> Class consciousness . . . is above all, the conscious understanding of these mechanisms: the realization by subordinate classes that it is necessary to transform the class structure if there are to be any basic changes in their capacities to act, and the realization by dominant classes that the reproduction of their power depends upon the reproduction of the class structure. Class formation, on the other hand, is the process by which individual capacities are organizationally linked together in order to generate a collective capacity to act, a capacity which can potentially be directed at the class structure itself. (28)

It is Gramsci's contention that changes in the current hegemony require a process whereby various constituencies come together for a common purpose, a matter quite similar to Wright's "class formation." Groups join together to seek change, a war of maneuver, in Gramsci's language, a joining together of intellectuals in the traditional sense and in the broader sense in order to foster change. And in some sense all of these distinctions are spurious.

The middle is not the top or the bottom. But where are most of us rooted, really? How many of us come from backgrounds in which our ancestors did not need to work but could live off the work of others because those ancestors owned the property and the tools (the historical definition of the bourgeoisie)? How many of us can claim to accumulate capital without laboring—and are able to accumulate sufficiently to invest with the overriding purpose of accumulating further (the contemporary definition of the bourgeoisie)? We are—all of us, whatever our other differences—in some fundamental sense the working class, just not all of us are conscious of so being.

VI

So how does this show up in the classroom? Well, this is a story I've told before (Villanueva 1993, 105–114; Villanueva 1994, 123–139). It has to do with our discussions of community building in classrooms. It has to do with Basil Bernstein. It's been my experience that although I can make long-term connections with my students in traditional first-year comp courses, and although I see that sometimes groups that I helped to form in the comp course stay together as friends, I don't seem to build community in the traditional classroom in the way I can with graduate students or basic writing students. Or better—communities form better in those situations (since I can't take credit). The bonding agent among graduate students is obvious—matters of like-mindedness, like toils, like economics. In terms of basic writers the typical reaction would be to think that the collective is formed over matters of race. But the races mix in traditional first-year classes, too, even in predominately white schools. The tradition in "traditional" first-year composition courses no longer applies.

In a research study I conducted some time back, I saw some indications of class formations and a growing class consciousness. For the study, I recorded a number of peer groups in two classes, targeting students of color in a traditional first-year class and students of color in a basic-writing class. Without exception, the students in the traditional course spoke in cosmetic, prescriptive grammar terms: what constitutes a properly formed paragraph, comma placement, spelling, what the teacher wants (one student saying aloud, "I'll just give her what she wants"). The basic writers thought in terms of what the teacher needs.

One instance out of many: The student is Edita—self-identified as white and Mexican, around thirty. Her group contains SreyNun, a Cambodian woman, first generation in America; Diana, another Chicana, though decidedly younger; Amo, a Native Alaskan about the same age as Edita, who was a high school dropout and was once nominated for public office, though he declined the nomination for fear that his limited literacy would be discovered. We catch them in mid-conversation about one of Edita's essays:

Amo: That. I thought *that* was your best paper. That you told your life's story in a very short time.

Diana: That's hard.

Amo: And you went into stuff that college ki. Um. I don't know. Yeah. Showed, showed to me your dri::ve, your determination. You kind of expressed the way you feel about your school. You, you discovered a feeling you had inside that helped you in all your jobs. And it put you above all the rest of those, *people* around . . .

Edita: Sure did.

Amo: You really describe for people who couldn't know the feelings, being sh::. Being pushed in the dummy section. Self-esteem. Being poor and being dumb. The paper gives me a [ri] an understanding.

Diana: I think you should, uh, I don't know. It sort of confuses me about your son. It's like you jus:: started your paper over. It's the feeling I get. It's the sound of it, I guess. I don't know how to say it.

Amo: Just say it.

Diana: I mean, it, it's good, but then at the end, you—saying that the reason. You know? You want your son to do what you did. Right? The ending was confusing to me.

Edita: No, I don't.

Diana: I mean, like, you didn't just put it there, but I didn't quite get it. I mean, I mean, I understand what you are saying about your son but I don't know. I don't know if I.

Edita: Yeah, sometimes it's hard. I know what you mean. But, um, but, you see, when you got kids . . .

Amo: It is that she. I can see the completeness, how it all fits into the, to your, what the message is to us. That just cause you're in college and computers and all, that the same thing could happen to your son, cause there still isn't the money so there's still the color or something. I, I *thought* that.

Diana: I mean like. You came out with a beginning. You should say something about your son then. I don't know if that would help.

Amo: Yeah, that could've been good. I, a good idea at the beginning. Your, you know, your theme.

Diana: I mean cause it, it's, you just brought it, about your son. You're talking about yourself all the way through, and then you bring your son in, in addition.

Edita: Yeah. But my *purpose* was *not* to talk about him at *all*. But my experience, the things *you* guys can fol, can understand, what you guys know something about, and how my experience would *change*, in, the way I would, raise *my* kid. So I have to talk about *my* self. Cause maybe in some way *we're* alike, but I'm not talking to *you*. I'm talking to people like *John* who don't move up from where we do. I wasn't talking about him. I was talking about myself. I think.

Of the members of the group, SreyNun, the Cambodian, is foreign to the context before her—matters of growing up in the United States She takes no part in the conversation. Though Diana is of the same ethnic background as Edita and even from the same school, she is decidedly younger than either Edita or Amo. Her part in the discussion is limited—more conventionally studentlike, text-centered, concerned with arrangement, the organization of Edita's essay. Amo and Edita have class-related experiences in common. They both have living as adults in poverty in common, although culturally, they're quite different. Edita is a child of the inner city, an Anglo-Latina mix; Amo, from a tribal life, with the Anglo influence more Canadian than American, he says in conversation. Class, more than culture, binds Amo to Edita.

Edita simply trails off in her attempt to tell Diana about the perspective that comes with being an adult who has had working-class related experiences and has a child. But Amo understands, how raising children is less at issue than explaining the difficulties in attempting to move within the class structure, the difference between "being poor and being dumb." Even Amo's one reference to race is more a matter of class, a play on the cliché that money knows no color: "there still isn't the money so there's still the color." Amo ends the conversation on Edita's essay with a note of support, given a particular worldview. He says:

> Well. Well. *Still.* You know, it's just the point of view. Because I. It fit in. The boy fit in. Uh. Your whole attitude about life now. You're treating him as basically your own attitude about college, about studying. It gave me a sense of completeness.

That is the view from the bottom of the class structure.

That Edita was conscious of how systemic forces can shape experience was reflected in her discussion of larger rhetorical matters contained in the texts under group discussion, discussions concerned with what a middle-class audience would not know.

And this recalls Basil Bernstein, but not exactly as he laid his theories out. In Bernstein's social matrix, a strictly hierarchical authority structure in the working-class's workplace gives rise to a hierarchical authority structure in the home. Authority is position-centered, more a matter of rank than of potential competence. Although there is no reason to presuppose that this reproduction is intentional, the nature of work involved in physical labor would affect home life, a sense that there isn't the time or that there aren't the conditions that allow for negotiation. Constraining conditions would be more pointed in a single-parent household.

Bernstein was substantiated in my research—but only so far. The majority of the basic writers came from single-parent households. All but one came from working-class households, all but one were not encouraged to speak out. Amo's mother never worked outside the home. His father was a laborer in a fish-processing plant. Amo's was a working-class, position-centered home.

Position-centered households make for a restricted speech code, according to Bernstein. Shared social contexts among speakers is assumed within the restricted code. Because meaning is implicitly understood, discourse is fragmented. Meaning is "particularistic," in Bernstein's terms (1977). Much of this could be heard in the interactions between Amo and Edita, in their understanding each other yet taking time to explain things to Diana. But Diana was not wholly "Other." She was included in "the things . . . you guys know something about."

So we begin to detect the twist in Bernstein. Members of the position-centered move away from the restricted code when they perceived themselves as no longer within their more familiar place within the class structure. More elaboration became necessary for the instructor, assumed to be from the middle class.

Elaboration marks the speech code of the middle class, an elaborated code, in Bernstein's terms. The workplace and preparing children, even if not always consciously, for survival in the workplace here, as in the working class, determines the code. In the middle-class workplace, authority boundaries are not drawn as clearly as they are in the physical-labor workplace. Some negotiation is possible—the committee replaces the suggestion box; explained tardiness replaces the punch clock. So it is that authority in the household is person-centered. Some negotiation becomes possible; rules can sometimes be bent, given a well-formed, well-articulated argument. The elaborated code is explicit, context free. It is universalistic, assuming little shared experience among speakers. The elaborated code parallels literate discourse. Since the white-collar and the professional workplace depend upon literate practices, literacy instruction takes on special importance in the middle-class household. The middle class's speech code is the school's code.

Again, Bernstein is verified to a point. Most of the students in the traditional course came from two-parent households, with both parents usually employed outside the house, performing white-collar or professional jobs. All could recall being encouraged to speak up at home. All had heard texts read aloud. All read at least magazines on their own. Lori, an Asian American student in the traditional classroom, believed she *heard* a run-on sentence, believed she heard a paragraph break. In one exchange within Lori's group, Hana, another member, commented on an essay in decidedly literary terms:

> You need to do something about the first two sentences. They sound like Gothic novels. [laughter] Seriously. I get images of cliffs overlooking the sea. But it's only a stupid track meet. [laughter]

The group appreciated the comment. The writer understood it. Theirs was a literate background. Theirs was a consensus born of a common literate background.

This consensus marks the twist of Bernstein. For Bernstein it should be the working class who base social interaction on consensus. Social interaction among the middle class is supposed to be based on difference. If no context is assumed and must thereby be provided in an elaborated code, a commonality must not be assumed, Bernstein reasons. Yet the opposite took place in the college composition classrooms I observed. The traditional believed themselves to be of the same class as the majority within the academic community. The traditional—including the traditional of color—really did share in the speech code of the majority, a code having substantial similarities to literate written discourse. This sense of being essentially no different from others in the classroom's discourse community, which would include the teacher, made for a certain ease among the traditional. There was no need to form a class identity, to raise a consciousness of class and class difference. The basic writers, however, assumed they had to teach their teacher the meaning of class.

In terms of culture, the traditional writing class was no more homogeneous than the basic one. Class was the overriding difference between the students and the community in which they found themselves. Their language, *la langue*, might have been the same as the majority in the university's discourse community, but the basic writers' class-structural determinants of speech code, *la parole*, were different. The basic writers were at least implicitly aware of the discourse differences.

So what lesson can we take from this? Well, there are many, detailed elsewhere. But for my purposes here is a suggestion that we let our Selves be known to our students. I'm not advocating being confessional, making ourselves TV-tellers-of-all as if we're on Oprah (or any of the countless others). Just making clear that we are not the same as them, the students, and not the same as one another either. The research suggests that students will take the teacher as a legitimate audience if there are understood differences beyond the power positions that play in any classroom. That is, students will recognize their own class status when they recognize some difference between theirs and their teachers'. I would venture that, made conscious, students would recognize their allegiances to as well as differences from their teachers, thereby willingly entering into a conversation—entering into the rhetorical situation.

Class consciousness and class formation are necessarily rhetorical acts. And as teachers we can be instrumental in those rhetorical acts that are fundamentally political. It is only through a raising of class consciousness, which includes a recognition of a class's history and its antagonistic relation to other classes, that a particular class (and now I'm being intentionally ambiguous) can recognize itself as engaged in class struggle. This recognition is requisite to altering the class structure, to creating a new hegemonic influence. This is at the very least a part of our business.

Works Cited

Balibar, E. 1991. "Class Racism." In *Race, Nation, and Class: Ambiguous Identities*, ed. E. Balibar and I. Wallerstein, 204–215. New York: Verso.

Bernstein, B. 1977. *Class, Codes, and Control: Towards a Theory of Educational Transmission,* 3 vols. 2d ed. New York: Routledge and Kegan Paul.

Ehrenreich, B., and J. Ehrenreich. 1978. "The Professional-Managerial Class." In *Class, Crises and the State*, ed. E. Olin Wright. London: Verso.

Freire, P. 1982. *Pedagogy of the Oppressed.* New York: Continuum.

Gouldner, A. 1979. *The Future of Intellectuals and the Rise of the New Class: A Frame of Reference, Theses, Conjectures, Arguments, and An Historical Perspective on the Role of Intellectuals and Intelligentsia in the International Class Contest of the Modern Era.* New York: Seabury.

Gramsci, A. 1971. *Selections from the Prison Notebooks.* Ed. and trans. Q. Hoare and G. N. Smith. New York: International.

Lukács, G. 1971. *History and Class Consciousness: Studies in Marxist Dialectics.* Trans. R. Livingstone. Cambridge, MA: MIT Press.

Marx, K. 1978a. "German Ideology." In *The Marx-Engels Reader*, ed. R. C. Tucker, 176–200. New York: Norton.

———. 1978b. "Manifesto of the Communist Party." In *The Marx-Engels Reader*, ed. R. C. Tucker, 469–500. New York: Norton.

Poulantzas, N. 1978. *Political Power and Social Classes.* Trans. T. O'Hagan. London: Verso.

Trotsky, L. 1945. *The Revolution Betrayed. What Is the Soviet Union and Where Is It Going?* New York: Pioneer.

Tuman, M. C. 1988. "Class Codes and Composition: Basil Bernstein and the Critique of Pedagogy." *College Composition and Communication* 89 (1): 42–51.

Villanueva, V. 1996a. "Literacy, Culture, and the Colonial Legacy." In *The Politics of Multiculturalism*, ed. R. Eddy, 79–99. Yarmouth, ME: Intercultural.

———. 1996b. "On Colonies, Canons, and Ellis Cose's *The Rage of a Privileged Class*." *JAC: A Journal of Comp Theory* 16 (1): 159–170.

———. 1994. "On Writing Groups, Class, and Culture: Studying Oral and Literate Language Features in Writing." In *Writing With: New Directions in Collaborative Teaching, Learning, and Research*, ed. S. B. Reagan, T. Fox, and D. Bleich, 123–139. New York: SUNY Press.

———. 1993. *Bootstraps: From an American Academic of Color.* Urbana, IL: National Council of Teachers of English.

———. 1992. "Hegemony: From an Organically Grown Intellectual." *PRE/TEXT: A Journal of Rhetorical Theory* 13 (1–2): 17–34.

Wallerstein, I. 1991. "Class Conflict in the Capitalist World Economy." In *Race, Nation, and Class: Ambiguous Identities*, ed. E. Balibar and I. Wallerstein, 115–124. New York: Verso.

Weber. M. 1968. *Economy and Society.* 3 vols. New York: Bedminster.

———. 1958. *From Max Weber: Essays in Sociology.* Trans. and ed. H. H. Gerth and C. W. Mills. New York : Oxford.

Wright, E. Olin. 1994. *Interrogating Inequality: Essays on Class Analysis, Socialism and Marxism.* New York: Verso.

———1985. *Classes.* London: Verso.

20

Class and Comfort
The Slums and the Greens

Edward M. White

I was in my fifth year of teaching at Wellesley College early in 1965 when a letter from California appeared in my mailbox. A new state college would be opening in a working-class city that fall and I was invited to apply for a position. My spine tingled at the thought and I applied without hesitation. When the job offer came, I had some difficulty explaining to myself, my family, and my friends why I wanted to leave the comforts of Wellesley, a wealthy and selective school for women, with a lovely campus (and lovely campus faculty housing) in a wealthy Boston suburb, for the uncertainties of the wild West. It took me several years of teaching in San Bernardino before I understood what had really motivated me. It was the buried issue in America: social class.

Some thirty years after that decision, I can look back and notice that issues of social class not only led to my move, but also to a change in direction of my teaching and writing. Several chapters of my Harvard Ph.D. thesis on Jane Austen had been published and I had completed some bibliographical articles on Thackeray; I was turning my thesis into a book on Austen and comic theory. I had become a nineteenth-century British lit man. But somehow, in California I began writing on composition, assessment, and program administration (I had become the English department chair). I continued to value, write about, and teach literature, but it no longer seemed to be the only subject that mattered. As years slipped by, I started to think of my time at Wellesley as rather like the section of Spenser's *Faerie Queene* we taught in our lit survey course: a Bower of Bliss perhaps, but fatally flawed and not connected to my reality.

When my first book was published in 1970, it was a composition textbook, *The Writer's Control of Tone*, not my Jane Austen book. The composition text probably would not have "counted" toward tenure at Wellesley, but by then I didn't care. I was comfortable with my working-class, first-generation students; more important, I felt useful and that my job was worth doing, emotions I had never felt at Wellesley. I had, in a sense, come home, though home was three thousand miles away from the slums of Brooklyn in which I grew up.

This essay looks at that homecoming and its aftermath not merely as one more American tale of the triumph of class, but also as a parable of composition studies, that recent specialization so imbricated with class issues that its very language is tinged with social striving.

Slum Kid Gets to College and Loses His Way

Neither of my parents had graduated from high school, and my father had left school in the sixth grade to help support his family. At thirteen he began working as a clerk for the post office, a job he doggedly held and hated his entire life. He was a strong union man and a fierce foe of management. His lack of education and his bristly antagonism to the world kept him from promotion, and he retired at age sixty-five on a small pension that, to his surprise, kept growing faster than his salary did when he worked. He did not know what to do with the extra income, resisting the purchase even of necessities as their cost inflated over the years. "No matter how much money I have, I'll always be a poor man," he told me, when I tried to get him to spend some of his money on sorely needed clothing. The proudest moment of his entire life, he said, during a rare moment of lucidity as he approached death at eighty-nine, was when his first post office paycheck let his family move into a modest New York apartment with inside plumbing. That was 1907, early spring, he told me, and nothing in his later life could diminish the glory of that day. His mother and four sisters adored him and he was the darling of an increasing yet small family circle, admiration not shared by outsiders, most particularly my mother, who, by the time I became aware, voiced steady contempt for his uneducated manners and uncultured habits. She was overwhelmingly ambitious, for her sons more than for herself, though she achieved a high school diploma at the age of forty-five by taking the GED examination. After I started school, she worked, at first in secret ("no wife of mine will ever work" echoed through the house of my childhood) as a legal secretary to provide money for college for my brother and me. She fought her husband fiercely when he declared that school was a waste of time, and she maintained that education was the ticket to success for their offspring. Her life was devoted to moving her sons firmly into the middle class.

Nonetheless, I went to college by accident, just as I became lost in the world of books as part of an effort to avoid the dangers of the streets. From earliest childhood, I was ordered to play outside, since the perilous New York air was supposed to be good for me. A scrawny, nearsighted, and unathletic kid, I would sneak around the block and wind up in sanctuary: the Brooklyn Public Library. There I would hide out until dinnertime, confident that the gangs and bullies who dominated the streets would never find me there. I could hardly help noticing the books on the shelves, and so I became a great reader, despite parental warnings that too much reading would damage my weak eyes. From the talking animals of Dr. Doolittle I graduated to the anthropomorphic collies of Albert Payson Terhune, and from there to the heroic exploits of the Three Musketeers. Unaware of the education I was acquiring by stealth, I smuggled Quasimodo and the Count of Monte Cristo into our book-free home to keep me company at night by flashlight. The bigger the book the better, and the more volumes in a series (how many others have read all five of the Musketeer volumes?) the more I could lose myself in its world. I think of my childhood (despite that cockeyed ill-dressed waif in the photo album) as a miasma of romantic fiction. When I encountered the dreamy Dublin boy in James Joyce's "Araby" years later, I saw myself as a kid in Brooklyn, also carrying my chalice proudly through a throng of foes.

Yet I knew I was going to college, even if no one else on my block was, and during my senior year of high school I filled in some applications and took some tests. And out of the blue fell a full-tuition scholarship to New York University, which I entered as a pre-law major, commuting by subway from home, clutching a bag lunch. And there I encountered in freshman composition Professor Hans Gottlieb, who took me under his wing. He unofficially placed me in his fiction writing workshop instead of comp and asked me questions no one had ever asked before.

"Why do you want to be a lawyer?"

"Well," I answered, giving the only answer my culture had prepared me for, "lawyers make lots of money."

"That's not a good enough reason," he responded.

I was stunned. What other reasons were there?

It was Professor Gottlieb who showed me that I could actually make a living at the subversive activity I had spent my childhood hiding: reading and writing. The line from his conversation led through Harvard straight to my job at Wellesley. I ought to have been happy.

I was, of course, lonely and unhappy at Harvard, but the issue of class never rose to the conscious level for me, even when I was teaching freshman composition. I was immersed in literature, and in those days of formal literary theory and aesthetic structures even such social novels as *Emma* or *Vanity Fair* were objects to be admired, not living reflections of historical or present reality. I learned next to nothing about my students' lives, though I did know that the governor's son was in one class and a famous entertainer's daughter in another, and little enough about my own. I read constantly, wrote analytic papers and a dissertation, grubbed to make ends meet by working in the library, and knew in my heart of hearts that ability and diligence would lead to success.

And, in a sense, it did. I saw my appointment to Wellesley as an appropriate culmination of my labors, a chance to teach literature to bright students, a well-paying job doing what I had come to enjoy most: reading, writing, and, increasingly, teaching. It never occurred to me that teaching at an elite women's college was anything but an intellectual enterprise or that my total immersion in books had imbued me with social naivete. It took me some years to realize that I was deeply uncomfortable in paradise. Though I was actually secretary of the faculty club, I slowly came to feel that I was an imposter. I knew nothing of wines or brandy; I had not been to Europe; my tennis game (the sport of the socially mobile) was from the streets, not the club. My clothes were not merely scruffy but actually shabby. I, alas, had no style, no *class*. I could not forget my job interview at Princeton, where I had been put up at Willard Thorpe's elegant residence. Coming downstairs in the morning, I found a maid putting an egg in an egg cup at my place. Was it, I wondered, to be eaten or simply admired? My polite hosts, wondering, watched me wondering. Where, they were thinking, I was thinking, is this barbarian from?

Class divisions, like gender and race divisions, are made up of a hundred tiny glances, none of them overt enough or important enough to be isolated and challenged. As year followed year at Wellesley, I became more and more aware that I did not belong, that induction into the upper reaches of social class was an essential extracurriculum that pervaded the institution. I did not react by becoming assertedly working class in dress and language, as did some of my colleagues, but I became hypersensitive to the environment. One of my worst times at Wellesley was the commencement procession that wound its way between lines of camera-snapping daddies through the beautiful spring campus, dotted with blueberries that my young daughters loved to pick and make into pies. Our caps and gowns were colorful and cheerful, as was everyone but me. "See what I have bought my daughter," I heard behind the laughter and cheers. "Look at the savage in the crimson gown who has taught our girls to understand poetry." I felt as if I were part of the groundskeeping crew.

Teaching Composition to the Elite

These were essentially pre-theoretical days for composition, the early 1960s. The Wellesley English department at that time took its responsibilities to teach writing seriously (I hear that in recent years it has shaken off that burden), although even rank beginning teachers were supposed to know what to do with no guidance. Most of my colleagues did then what some uninformed English departments continue to do in these more enlightened years: teach writing to first-year students by designing an introductory literature course, assigning regular papers, and hoping that somehow students will absorb the mystery of writing from the experience. The students, on their part, were supposed to have learned "how to write" (whatever that was—we were a selective school and most of the important definitions and rules were unwritten) in secondary school, and they expected to be praised for their unassertive good taste and their correct spelling and grammar. In fact, the students did seem to improve as they matured, but that was probably at least as much owing to the maturing experience of college and of their other course work as to the composition course. An inadequate writer was rare and a remedial one was unknown; we were teaching critical reading and creative thinking to students who had grown up speaking the prestige dialect at home and who had been drilled in how to write formal papers at school. Almost all of these students knew already what first-year writing courses teach in less privileged circumstances: the codes and dialect of college discourse. We had plenty to teach, of course, to these complacent adolescents, but that is not the same as inducting strangers to the discourse into the way ideas are handled in college.

Freshman composition was rather fun in those days, with those students. I had no real idea of what I was doing, of course, since I had never had a college writing course, with the single exception of the fiction class with Professor Gottlieb, and almost all modern composition scholarship lay in the future. But it didn't seem to matter, since I could take the idea of language as a form of creativity into the classroom, to delight the well-schooled students expecting more drill and practice. They were in fact quite ready for writing as a form of play, an element of freshman writing that has, sadly, largely disappeared in these more enlightened times. As an outsider, I felt comfortable teaching literature and creative writing; I could play the artist, and artists have never fit well into conventional class structures. And meanwhile, the students did very well with conventional argument papers. It is much easier, I have since come to realize, to teach something to someone who already knows it than to someone who does not.

The most important class issue in composition for the elite, as I look back at my time at Wellesley, is that good writing is seen as a *social* skill that students are supposed to have learned elsewhere, like their moral codes or their ability to dress appropriately for different occasions. Their job in freshman composition was to demonstrate their good linguistic manners in a pleasing variety of ways. The instructor's task was to give challenging opportunities to the students to show off their skills and to refine them. The papers rarely had much to say, but they were invariably neat and well spelled. I remember sitting in our faculty coffee lounge (an important locus of learning for me, the place where I learned that the sugar and cream I poured into my cup was a sign of moral decay), talking with other young teachers about the superficiality of the student papers we received. We argued for hours over how "to get them to think." But we were looking for quality in all the wrong places, as one song of the day had it. The problem was much more complicated than that, tied up as it was in the limited experience and the multiple protections privileged girls routinely receive. Composition teaching to the well-trained elite students at Wellesley and similar selective schools is thus not much different from the dating scene that occupies so much student attention in the first year. Students were supposed to know how to behave according to the mores of their class, and every paper, like every dance, was a kind of politeness test as well as a chance to hone their skills. I remember taking a turn as chaperone for one of the freshman dances, in those ancient days, and noticing a brightness and vivacity in faces I had been accustomed to see as dull and sleepy in class. The dance presented a more stressful and more important performance assessment than any writing assignment could hope to do. Those were the days of couple dancing, and the last thing a young woman could do was attempt to take the lead.

Writing for freshman composition (as opposed to the privileged and arty writing of poetry and fiction) was not seen by students or most faculty as a means of learning, as a crucial tool of intellectual development, or as a process of discovery of meaning—rather, it was one among many social skills that demonstrated that the student belonged to the elite. Thus, I never imagined that I should challenge the tenured professor whose freshman composition text was James Joyce's *Ulysses,* nor did I protest when he declared that my course spent too much time dealing with argument and with creative writing, both "low-level" and "high school" subjects. After all, Dartmouth was breaking new ground by seeking to admit underprepared racial minorities and had decided that Milton's *Paradise Lost* (the custom-

ary freshman composition reading material for the usual privileged
students) might not be appropriate for this hitherto unknown breed of
individual; after due deliberation, the course committee solemnly
determined that Milton's shorter poem "Samson Agonistes" would
more directly speak to these new students and their concerns. Very little has changed in this regard, by the way, despite the passing of thirty years dominated by social issues. In general, the higher the social
class of the first-year students, the higher the prestige of the institution, and the more emphasis there is on literature in the required writing course; as we move to state colleges and then to community colleges, literature almost disappears from the composition curriculum,
in favor of nonfiction prose, dominated by argumentative essays on
controversial issues of the day. Ironically, literature—the imagination in verbal free flight—in freshman composition seems to function
like the old hoop skirts, designed to keep the wealthy immobilized
and decorative; modern compositionists share a bias against literature in the writing curriculum for this reason, not because literature
itself is irrelevant. Neither the slum kid nor the debutante struggling
with the implications of Miltonic verse is likely to become personally
involved or socially troubled as a result of reading this poetry, particularly when it is the flower imagery in "Lycidas" and the theological
issues of the epics that receive the most attention in class. I hope the
teaching of Milton to elite freshmen has changed in more recent days,
with some attention to the rough originality of his rebelliousness, particularly in his essays. But I would be surprised to find that the case.
The social function of Renaissance poetry in the writing class is usually to distance and sanitize writing assignments, to confirm aesthetic
issues as the most important material for those with money.
Incidentally, the usual tension in English departments between those
who consider themselves lit people and the compositionists has this
same shadow of class warfare: the exploited proletariat of writing
teachers (often female) versus the privileged aristocracy of male literary scholars.

At one point during my time at Wellesley, I taught a unit on the
nature of assumptions. The freshmen were accustomed to talking
about religious and political assumptions behind their beliefs and they
rather enjoyed writing a paper on the assumptions behind advertise-
ments, particularly those, like cigarette and perfume ads, that suggested certain sex roles. But then I made a mistake. I asked about the
assumptions behind the "honor code" at the college, a code that
required students to turn in for discipline anyone they observed cheat-
ing. Coming as I did from my neighborhood in Brooklyn, where
Wellesley was as exotic as West Point or, for that matter, the planet
Jupiter, the social compulsions of the honor code jumped out at me:

Allegiance to the institution and its rules was far more important than allegiance to your friends and colleagues. (Try that in the slums and you are dead.) But the students, despite their high SAT scores, couldn't see this kind of assumption at all; that is, they could not see that a class assumption about loyalty lay behind the code. "Well," one student ventured, from her well-trained perplexity at what she took to be my idiotic question, "We wouldn't have been allowed to come to Wellesley if we couldn't tell Right from Wrong."

"Aha," I declared, seeing the teaching moment, "but we need to look at the social assumptions that determine what is Right and Wrong here. What makes it 'right' to turn in your friends?"

The class had turned stony. Who was I to question their values, their morals, their honor? No, let's return to easier matters for class discussion, like abortion rights, capital punishment, the legal drinking age, or even the problem of evil. Better still, let's analyze Renaissance poetry and the courtly love tradition and then write a sonnet of our own.

At another point, I decided to ask the students to write a satire. We were reading satiric pieces by Swift and Austen, and I thought that the assignment could yield thoughtful creativity. As we discussed the assignment, I pointed out that satire has only one essential requirement: The writer needs to be angry about something. After class, half a dozen students gathered around my desk, concerned that they could not do the required work: "We're not angry about *anything*," one of them said plaintively. Contrary to my intentions and my explicit teaching, they were enjoying eighteenth- and nineteenth-century satire because they felt its concerns were distant from contemporary life.

Most prominent of all my Wellesley memories is the intelligent and talented student who refused to write *A* papers. Throughout the year, she turned in clear, competent, conventional work, obviously restricted to the surface of the assignment. I would praise the dutiful writing, grade it *B*, and request the kind of revision that would show enough original thought to earn an *A*. Toward the end of the term, she showed up during office hours, angry.

"I want you to leave me alone," she said.

"But you could certainly do better work. We both know that," I replied.

"I know exactly what you mean," she continued. And she did indeed. She told me of the Harvard business school student she would marry as soon as they graduated and the house in Shaker Heights their parents had bought for them. But her lower lip trembled a bit as her vision of contented suburban housewifery clouded over. After some moments of silence, she went on: "If I started to write the papers you want me to write, if I *really* went deep, I don't think I could go through with it. So get out of my life and let me be." And she fled my office before I could see the tears.

Just last year, to jump ahead some decades, a graduating senior from our state college business school gave a twenty-minute talk to community business leaders at a breakfast honoring me as that year's "outstanding university professor." I sat at the head table, grinding my teeth, as this articulate young man, with the greatest sincerity, assured the assembled business men (there was but one woman in the large room) that he had gone all the way through college and was nonetheless entirely untouched by anything I recognized as education. Like a modern warrior negotiating a mine field, he had survived philosophy and history without ever thinking twice about the faith of his fathers; economics and business ethics had been passed and neatly passed over; he had taken the required art and lit courses but still hated the arts for their inherent immorality. He had maintained his working-class prejudices and beliefs despite the efforts of the faculty to corrupt him, and he was proudly ready to take his place as a middle manager in any of the businesses represented in the room. His business cards were stacked on the table by the door, and he was ready for job interviews.

Agonizing as the student's self-congratulatory speech was, it took me back to my Wellesley days. We try to free our students from the biases of their class, nowhere more overtly than in our composition classes these days, but all too often we barely make a dent. Which was actually better, the upper-class complacencies at Wellesley or the lower-class assumptions at state college? Hard to say. We inevitably teach our students how to fit in to their society, to know their places, despite our best intentions. But we want to carry out another, harder, even contradictory goal as well: to help them see the emptiness of the systems they strive so hard to enter. And here we routinely fail, as, I suppose, we must. It is, after all, the essence of assumptions, as I tried to show my Wellesley class, that they be buried, undiscussable, natural, *assumed*.

Teaching Composition to the Lower Middle Class

I had been a teaching assistant in the writing course at Harvard for two years and, with uncommon good luck, had worked under the direction of two scholars who actually took composition seriously: Harold Martin and Richard Ohmann. Their textbook, *The Logic and Rhetoric of Exposition,* had become my Bible, my first acquaintance with anything approaching the scholarship of composition studies. It was from Martin and Ohmann, the people and the book, that I learned about key issues in writing and writing instruction: coherent development of voice, thoughts, arguments. I learned the crucial underlying problem for college writers: to learn to use evidence to demonstrate concepts, not merely to assert and reassert them. With these goals, I battered the complacencies of the elite students at Harvard and then at Wellesley, without much success. Many of the students I encountered at state college were not different in intelligence from the privileged students I had taught for seven years. But now I encountered as well a group, sometimes close to half a freshman class, for whom the dialect of the streets was much more familiar than the Edited American English that approached native speech for the elite. So in addition to the issues and goals I have just mentioned, I now had to help many students learn a new dialect for use in school and, later, on the job. If they had done much reading, the active acquisition of the school dialect was not too difficult, but television had become the new form of literacy, and many students no longer had the ring of the written English sentence in the back of their minds. Nonetheless, these were interesting people, with a much wider variety of experience and education than I had seen before; they came in many colors and from many backgrounds, making generalizations about them risky. Some of them had managed to read all of Proust; others had traveled around the world in the military or on their own; one quiet elderly woman in the back of the room turned out to have published a half a dozen books. But for many of them writing was purely a school exercise in a mysterious dialect, an activity that had no relation to real communication or to their lives.

Hilary, for example. She was not typical, but still a familiar type. Her writing was, to me, unreadable, the kind of error-filled prose that Mina Shaughnessey would teach us all to learn from, a decade later. I had no idea what to do with Hilary at our first conference, so I tried suggesting that she take "remedial writing" at the local community college. Through her tears she told me that she had already done that three times and she would rather die than do it again. I was speechless, yet, unschooled in composition though I was, I saw I would need to try something different.

"Tell me," I said gently. "Just tell me what you were saying to me in the first paragraph."

"I checked the spelling twice," she replied, weeping.

"No, forget that. What were you trying to say?"

"Say? What do you mean? Every sentence has a verb."

And then it came to me with blinding clarity: For Hilary, writing was not a means of communication at all, and not really connected with learning. Communication took place face to face or over the telephone. Writing was a teacher's trap, a cruel exercise to expose her inadequacies. As she wrote in a later paper about the purpose of writing, "They make you write so they can *getcha*." So her job as a writer, as she saw it, was to avoid making errors, and her repeated forays into remedial workbook instruction had solidified that view.

I worked hard with Hilary, who wound up with a C and some sense that college reading and writing had to do with developing ideas by the end of the term. She reminded me in some ways of the Wellesley students I had left behind, though she would have been next to invisible to them: She was intelligent and articulate in person, polite and interested in doing well in school, eager to make a good impression and to get good grades. But the class differences were plain. Her family was not contributing any money to her college expenses, and she was working forty hours a week as a checkout clerk to send herself through school. She had never traveled much, except to the nearby beaches and mountains, and books were not part of her life. She spoke in the dialect of the inner city. Her goals were modest: She hoped to get a degree in business and move up to a middle-management job in retailing. Her fiancé was a mechanic, and she knew that she would need to help support the family even after the children came.

As with the privileged, private college students, writing was a performance for Hilary, but not a performance for which she had been prepared. It was more of an irrational and useless *rite de passage* for her, one of many in a higher education system not really designed for people like her. She was ready to be called "remedial" and to experience repeated failure, but she had a dogged determination that went beyond anything I had seen at Wellesley. My job now was to make writing a meaningful activity for her, if I could, not just a series of conventional motions. Until that happened, and it did, Martin and Ohmann and all my prior experience were of no use at all. I was reading the critic R. P. Blackmur at the time, and I was well aware of his caution (later amplified by Richard Ohmann) that the teaching of "basic skills" can actually give just enough reading and writing ability for a population to be effectively controlled. If all that Hilary took from the composition class was a sense of neatness and linguistic propriety—the goals of "remedial writing" in those days and of too many of its descendants in these—the class would be neither liberal nor educating, merely confirming her class status and helplessness.

The reading and the writing assignments were crucial, as, indeed, they always are for any group of students. I had developed a source paper assignment for my Wellesley students based on popular culture. I had asked them to pick some form of popular art—an advertisement, a comic strip, a type of pop music, even pop architecture (like the tract house) or literature (like the hard-boiled detective story)— and to describe it carefully as they analyzed its values. Finally, they were to contrast it with high art, using the generalizations that high art challenges convention while pop art reassures clichéd thinking, and that all definitions of art are culturally constructed. My students were uneasy with the topic, accustomed as they were to formal analyses of literature as the pattern for "research." But they dutifully went about the job, developing interest—even some passion—as their drafts developed. The pictures of themselves that popular art gave them, the vision of life as seen by Nancy Drew or Mary Worth or the Marlboro Man, drove them to find other visions in Jane Austen or Anne Tyler or Richard Wright. Their experiences with art in European trips with their parents came into play, as did their careers as clothing shoppers. They had in general enough experience with various levels of art in their lives to draw upon for an inquiry into the meaning and values of a specific art form.

But the assignment was much less successful with state college freshmen, whose lives (like all of our lives) had been spent floating on the sea of popular art, but with little else to vary the commercial culture. Without much experience with the traditional arts, still one of the major criteria for class, the analysis of popular art felt thin. Where, I began to ask, is the topic that allows these working-class students to use more of their rich experience fruitfully in writing? I don't mean to suggest that literature or the arts are beyond my students; far from it. They often respond to them with enthusiasm. But in the first-year writing course we need to offer writing topics that directly engage students' interests and then urge our students as writers to develop these topics as far as they can. The most successful assignments are based on existing strengths, not weaknesses.

The answer, offered by Erika Lindemann in conversation, was the "family history" source paper. I found that my students were intensely family-oriented, many with large extended families in several countries. My Wellesley students had little to say about their families, distant from them in many ways. But the family is the treasure for my commuting students, a trove of values, character, and meaning that can open into splendid writing. So I now ask my students to gather source material about their family: interview the oldest surviving member; discover old letters, diaries, pictures, deeds, and the like; find out where their religion, values, traditions, came from. I ask them to consider throughout the paper the effects of their family on who they are and what they intend to be. And I require some consultation of scholarly journals, in which students locate studies relevant to their topic, such as analyses of the urban black family, the migrant farm worker family, or the effects of child abuse on later development. Most of my students hand in extended papers, with appendices, complaining about the too-short page limits I must set so I can read them all before the term ends. They produce writing that embodies discovery and meaning, a process of inquiry that catches them up in its sweep, and a final product to hand down to their own children.

This is the meaning of the homecoming that I felt when I came to state college, a homecoming that I have slowly come to understand as a matter of social class. I see my multicolored classroom, dotted with second-language students, working part- or even full-time to make expenses, as my kind of people. They do not have bright prospects in our society, nor do they own the world, as do so many of the students at elite institutions. But they know and I know that writing can improve their lives in countless ways, and they look at me with a familiar combination of hope and suspicion at the start of each term. State college offers them social mobility and opportunity in ways they hardly know. I pay my debt to Professor Gottlieb by asking my most talented students the questions he asked me about my own life more than four decades ago. I have spent some thirty years of useful work with these people, and I can retire from teaching with a sense of purpose accomplished.

But in my imaginary conversations with my father I do not triumph. When I switched majors in college he had only scorn for my decision: "An English major! What's that? And what will you do to earn your living, be an Englishman?" He took no pride in my degrees, or my jobs, not even in my books, which he refused to read or recognize. As far as he was concerned, I was still in school, endlessly preparing for a real job, which never came. He tells me now, in my fantasy, that I have betrayed my class by accepting privileges and responsibilities and salaries to which I am not entitled. But his voice is less strident at state college than it was in the halls of privilege, and his harshness is mellowed in the afterlife that began two decades ago with his senility. And I do my work, though I am not a working man, with guilt and exultation, in the knowledge that I am, like all of us, defined by class yet not, I want to believe, trapped by it.

Works Cited

Blackmur, R. P. 1955. "Towards a Modus Vivendi." In *The Lion and the Honeycomb: Essays in Solicitude and Critique.* Orlando, FL: Harcourt Brace.

Martin, H. C., and R. M. Ohmann. 1958. *The Logic and Rhetoric of Exposition.* New York: Holt, Rinehart, and Winston.

Ohmann, R. M. 1976. *English in America: A Radical View of the Profession.* New York: Oxford University Press.

White, E. M. 1970. *The Writer's Control of Tone: Readings, with Analysis, for Thinking and Writing About Personal Experience.* New York: Norton.

21

The Job, The Job
The Risks of Work and the Uses of Texts[1]

Janet Zandy

> "Work! Sure! For America beautiful will eat you and spit your bones into the earth's hole! Work!"
>
> Pietro di Donato, *Christ in Concrete*[2]

> "I shall never forget where I came from, and I shall never deny that I was privileged to learn."
>
> Rosa Crane, unpublished memoir[3]

> "Ever—the Human Document to keep the present and future in touch with the past."
>
> Lewis Hine, *America & Lewis Hine*

The documentary photographer Lewis Hine never won a major grant, fellowship, or prize. In 1938, strapped for cash, his son Corydon hospitalized, his wife, Sara, suffering from chronic asthma, facing foreclosure on his house in Hastings-on-Hudson, he applied for a Guggenheim Foundation grant. His proposal, "Our Strength is Our People," said simply, "This project should give us light on the kinds of strength we have to build upon as a nation. Much emphasis is being put upon the dangers inherent in our alien groups, our unassimilated or even partly Americanized citizens—criticism based upon insufficient knowledge. A corrective for this would be better facilities for seeing and so understanding, what the facts are. . . ." (Rosenblum 1977, 10) The Guggenheim Committee considered, considered, promised,

promised, and then finally turned him down. Hine then applied to the Carnegie Foundation with a proposal for a project on American craftsmen. That, too, was rejected. The bank foreclosed on his house, and Hine was forced to go on relief. Then on Christmas morning 1938 his wife, Sara, died, and two years later, Lewis Hine, broke and, perhaps, broken, died. Such is the cruel, ironic conclusion to the life of America's greatest documentary photographer, Lewis Hine.

Lewis Hine died five years before I was born. I cannot recall when I first saw a Hine photo. Somehow I knew the familiar images before I knew anything about the man who created them. I say "created" because of the craft and beauty of Hine's images and because of the relationship between photographer and subject in his pictures.[4] More often than not, his work has been publicly used for some national self-congratulatory celebration without credit to Hine or recognition of his deep commitment to social justice. But, for me, Hine has been an essential guide exactly because his photographs are about illumination not celebration. His "photo stories" are both public and private: historical documentation and family album. I can close my eyes and see Hine's photos of immigrants in Ellis Island, his "sky boys" building the Empire State Building, his street children and tenement mothers. Sometimes the portraits convey the blank look of exhaustion, sometimes the newcomer's shyness, sometimes an unexpected posture, even bravado, but almost always there is the mark of labor on the human body.

Consider Hine's photographs of the "breaker boys" in the coal mines of Pennsylvania (Figure 21–1). Boys, seven, eight, nine years old, wedged in tight rows, covered with soot, hunched over, are pushed to work and work, faster and faster, sorting and breaking, hour after hour.[5] In a 1913 Child Labor Bulletin, the anonymous "Mr. Coal's Story" reports: "These boys picked out the pieces of slate and stone that cannot burn. It's like sitting in a coal bin all day long, except the coals is always moving and clattering and cuts their fingers. Sometimes the boys wear lamps in their caps to help them see through the thick dust. They bend over the chutes until their backs ache, and they get tired and sick because they have to breathe coal dust instead of pure air" (in Trachtenberg 1977, 58).

What happens to bodies that never unbend, that never feel the heat of the sun? These young lads, grown into men, were said to carry their "boy on their back." Their spines were often permanently crooked, and their shoulders forever carried the hump of work. This is not a birth deformity. This is a work deformity[6] (Figure 21–2).

I do not carry the hump of childhood work on my back. I was allowed, even encouraged, to study. Today I have cuts on my hands from working in my garden, calluses from carrying my briefcase, but

Figure 21–1
"Coal Breakers, 1910" by Lewis W. Hine
(Courtesy George Eastman House)

Figure 21–2
"Coal Breakers, PA 1910" by Lewis W. Hine
(Courtesy George Eastman House)

my fifty-one-year-old body does not bear the mark of labor as my parents' bodies did, as their parents' and grandparents' bodies did before them. In snapshots of significant occasions in my parents' lives, the work clothes are gone, the injuries are hidden, and they smile into the camera. They choose to smile. I choose to look behind the smile, not because the smile is false; it is as genuine and real as what lies behind the smile. I choose to look behind, beneath, and around the smile exactly because I am safe. I will not be injured on the job; no chemical burns will tattoo my skin; no knife will slip and cut off my finger. I am physically safe and have time and space to think and to write. In every sense, I can afford to do this and they could not—at least not in this textual way. I do not feel guilt; I feel responsibility. I have a responsibility to carry this hump of memory and knowledge of the brutal physical reality of work out and into the world.

How do I proceed without domesticating or, worse, betraying the lives of working people? How can I both *feel* and *use* private and historical memory? How do I carry it, negotiate its weight and density? How do I bring it into other cultural spaces and knit small private memories into large collective voices? How can I forge new cultural spaces and create not only discursive but also political and economic possibilities? How does memory live in the present and act for the future?

A Living Memory

I am standing in the doorway to my parents' bedroom in our small apartment in Union City, New Jersey. Each room has a doorway but no door. Only the bathroom with a tub and no sink has a door. My parents' bedroom is in the center of the apartment. On the right is the front or living room with its elaborate 1950s wallpaper of ferns and ivy. On the left is the tiny closet of a room I share with my sister. The center of our home is, of course, not the living room, but the kitchen. Every corner of this crowded apartment is clean and tidy.

I am standing in the doorway to my parents' bedroom because I am afraid to enter that space. Accustomed to my father's shift work at the chemical plant, I knew there were times when he had to sleep in the daytime because he worked all night. So, I was used to playing quietly, unseen, hushed, so Papa could rest. On this particular day, when I was perhaps seven or eight, something felt different. Papa was in bed in the middle of the day but he wasn't trying to sleep. He was trying to get better. From what? And then, standing in the doorway, I saw it: the ugly red burns gouged into his chest. I remember he looked at me—maybe he smiled, that would be like him—but did I smile back or did I run away too scared by what I saw to speak?

This was a family where the children were not encouraged to speak up or back or question. From a very young age I knew the boundaries of what could be named and what was permissible for family kitchen talk. Papa getting burned at work was not for the children to hear about or know . . . But I saw! I saw! . . .

How do I carry this memory?

Our Strength Is Our People

Academics from the working class experience a psychological, social, and linguistic dislocation, a different subjectivity rarely recognized by their privileged class colleagues. Fortunately, these differences are no longer closeted. We now have stories aplenty written by women and men who were born into the working class and were able, often because of their capacity to learn, their tenacity, and, perhaps, their good fortune, to acquire academic jobs that may offer physical safety and security not even imagined by their own families.[7]

The challenge for academic working-class intellectuals is to craft curriculum and change classroom practices so that working people are at the center of study rather than at the margins of a syllabus or not on the page at all. In order to practice a working-class democratic pedagogy one has to engage and expand one's own story (either voiced or silently remembered), draw strength and knowledge from it, connect it historically and narratively to other stories, and then use these multiple voices to transform the present and imagine a future of transnational economic justice.

In my own life, I know that I would be violating and betraying the family if I told a family story about class difference only for the sake of my own academic career. I do not have an academic "career." I have privileged space and opportunity, and I must struggle to use these small powers and occasions in ways that serve not just my own family but all working people. I am very clear about this, although I am not always so clear about the means to do it or whether I can ever get it right. I feel this difference because I have been negotiating death and grief most of my adult life. By negotiating I do not mean "closure" in the popular media sense of forty-five seconds of bad news reporting and now on to today's "bright spot." By negotiating I do not mean silencing, forgetting or hiding the grief for the comfort level of other people. I mean instead the difficult task of putting personal grief to collective, democratic use.

I can't go home again because there is no home there. My parents, grandparents, most of my aunts and uncles are dead, the cousins scattered across the country. When I was a very young woman struggling with my father's sudden death, I thought my family was just unlucky, cursed like the Kennedys only without the millions. And then, something happened. I came to understand that my circumstances were class(ed) circumstances. What I experienced was not so much a change in consciousness as a recovery of consciousness, what I might call now a reclamation of working-class epistemology. But at the time I understood it in blunter language as "so that's why they died." Long before I entered the community of readers of working-class literatures and theories, I was developing class consciousness out of the necessity of coping with the physicalilty of grief and loss. I think now this is a kind of cultural haunting. I used to joke about how I would hear voices of family members reprimanding, scolding, urging, and encouraging me to work hard (intellectually) for us all.

Kathleen Brogan (1995), in a fine essay, "American Stories of Cultural Haunting," speaks of the ghost in literature as "go-between, an enigmatic transitional figure moving between past and present, death and life, one culture and another" (152). To be sure, I am not a ghost, but I am a teacher-writer-intellectual moving between death and life, past and present, one culture and another, and struggling to create spaces of reciprocal visibility, to provide, in Lewis Hine's words, "better facilities for seeing." In order for me to do my work in the academy, I have to claim an epistemological grounding outside the traditional, privileged-class university.

All of us (even the owning class) carry within us traces of our families' work histories: paid or unpaid labor, underemployment or unemployment, seasonal work or steady work, legal work or illegal work. Consciously or not, this work inheritance shapes our own attitudes about work, sometimes in imitation, sometimes in rejection. From my parents I have inherited a strong work ethic as I have inherited brown eyes. I see my mother breaking the eggs, rolling the dough, shaping the raviolis. I also see her at the window, waiting anxiously for my father's safe return from work. I realize that their sense of pride in their work could also be used against them on the paid job, facing working conditions that were unfair, and possibly damaging and dangerous.[8] Work also kills. Would my father have died at the age of forty-nine if he were a professor instead of a pre-OSHA chemical plant worker? Possibly, but not probably. Work also kills.

Studs Terkel begins his classic *Working* (1975) with "This book, being about work, is, by its very nature, about violence—to the spirit as well as to the body." But Terkel, with his usual brilliant dialectical acumen, also says, "Perhaps it is time the 'work ethic' was redefined and its idea reclaimed from the banal men who invoke it. In a world of cybernetics, of an almost runaway technology, things are increasingly making things. It is for our species, it would seem, to go on to other matters. Human matters" (xxviii).

Human Matters

Every third Thursday of the month I attend a meeting of ROCOSH. ROCOSH is a local "COSH," one of the many councils on occupational safety and health that exist all over the country. I have been a member of ROCOSH for more than a decade and march with them every Labor Day and mourn with them on April 28, every Workers Memorial Day. This is my first year as an at-large board member. I am an outsider to this group, but I do not feel unwelcomed. Almost everyone is a union member. (My university has no union.) The board is a good mix of men and women. The women do not defer to the men. Most of us come in our work clothes, jackets and trousers, jeans and flannels, some wear union T-shirts with bulging cigarette packs in the front pockets. People arrive on time and get right to the evening's agenda: no posturing, no elaborated, abstracted language, no phony politeness. Speakers get interrupted and people openly disagree. Everyone has a say and everyone has a common purpose: the health and safety of workers. I attend these meetings to listen and learn and to bring this information back to my literature and writing classes.

The December 22, 1996 issue of the *New York Times* reports 6,210 work-related fatalities in 1995 or five for every 100,000 workers (Nordheimer, 1). The National Safety Council, in its 1996 edition of *Accident Facts,* lists 5,300 work deaths and 3,600,000 disabling injuries in 1995. Also, it reports that more than 514,000 occupational illnesses were recognized and diagnosed in 1994, according to the Bureau of Labor Statistics. The overall incidence rate of occupational illness for all workers was 63.7 per 10,000 full-time workers. Disorders associated with repeated trauma were the most common illness, with more than 330,000 cases, followed by skin diseases and disorders (more than 65,000), and respiratory conditions due to toxic agents (more than 25,000) (72).[9] These are the officially sanctioned figures.

America's Forgotten Environment (1989), a pamphlet published by a coalition of labor, minority, and environment groups, reports 100,000 worker deaths each year from occupationally caused disease and 10,000 deaths from preventable accidents at the job. OSHA, which is currently under attack in the Republican congress, spends only $4 per year for every one of its 65,000,000 covered workers (Bell and Wallick, 6).

How can these human matters, the safety and health of workers, surface in a literature course?

Humans Matter: On the Job in Academe

"Humans matter." And they matter not in an abstract, idealized, romanticized way, but in a physical, gritty, tactile way. I carry my working-class inheritance, a knowledge of the physicality of work, into the classroom by creating spaces for a discourse of the working body in a context where machines and technology and market forces matter most.

My technical institute is often on the cutting edge of new techniques in imaging science or computer engineering; it is also on the
cutting edge of the brave new university serving the technical needs
of corporations and the careerist aspirations of students. All the solid
brick modern buildings on campus have hard edges (except for the
circular base of the college of liberal arts). This is a contemporary
architectural style called "brutalism" (McCrank 1991). And the name
fits. Students keep their heads down as they face the cutting wind
between the sharp edges of the campus buildings. There is a clarity on
the campus about goals and purposes: Students take their courses,
pass their tests, work their co-ops (making money and valuable con-
tacts), get their degrees, and land well-paying jobs. Whatever their
major—graphic arts, information systems, civil engineering, printing, packaging science—these students have a strong work ethic; they
have to or they wouldn't make it over the finish line to graduation.[10]
Here there are no English or history majors, and scarce talk of students finding themselves. They know exactly where they are. And so
must I if I am to do my work of providing a catalyst for students to
develop and expand their own humanity, a humanity that is inseparable from the history of work and class struggle.

My students are historically situated in the world of training for
and acquiring jobs in a context where the national political rhetoric is
of expansion and growth but the lived reality is of scarcity and huge
college loan debts. My students are not automatons. Student artists
speak knowingly about splitting their future work lives between art
for the market and art for themselves; many engineering students also
take photographs, play instruments, climb mountains. But some students, especially the younger ones, who have logged innumerable
hours before televisions, terminals, videos, and who have never eaten
a meal without a humming machine in the foreground or background,
are not accustomed to imagining or dialoguing with other people who
are not copies of themselves. But even these students, who seem to
possess the most metallic hearts, who are the most indifferent to politics and history, who are most centered on their immediate needs,
who are most captured by the latest techno toy, have a work legacy I
can tap. And then there are those students, a little older, who are split
between jobs, family, and school. Often the women have business
ambitions and want the degree to get to the next wage grade; the men
may be technicians in local plants or recent sailors or soldiers returning to school not to acquire skills they already possess but to have
those skills warranted, certified, credentialed, and degreed. These students have little patience with what they may perceive as liberal arts
blather. Their lives are one long time clock. Invariably, these are the
students most responsive to working-class texts, and I rely on them to

convey this understanding to other, perhaps more economically privileged, students.

Mike is a good example. Recently married and discharged from the Navy, he signed up for my upper-division writing course. His first essay was a beautifully written narrative recalling his father's suicide from the perspective of his twelve-year-old self. When he submitted his first draft for my comments, he remarked on how he expected me "to tear it up." He was worrying about punctuation; I was staggered by his capacity to write so powerfully and personally. I returned it to him, telling him there was nothing to tear. I do not think he believed me at first. At the end of the quarter he sought me out as I was ending another class. He blurted out: "I didn't expect to like your class. You seemed liberal and the other students seemed liberal, and I'm very conservative. But I love this class." Why? I cannot in good faith put words in Mike's mouth, but I can safely surmise that three things appealed to him: the course seemed *real*; the "real world" was not out there somewhere. We tested how reality is shaped by language. And we read books and had writing assignments (including oral histories) that considered the lives of working-class people. One of Mike's favorite texts in this course was Michael Wilson's screenplay *Salt of the Earth* ([1953] 1978). Mike had no difficulty seeing the parallel work lives of the husband and wife protagonists, the unsafe, exhausting paid work in the mines, and the unsanitary, exhausting unpaid work of the Mexican wives and mothers at home. Unlike some of the other, more economically privileged students, he could identify with the characters on the basis of work and class and not feel outside the text because of ethnic or gender difference. Other students have to negotiate their own class positions vis-à-vis a text that challenges their unstated, market-shaped assumptions about business and that presents the characters they're most inclined to identify with—managers, owners, and the local sheriff—as oppressors. Rather than investigate their own ideological assumptions, these students would rather write off the film as hokey or dated. It is ideologically safer. Relating the film to contemporary economic realities, such as the huge wage differential between CEOs and workers, I can see that I am trespassing on sacred ground. Recently, one student challenged me, "Do you have a problem with that?" ("that" being CEO salaries). "Yes, I have a problem with that because my work as a teacher is connected to the struggle for economic justice," I answer.

"God Job"[11]

In recovering working-class stories, with their frequent descriptions of the physicality and dangers of work, I am recovering not only a lost American labor history, but also students' own transgenerational fam-

ily work histories. (It is important to note to students, however, that
dangerous work is not ancient history but part of the daily work lives
of million of workers all over the world—today.) Accustomed to
sweaty bodies on the running track, in the weight room, or in an aer-
obic class, many students, like many professors, managers, and tech-
nocrats, are not accustomed to acknowledging visually the working
bodies in their daily lives—the men and women who clean their toilets, repair their machines, or pick up their litter. Just as consumers
resist acknowledging the machine-tending human hand behind the
products they buy, students resist the disquieting confrontation with
this fourth dimension of reality—physical work. As a working-class
cultural worker, I try to use texts the way Hine created photo stories
in order to structure a reciprocal and democratic visibility. This does
not happen without resistance. Some students are plainly uncomfortable with this approach and they complain about "this book being
depressing and not fun." I am asking students—often very privileged
ones—to look at the physicality and dangers of work and to risk a discomfort to their own subjectivity. Students who have cut their teeth
on violence in every medium (TV, film, video games, music, dance)
are squeamish in the face of industrial and work-related violence.
The connections I seek are emotional as much as intellectual. I want
these young civil engineers and future managers to carry with them
out into the future world of their own jobs knowledge about bodies at
work—the risks, the exhaustion, the dangers working people face.

One of the ways working-class literature is distinct from bourgeois literature is in its emphasis on the physicality of work. The
white-gloved serving hand that might be glimpsed on the periphery in
a middle-class novel is fully attached to the working body in working-
class literature. Workers and the physicality of labor are foregrounded
in working-class autobiographies, novels, poems, and songs.
Characters get hurt and die because of the work they do. Work kills
and maims. Whatever their differences of gender, ethnicity, race, and
regional perspective, Agnes Smedley's *Daughter of Earth* ([1929]
1973), Tillie Olsen's *Yonnondio* (1975), William Attaway's *Blood
on the Forge* ([1941] 1993), Audre Lorde's *Zami* (1982), Thomas
Bell's *Out of This Furnace* ([1941] 1976), Pietro di Donato's *Christ
in Concrete* ([1939] 1993), Maxine Hong Kingston's *China Men*
(1980), Edith Summers Kelley's *Weeds* ([1923] 1982), Helena Maria
Viramontes's *Under the Feet of Jesus* (1995), Jim Daniels's *Punching
Out* (1990), Sue Doro's *Blue Collar Goodbyes* (1992), Alice Walker's
The Color Purple (1982) are all literatures (to name a few) grounded
in the physicality of work.

Working-class writing often creates a spatial and emotional intimacy between paid and unpaid work: the sustaining, unceasing work

at home and the (un)living-wage work on the job. Michael Wilson, blacklisted author of the screenplay for *Salt of the Earth,* remarked in 1953 that his film was an alternative to the current Hollywood 3-D fad. *Salt of the Earth* illuminated the "fourth dimension . . . called reality—the reality of working people's lives" (Rosenfelt, 109). When the men can no longer "man" the picket line because of a court injunction based on the Taft-Hartley Act, the women take over and hold the line while the men, who are wrestling with their own macho opinions about the division of labor, take up the women's work of chopping the wood, scrubbing the laundry, and caring for the children. The women's demands for sanitation (running water, indoor plumbing like the Anglo miners) finally seem crucial to the men, who are so sick of chopping wood that they are ready to form a wood-chopping union.

Likewise, Tillie Olsen in *Yonnondio* (1975) structures a parallel work day in the lives of Anna and Jim Holbrook, who face the oppression of work and summer's heat: he in the packing house; she in the kitchen on "the fifth day of hell-heat" with the temperature 104 degrees outside, 112 in casings (135). At "God Job" Jim must do the workers' speed-up dance, "choreographed by Beedo, the B system, speed-up stopwatch, convey. Music by rasp crash screech knock steamhiss thud machinedrum. . . . Become component part, geared, meshed, timed, controlled" (133). In the humid kitchen Anna "works on alone," canning the last of the fruit for jelly, tending the sweaty, heat-cranky children. "Between stirring and skimming, and changing the wet packs on Ben, Anna peels and cuts the canning peaches—two more lugs to go. . . . Skim, stir; sprinkle; change the wet packs on Ben; pit, peel and cut; sponge" (148–149). In these parallel scenes, Olsen brilliantly conveys the body forced to work as a machine, but she never relinquishes the humanity of her characters to the machine. Nor is their suffering labor aestheticized and distanced. With her beautiful rhythmic language, Olsen pays tribute to the courage and endurance of Anna and Jim. Above all else, humans matter.

Mike Wallace, in his *Mickey Mouse History and Other Essays on American Memory* (1996), demonstrates the paradoxical relationship many Americans have to history. On the one hand, there is tremendous enthusiasm for the present, the new and the now,[12] and pressure to move on and "achieve closure." On the other hand, as Wallace points out, "we have been on a heritage binge and remain thoroughly obsessed with the past" (x). My students may have had vacation stops at Colonial Williamsburg or Old Sturbridge, even field trips to historical sites, but very few have faced the dangers of work or the disturbing descriptions of physical labor from a worker's perspective found in working-class literature. When I ask them to read

Yonnondio or *Salt of the Earth,* I know I am also asking them to relin-
quish the pleasant stance of the distanced tourist and to take up the
emotional burden of these stories and these histories.

Two working-class autobiographical novels that address the
unaccidental nature of industrial deaths and injuries are Thomas
Bell's *Out of This Furnace* ([1941] 1976) and Pietro di Donato's
Christ in Concrete ([1939] 1993). Both novels, like *Yonnondio* and
Salt of the Earth, illuminate the interdependence between domestic
work and paid work (Bell more so than di Donato), and both convey
the economic and emotional aftermath of an industrial death on a
family. At the literal center of *Out of This Furnace*, an immigrant
novel of three generations of steelworkers, is the story of Mary and
Mike Dobrejack, Slovakians living in the steel town of Braddock,
Pennsylvania, in the first decade of the twentieth century. "With
July's heat baking the streets and courtyards of the First Ward,"
Mary collapses in her kitchen and the doctor is summoned. She is
pregnant again. The doctor advises bed rest and no exertion and
"Mary stared up at him. With six boarders, three children and a husband to look after, meals to cook, clothes to wash, her hours were
from four-thirty in the morning to nine at night, seven days a week"
(173)—how could she rest? There is no rest for her husband, Mike,
either—now old at thirty—as he faces another twenty-four-hour
work shift: "The first twelve hours were much like any day turn
except that sometimes, through a break in the mill's rumble, he could
hear church bells. . . . The second twelve hours were like nothing
else in life. Exhaustion slowly numbed his body, mercifully fogged
his mind; he ceased to be a human being, become a mere appendage
to the furnace, a lost damned creature. 'At three o'clock in the morning of a long turn a man could die with knowing it'" (167). Working-
class novels like *Out of This Furnace* are more than an accumulation
of work horrors; they also document again and again the human
capacity for resistance and for insisting humans are not "its," merely
"check number[s]," "Hunky laborer[s]," or human appendages to the
machine. In a drunken monologue, Mike proclaims to his friend
Stefan and to the larger world:

> It's a terrible and beautiful thing to make iron. It's honest work, too,
> work the world needs. They should honor us, Stefan. Sometimes
> when the bosses bring their friends through the mill they watch us
> make a cast and when the iron pours out of the furnace, you know
> how wonderful it is, especially at night, I feel big and strong with
> pride. . . . I don't mind work. But a man should be allowed to love
> his work and take pride in it. There's good in all of us that would
> make our lives happier and the world a better place for everybody.
> But it's never asked for. We're only Hunkies. (196)

The next day Mike kisses Mary good-bye, heads for the steel mill on a springlike, mild evening, enters the mill gate, and goes to work. Before he can finish his shift, a furnace blows and Mike Dobrejack is dead. Mike's death is reported to Mary; the reader "overhears" the details of the explosion and experiences the aftermath—the burial, the paltry compensation, and then Mary's and the children's struggle to survive.

In Pietro di Donato's *Christ in Concrete*, workers' lives are also sacrificed to "God Job," but in this 1939 novel of Italian immigrant bricklayers, there is no reader comfort zone. The novel begins on the job site with Italian immigrant bricklayers on a brisk March day of Easter week. Immediately, the reader confronts the physicality of humanity: "Old Nick, the 'Lean,' stood up from over a dust-flying brick pile, tapped the side of his nose and sent an oyster directly to the ground" (3). One by one we are introduced to the other bricklayers through their ribald language, jokes, physical descriptions—Burly Julio known as "Snoutnose" (3) or Mike the "Barrel-mouth" (4)—and to Geremio their foreman, proud husband to Annunziata, father of six children, and one more soon to come. Geremio is torn between the intensity of his pride in and duty to his family and the realization that the construction job is unsafe. He tries to stop the work: "Padrone— padrone, the underpinning gotta be make safe and . . ." And gets the expected response: "Lissenyawopbastard! if you don't like it, you know what you can do!" (9). And what can Geremio do? "The new home, the coming baby, and his whole background, kept the fire from Geremio's mouth and bowed his head [and he became] no longer Geremio, but a machinelike entity. The men were transformed into single, silent beasts" (9). On Good Friday, Geremio "stared dumbly at the structure and mechanically listed in his mind's eye the various violations of construction safety" (11), and the concrete was poured. The inadequate building supports burst and the "floor vomited upward" (14). Geremio is catapulted in "directionless flight," landing upright with arms outstretched, crucified, and facing the huge concrete hopper and the gray gushing concrete. In five long pages, di Donato describes the agony of Geremio's death:

> His genitals convulsed. The cold steel rod upon which they were impaled froze his spine. He shouted louder and louder. "Save me! I am hurt badly! I can be saved I can—save me before it's too late!" But the cries went no farther than his own ears. The icy wet concrete reached his chin. His heart appalled. "In a few seconds I will be entombed. If I can only breathe, they will reach me. Surely they will!" . . . He had bitten halfway through when his teeth snapped off to the gums in the uneven conflict. The pressure of the concrete was such, and its effectiveness so thorough, that the wooden splinters, stumps of teeth, and blood never left the choking mouth. . . .

> He tried to breathe, but it was impossible. The heavy concrete
> was settling immutably and its rich cement-laden grout ran into his
> pierced face. His lungs would not expand and were crushing in
> tighter and tighter under the settling concrete. . . . He screamed,
> "Show yourself now, Jesu!". . . . and the fighting brain disintegrated
> and the memories of a baffled lifetime sought outlet. (16–18)

Pietro di Donato sums up the day after Geremio's funeral in this
understated, powerful way: "The day that followed was lived" (30).

I know of no other working-class novel that so powerfully confronts the reader with the horror of death on the job.[13] In teaching this
material, I wish to carry responsibly the lives of working people into
the classroom. It is difficult, perhaps impossible, to measure the
impact of working-class literature like *Christ in Concrete* on students.
To be sure, this is not about evoking their guilt; rather, it is about, as
Hine might put it, naming the guilty. Students are asked to be brave
enough to take in, subjectively, the lived reality of these stories. And
many do, as revealed in these written responses from my 1997 course,
New American Literature:

> We know that our ancestors, immigrant workers built this country,
> yet the stories and injustices are not always readily available to learn
> from. *Christ in Concrete* exposes harsh and often dissimilar experi-
> ences from our own, but . . . we may relate in personal ways. It
> made me consider my position in society as a worker, my economic
> position, the modern workplace conditions. What is my status? Who
> is in control? God? Boss? (Rachel Heinold-Belock)

> I can relate to Paul's feeling of pride and accomplishment during the
> scene where he constructs his first corner. I can understand the
> importance of his obtaining a job to support his family because my
> grandparents did the same thing. In *Christ in Concrete* Geremio's
> work leaves behind a legacy as evidenced by the way Nazone calls
> him "Little Master Paul." Though to a lesser extent and under much
> different circumstances, I also feel the pressure to live up to the
> hard-working image of my father. (Rich Gille)

> I really liked the novel. I was drawn into the book from the first
> word. My grandfather was a bricklayer and also the first generation
> of his family born in America, although he was Irish not Italian. He
> told many stories about his job, and this may sound really funny but
> I appreciate the architecture of RIT because my grandfather laid the
> bricks for many of the buildings. I, however, have a different take on
> the Job. Besides the danger of falling off scaffolds, there is also a
> hidden danger which ended up taking my grandfather's life. Years of
> working with cement and dust and asbestos, caused my grandfather
> to develop emphysema, which took his life at age 63. My grandfa-
> ther's story is much like Geremio's. He was taken advantage of by
> the Job, safety precautions were never taken and they both experi-

enced discrimination by the American bosses. . . . The Job took both of their lives and left little in return. My family as well as Geremio['s] had to say good bye way too early and the compensation board offered little support, . . . [leaving] both families struggling to survive in this great country of America, the land of opportunities and dreams. (Gretchen Bush)

In a 1933 letter to Florence Kellogg about the "value of human values in photography beyond mere illustration," Lewis Hine writes:

> Just now I think it is a very important offset to some misconceptions about industry. One is that many of our material assets, fabrics, photographs, motors, airplanes and whatnot "just happen," as the product of a bunch of impersonal machines under the direction, perhaps, of a few human robots. You and I may know that it isn't so, but many are just plain ignorant of the sweat and service that go into all these products of the machine.
>
> One more "thought"—I have a conviction that the design, registered in the human face thro years of life and work, is more vital for purposes of permanent record, tho it is more subtle perhaps, than the geometric patterns of lights and shadows that passes in the taking, and serves (so often) as mere photographic jazz (Kaplan 1992, 49–50).

Human matters. Humans matter.

Notes

1. This essay is dedicated in loving memory to Constance Coiner and Ana Duarte-Coiner. On July 17, 1996, Constance Coiner, scholar, teacher, and activist, was killed on TWA flight 800 with her daughter, Ana Duarte-Coiner. A champion of economic justice, Constance Coiner advanced the study of U.S. working-class literature and culture. She is profoundly missed.

2. Such is the unromanticized view of work of "The Lean" one of the bricklayers in Pietro di Donato's *Christ in Concrete* ([1939] 1993).

3. From an unpublished memoir by Rosa Crane, high school teacher.

4. In his introduction to *Portraits in Steel*, a collection of photographs of former steelworkers by Milton Rogovin and interviews by Michael Frisch (1993), Frisch comments on the *collaboration* between photographer and subject in Milton Rogovin's work: "portraits *do* represent and express a collaboration of their own between subject and artist/historian, a collaboration in which the subject is anything but mute and powerless, a mere object of study. . . . Rogovin . . . is the sort of photographer who does not 'take' photographs; rather, his subjects 'give' them to him" (3). The same relationality applies to the process and product of Lewis Hine's work.

5. These images are reminiscent of William Blake's 1789 poem, "The Chimney Sweeper."

6. Lewis Hine writes: "There is a prevailing impression that in the matter of child labor the emphasis on the labor must be very slight, but let me tell you right here that these processes involve work, hard work, deadening in its monotony, exhausting physically, irregular, the workers' only joy the closing house. We might even say of these children that they are condemned to work" (Hine 1977, 58). Also, it should be noted that Hine's photographs should inform and remind us of the wide use of child labor in the transnational market place. As recent boycott campaigns against the Gap and other clothing merchants prove, the clothes we purchase are often made by children and young women under the most horrific conditions.

7. Roxanne Rimstead offers a penetrating analysis of these narratives in the context of their potential and their limitations to develop political consciousness and transformative power. Rimstead emphasizes the importance of not merely displaying one's working-class "identity credentials" in order to speak for the missing voices in academic circles (Rimstead 1996, 128).

8. Although not dangerous, my working conditions as a longtime adjunct faculty member in a community college were certainly exploitative. I was torn between my commitment to working-class students, my sense of craft and dignity in my own labor, and my outrage at being treated as an inexpensive appendage. I describe my efforts to organize adjunct faculty in Zandy 1995.

9. The National Safety Council, chartered by Congress, is a nongovernmental, not-for-profit public service organization, devoted solely to educating and influencing society to adopt safety, health, and environmental policies, practices, and procedures that prevent and mitigate human suffering and economic losses arising from preventable causes.

10. Faculty must have a strong work ethic as well, since most of us teach nine courses a year on the quarter system.

11. In *Yonnondio* Tillie Olsen (1975) describes "the crap" humans have to take in order to support their families on "God Job." Olsen and Pietro di Donato ([1939] 1993) both describe the/a job as JOB, a ruthless deity ready to consume the lives of workers. With families to support, workers have no choice but to obey God JOB.

12. This attraction of the "new" surfaced recently in the renaming of my course, Multi-Cultural North American Literature. The first time the course was offered, two students enrolled; the second time, about twelve students; the third time, with the new title "New American Literature," thirty-three students enrolled. Same professor, same course, but now NEW!

13. It is true that because of better building codes and OSHA regulations, fewer Geremios die laying bricks today. But it is also true that the deaths of five or six thousand workers a year in the United States (and who knows how many on the global assembly line?), often in preventable accidents, are intolerable. Would these deaths be tolerated if they were celebrities, CEOs or other members of the owning class?

Works Cited

Attaway, W. [1941] 1993. *Blood on the Forge*. New York: Doubleday.

Bell, J., and F. Wallick. 1989. *America's Forgotten Environment*. Washington, D.C.: Urban Environment Conference.

Bell, T. [1941] 1976. *Out of This Furnace*. Pittsburgh: University of Pittsburgh Press.

Brogan, K. 1995. "American Stories of Cultural Haunting: Tales of Heirs and Ethnographers." *College English* 57 (2) (February): 149–195.

Crane, R. 1996. Unpublished memoir. Rochester, New York.

Daniels, J. 1990. *Punching Out*. Detroit, MI: Wayne State University Press.

di Donato, P. [1939] 1993. *Christ in Concrete*. New York: Signet.

Doro, S. 1992. *Blue Collar Goodbyes*. Watsonville, CA: Papier-Mâché Press.

Hine, L. 1977. "Baltimore to Biloxi and Back." In *America & Lewis Hine*, ed. A. Trachtenberg. Millerton, NY: Aperture.

Kaplan, D. 1992. *Photo Story: Selected Letters and Photographs of Lewis W. Hine*. Washington, D.C.: Smithsonian Institution Press.

Kelley, E. S. [1923] 1982. *Weeds*. New York: The Feminist Press.

Kingston, M. H. 1980. *China Men*. New York: Knopf.

McCrank, M. 1991. "Architect Lists RIT Campus 9th in Nation for Aesthetics." *Democrat and Chronicle* (12 December).

Nordheimer, J. 1996. "One Day's Death Toll on the Job." *The New York Times* (22 December) Sec. 3: 1, 10–11.

Olsen, T. 1975. *Yonnondio*. New York: Laurel.

Rimstead, R. 1996. "What Working-Class Intellectuals Claim to Know." *Race, Gender and Class: Working-Class Intellectual Voices*. 4 (1): 119–141.

Rogovin, M., and M. Frisch. 1993. *Portraits in Steel*. Ithaca, NY: Cornell University Press.

Rosenblum, W. 1977. "Foreword." In *America & Lewis Hine*, ed. A. Trachtenberg. Millerton, NY: Aperture.

Rosenfelt, D. S. 1978. "Commentary." In *Salt of the Earth* by M. Wilson. New York: The Feminist Press.

Smedley, A. [1929] 1973. *Daughter of Earth*. New York: The Feminist Press.

Terkel, S. 1975. *Working*. New York: Avon.

Trachtenberg, A. 1977. "Ever the Human Document." In *America & Lewis Hine*, ed. A. Trachtenberg. Millerton, NY: Aperture.

———, ed. 1977. *America & Lewis Hine: Photographs 1904–1940*. Millerton, NY: Aperture.

Viramontes, H. 1995. *Under the Feet of Jesus*. New York: Dutton.

Walker, A. 1982. *The Color Purple*. New York: Washington Square Press.

Wallace, M. 1996. *Mickey Mouse History and Other Essays on American Memory*. Philadelphia: Temple University Press.

Wilson, M. [1953] 1978. *Salt of the Earth*. New York: The Feminist Press.

Zandy, J. 1995. "Liberating Memory." In *Liberating Memory: Our Work and Our Working-Class Consciousness*, ed. J. Zandy. New Brunswick, NJ: Rutgers University Press.

Contributors

Jim Daniels's most recent book of poetry is *Blessing the House*. He is a professor of English at Carnegie Mellon University, where he won the 1996–97 Elliot Dunlap Smith Award for Teaching and Educational Service.

Louise DeSalvo, Professor of English and Creative Writing at Hunter College in New York City, is best known for *Virginia Woolf: The Impact of Childhood Sexual Abuse on Her Life and Work* and her own memoir *Vertigo*, about growing up Italian American and working-class. Her most recent book is *Breathless*, a memoir about illness. She is completing *Writing as a Way of Healing*, an inquiry into the ways in which writing has been and can be used to address psychic and physical woundedness.

John Ernest is Associate Professor of English and Coordinator of the African American Studies minor at the University of New Hampshire. He is the author of *Resistance and Reformation in Nineteenth-Century African-American Literature: Brown, Wilson, Jacobs, Delany, Douglass, and Harper.* His work has appeared in *American Literature, American Literary History, PMLA,* and elsewhere. He is currently working on a book about nineteenth-century African American historians.

Carol Faulkner received a Ph.D. from the University of Oregon in 1992. Most recently, she has taught American literature and culture at Lund University in southern Sweden.

Karen Fitts, Assistant Professor in the Writing and Media Department at Loyola College in Maryland, teaches first-year writing and upper-division rhetoric courses. With Alan W. France, she has published articles on writing instruction and has edited *Left Margins: Cultural Studies and Composition Pedagogy.* Her most recent essay, "The Pathology and Erotics of Breast Cancer," is forthcoming in *Discourse.*

Alan W. France teaches introductory composition at West Chester University of Pennsylvania. His work includes a book, *Composition as a Cultural Practice*; an anthology coedited with Karen Fitts, *Left Margins: Cultural Studies and Composition Pedagogy;* essays; and shorter commentary, all concerned with the politics of writing instruction.

Olivia Frey is an associate professor of English at St. Olaf College. She has published articles on education and writing, most notably "Beyond Literary Darwinism: Women's Voices and Critical Discourse" (*College English*) and an anthology edited with Diane Freedman and Frances Murphy Zauhar, *The Intimate Critique: Autobiographical Literary Criticism.* She is currently working with Diane Freedman on a second anthology, *Personal Thoughts: The Autobiographical Nature of Research, Scholarship and Knowledge Across the Disciplines.*

Donald Lazere, Professor of English at Cal Poly, San Luis Obispo, held the Cardin Chair in the Humanities at Loyola College of Maryland in 1996–97. He is author of *The Unique Creation of Albert Camus* and editor of *American Media and Mass Culture: Left Perspectives.* He is also author of the forth-coming textbook *Reading and Writing for Critical Citizenship.*

Lawrence MacKenzie is Professor of English at the Community College of Philadelphia, where he has won the Collos Award for excellence in teaching and serves on a team that helps faculty develop new courses. He teaches composition, literature, and creative writing. His most recent work is *Oiseau? Wazzat?,* a play about art on trial.

Christina Russell McDonald is Assistant Professor of English and Director of the Writing Program at James Madison University. She teaches introductory and advanced writing courses, as well as a graduate seminar in composition studies. With Robert L. McDonald, she is coeditor of *Teaching Composition in the 90s: Sites of Contention.* Her current research focuses on the history of writing instruction in American women's colleges.

Robert L. McDonald is Associate Professor of English and Fine Arts and Director of Writing Across the Curriculum at the Virginia Military Institute. He teaches a variety of courses in American literature and drama as well as composition, and helped establish a minor in writing in his department. With Christina Russell McDonald, he is coeditor of *Teaching Composition in the 90s: Sites of Contention.* His most recent work is *The Critical Response to Erskine Caldwell.*

John McMillan is completing doctoral work in composition studies at TCU. His dissertation focuses on narrative and pedagogy.

Cecilia Rodríguez Milanés teaches writing, multicultural literature, and women's studies at Indiana University of Pennsylvania. Her writing ranges from topics in teaching writing and social issues in the classroom to cross-genre writing, Latina poetics, and short stories.

Beverly J. Moss is Associate Professor of English and Director of the Writing Center at The Ohio State University. She is the editor of *Literacy Across Communities* and the author of the forthcoming *A Community Text Arises.*

Kevin Railey is Associate Professor of English at Buffalo State College, where he teaches American literature and contributes to the English education program. His published writings include articles about composition theory/pedagogy, edited collections about urban and multicultural education, and articles about William Faulkner. His book, *Natural Aristocracy: History, Ideology, and the Production of William Faulkner,* has been accepted for publication by the University of Alabama Press.

Carol Reeves is Associate Professor of English at Butler University, where she directs Freshman writing, runs the University Lampoon Magazine, and teaches writing and literature courses. Her scholarly essays in the rhetoric of science have been published in various journals, most recently in *The Quarterly Journal of Speech.*

Hephzibah Roskelly teaches at the University of North Carolina, Greensboro, where she directs the composition program and teaches courses in rhetoric and composition, American literature, and pedagogy. Her most recent book, forthcoming in 1998, is *Reason to Believe: Romanticism, Pragmatism and the Possibility of Teaching*, coauthored with Kate Ronald.

Alan Shepard is Associate Professor of English at TCU. He teaches and writes about sixteenth- and seventeenth-century literature, literature and science in the early modern period, and contemporary drama.

Patricia A. Sullivan is Associate Professor of English and Director of Composition at the University of New Hampshire, where she teaches graduate and undergraduate courses in composition studies, critical theory, and American literature. Recipient of the 1991 James L. Kinneavy Award, she is coeditor, with Donna J. Qualley, of *Pedagogy in the Age of Politics.* Her work has appeared in journals and essay collections that explore both ideological and practical issues in the study and teaching of writing.

Gary Tate is Professor of English at TCU, where he teaches courses in composition theory/pedagogy and working-class literature. With Amy Rupiper and Kurt Schick, he is coediting a collection of original essays, *A Bibliographical Guide to Composition Pedagogies.*

Victor Villanueva teaches writing, writing theory, and rhetoric at Washington State University. His books include the award-winning *Bootstraps: From an American Academic of Color.*

Edward M. White is an emeritus professor of English at California State University, San Bernardino, and a senior lecturer in English at the University of Arizona. He is editor or author of nine books on writing, including his award-winning *Teaching and Assessing Writing* and *Assessment of Writing.* Current projects include a book-length autobiography based in part on the essay in this collection.

Janet Zandy is the editor of two collections on class and culture, *Calling Home: Working-Class Women's Writing* and *Liberating Memory: Our Work and Our Working-Class Consciousness*; and of a special issue of *Women's Studies Quarterly* on working-class studies. She is Associate Professor of Language and Literature at the Rochester Institute of Technology.